All the pages in this book were created—and are printed here—in Japanese RIGHT-to-LEFT format. No artwork has been reversed or altered, so you can read the stories the way the creators meant for them to be read.

RIGHT TO LEFT?!

Traditional Japanese manga starts at the upper right-hand corner, and moves right-to-left as it goes down the page. Follow this guide for an easy understanding.

For more information and sneak previews, visit cmxmanga.com. Call 1-888-COMIC BOOK for the nearest comics shop or head to your local book store.

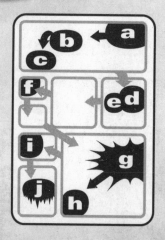

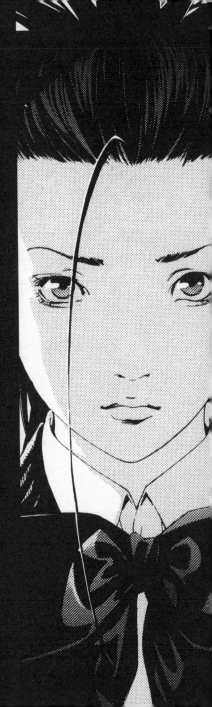

TENJHO TENGE © 1997 by Oh! great. All rights reserved.
First published in Japan in 1997 by SHUEISHA Inc.

TENJHO TENGE Volume 17, published by WildStorm
Productions, an imprint of DC Comics, 888 Prospect St.
#240, La Jolla, CA 92037. English Translation © 2008. All
Rights Reserved. English translation rights in U.S.A. and
Canada arranged by SHUEISHA Inc. CMX is a trademark of
DC Comics. The stories, characters, and incidents
mentioned in this magazine are entirely fictional. Printed on
recyclable paper. WildStorm does not read or accept
unsolicited submissions of ideas, stories or artwork.
Printed in Canada.

DC Comics, a Warner Bros. Entertainment Company.

Sheldon Drzka – Translation and Adaptation
Saida Temofonte – Lettering
Larry Berry – Design
Jim Chadwick – Editor

ISBN: 978-1-4012-1532-3

KNOW WHAT'S INSIDE

With the wide variety of manga available, CMX understands it can be confusing to determine age-appropriate material. We rate our books in four categories: EVERYONE, TEEN, TEEN + and MATURE. For the TEEN, TEEN + and MATURE categories, we include additional, specific descriptions to assist consumers in determining if the book is age appropriate. (Our MATURE books are shipped shrink-wrapped with a Parental Advisory sticker affixed to the wrapper.)

EVERYONE

Titles with this rating are appropriate for all age readers. They contain no offensive material. They may contain mild violence and/or some comic mischief.

TEEN

Titles with this rating are appropriate for a teen audience and older. They may contain some violent content, language, and/or suggestive themes.

TEEN PLUS

Titles with this rating are appropriate for an audience of 16 and older. They may contain partial nudity, mild profanity and more intense violence.

MATURE

Titles with this rating are appropriate only for mature readers. They may contain graphic violence, nudity, sex and content suitable only for older readers.

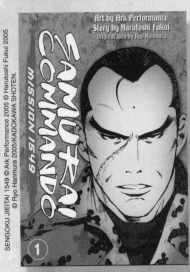

WANT TO TRY A NEW SERIES? START HERE!

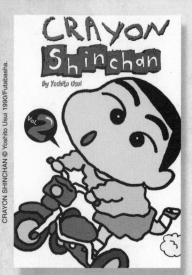

CRAYON SHINCHAN © Yoshito Usui 1990/Futabasha.

By Yoshito Usui
3 volumes available

SUMEBA MIYAKO NO KOSUMOSUSOU
© TARO ACHI•YU YAGAMI/ASCII MEDIA WORKS Inc.

By Y. YAGAMI and T. ACHI
2 volumes available

ORFINA © KITSUNE TENNOUJI/FUJIMISHOBO.

By Kitsune Tennouji
3 volumes available

GON © 1992 Masashi Tanaka/Kodansha Ltd.

By Masashi Tanaka
5 volumes available

KIKAIDER IS BACK FOR ONE FINAL BATTLE!

KIKAIDER02

CODE: ZERO TWO

Volume 7

By Shotaro Ishinomori and MEIMU. In a bleak, future world, a young man named Jiro is really the robot called Kikaider. Created by a scientist who built robots for an evil organization, Jiro was given a special, humanizing chip to keep him from being used for destructive purposes. This sequel picks up on the fast-paced robot action of the cult CMX series and addresses some unanswered questions.

KIKAIDER 02 Vol. 7 © Shotaro Ishimori Pro.

DOROTHEA'S CRUSADE CONTINUES NOW!

Volume 2

By Cuvie. When she finally gets her initial taste of war, Dorothea is forced to kill for the first time. She's not able to shake off the experience, despite attempts to rationalize her actions as necessary. Later, she confronts a band of soldiers trying to loot a home and attack the widow who lives there. But her savior role is short-lived when she is forced to face the consequences of her earlier actions.

DOROTHEA - MAJYO NO TETTSUI Vol. 3 © 2006 Cuvie/FUJIMISHOBO.

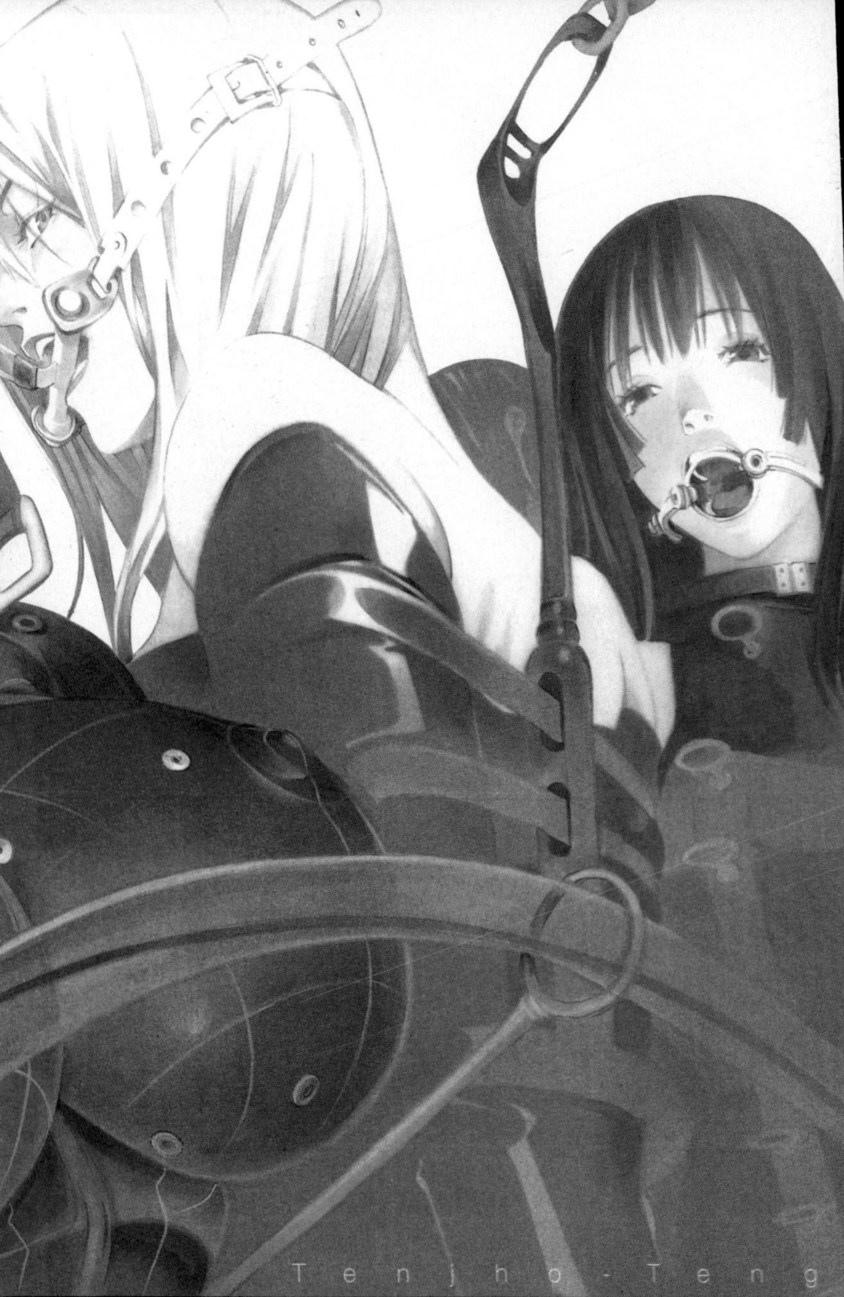
T e n j h o - T e n g

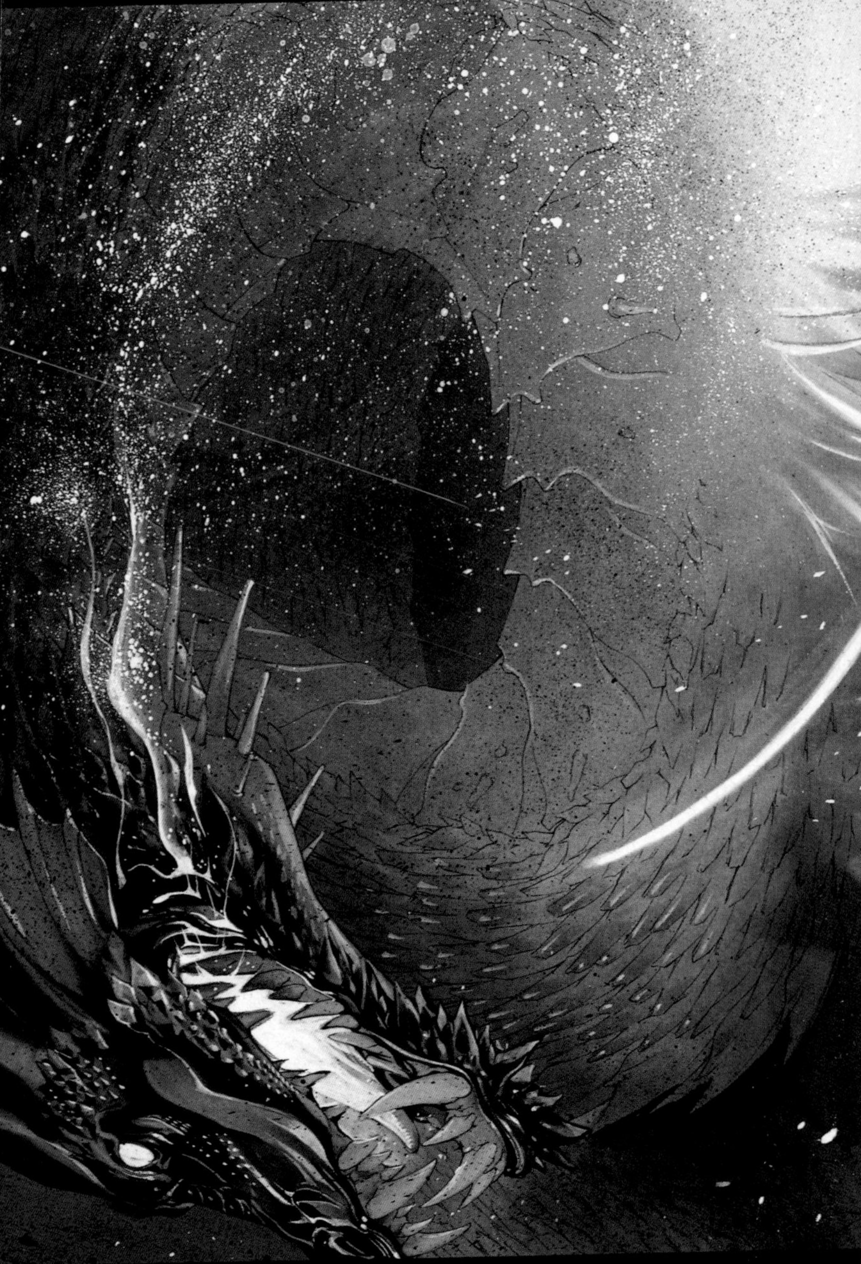

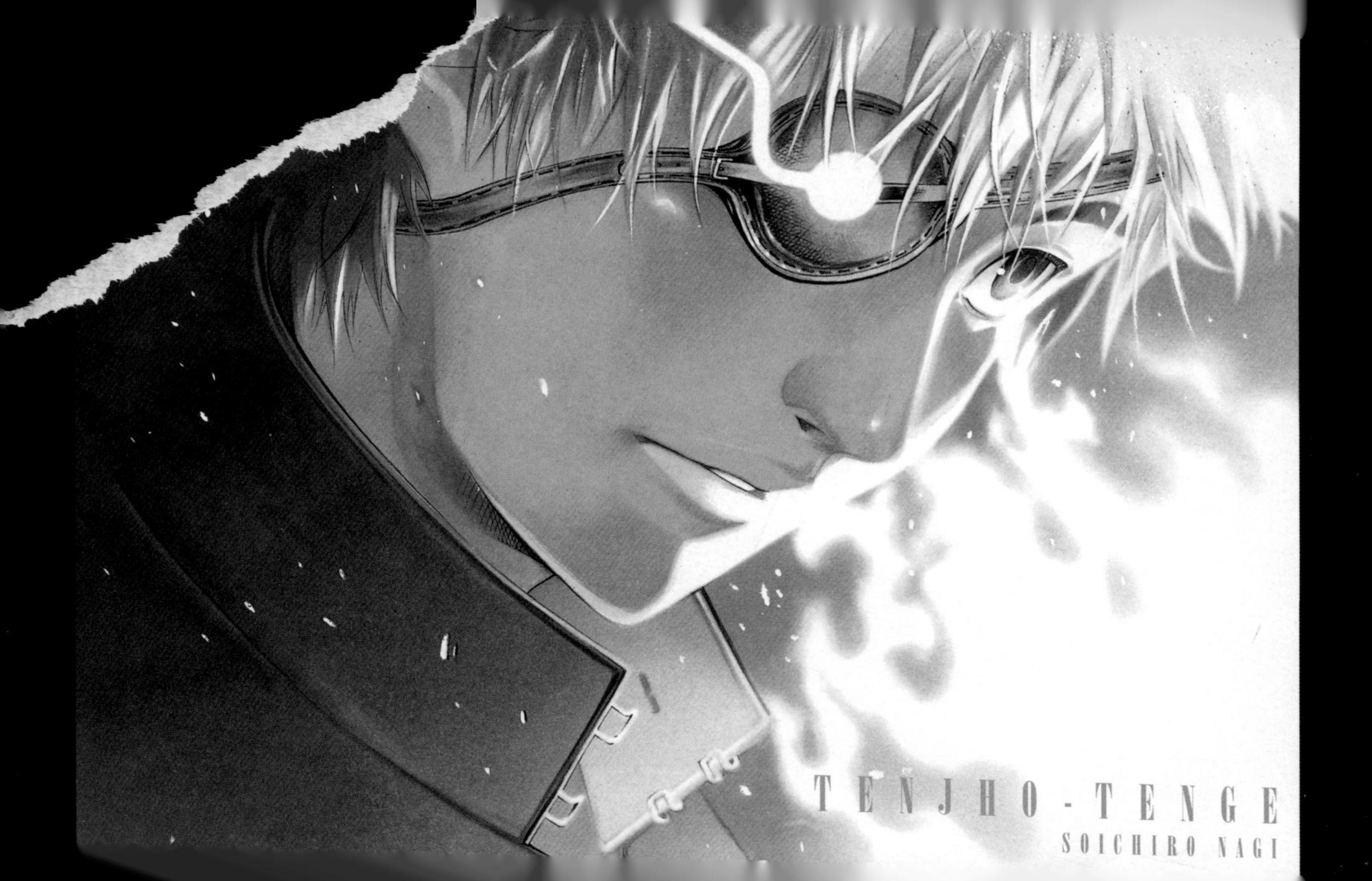
TENJHO-TENGE
SOICHIRO NAGI

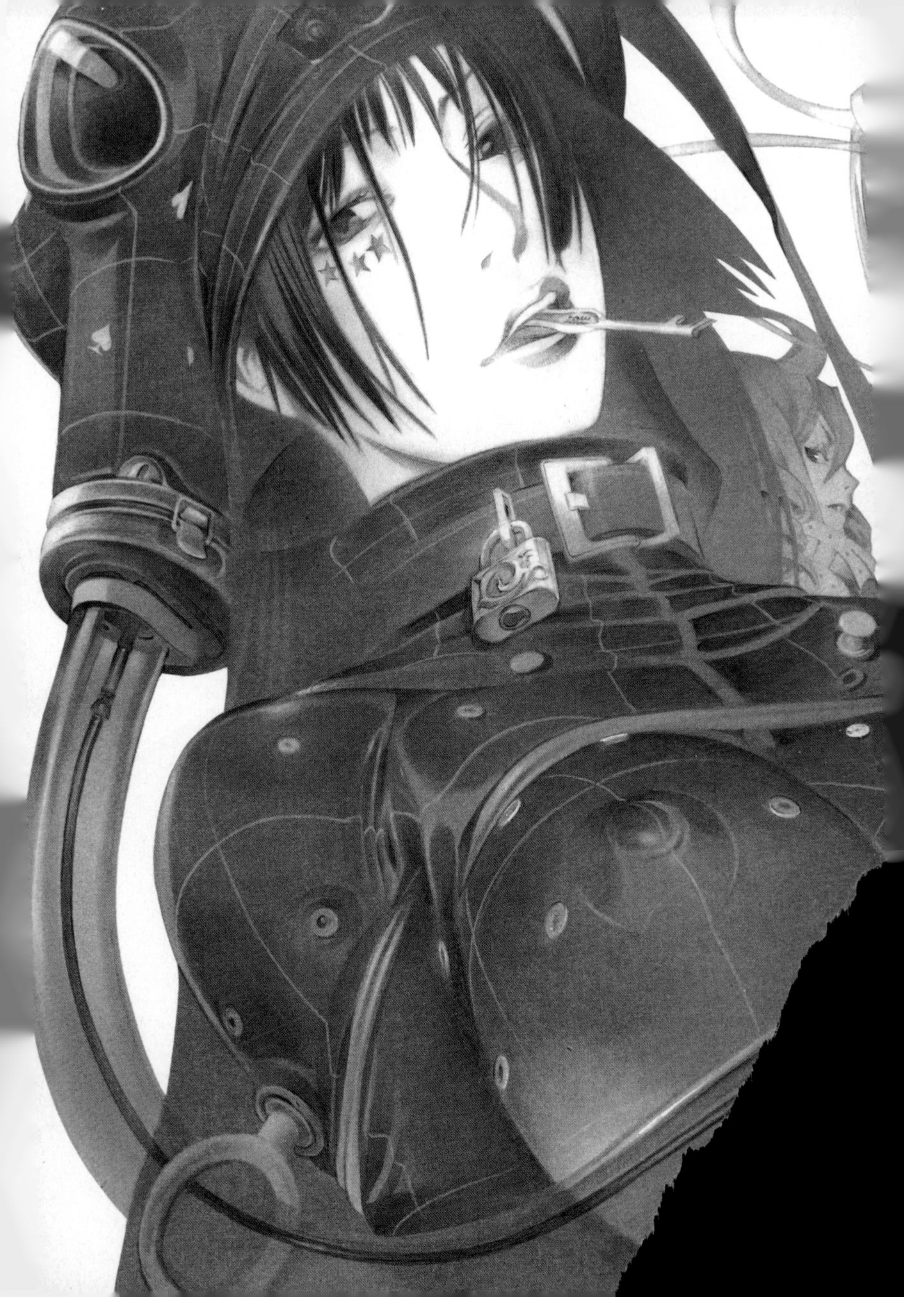

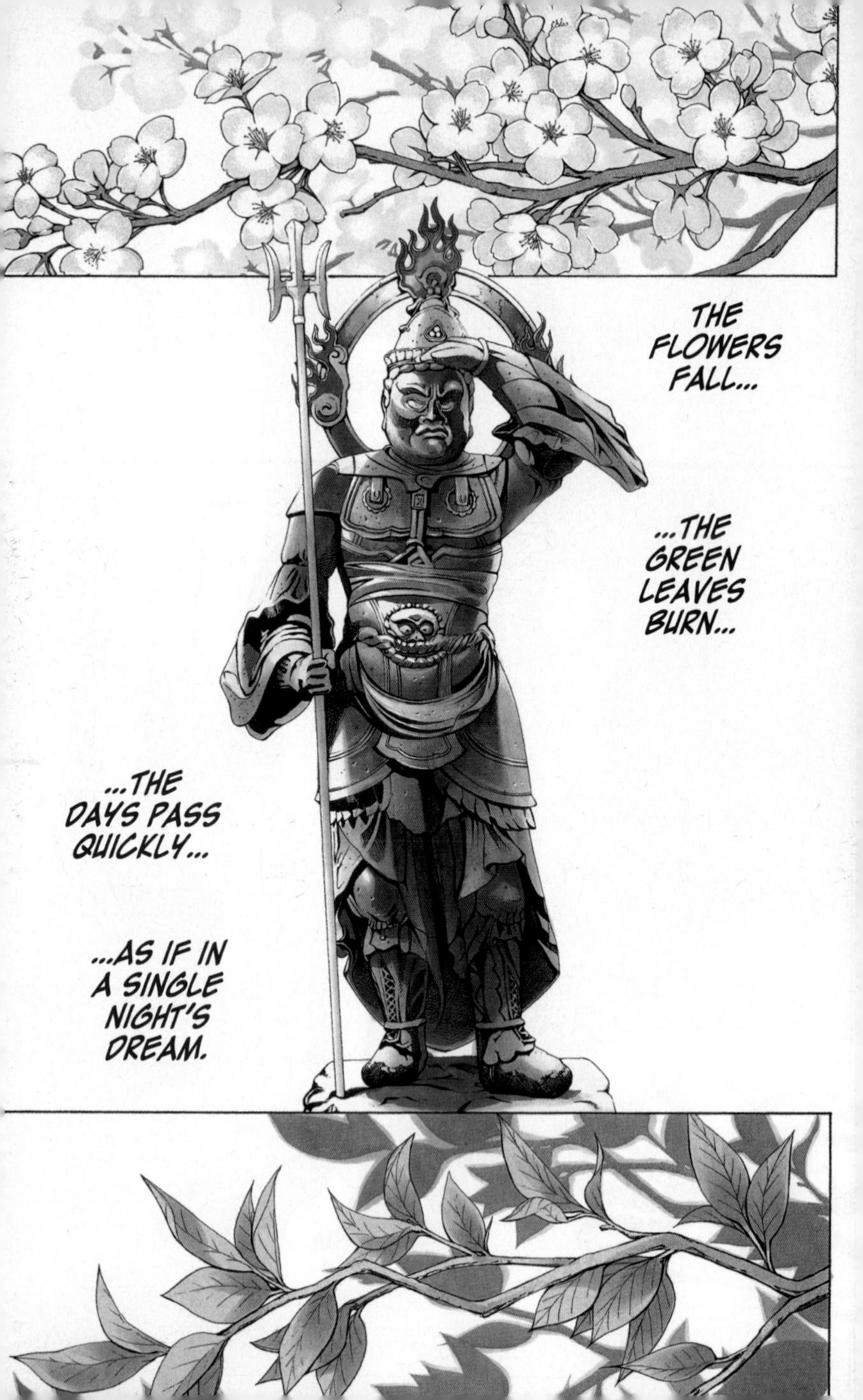
THE FLOWERS FALL...
...THE GREEN LEAVES BURN...
...THE DAYS PASS QUICKLY...
...AS IF IN A SINGLE NIGHT'S DREAM.

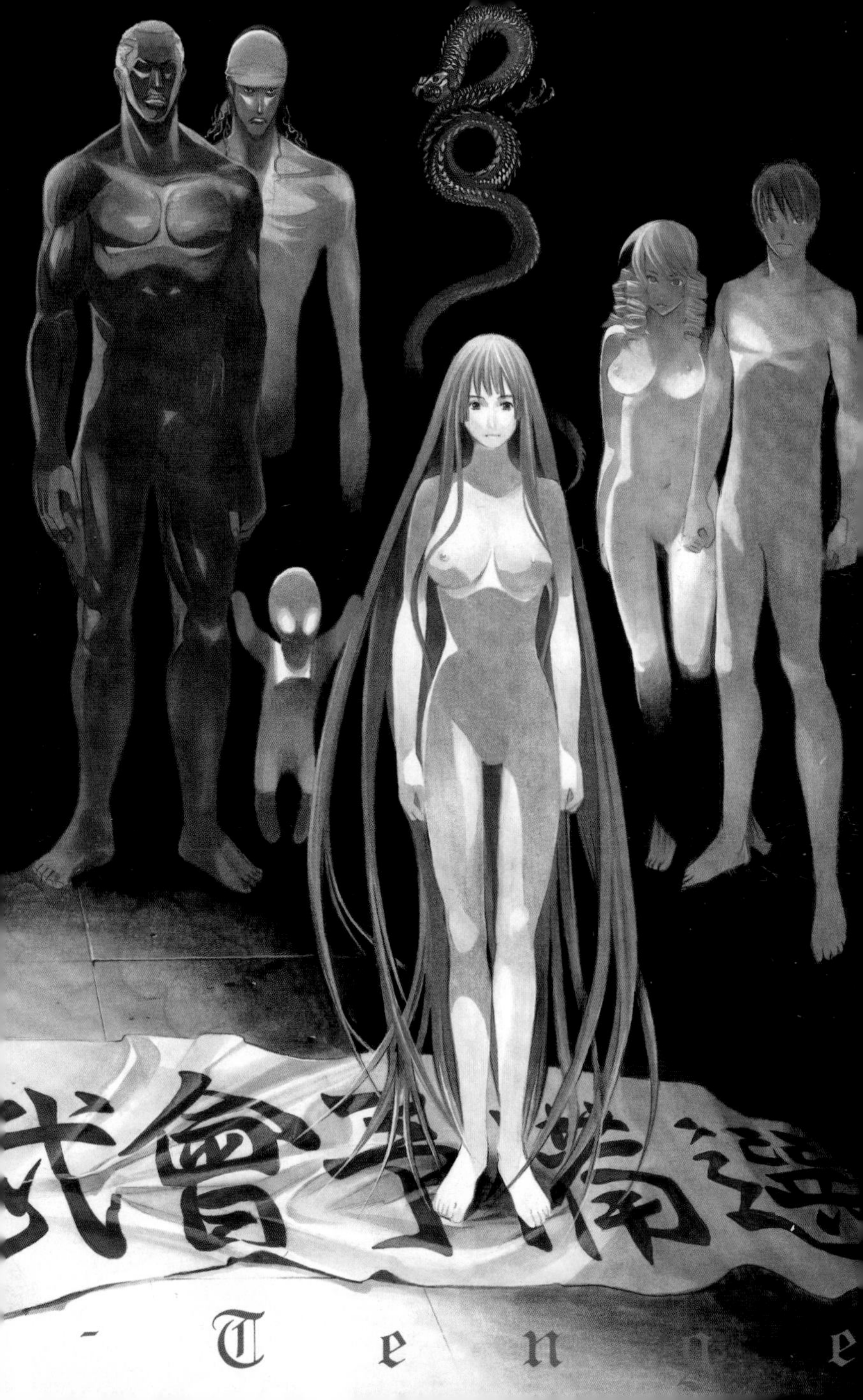
- T e n g e

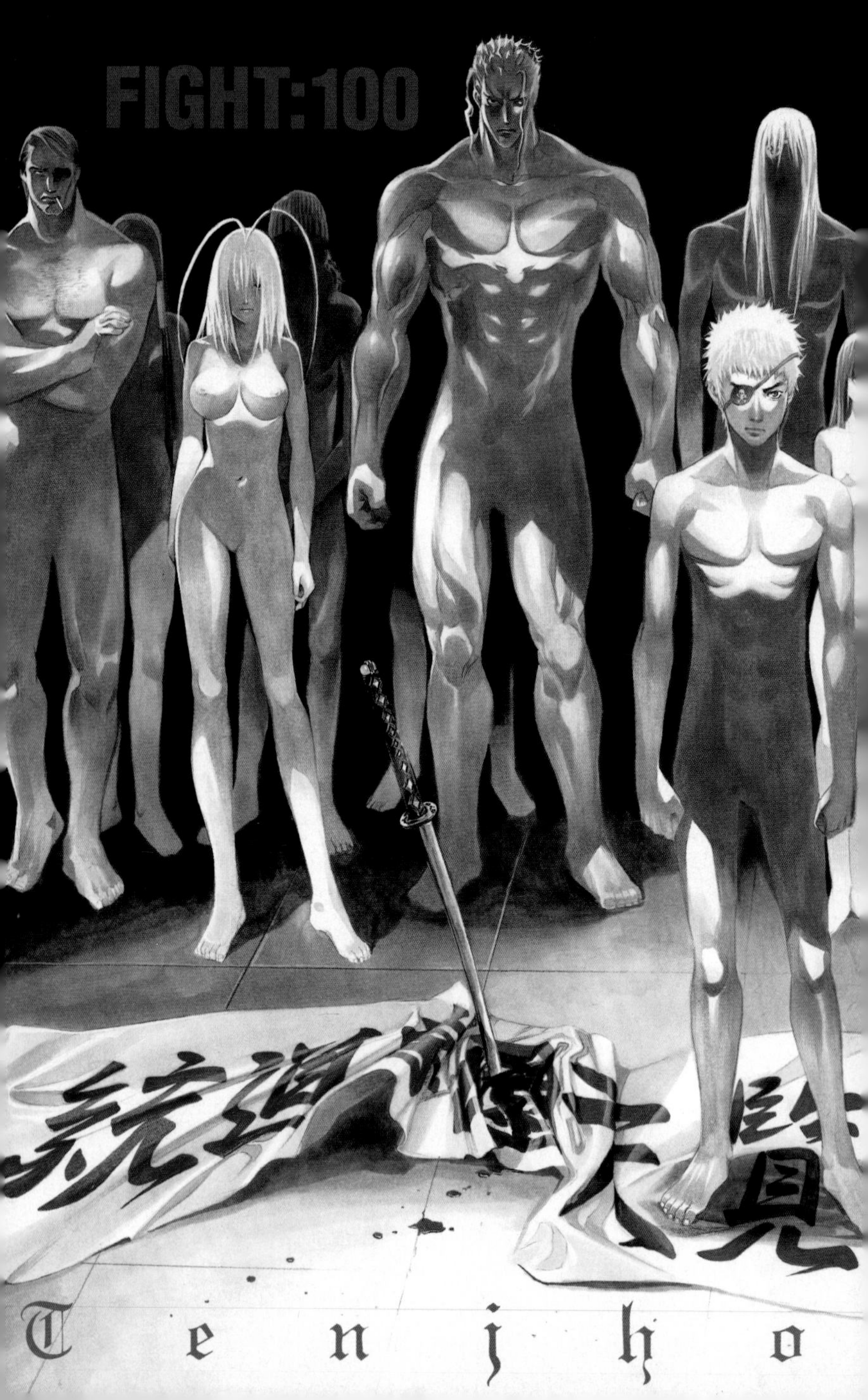
FIGHT:100
Tenjho

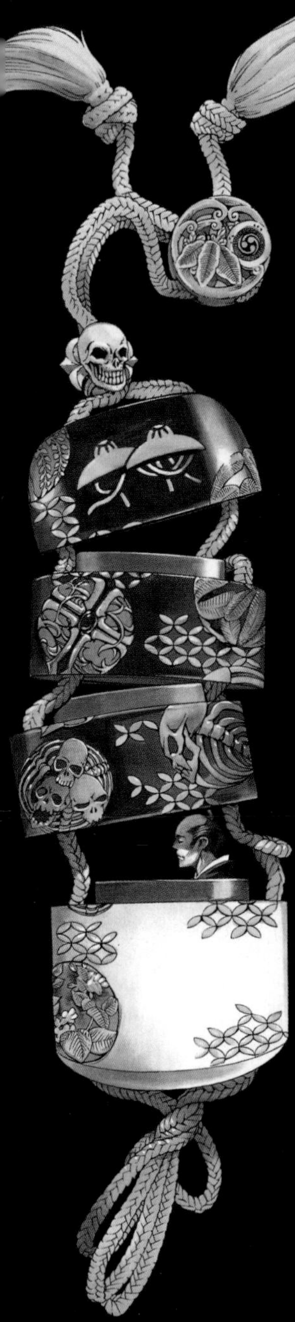

Contents 17

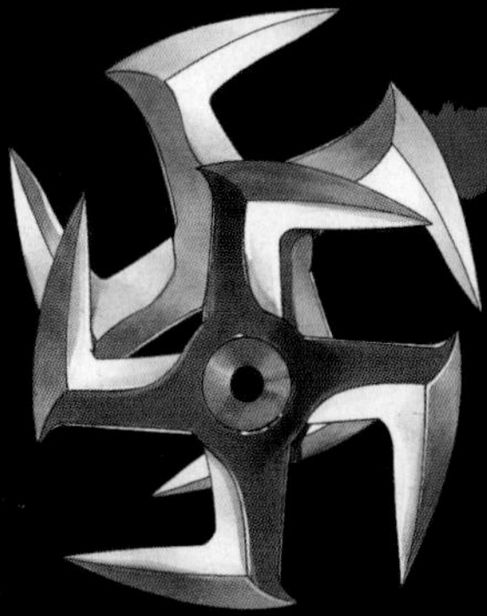

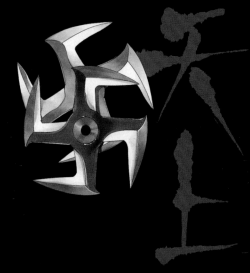

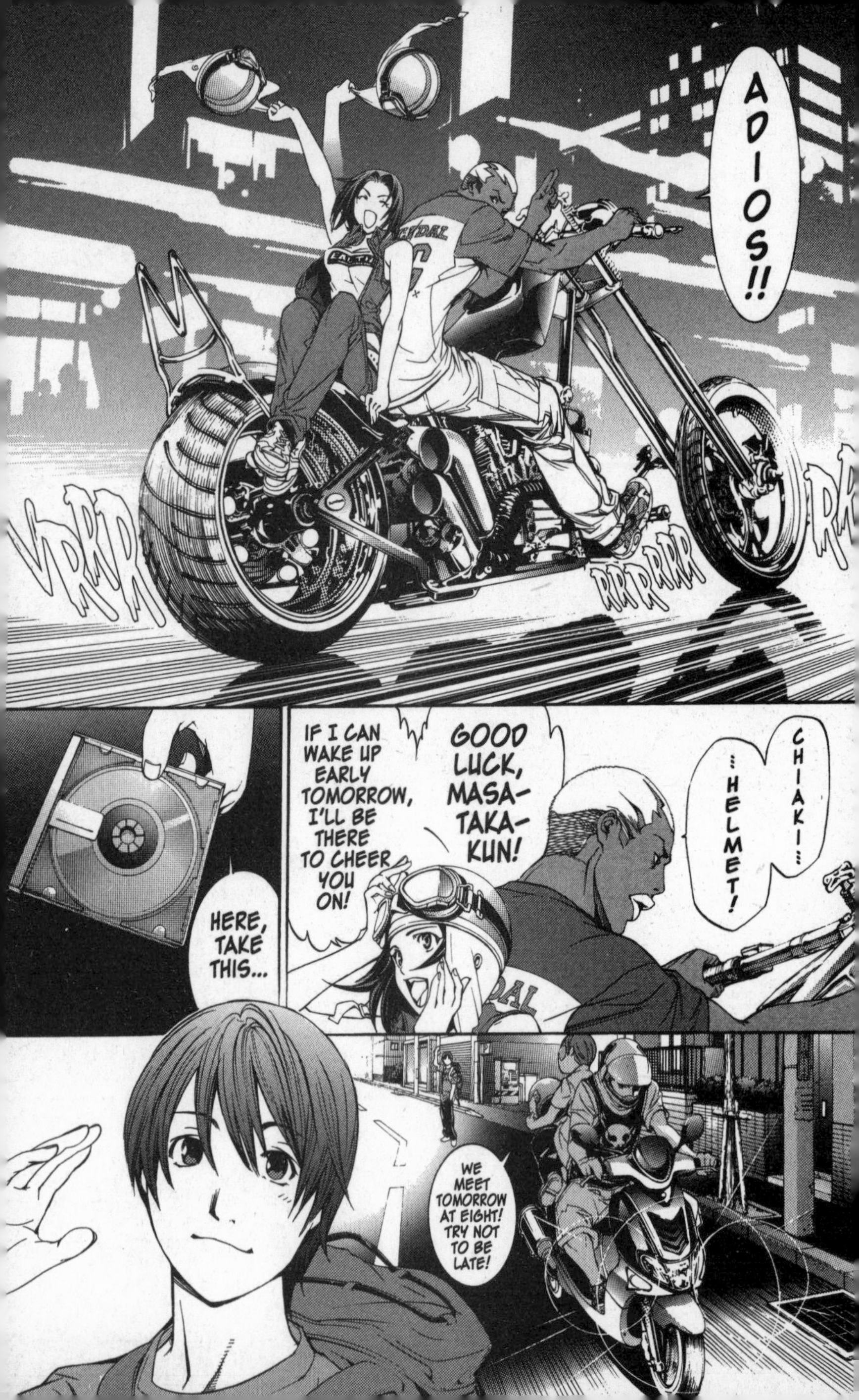
ADIOS!!
VRRRR
RRRRRR
CHIAKI... ...HELMET!
GOOD LUCK, MASA-TAKA-KUN!
IF I CAN WAKE UP EARLY TOMORROW, I'LL BE THERE TO CHEER YOU ON!
HERE, TAKE THIS...
WE MEET TOMORROW AT EIGHT! TRY NOT TO BE LATE!

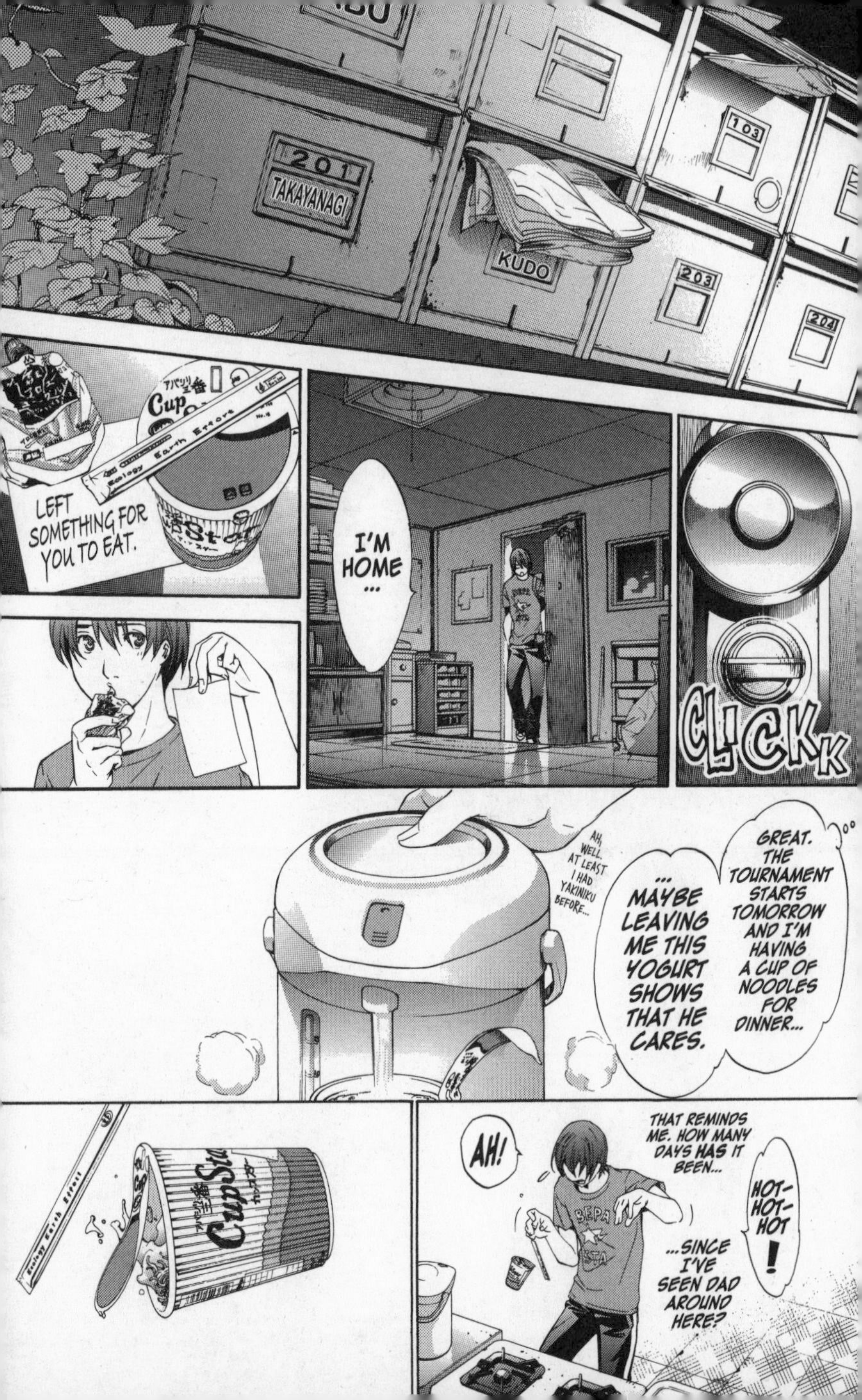
201
TAKAYANAGI
KUDO
103
203
204
CLICKK
I'M HOME ...
LEFT SOMETHING FOR YOU TO EAT.
GREAT. THE TOURNAMENT STARTS TOMORROW AND I'M HAVING A CUP OF NOODLES FOR DINNER...
... MAYBE LEAVING ME THIS YOGURT SHOWS THAT HE CARES.
AH, WELL. AT LEAST I HAD YAKINIKU BEFORE...
HOT-HOT-HOT!
AH!
THAT REMINDS ME. HOW MANY DAYS HAS IT BEEN...
...SINCE I'VE SEEN DAD AROUND HERE?

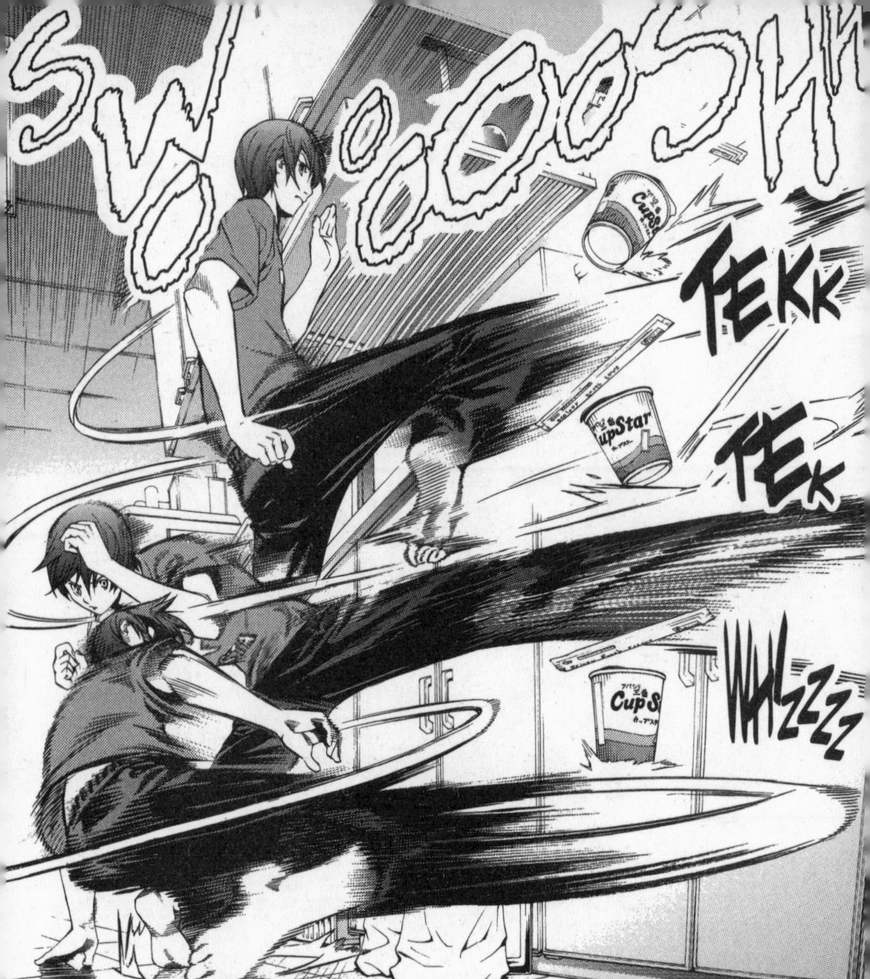
SWOOOOSH
TEKK
TEK
WHIZZZZ

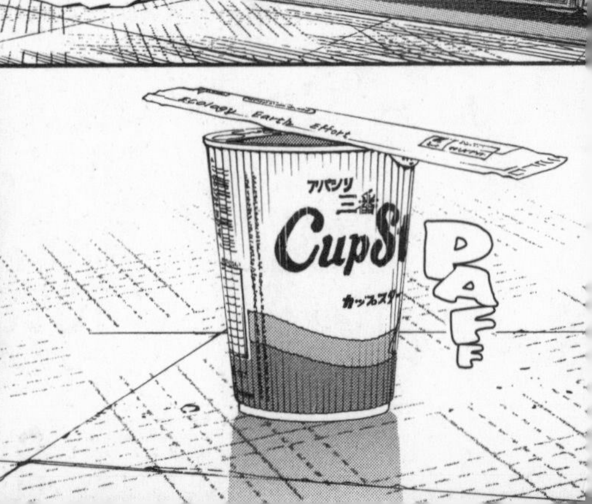
PAF

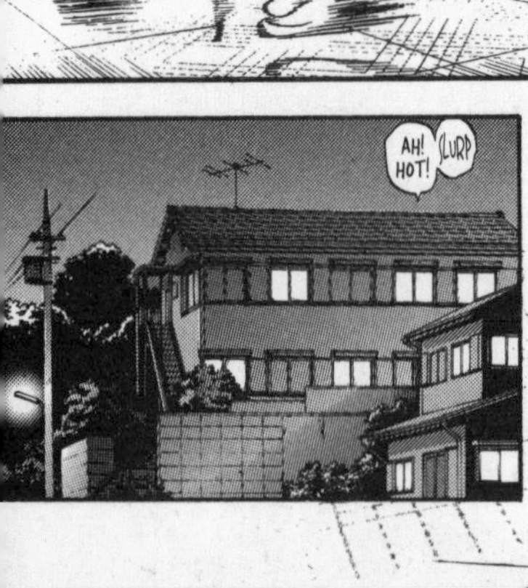
SLURP
AH! HOT!

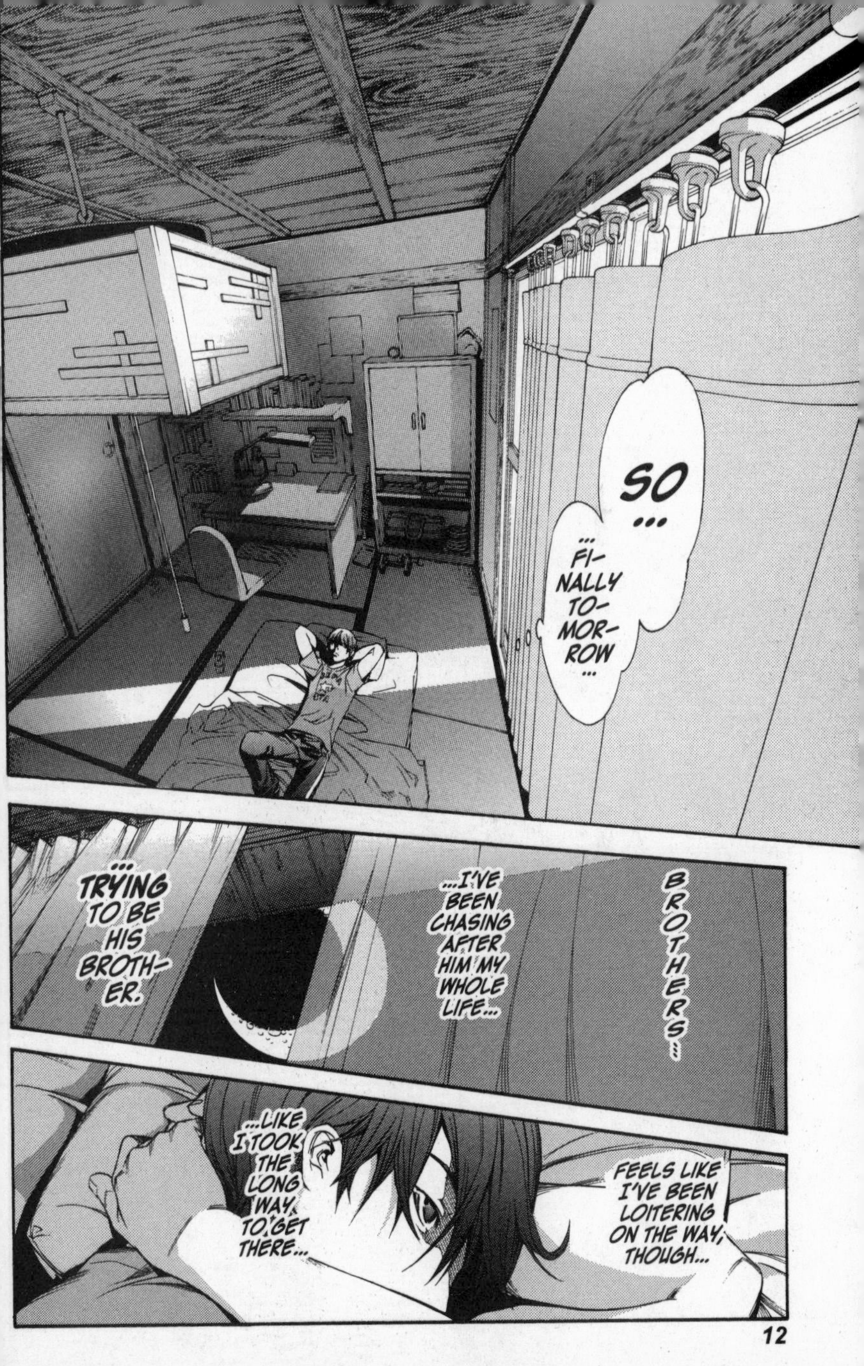
SO...
...FINALLY TOMORROW...
BROTHERS...
...I'VE BEEN CHASING AFTER HIM MY WHOLE LIFE...
...TRYING TO BE HIS BROTHER.
FEELS LIKE I'VE BEEN LOITERING ON THE WAY, THOUGH...
...LIKE I TOOK THE LONG WAY TO GET THERE...

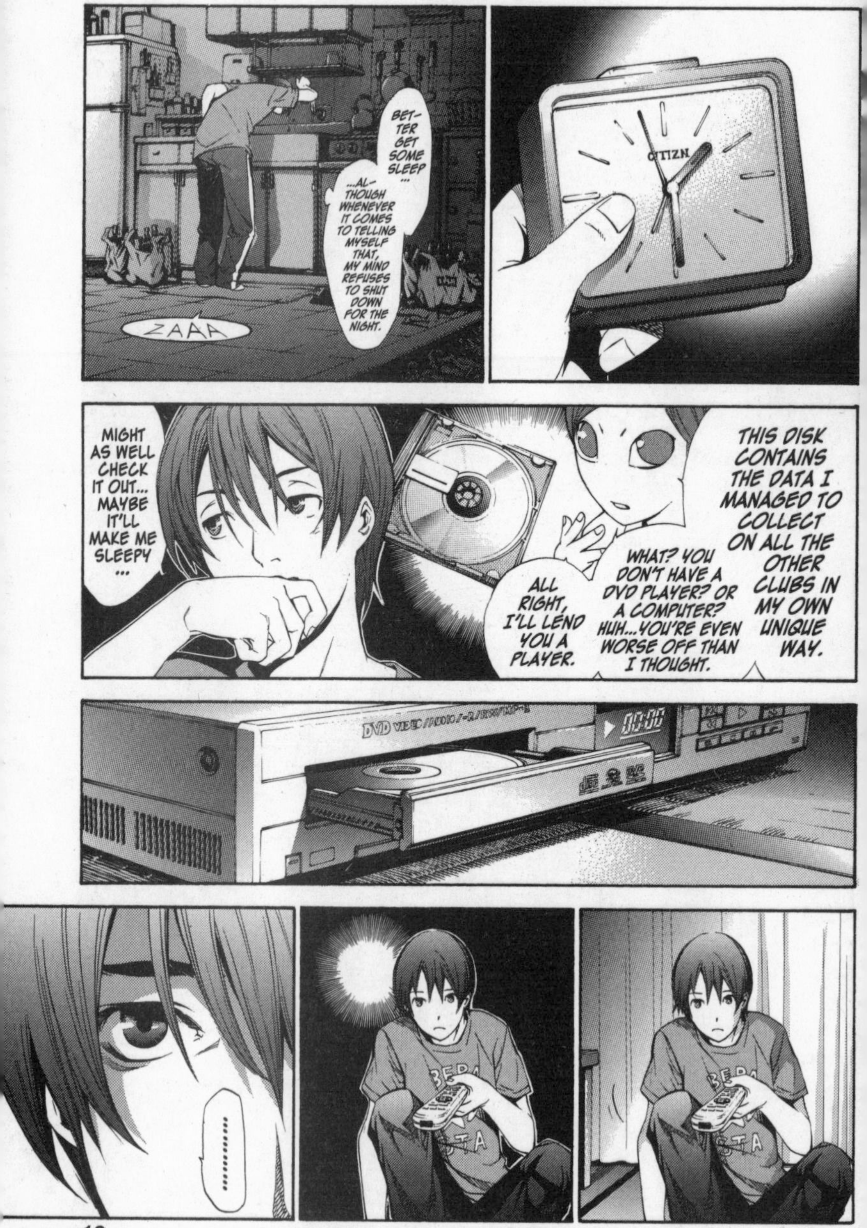
CITIZN
BET-TER GET SOME SLEEP ...
...AL-THOUGH WHENEVER IT COMES TO TELLING MYSELF THAT, MY MIND REFUSES TO SHUT DOWN FOR THE NIGHT.
ZAAA
THIS DISK CONTAINS THE DATA I MANAGED TO COLLECT ON ALL THE OTHER CLUBS IN MY OWN UNIQUE WAY.
WHAT? YOU DON'T HAVE A DVD PLAYER? OR A COMPUTER? HUH...YOU'RE EVEN WORSE OFF THAN I THOUGHT.
ALL RIGHT, I'LL LEND YOU A PLAYER.
MIGHT AS WELL CHECK IT OUT... MAYBE IT'LL MAKE ME SLEEPY ...
....

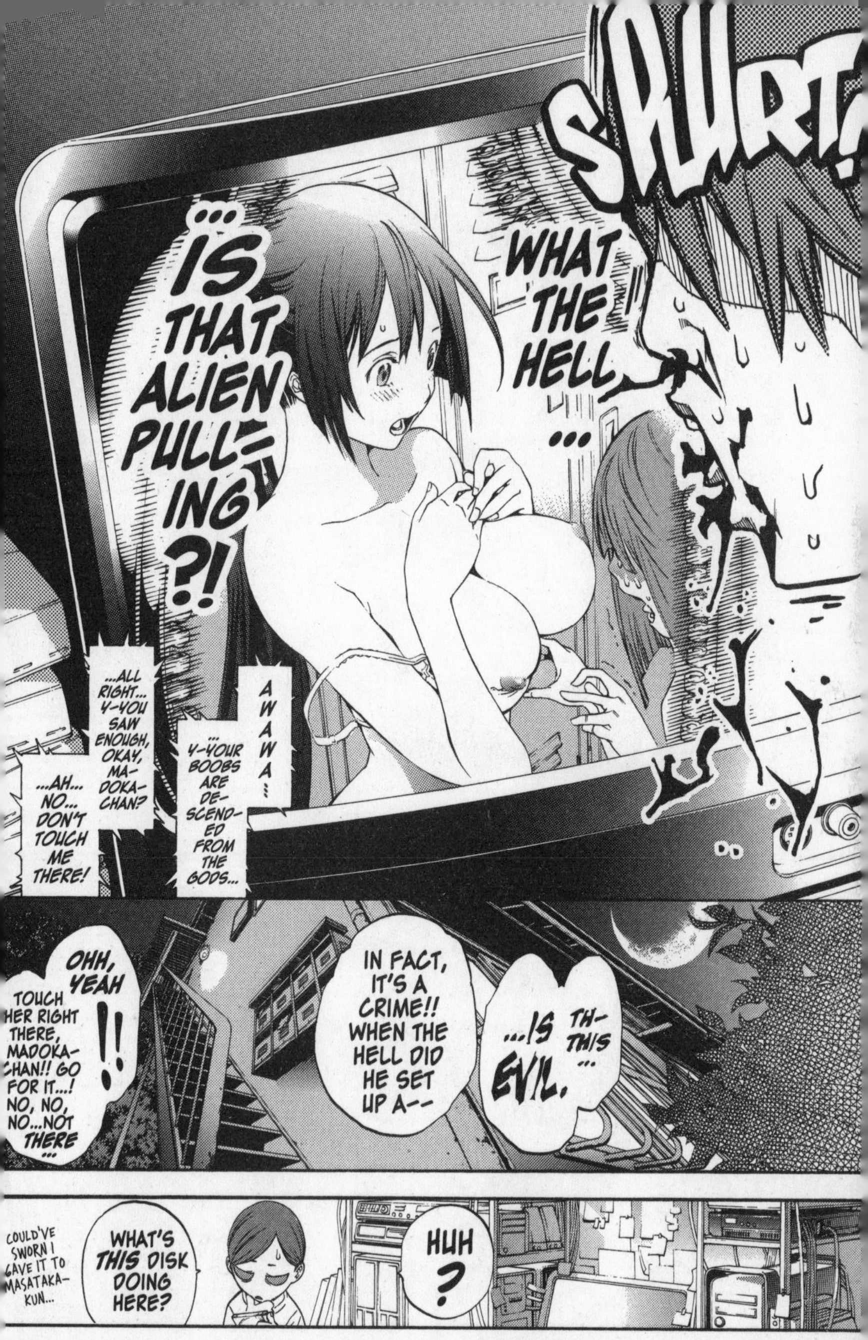
SPLURT!
WHAT THE HELL...
...IS THAT ALIEN PULLING?!
AWAWA...
...Y-YOUR BOOBS ARE DESCENDED FROM THE GODS...
...ALL RIGHT... Y-YOU SAW ENOUGH, OKAY, MADOKA-CHAN?
...AH... NO... DON'T TOUCH ME THERE!
TH-THIS...
...IS EVIL.
IN FACT, IT'S A CRIME!! WHEN THE HELL DID HE SET UP A--
OHH, YEAH!!
TOUCH HER RIGHT THERE, MADOKA-CHAN!! GO FOR IT...! NO, NO, NO...NOT THERE...
HUH?
WHAT'S THIS DISK DOING HERE?
COULD'VE SWORN I GAVE IT TO MASATAKA-KUN...

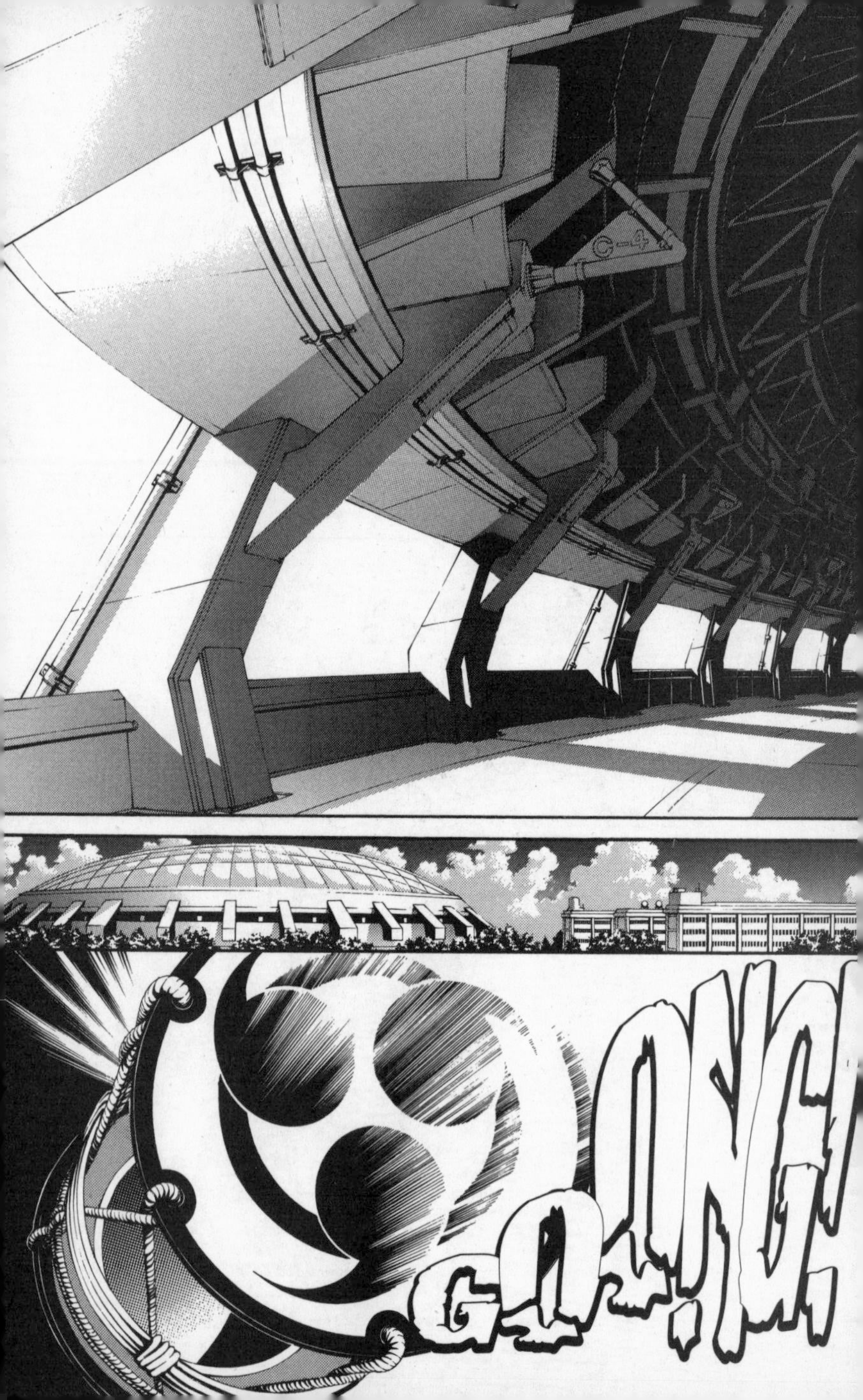
GOONG!

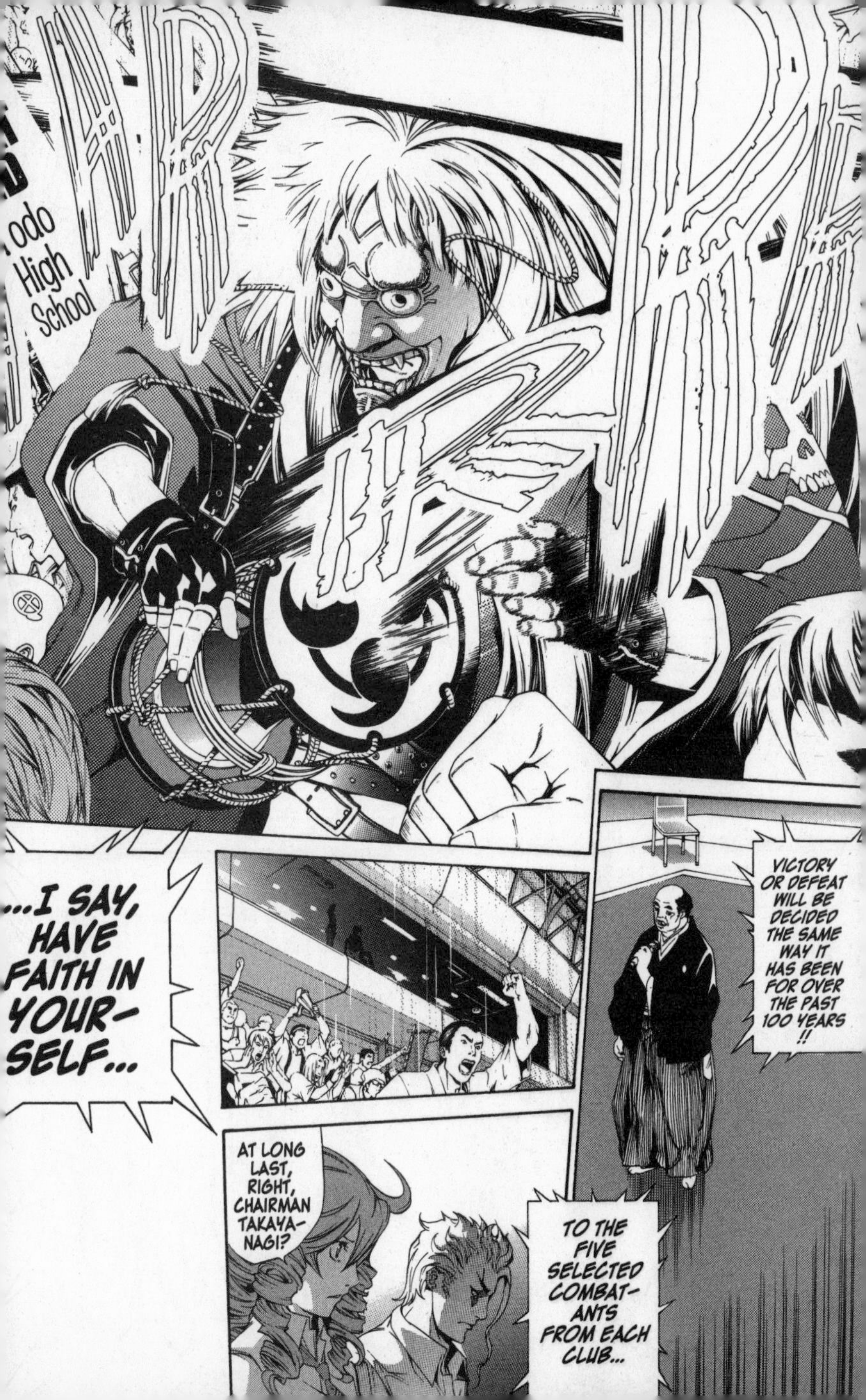
odo High School
VICTORY OR DEFEAT WILL BE DECIDED THE SAME WAY IT HAS BEEN FOR OVER THE PAST 100 YEARS !!
TO THE FIVE SELECTED COMBAT-ANTS FROM EACH CLUB...
...I SAY, HAVE FAITH IN YOUR-SELF...
AT LONG LAST, RIGHT, CHAIRMAN TAKAYA-NAGI?

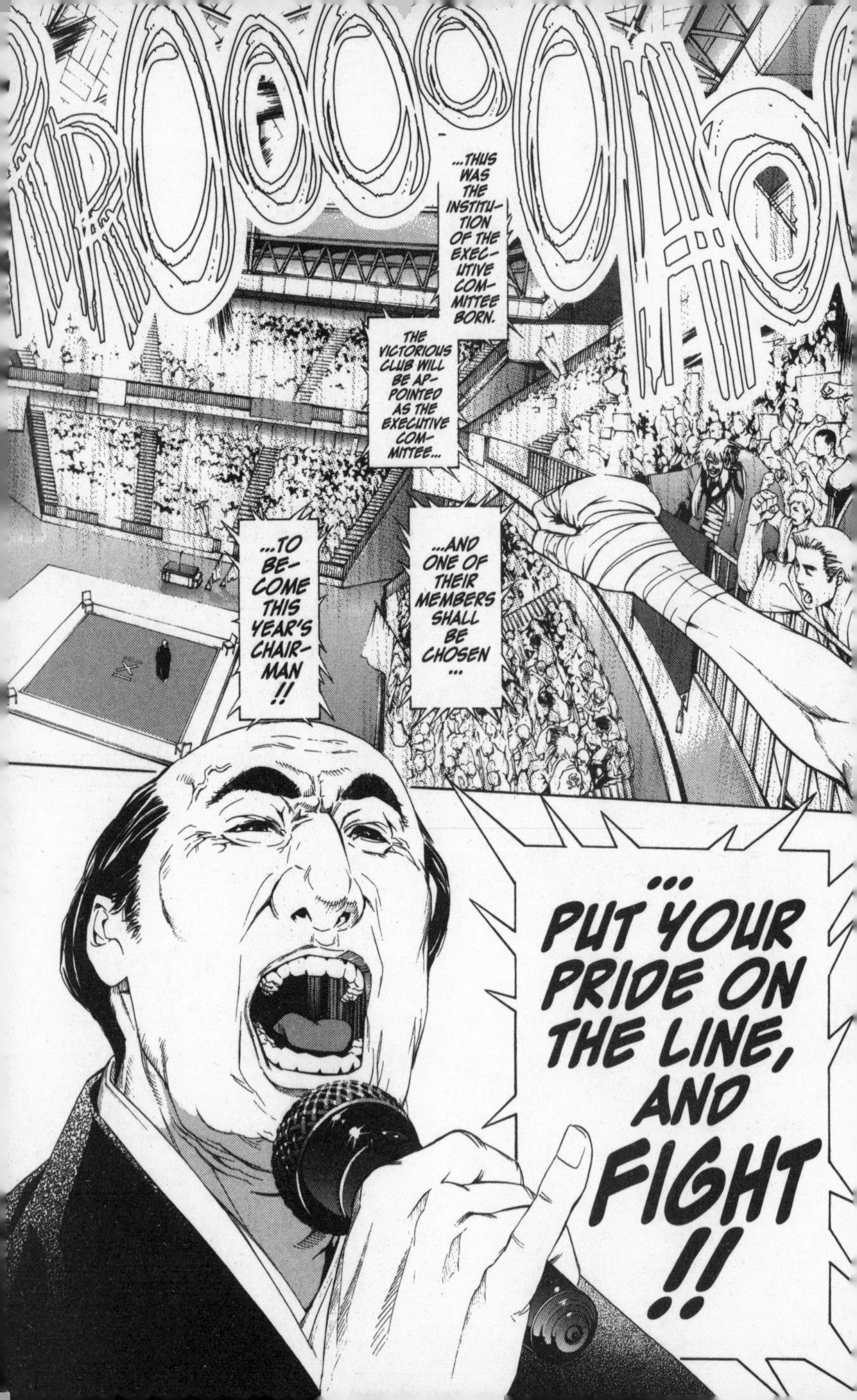
...THUS WAS THE INSTITUTION OF THE EXECUTIVE COMMITTEE BORN.
THE VICTORIOUS CLUB WILL BE APPOINTED AS THE EXECUTIVE COMMITTEE...
...AND ONE OF THEIR MEMBERS SHALL BE CHOSEN...
...TO BECOME THIS YEAR'S CHAIRMAN!!
...PUT YOUR PRIDE ON THE LINE, AND FIGHT!!

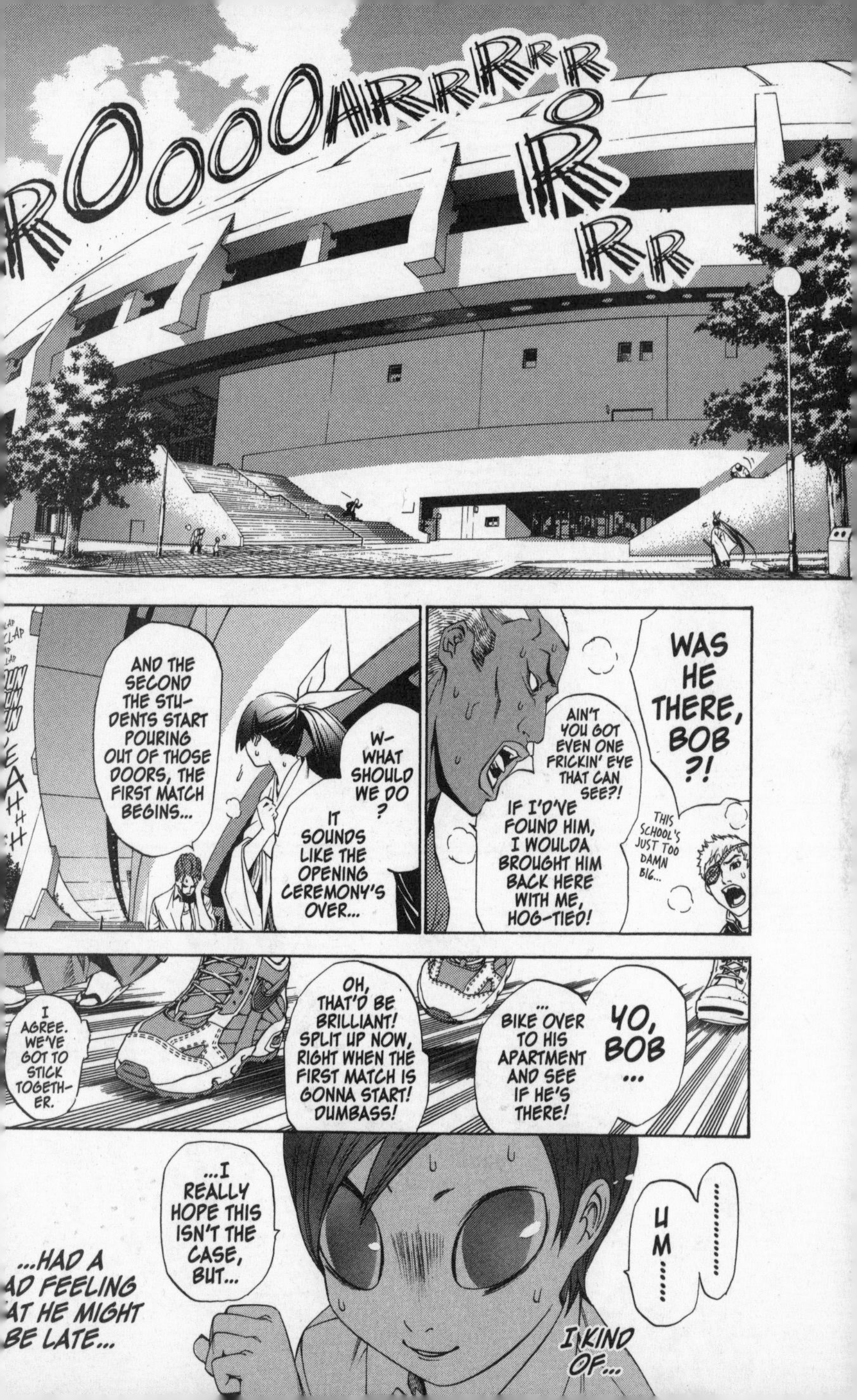
ROOOOARRRRRR
ORRR
WAS HE THERE, BOB?!
THIS SCHOOL'S JUST TOO DAMN BIG...
AIN'T YOU GOT EVEN ONE FRICKIN' EYE THAT CAN SEE?!
IF I'D'VE FOUND HIM, I WOULDA BROUGHT HIM BACK HERE WITH ME, HOG-TIED!
W-WHAT SHOULD WE DO?
IT SOUNDS LIKE THE OPENING CEREMONY'S OVER...
AND THE SECOND THE STUDENTS START POURING OUT OF THOSE DOORS, THE FIRST MATCH BEGINS...
YO, BOB...
...BIKE OVER TO HIS APARTMENT AND SEE IF HE'S THERE!
OH, THAT'D BE BRILLIANT! SPLIT UP NOW, RIGHT WHEN THE FIRST MATCH IS GONNA START! DUMBASS!
I AGREE. WE'VE GOT TO STICK TOGETHER.
UM.........
I KIND OF...
...I REALLY HOPE THIS ISN'T THE CASE, BUT...
...HAD A
AD FEELING
AT HE MIGHT
BE LATE...

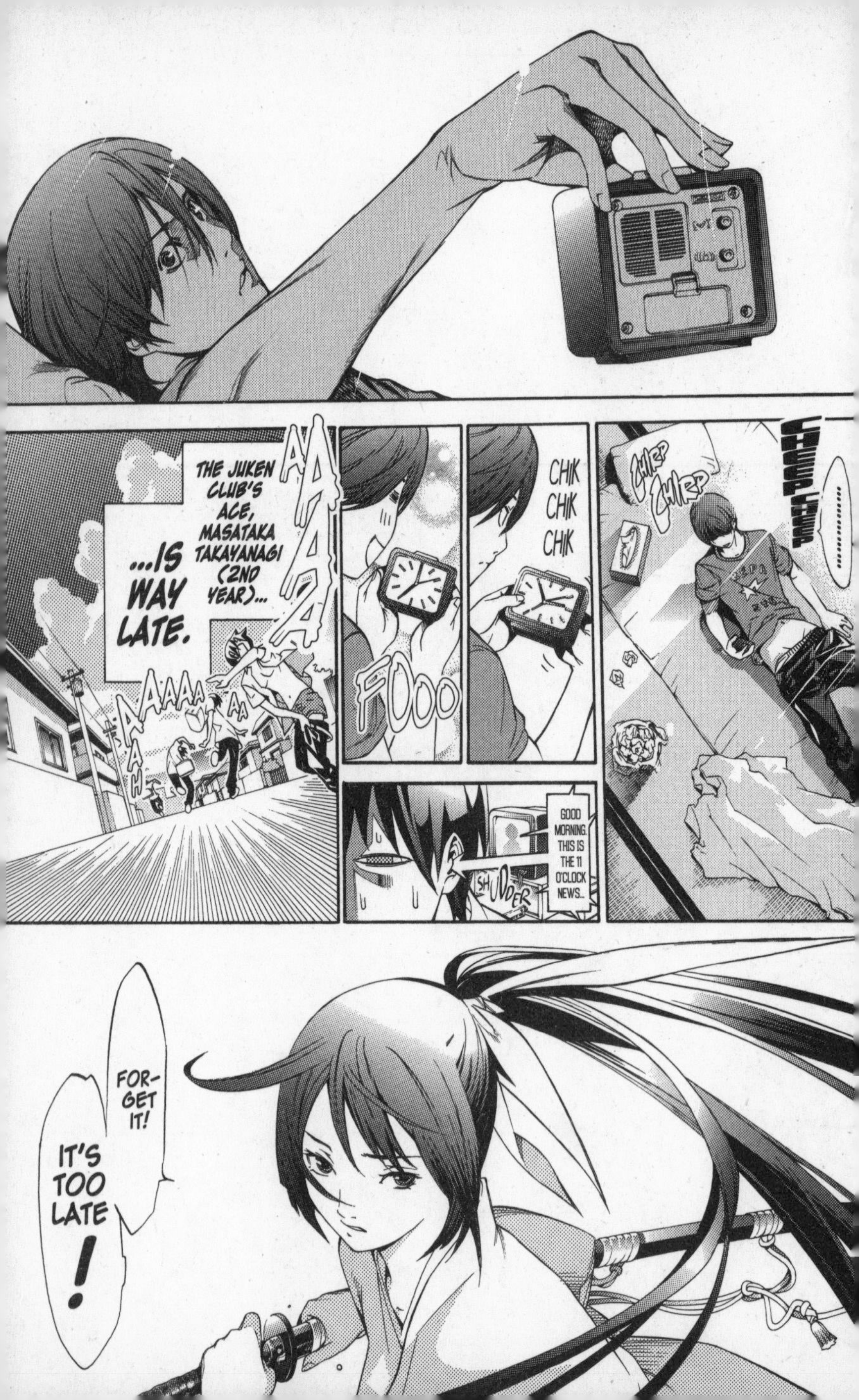

CHEEP CHEEP
......
CHIRP CHIRP
CHIK CHIK CHIK
FOOO
GOOD MORNING. THIS IS THE 11 O'CLOCK NEWS...
SHUDDER
THE JUKEN CLUB'S ACE, MASATAKA TAKAYANAGI (2ND YEAR)...
...IS WAY LATE.
AAAAAA
AAAA AA AAAH
FOR-GET IT!
IT'S TOO LATE!

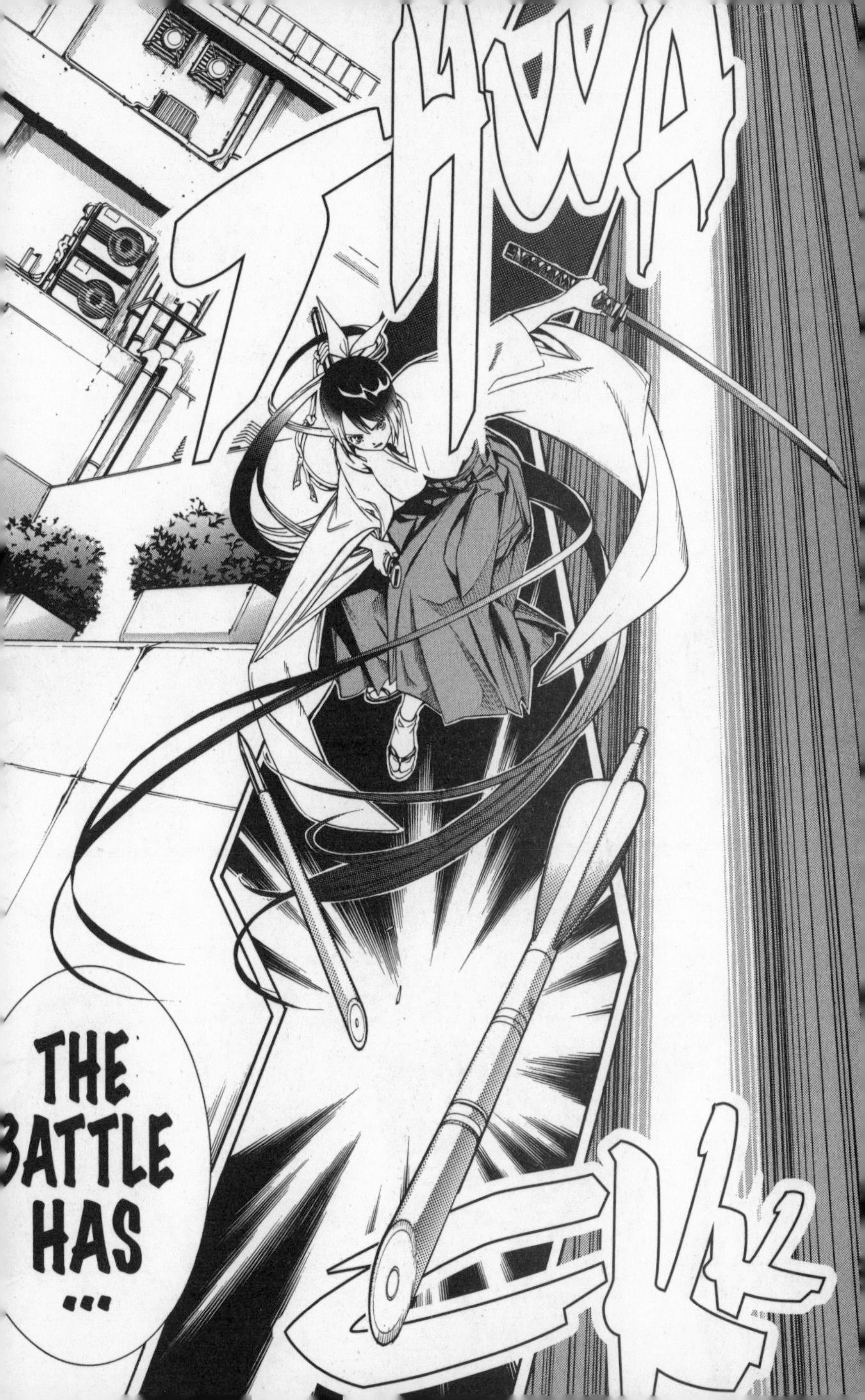
THE BATTLE HAS ...

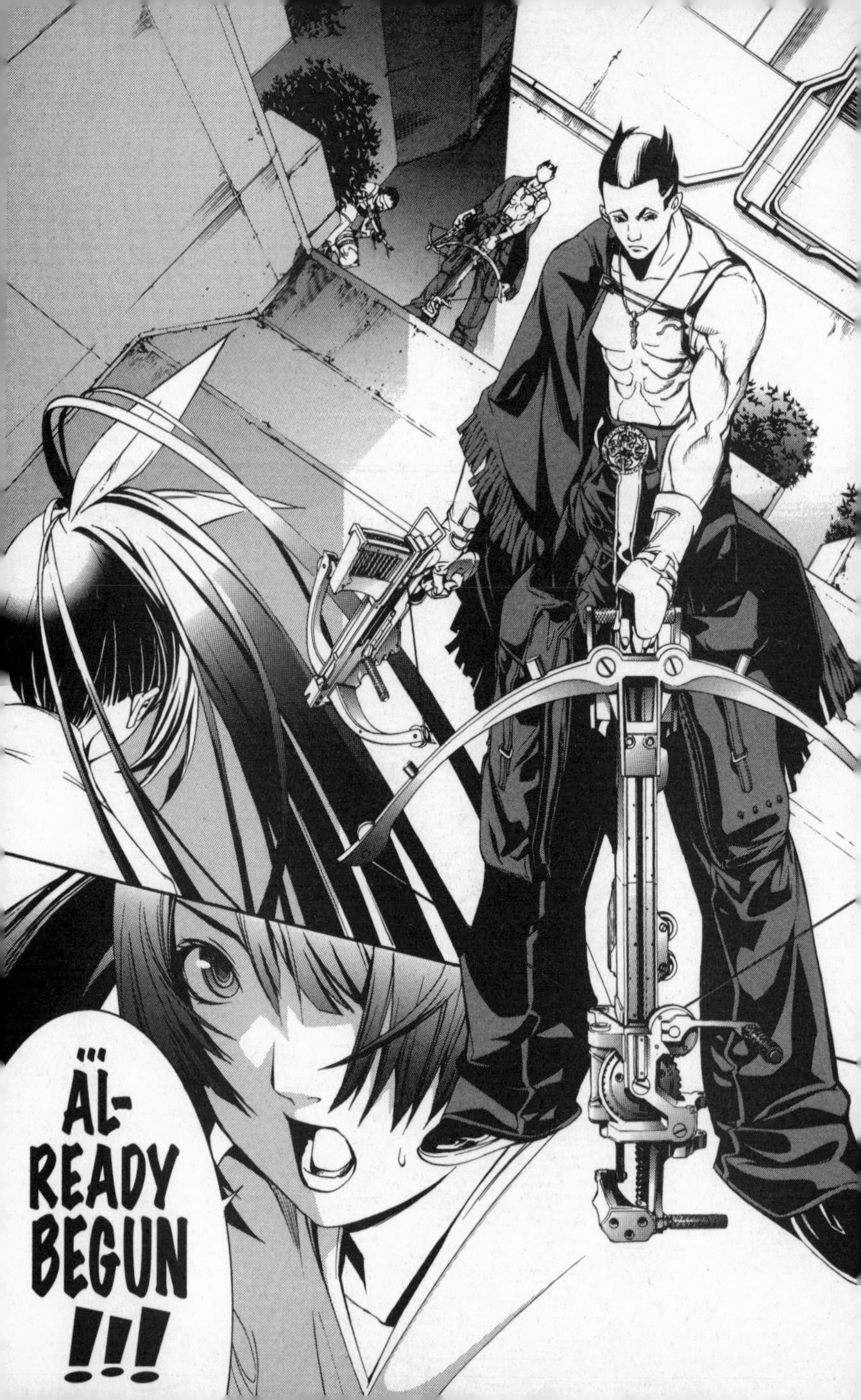
...ÄL-READY BEGUN!!!

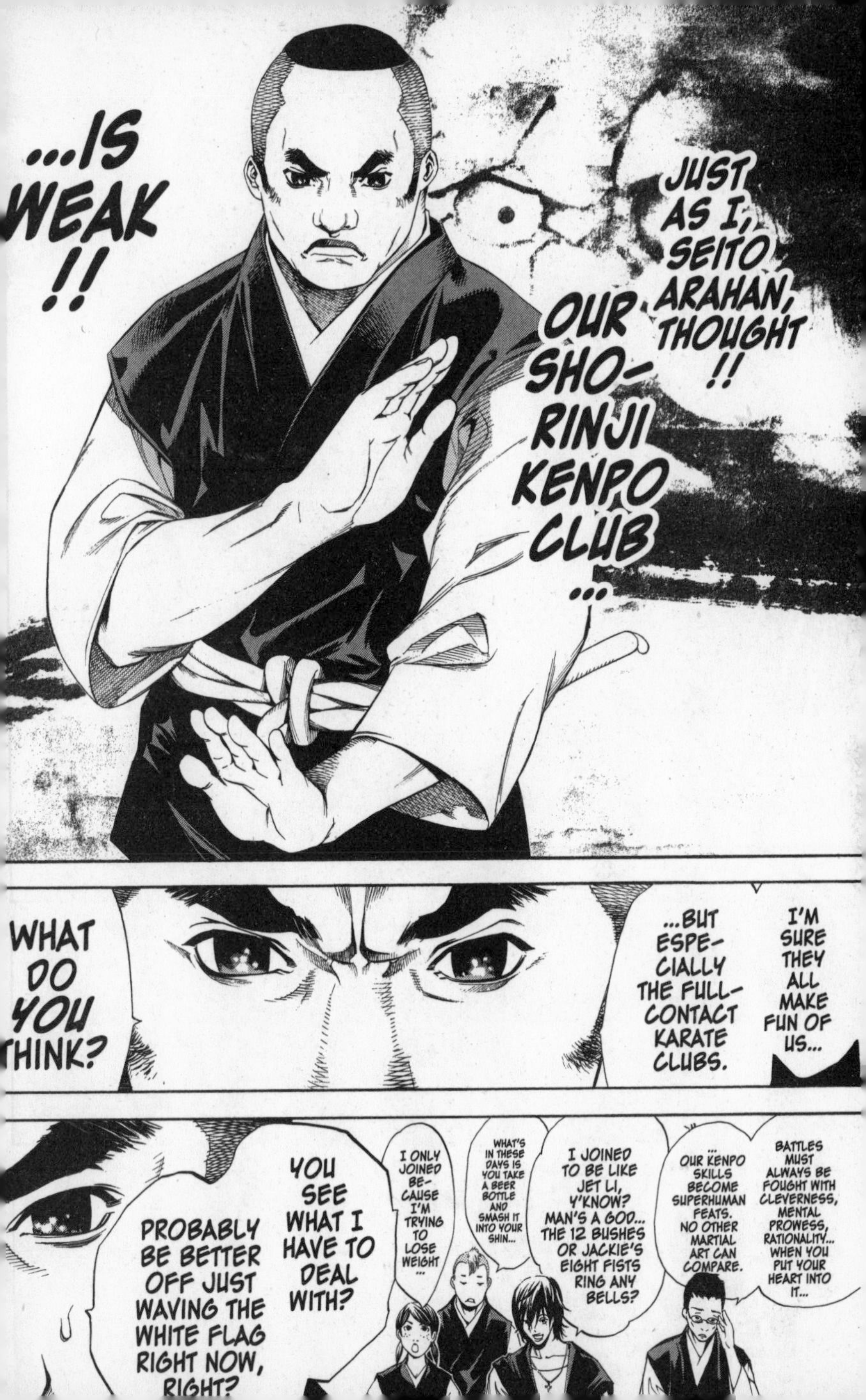
JUST AS I, SEITO ARAHAN, THOUGHT!!
OUR SHO-RINJI KENPO CLUB...
...IS WEAK!!
I'M SURE THEY ALL MAKE FUN OF US...
...BUT ESPE-CIALLY THE FULL-CONTACT KARATE CLUBS.
WHAT DO YOU THINK?
BATTLES MUST ALWAYS BE FOUGHT WITH CLEVERNESS, MENTAL PROWESS, RATIONALITY... WHEN YOU PUT YOUR HEART INTO IT...
...OUR KENPO SKILLS BECOME SUPERHUMAN FEATS. NO OTHER MARTIAL ART CAN COMPARE.
I JOINED TO BE LIKE JET LI, Y'KNOW? MAN'S A GOD... THE 12 BUSHES OR JACKIE'S EIGHT FISTS RING ANY BELLS?
WHAT'S IN THESE DAYS IS YOU TAKE A BEER BOTTLE AND SMASH IT INTO YOUR SHIN...
I ONLY JOINED BE-CAUSE I'M TRYING TO LOSE WEIGHT...
YOU SEE WHAT I HAVE TO DEAL WITH?
PROBABLY BE BETTER OFF JUST WAVING THE WHITE FLAG RIGHT NOW, RIGHT?

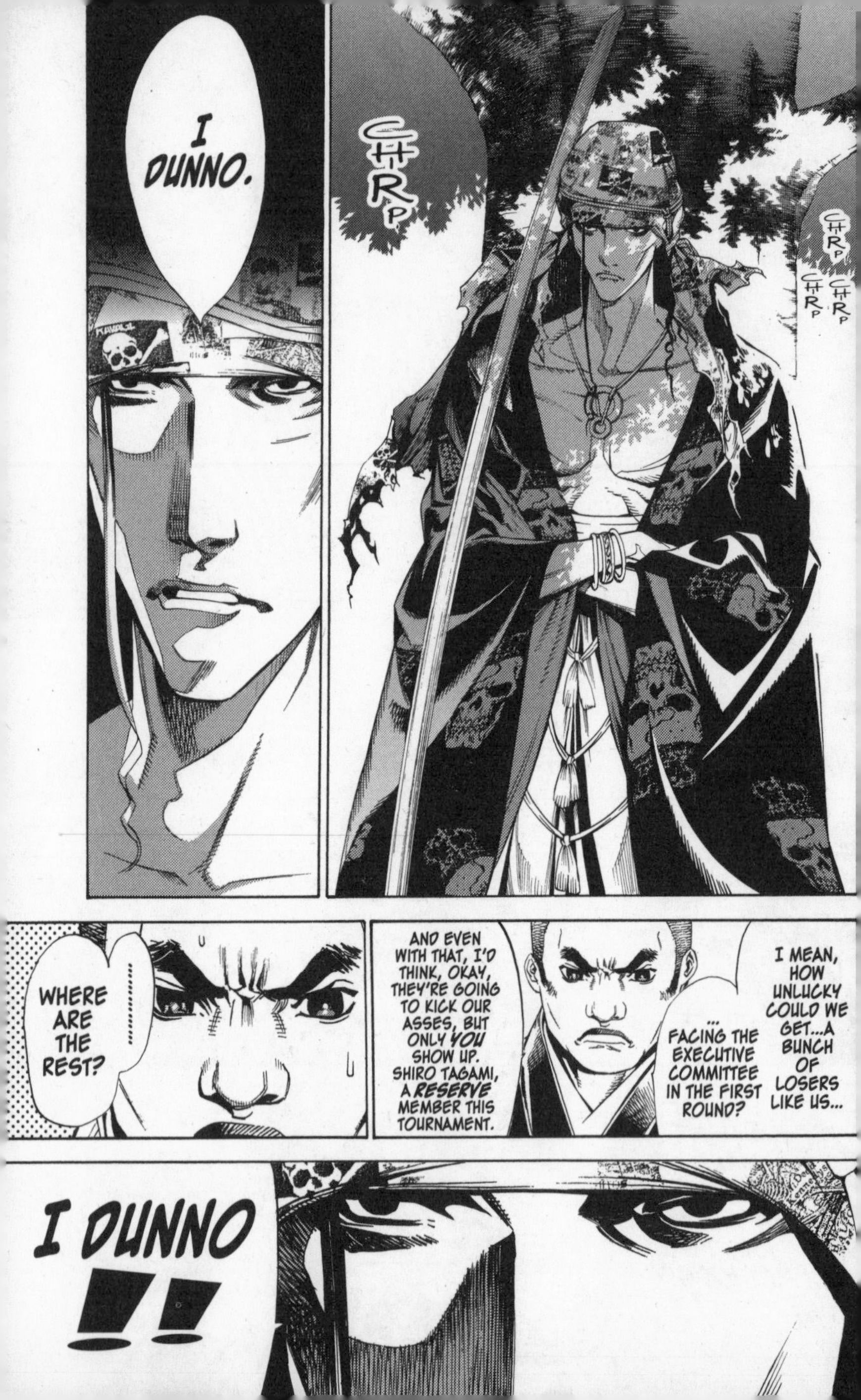
CHIRP
CHIRP
CHIRP
CHIRP
I DUNNO.
I MEAN, HOW UNLUCKY COULD WE GET...A BUNCH OF LOSERS LIKE US...
...FACING THE EXECUTIVE COMMITTEE IN THE FIRST ROUND?
AND EVEN WITH THAT, I'D THINK, OKAY, THEY'RE GOING TO KICK OUR ASSES, BUT ONLY YOU SHOW UP. SHIRO TAGAMI, A RESERVE MEMBER THIS TOURNAMENT.
......
WHERE ARE THE REST?
I DUNNO!!

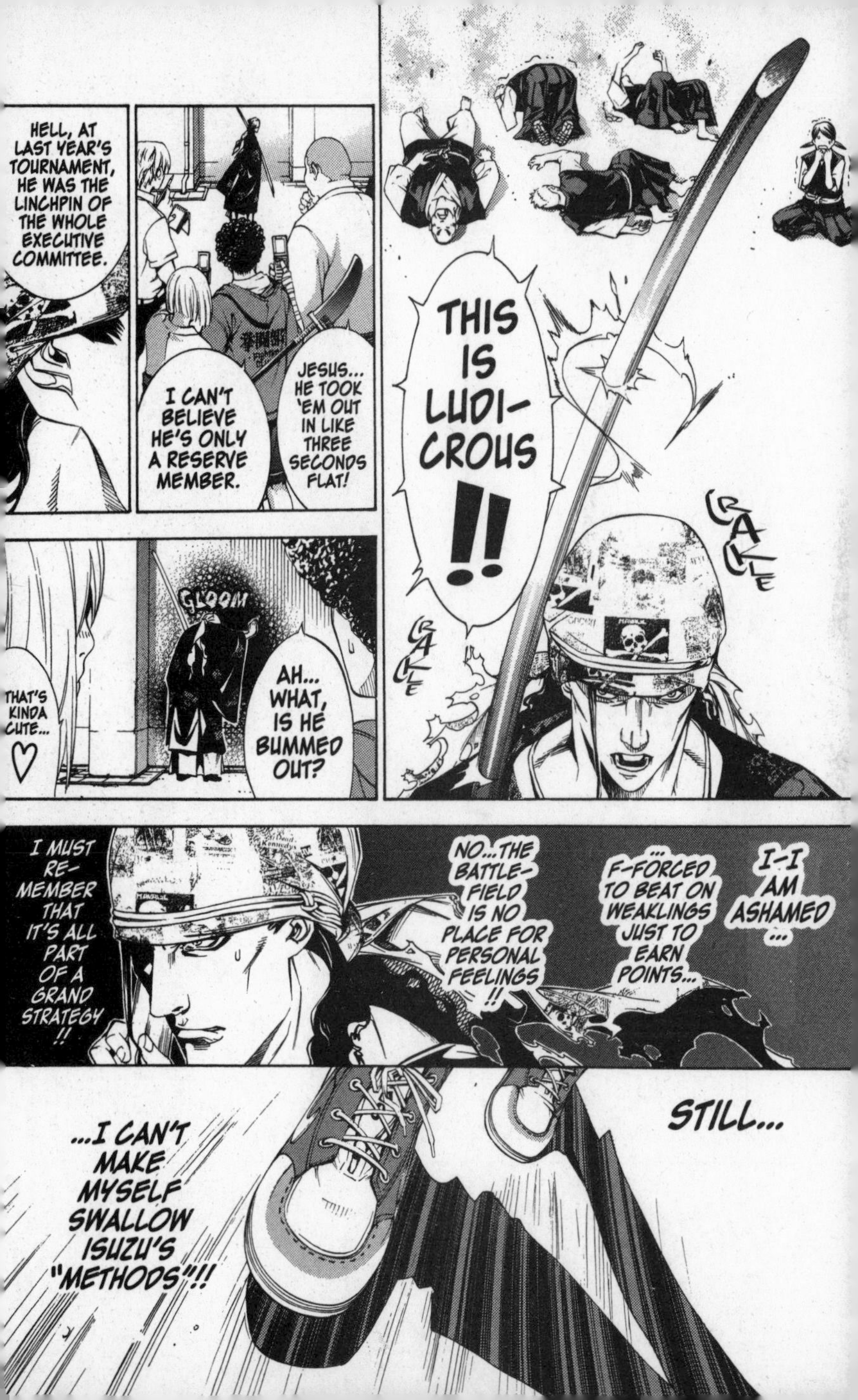
THIS IS LUDI-CROUS!!
CRACKLE
CRACKLE
JESUS... HE TOOK 'EM OUT IN LIKE THREE SECONDS FLAT!
I CAN'T BELIEVE HE'S ONLY A RESERVE MEMBER.
HELL, AT LAST YEAR'S TOURNAMENT, HE WAS THE LINCHPIN OF THE WHOLE EXECUTIVE COMMITTEE.
AH... WHAT, IS HE BUMMED OUT?
GLOOM
THAT'S KINDA CUTE... ♡
I-I AM ASHAMED...
... F-FORCED TO BEAT ON WEAKLINGS JUST TO EARN POINTS...
NO...THE BATTLE-FIELD IS NO PLACE FOR PERSONAL FEELINGS!!
I MUST RE-MEMBER THAT IT'S ALL PART OF A GRAND STRATEGY!!
STILL...
...I CAN'T MAKE MYSELF SWALLOW ISUZU'S "METHODS"!!

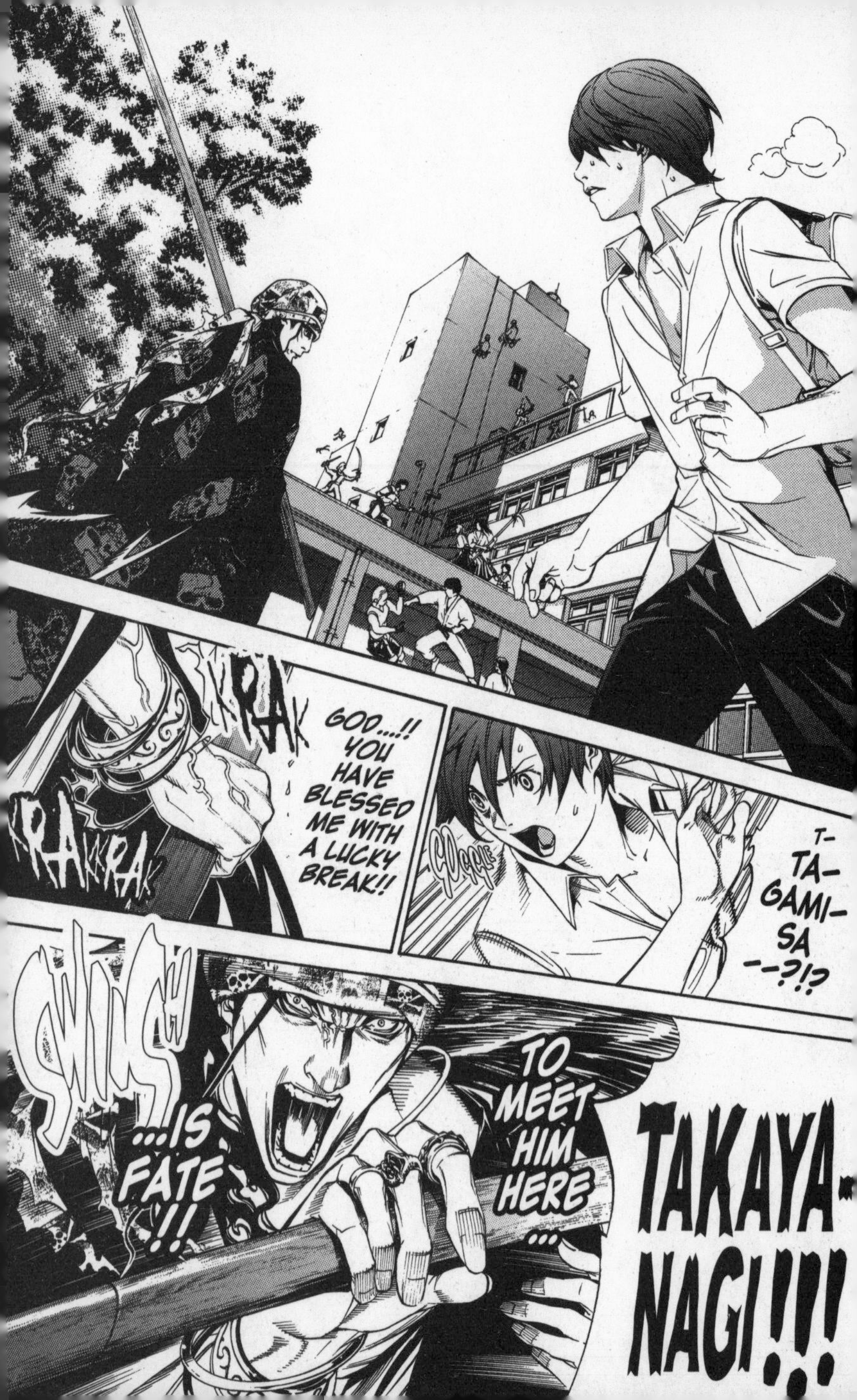
T-TA-GAMI-SA--?!?
GOD...!! YOU HAVE BLESSED ME WITH A LUCKY BREAK!!
TAKAYA-NAGI!!!
TO MEET HIM HERE...
...IS FATE!!

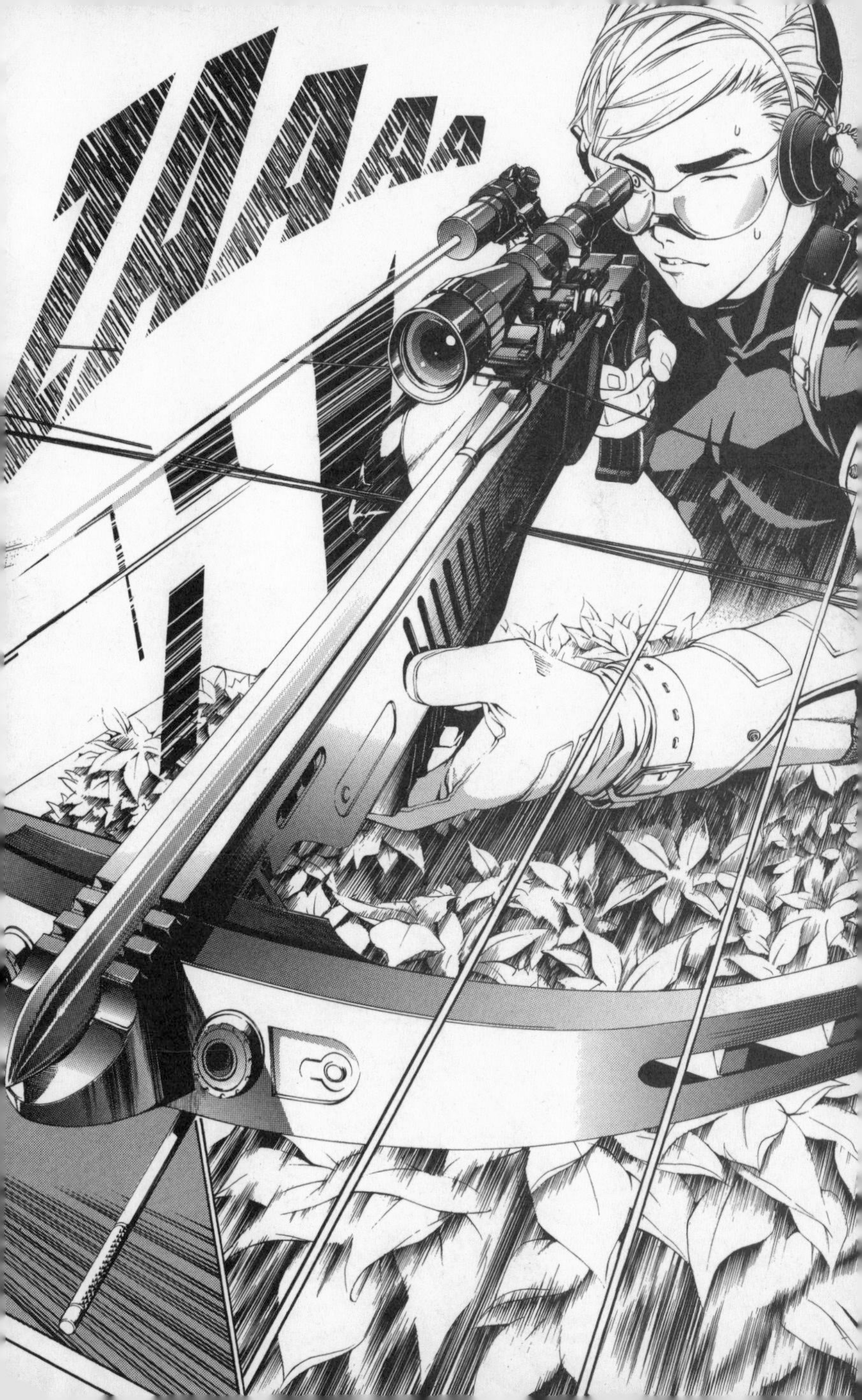

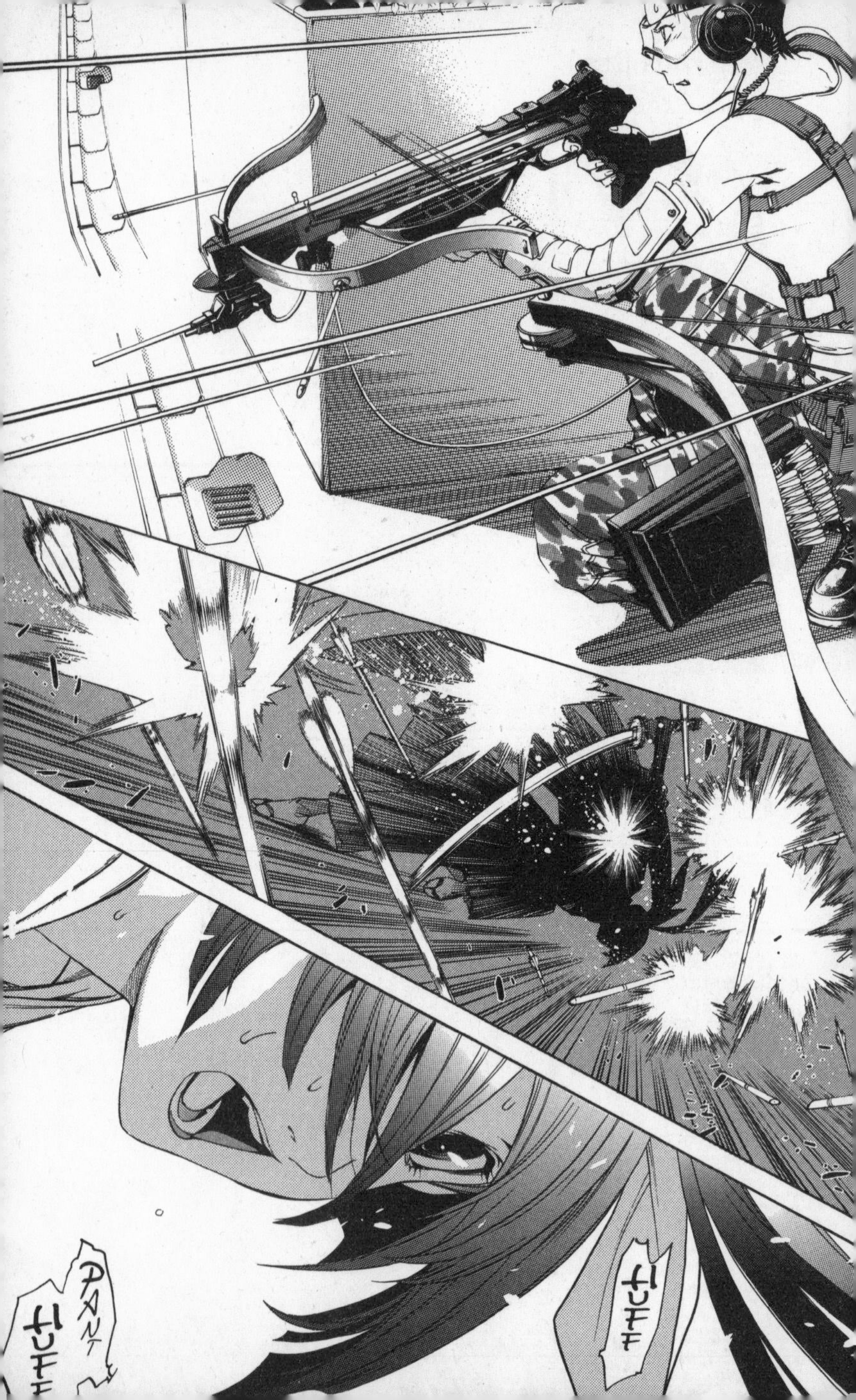
HUFF
PANT
HUFF

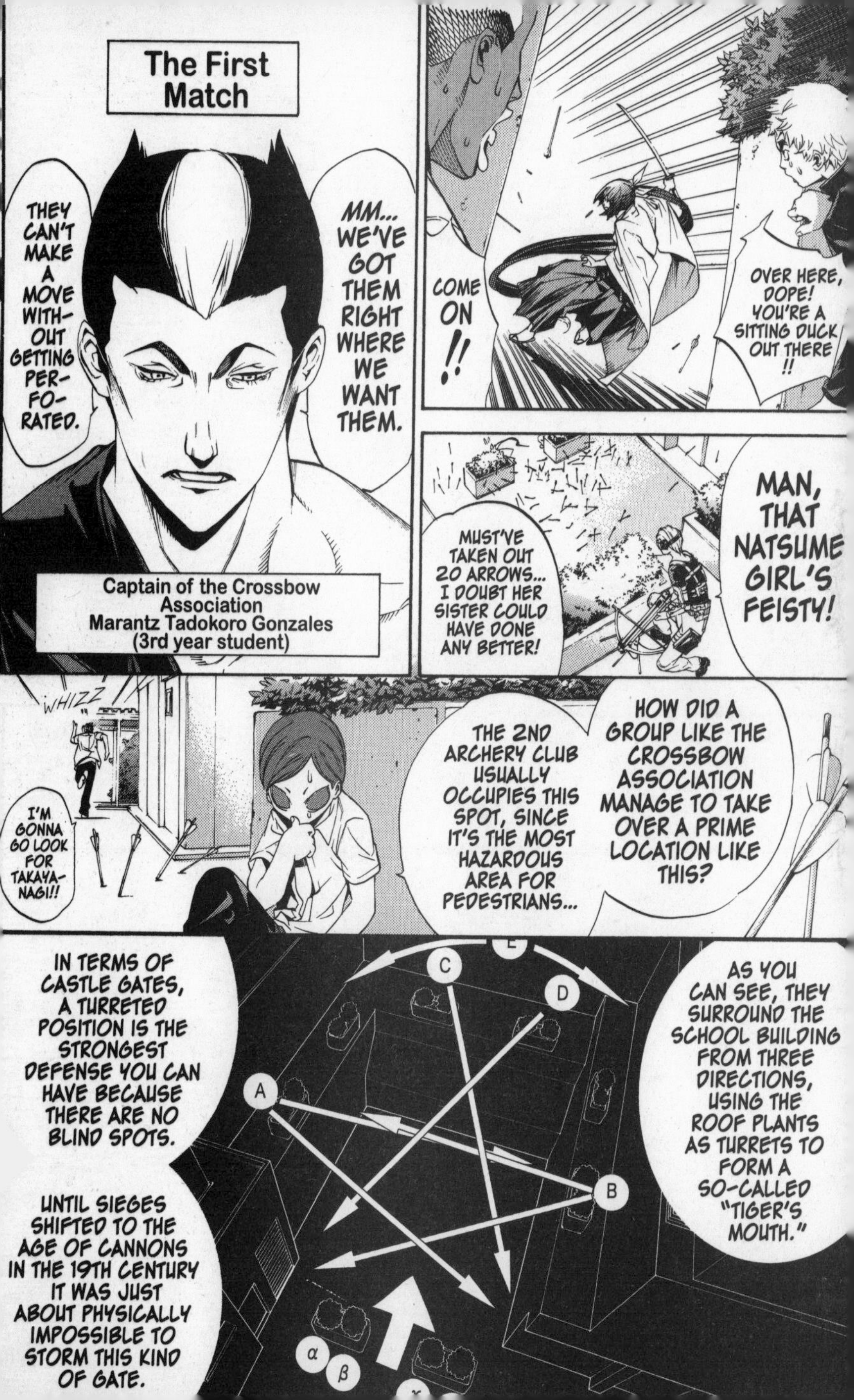
OVER HERE, DOPE! YOU'RE A SITTING DUCK OUT THERE!!
COME ON!!
MAN, THAT NATSUME GIRL'S FEISTY!
MUST'VE TAKEN OUT 20 ARROWS... I DOUBT HER SISTER COULD HAVE DONE ANY BETTER!
The First Match
MM... WE'VE GOT THEM RIGHT WHERE WE WANT THEM.
THEY CAN'T MAKE A MOVE WITH-OUT GETTING PER-FO-RATED.
Captain of the Crossbow Association
Marantz Tadokoro Gonzales
(3rd year student)
HOW DID A GROUP LIKE THE CROSSBOW ASSOCIATION MANAGE TO TAKE OVER A PRIME LOCATION LIKE THIS?
THE 2ND ARCHERY CLUB USUALLY OCCUPIES THIS SPOT, SINCE IT'S THE MOST HAZARDOUS AREA FOR PEDESTRIANS...
WHIZZ
I'M GONNA GO LOOK FOR TAKAYA-NAGI!!
AS YOU CAN SEE, THEY SURROUND THE SCHOOL BUILDING FROM THREE DIRECTIONS, USING THE ROOF PLANTS AS TURRETS TO FORM A SO-CALLED "TIGER'S MOUTH."
C
D
A
B
α
β
IN TERMS OF CASTLE GATES, A TURRETED POSITION IS THE STRONGEST DEFENSE YOU CAN HAVE BECAUSE THERE ARE NO BLIND SPOTS.
UNTIL SIEGES SHIFTED TO THE AGE OF CANNONS IN THE 19TH CENTURY IT WAS JUST ABOUT PHYSICALLY IMPOSSIBLE TO STORM THIS KIND OF GATE.

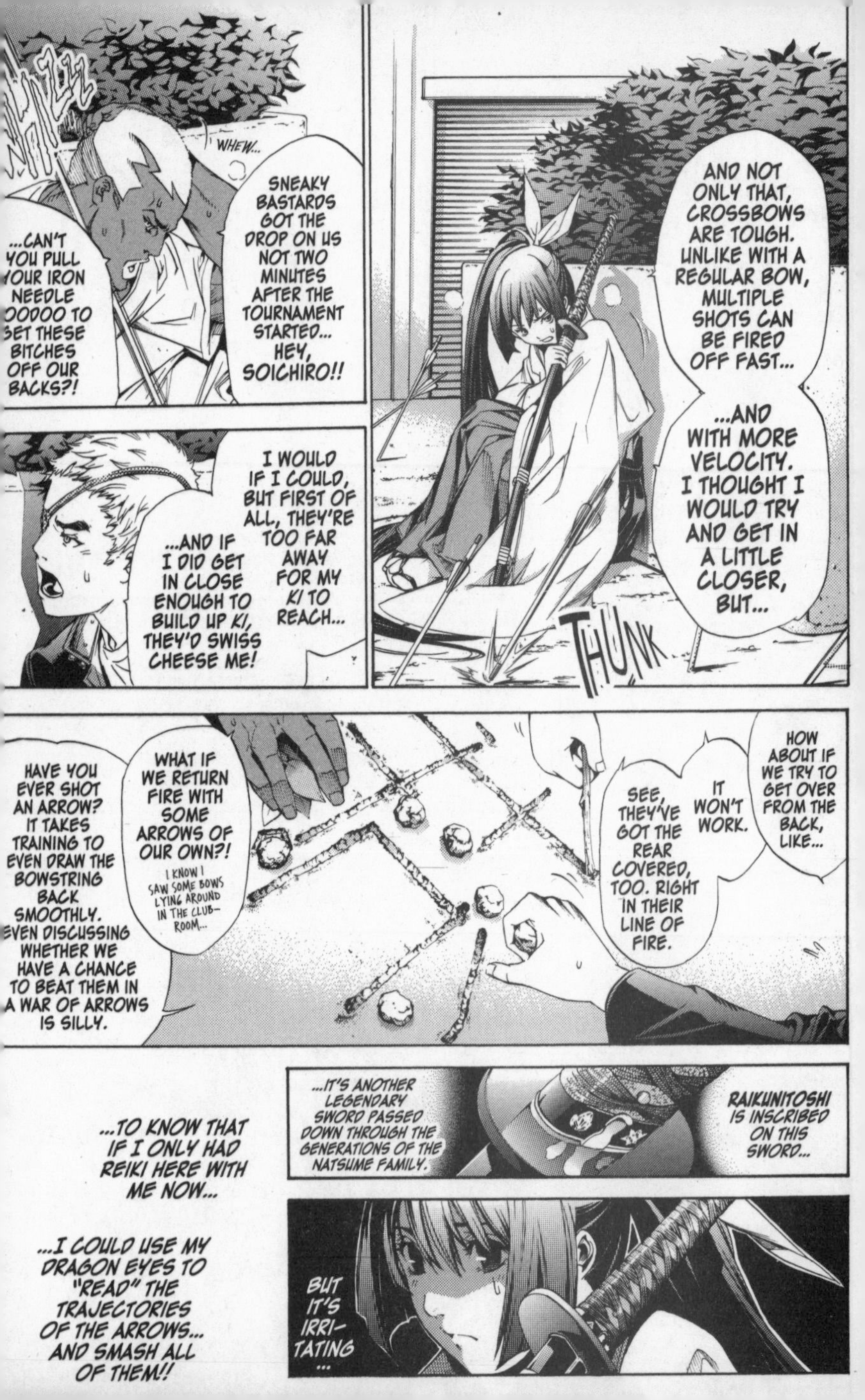
AND NOT ONLY THAT, CROSSBOWS ARE TOUGH. UNLIKE WITH A REGULAR BOW, MULTIPLE SHOTS CAN BE FIRED OFF FAST...
...AND WITH MORE VELOCITY. I THOUGHT I WOULD TRY AND GET IN A LITTLE CLOSER, BUT...
THUNK
WHEW...
SNEAKY BASTARDS GOT THE DROP ON US NOT TWO MINUTES AFTER THE TOURNAMENT STARTED... HEY, SOICHIRO!!
...CAN'T YOU PULL YOUR IRON NEEDLE VOODOO TO GET THESE BITCHES OFF OUR BACKS?!
I WOULD IF I COULD, BUT FIRST OF ALL, THEY'RE TOO FAR AWAY FOR MY KI TO REACH...
...AND IF I DID GET IN CLOSE ENOUGH TO BUILD UP KI, THEY'D SWISS CHEESE ME!
HOW ABOUT IF WE TRY TO GET OVER FROM THE BACK, LIKE...
IT WON'T WORK.
SEE, THEY'VE GOT THE REAR COVERED, TOO. RIGHT IN THEIR LINE OF FIRE.
WHAT IF WE RETURN FIRE WITH SOME ARROWS OF OUR OWN?!
I KNOW I SAW SOME BOWS LYING AROUND IN THE CLUB-ROOM...
HAVE YOU EVER SHOT AN ARROW? IT TAKES TRAINING TO EVEN DRAW THE BOWSTRING BACK SMOOTHLY. EVEN DISCUSSING WHETHER WE HAVE A CHANCE TO BEAT THEM IN A WAR OF ARROWS IS SILLY.
RAIKUNITOSHI IS INSCRIBED ON THIS SWORD...
...IT'S ANOTHER LEGENDARY SWORD PASSED DOWN THROUGH THE GENERATIONS OF THE NATSUME FAMILY.
BUT IT'S IRRI-TATING...
...TO KNOW THAT IF I ONLY HAD REIKI HERE WITH ME NOW...
...I COULD USE MY DRAGON EYES TO "READ" THE TRAJECTORIES OF THE ARROWS... AND SMASH ALL OF THEM!!

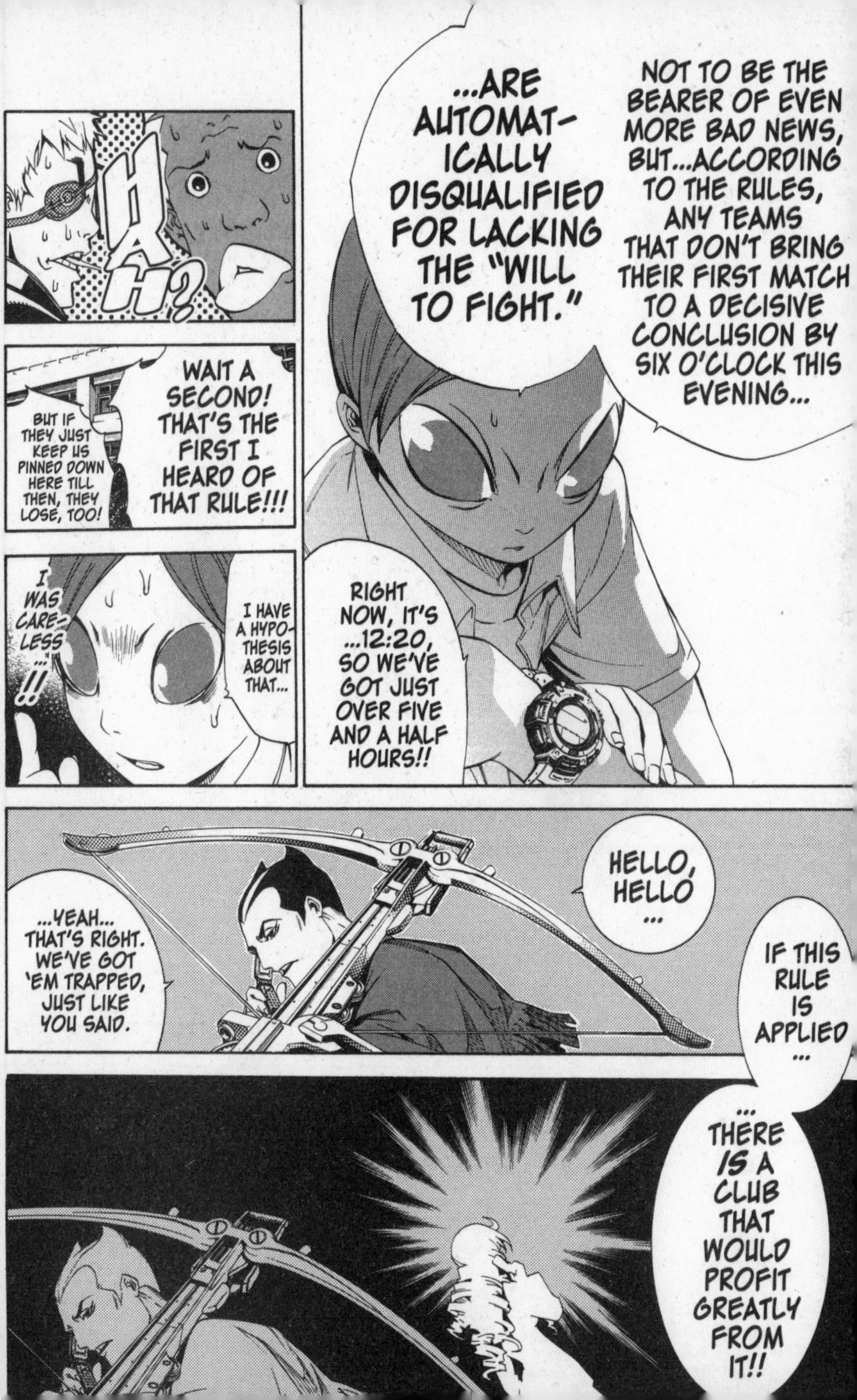
NOT TO BE THE BEARER OF EVEN MORE BAD NEWS, BUT...ACCORDING TO THE RULES, ANY TEAMS THAT DON'T BRING THEIR FIRST MATCH TO A DECISIVE CONCLUSION BY SIX O'CLOCK THIS EVENING...
...ARE AUTOMATICALLY DISQUALIFIED FOR LACKING THE "WILL TO FIGHT."
RIGHT NOW, IT'S ...12:20, SO WE'VE GOT JUST OVER FIVE AND A HALF HOURS!!
HAH?
WAIT A SECOND! THAT'S THE FIRST I HEARD OF THAT RULE!!!
BUT IF THEY JUST KEEP US PINNED DOWN HERE TILL THEN, THEY LOSE, TOO!
I HAVE A HYPOTHESIS ABOUT THAT...
I WAS CARELESS...!!
HELLO, HELLO...
...YEAH... THAT'S RIGHT. WE'VE GOT 'EM TRAPPED, JUST LIKE YOU SAID.
IF THIS RULE IS APPLIED...
...THERE *IS* A CLUB THAT WOULD PROFIT GREATLY FROM IT!!

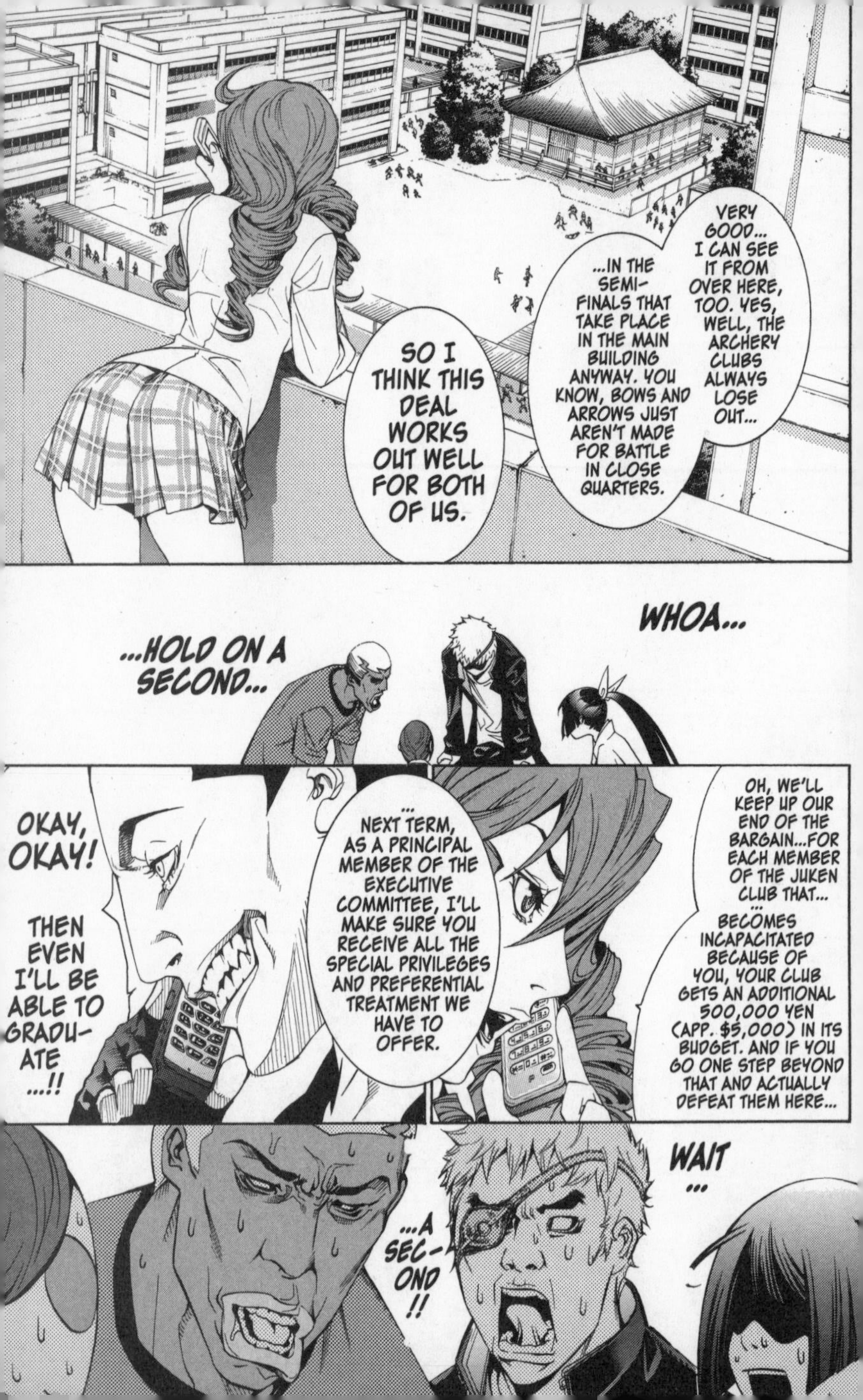
VERY GOOD... I CAN SEE IT FROM OVER HERE, TOO. YES, WELL, THE ARCHERY CLUBS ALWAYS LOSE OUT...
...IN THE SEMI-FINALS THAT TAKE PLACE IN THE MAIN BUILDING ANYWAY. YOU KNOW, BOWS AND ARROWS JUST AREN'T MADE FOR BATTLE IN CLOSE QUARTERS.
SO I THINK THIS DEAL WORKS OUT WELL FOR BOTH OF US.
WHOA...
...HOLD ON A SECOND...
OH, WE'LL KEEP UP OUR END OF THE BARGAIN...FOR EACH MEMBER OF THE JUKEN CLUB THAT... ...BECOMES INCAPACITATED BECAUSE OF YOU, YOUR CLUB GETS AN ADDITIONAL 500,000 YEN (APP. $5,000) IN ITS BUDGET. AND IF YOU GO ONE STEP BEYOND THAT AND ACTUALLY DEFEAT THEM HERE...
... NEXT TERM, AS A PRINCIPAL MEMBER OF THE EXECUTIVE COMMITTEE, I'LL MAKE SURE YOU RECEIVE ALL THE SPECIAL PRIVILEGES AND PREFERENTIAL TREATMENT WE HAVE TO OFFER.
OKAY, OKAY!
THEN EVEN I'LL BE ABLE TO GRADU-ATE ...!!
WAIT ...
...A SEC-OND !!

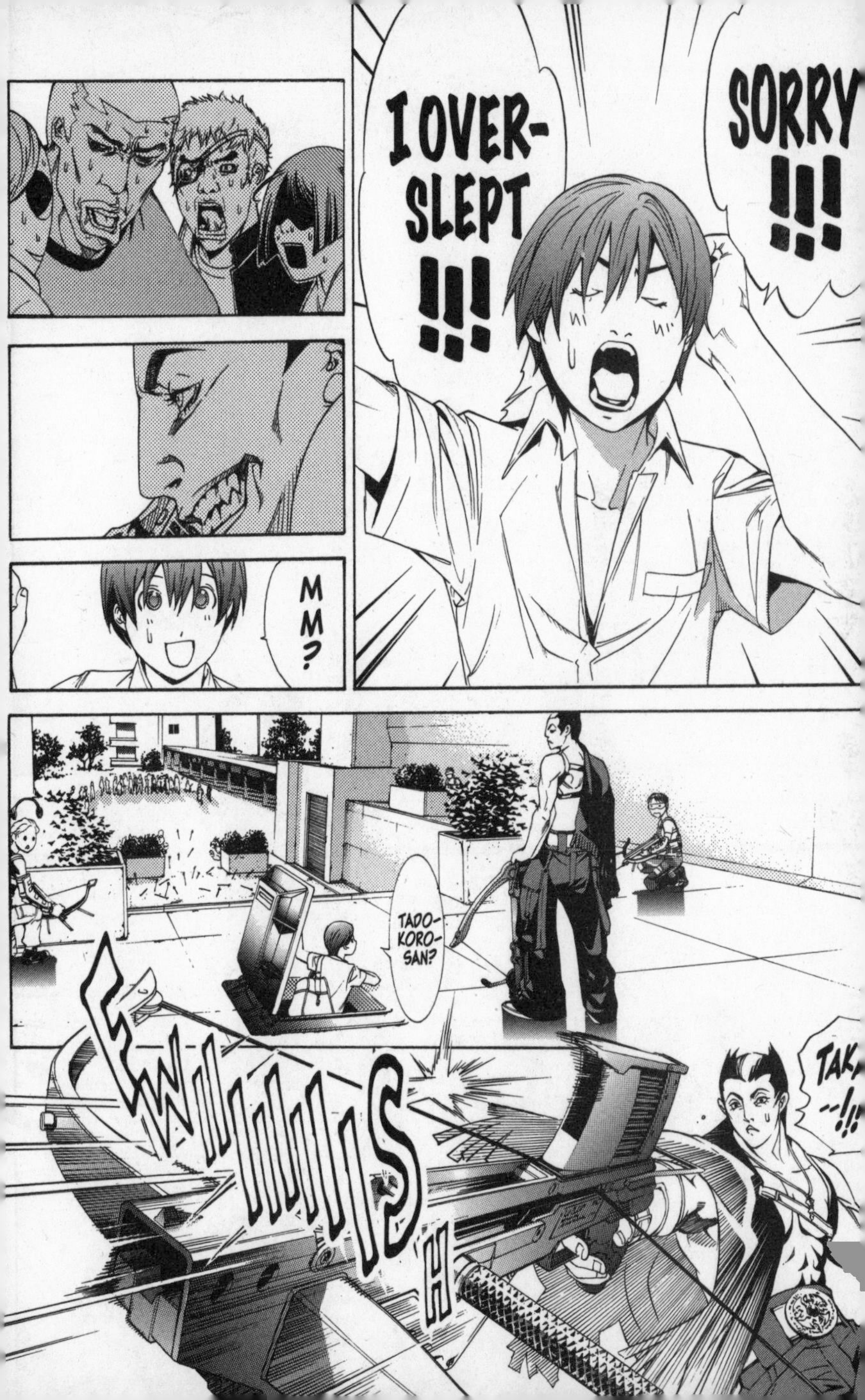
SORRY!!!
I OVER-SLEPT!!!
MM?
TADO-KORO-SAN?
TAKA--!!
WHIIIIISH

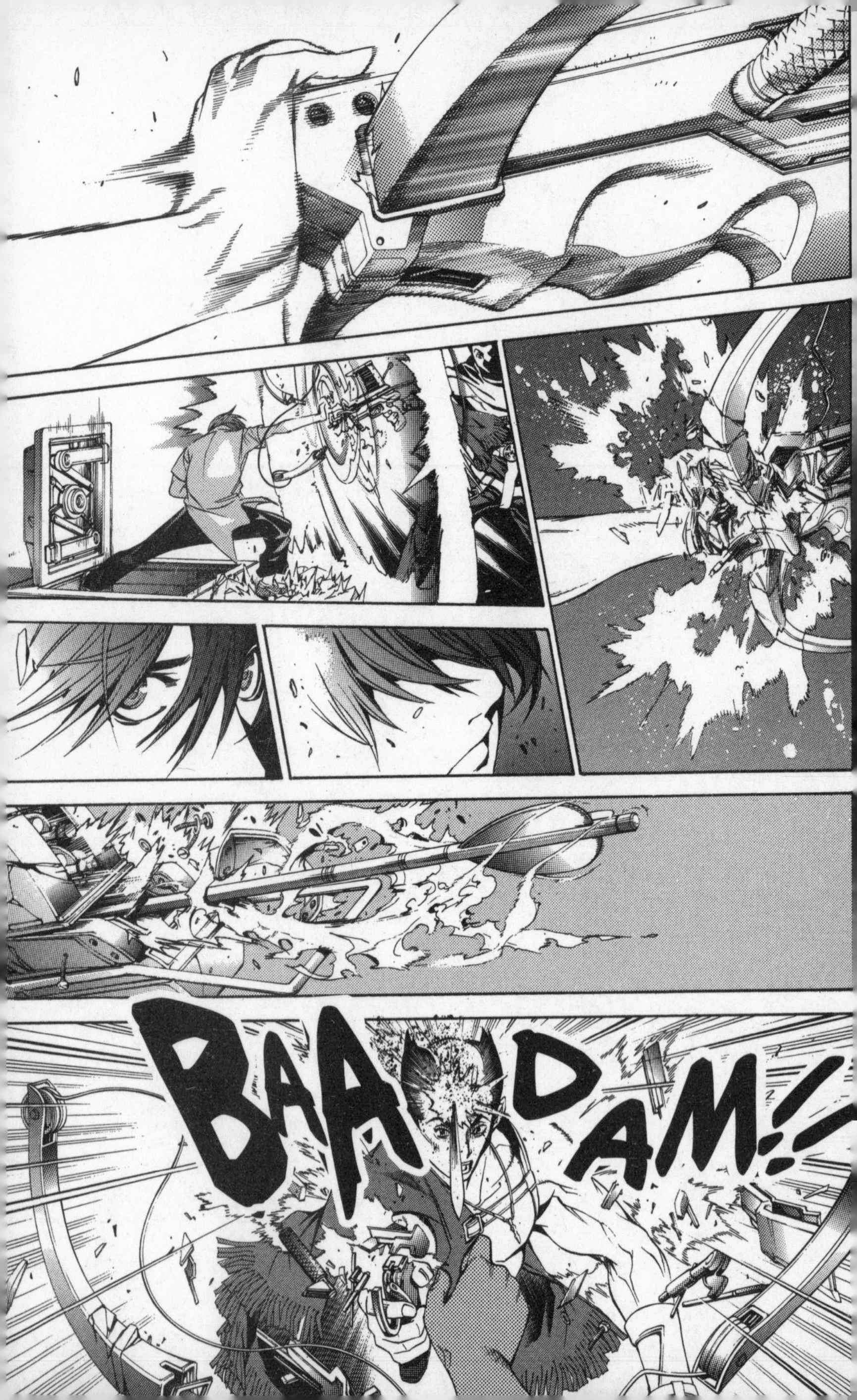
BAADAM!!

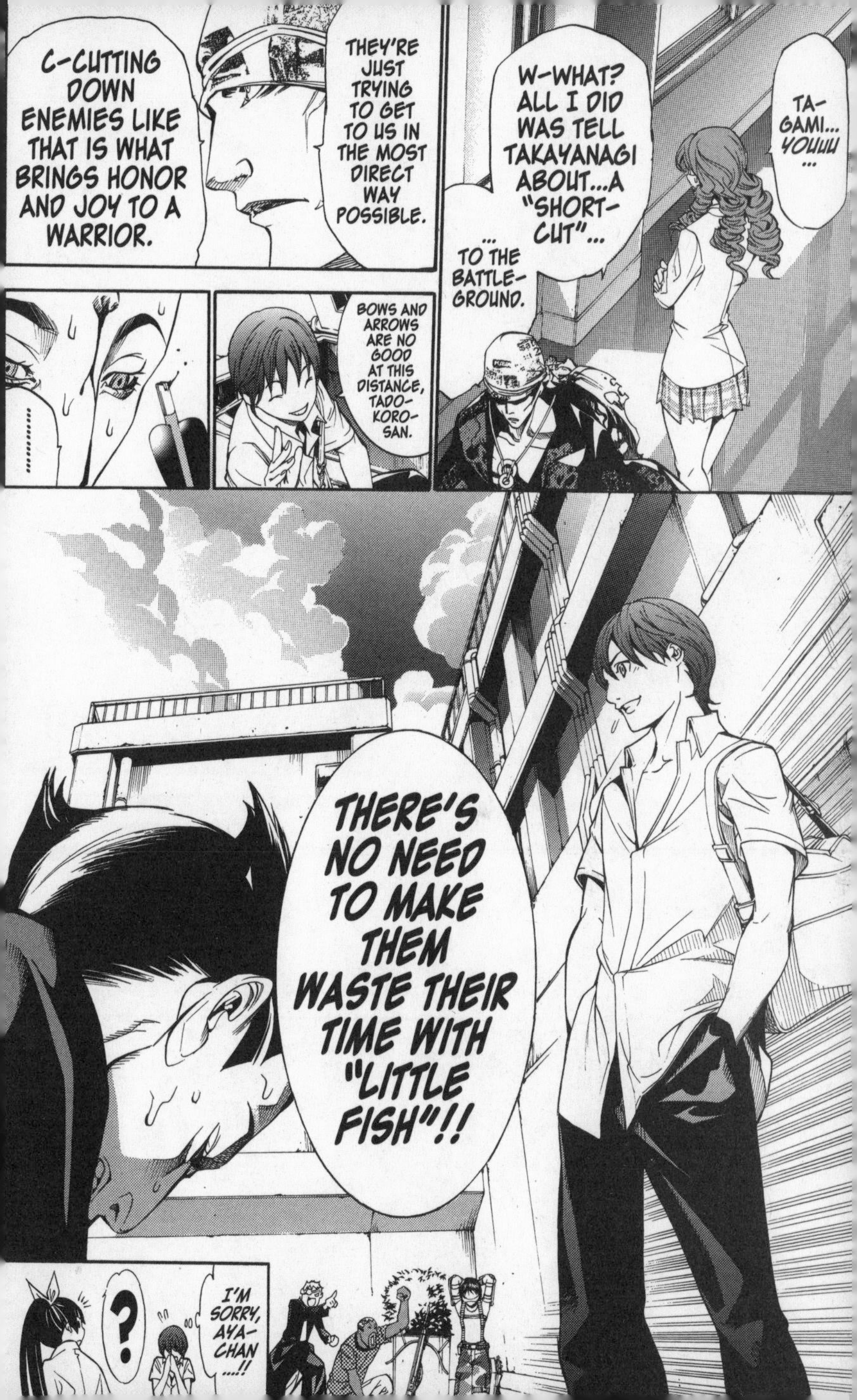
TA-GAMI... YOUUU...
W-WHAT? ALL I DID WAS TELL TAKAYANAGI ABOUT...A "SHORT-CUT"...
... TO THE BATTLE-GROUND.
THEY'RE JUST TRYING TO GET TO US IN THE MOST DIRECT WAY POSSIBLE.
C-CUTTING DOWN ENEMIES LIKE THAT IS WHAT BRINGS HONOR AND JOY TO A WARRIOR.
BOWS AND ARROWS ARE NO GOOD AT THIS DISTANCE, TADO-KORO-SAN.
......
THERE'S NO NEED TO MAKE THEM WASTE THEIR TIME WITH "LITTLE FISH"!!
I'M SORRY, AYA-CHAN ....!!
?

FIGHT:101

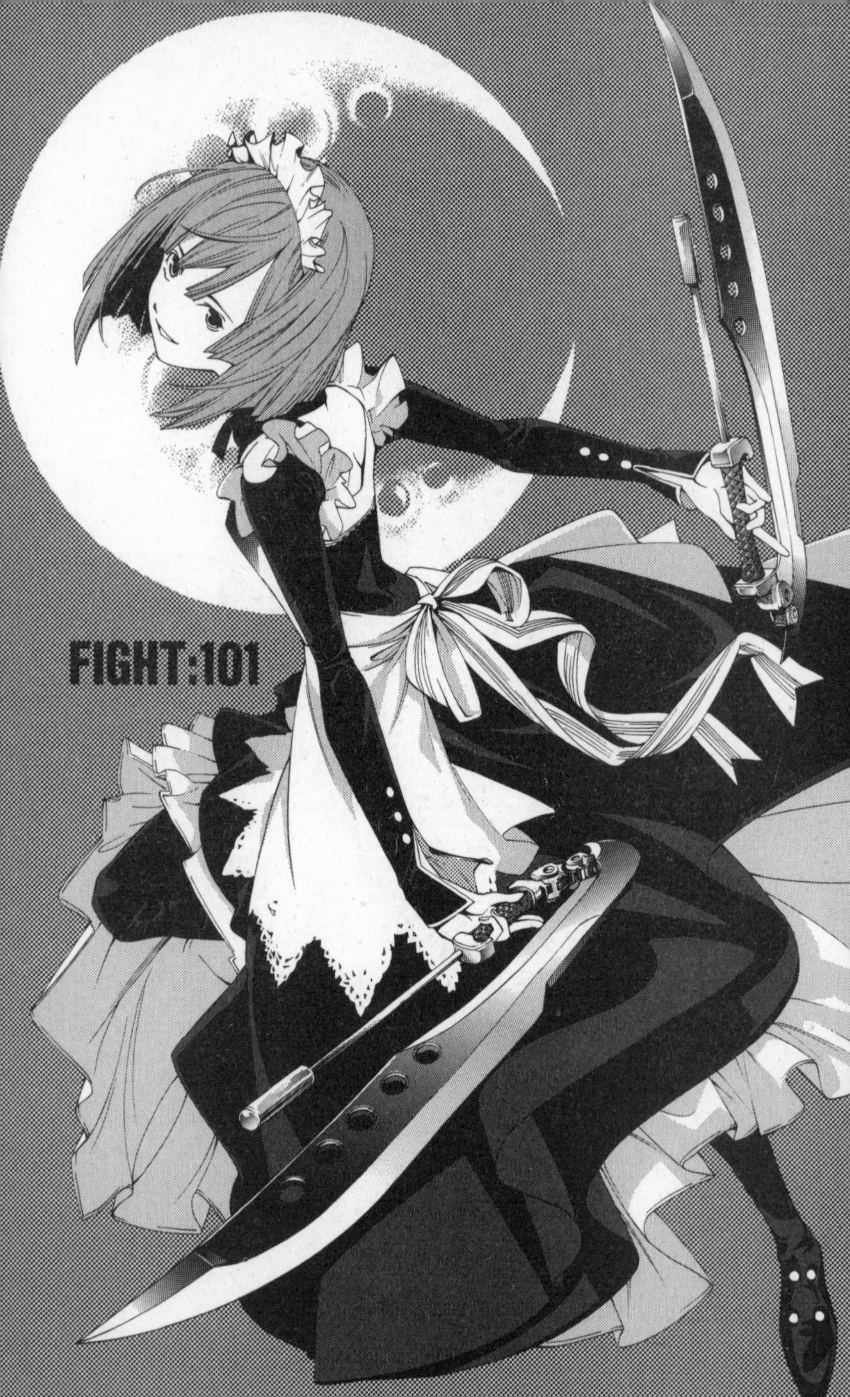

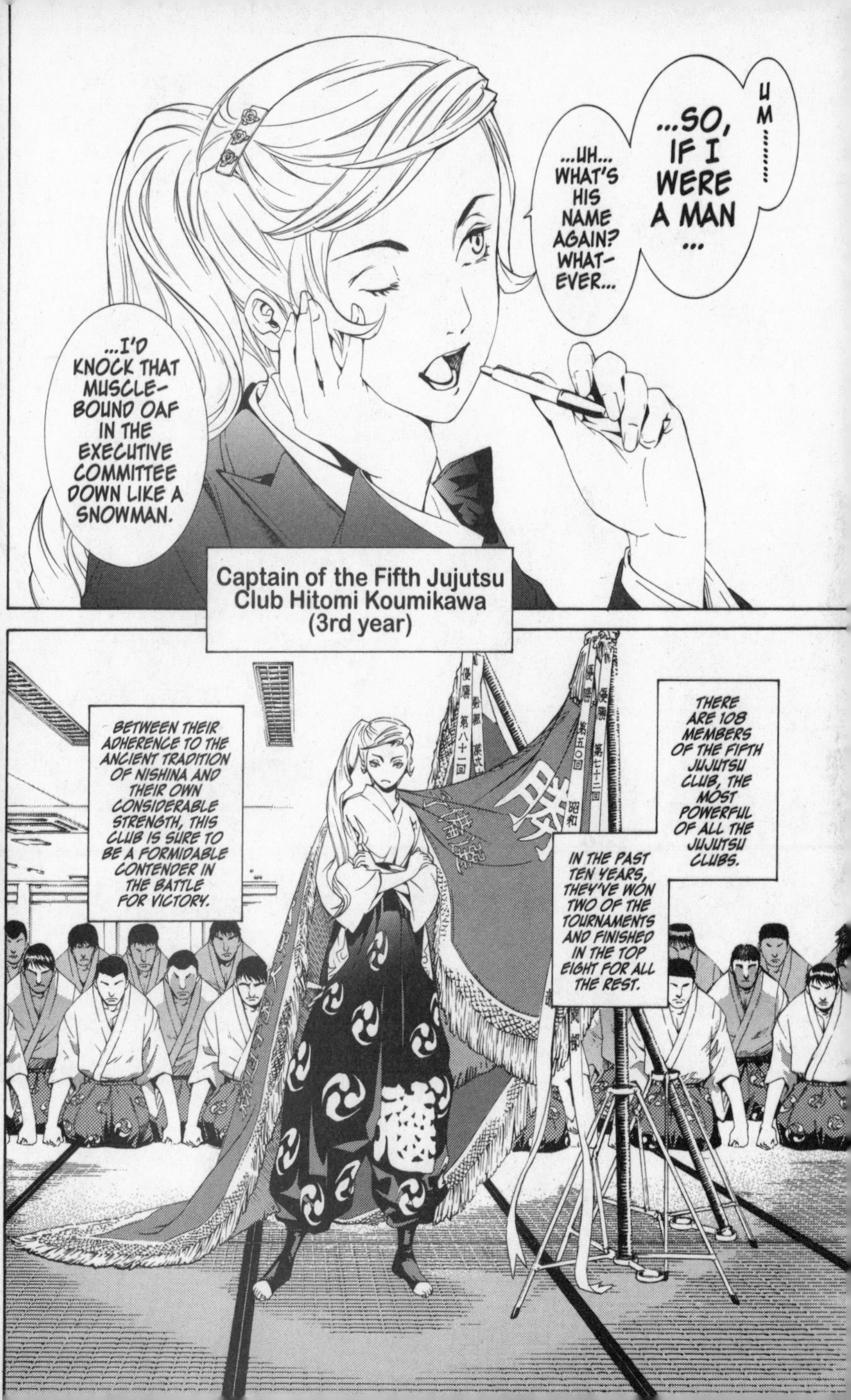
UM......
...SO, IF I WERE A MAN ...
...UH... WHAT'S HIS NAME AGAIN? WHAT-EVER...
...I'D KNOCK THAT MUSCLE-BOUND OAF IN THE EXECUTIVE COMMITTEE DOWN LIKE A SNOWMAN.
Captain of the Fifth Jujutsu Club Hitomi Koumikawa (3rd year)
THERE ARE 108 MEMBERS OF THE FIFTH JUJUTSU CLUB, THE MOST POWERFUL OF ALL THE JUJUTSU CLUBS.
IN THE PAST TEN YEARS, THEY'VE WON TWO OF THE TOURNAMENTS AND FINISHED IN THE TOP EIGHT FOR ALL THE REST.
BETWEEN THEIR ADHERENCE TO THE ANCIENT TRADITION OF NISHINA AND THEIR OWN CONSIDERABLE STRENGTH, THIS CLUB IS SURE TO BE A FORMIDABLE CONTENDER IN THE BATTLE FOR VICTORY.

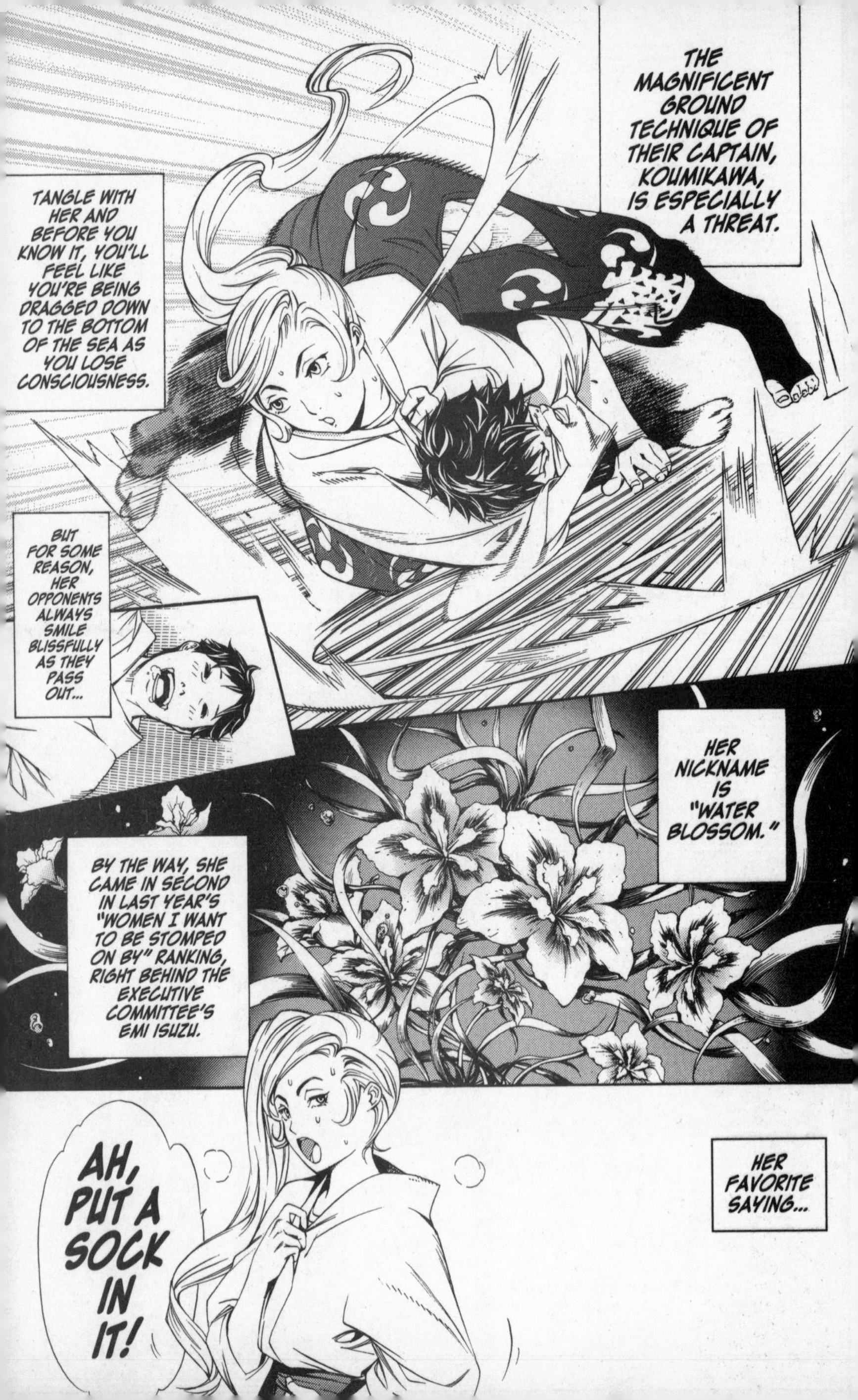
THE MAGNIFICENT GROUND TECHNIQUE OF THEIR CAPTAIN, KOUMIKAWA, IS ESPECIALLY A THREAT.
TANGLE WITH HER AND BEFORE YOU KNOW IT, YOU'LL FEEL LIKE YOU'RE BEING DRAGGED DOWN TO THE BOTTOM OF THE SEA AS YOU LOSE CONSCIOUSNESS.
BUT FOR SOME REASON, HER OPPONENTS ALWAYS SMILE BLISSFULLY AS THEY PASS OUT...
HER NICKNAME IS "WATER BLOSSOM."
BY THE WAY, SHE CAME IN SECOND IN LAST YEAR'S "WOMEN I WANT TO BE STOMPED ON BY" RANKING, RIGHT BEHIND THE EXECUTIVE COMMITTEE'S EMI ISUZU.
HER FAVORITE SAYING...
AH, PUT A SOCK IN IT!

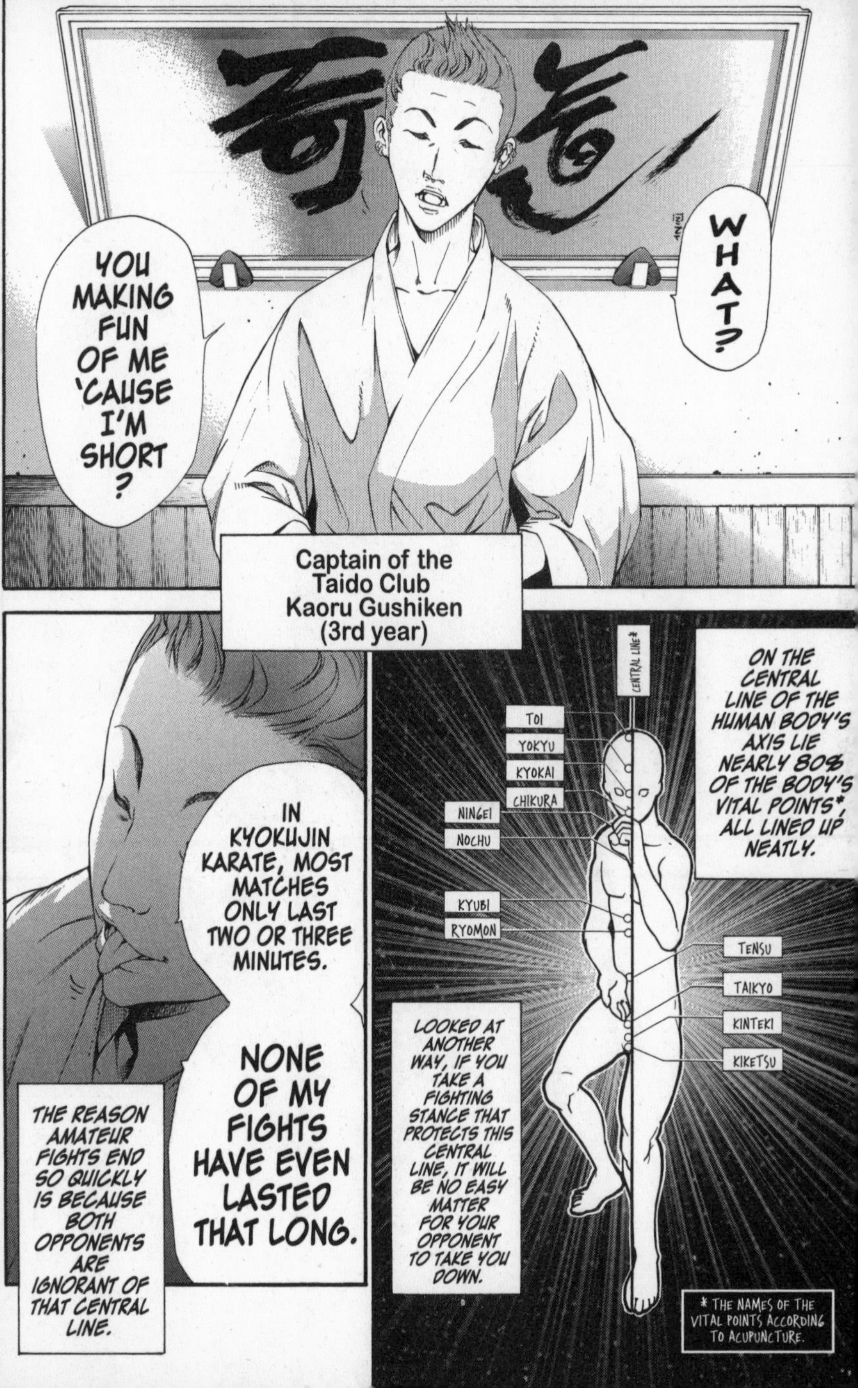
WHAT?
YOU MAKING FUN OF ME 'CAUSE I'M SHORT?
Captain of the Taido Club Kaoru Gushiken (3rd year)
ON THE CENTRAL LINE OF THE HUMAN BODY'S AXIS LIE NEARLY 80% OF THE BODY'S VITAL POINTS*, ALL LINED UP NEATLY.
CENTRAL LINE*
TOI
YOKYU
KYOKAI
CHIKURA
NINGEI
NOCHU
KYUBI
RYOMON
TENSU
TAIKYO
KINTEKI
KIKETSU
LOOKED AT ANOTHER WAY, IF YOU TAKE A FIGHTING STANCE THAT PROTECTS THIS CENTRAL LINE, IT WILL BE NO EASY MATTER FOR YOUR OPPONENT TO TAKE YOU DOWN.
* THE NAMES OF THE VITAL POINTS ACCORDING TO ACUPUNCTURE.
IN KYOKUJIN KARATE, MOST MATCHES ONLY LAST TWO OR THREE MINUTES.
NONE OF MY FIGHTS HAVE EVEN LASTED THAT LONG.
THE REASON AMATEUR FIGHTS END SO QUICKLY IS BECAUSE BOTH OPPONENTS ARE IGNORANT OF THAT CENTRAL LINE.

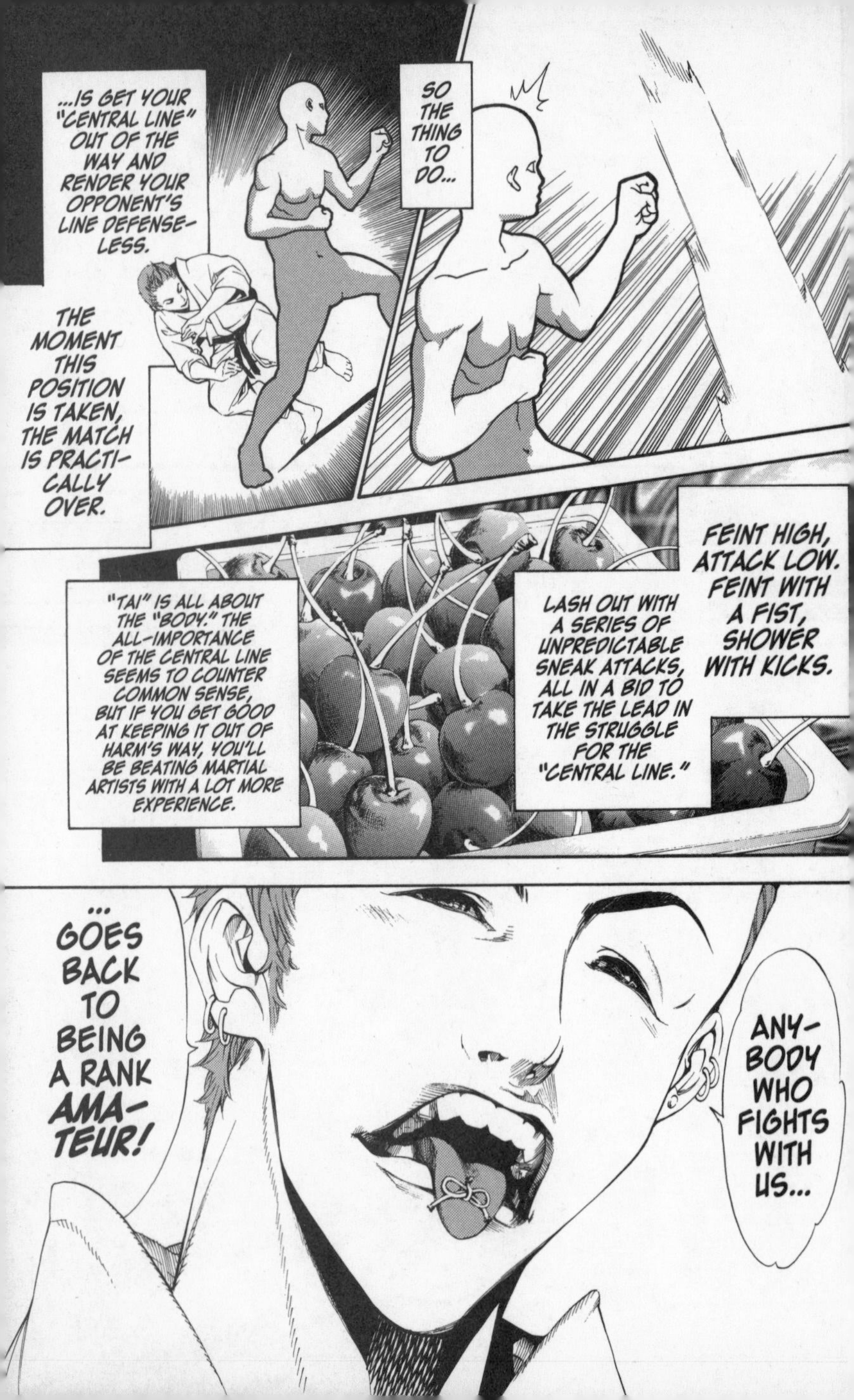
SO THE THING TO DO...
...IS GET YOUR "CENTRAL LINE" OUT OF THE WAY AND RENDER YOUR OPPONENT'S LINE DEFENSELESS.
THE MOMENT THIS POSITION IS TAKEN, THE MATCH IS PRACTICALLY OVER.
FEINT HIGH, ATTACK LOW. FEINT WITH A FIST, SHOWER WITH KICKS.
LASH OUT WITH A SERIES OF UNPREDICTABLE SNEAK ATTACKS, ALL IN A BID TO TAKE THE LEAD IN THE STRUGGLE FOR THE "CENTRAL LINE."
"TAI" IS ALL ABOUT THE "BODY." THE ALL-IMPORTANCE OF THE CENTRAL LINE SEEMS TO COUNTER COMMON SENSE, BUT IF YOU GET GOOD AT KEEPING IT OUT OF HARM'S WAY, YOU'LL BE BEATING MARTIAL ARTISTS WITH A LOT MORE EXPERIENCE.
ANYBODY WHO FIGHTS WITH US...
...GOES BACK TO BEING A RANK AMATEUR!

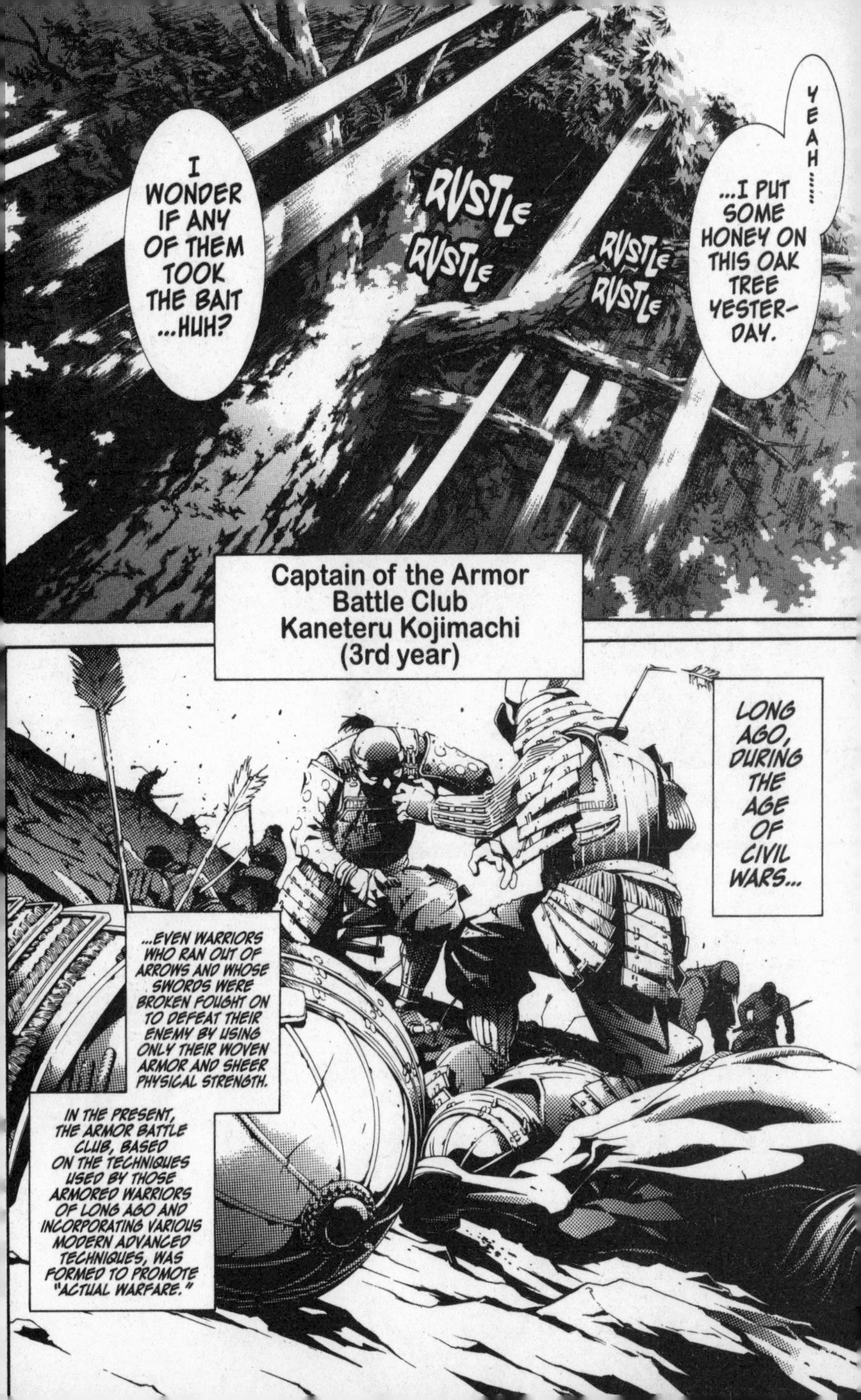
YEAH...... ...I PUT SOME HONEY ON THIS OAK TREE YESTER-DAY.
RUSTLE RUSTLE
RUSTLE RUSTLE
I WONDER IF ANY OF THEM TOOK THE BAIT ...HUH?
Captain of the Armor Battle Club Kaneteru Kojimachi (3rd year)
LONG AGO, DURING THE AGE OF CIVIL WARS...
...EVEN WARRIORS WHO RAN OUT OF ARROWS AND WHOSE SWORDS WERE BROKEN FOUGHT ON TO DEFEAT THEIR ENEMY BY USING ONLY THEIR WOVEN ARMOR AND SHEER PHYSICAL STRENGTH.
IN THE PRESENT, THE ARMOR BATTLE CLUB, BASED ON THE TECHNIQUES USED BY THOSE ARMORED WARRIORS OF LONG AGO AND INCORPORATING VARIOUS MODERN ADVANCED TECHNIQUES, WAS FORMED TO PROMOTE "ACTUAL WARFARE."

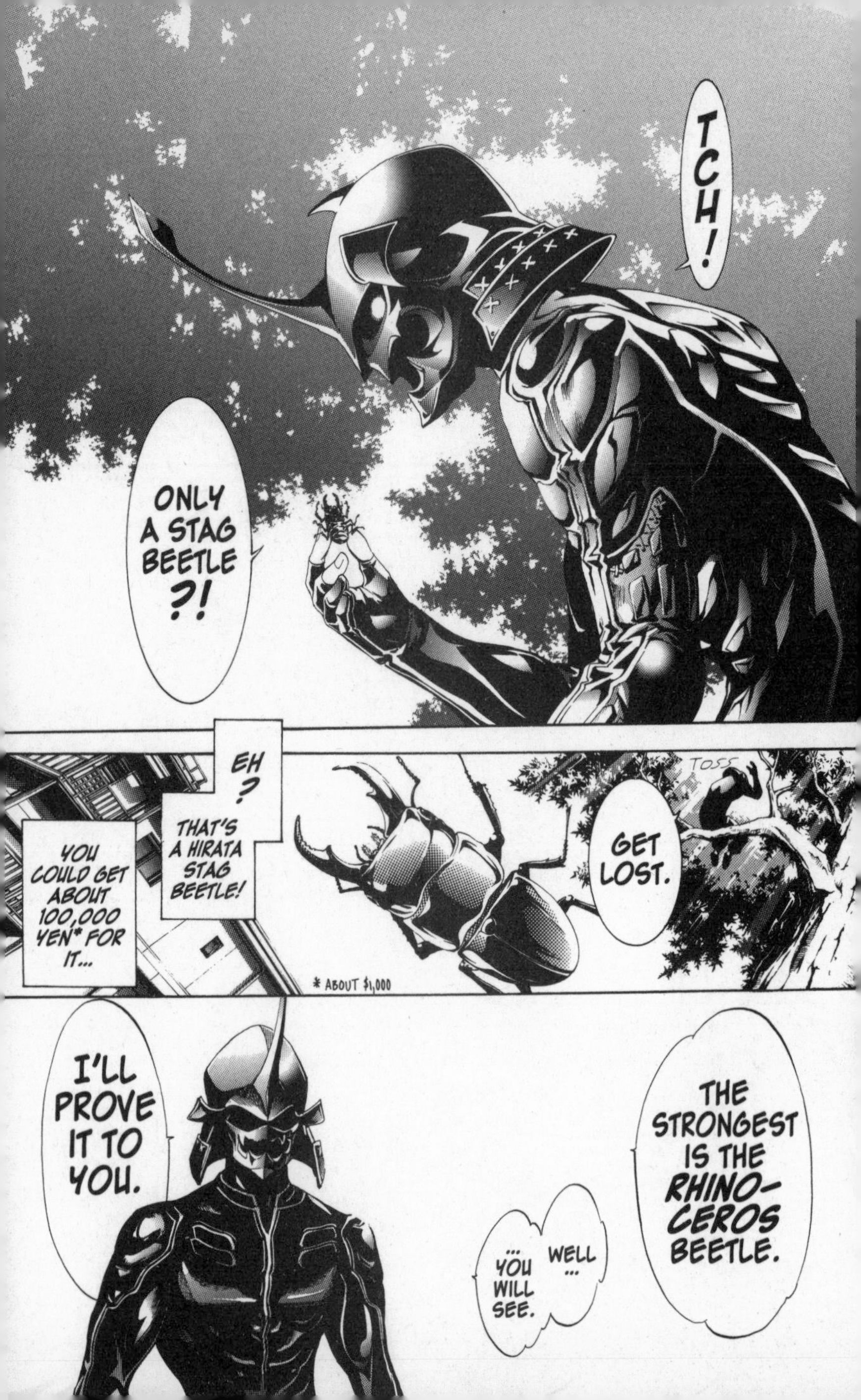
TCH!
ONLY A STAG BEETLE?!
TOSS
GET LOST.
EH? THAT'S A HIRATA STAG BEETLE!
YOU COULD GET ABOUT 100,000 YEN* FOR IT...
* ABOUT $1,000
THE STRONGEST IS THE RHINO-CEROS BEETLE.
WELL...
...YOU WILL SEE.
I'LL PROVE IT TO YOU.

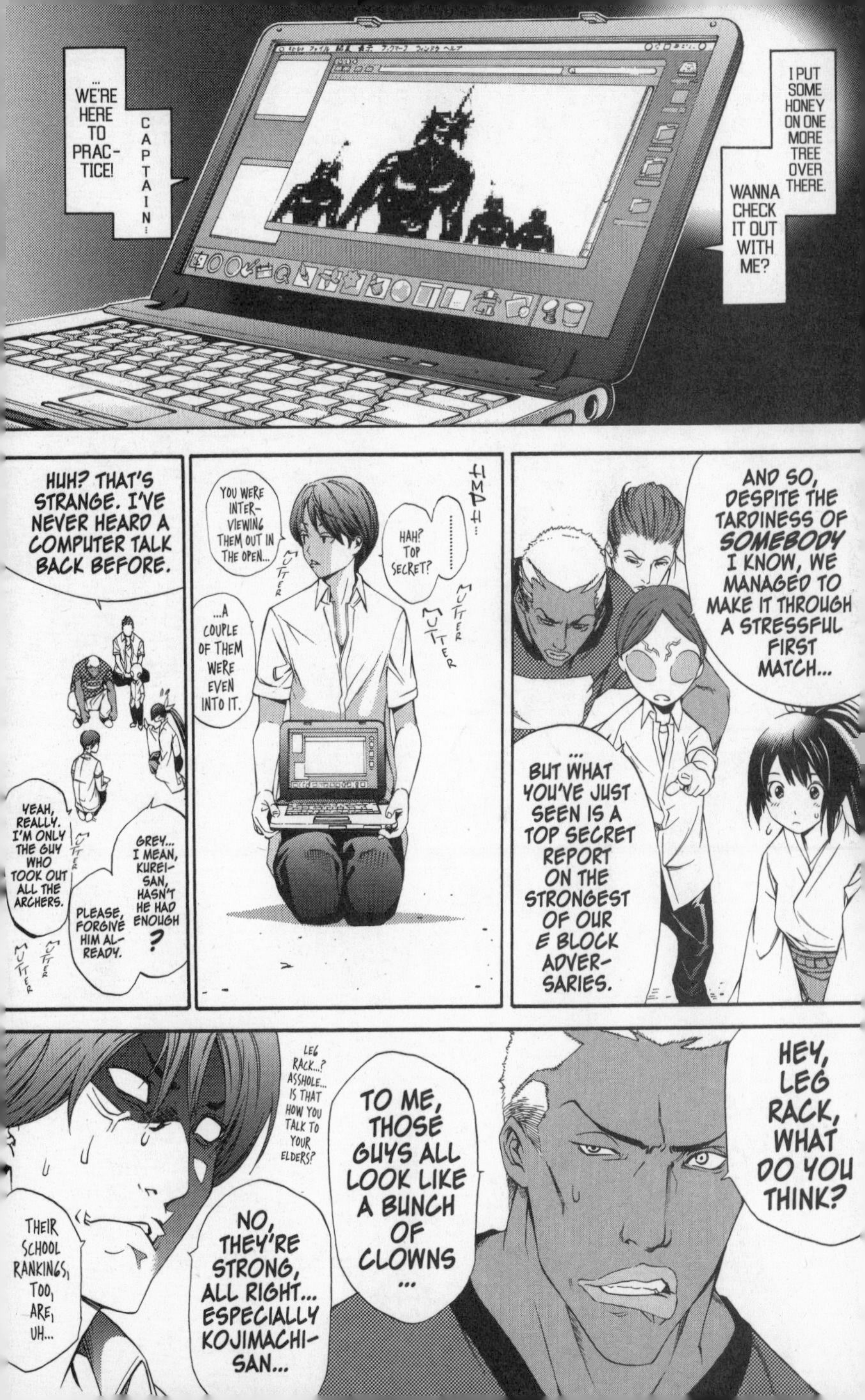
I PUT SOME HONEY ON ONE MORE TREE OVER THERE.
WANNA CHECK IT OUT WITH ME?
CAPTAIN...
...WE'RE HERE TO PRAC-TICE!
AND SO, DESPITE THE TARDINESS OF *SOMEBODY* I KNOW, WE MANAGED TO MAKE IT THROUGH A STRESSFUL FIRST MATCH...
...BUT WHAT YOU'VE JUST SEEN IS A TOP SECRET REPORT ON THE STRONGEST OF OUR E BLOCK ADVER-SARIES.
HMPH...
HAH? TOP SECRET?
....
YOU WERE INTER-VIEWING THEM OUT IN THE OPEN...
MUTTER
MUTTER
MUTTER
...A COUPLE OF THEM WERE EVEN INTO IT.
HUH? THAT'S STRANGE. I'VE NEVER HEARD A COMPUTER TALK BACK BEFORE.
GREY... I MEAN, KUREI-SAN, HASN'T HE HAD ENOUGH?
PLEASE, FORGIVE HIM AL-READY.
MUTTER
YEAH, REALLY. I'M ONLY THE GUY WHO TOOK OUT ALL THE ARCHERS.
MUTTER
MUTTER
HEY, LEG RACK, WHAT DO YOU THINK?
TO ME, THOSE GUYS ALL LOOK LIKE A BUNCH OF CLOWNS...
LEG RACK...? ASSHOLE... IS THAT HOW YOU TALK TO YOUR ELDERS?
NO, THEY'RE STRONG, ALL RIGHT... ESPECIALLY KOJIMACHI-SAN...
THEIR SCHOOL RANKINGS, TOO, ARE, UH...

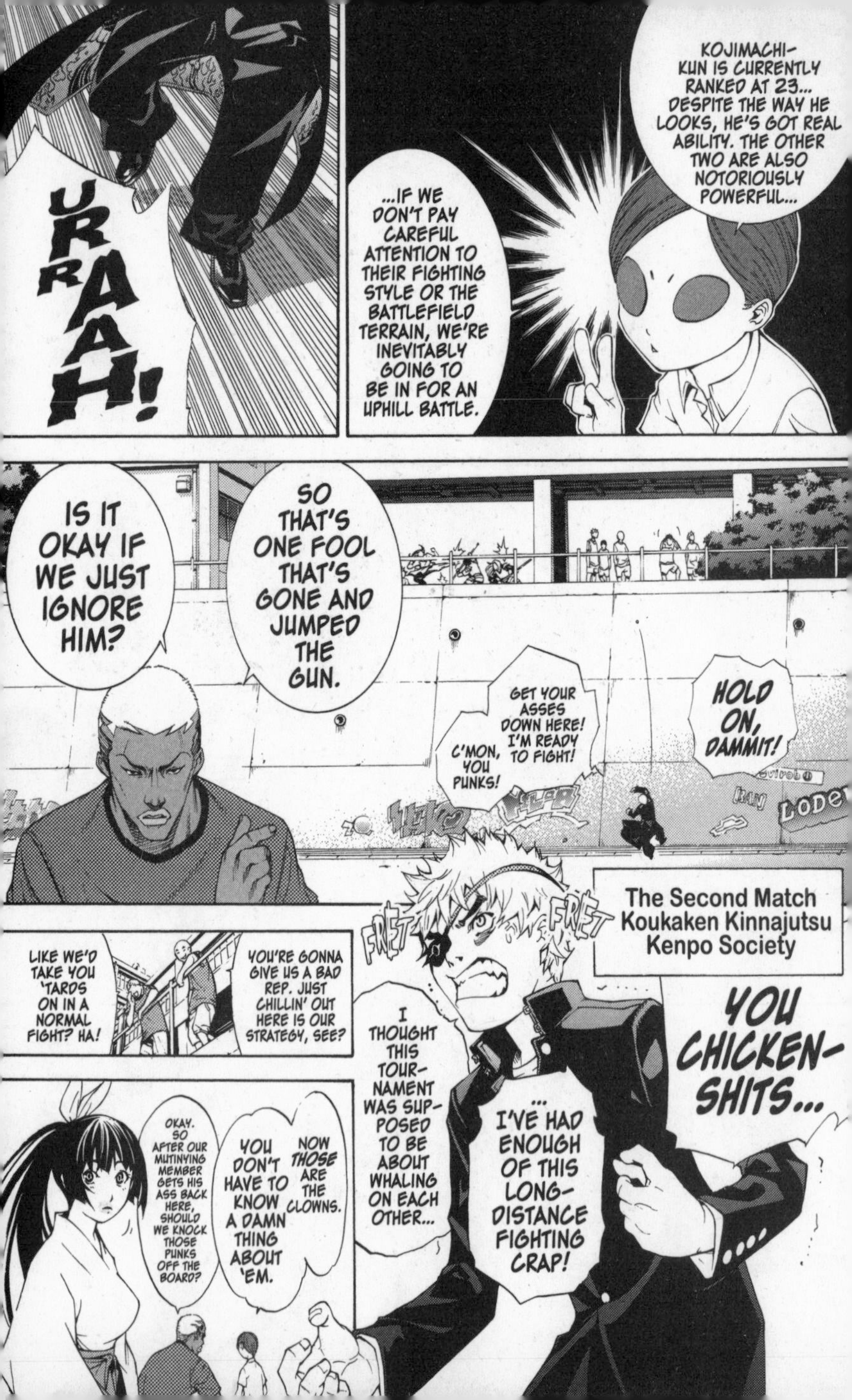

KOJIMACHI-KUN IS CURRENTLY RANKED AT 23... DESPITE THE WAY HE LOOKS, HE'S GOT REAL ABILITY. THE OTHER TWO ARE ALSO NOTORIOUSLY POWERFUL...
...IF WE DON'T PAY CAREFUL ATTENTION TO THEIR FIGHTING STYLE OR THE BATTLEFIELD TERRAIN, WE'RE INEVITABLY GOING TO BE IN FOR AN UPHILL BATTLE.
URRAAH!
HOLD ON, DAMMIT!
GET YOUR ASSES DOWN HERE! I'M READY TO FIGHT!
C'MON, YOU PUNKS!
SO THAT'S ONE FOOL THAT'S GONE AND JUMPED THE GUN.
IS IT OKAY IF WE JUST IGNORE HIM?
The Second Match Koukaken Kinnajutsu Kenpo Society
YOU CHICKEN-SHITS...
FRET FRET
...I'VE HAD ENOUGH OF THIS LONG-DISTANCE FIGHTING CRAP!
I THOUGHT THIS TOURNAMENT WAS SUPPOSED TO BE ABOUT WHALING ON EACH OTHER...
YOU'RE GONNA GIVE US A BAD REP. JUST CHILLIN' OUT HERE IS OUR STRATEGY, SEE?
LIKE WE'D TAKE YOU 'TARDS ON IN A NORMAL FIGHT? HA!
NOW THOSE ARE THE CLOWNS.
YOU DON'T HAVE TO KNOW A DAMN THING ABOUT 'EM.
OKAY. SO AFTER OUR MUTINYING MEMBER GETS HIS ASS BACK HERE, SHOULD WE KNOCK THOSE PUNKS OFF THE BOARD?

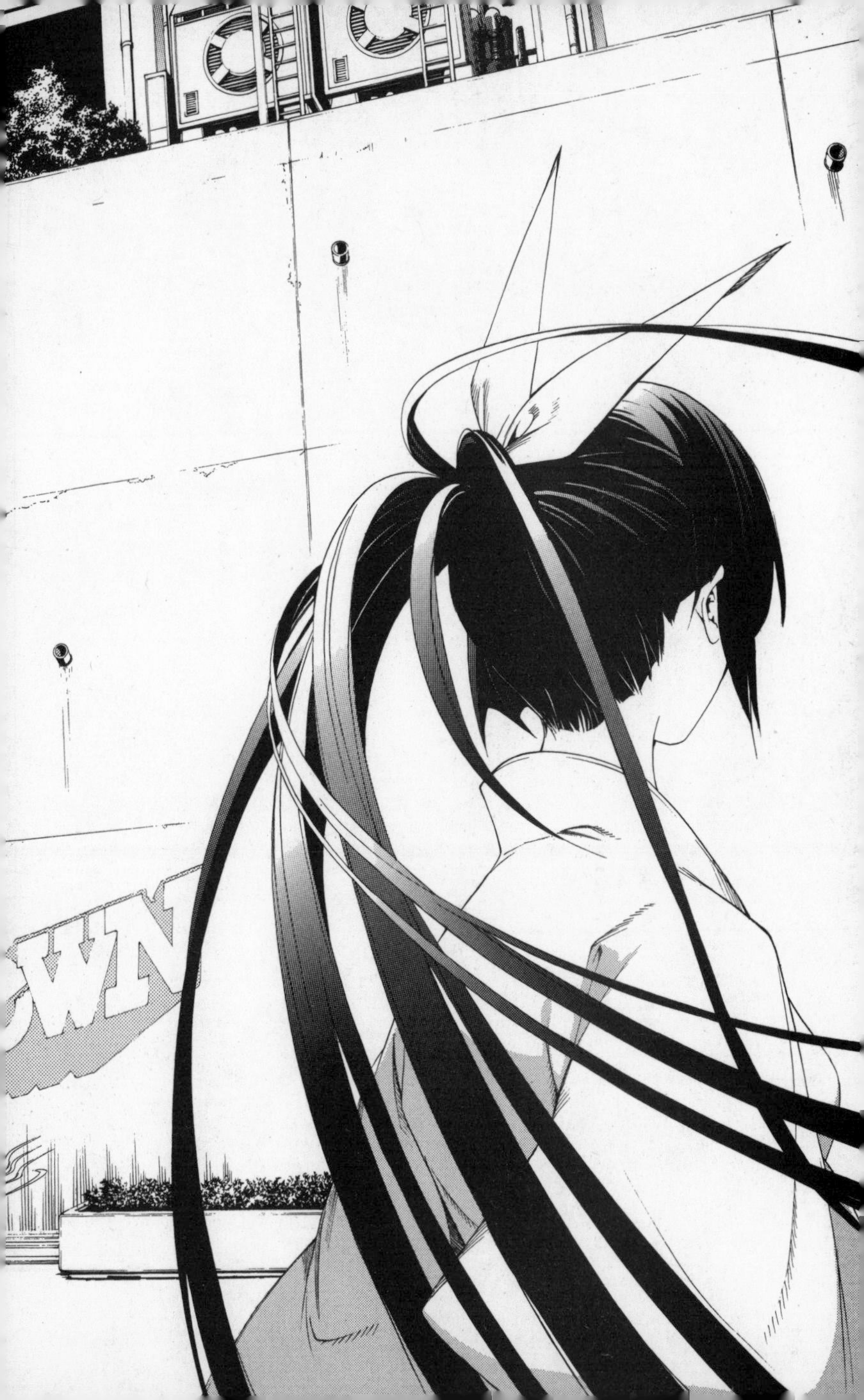

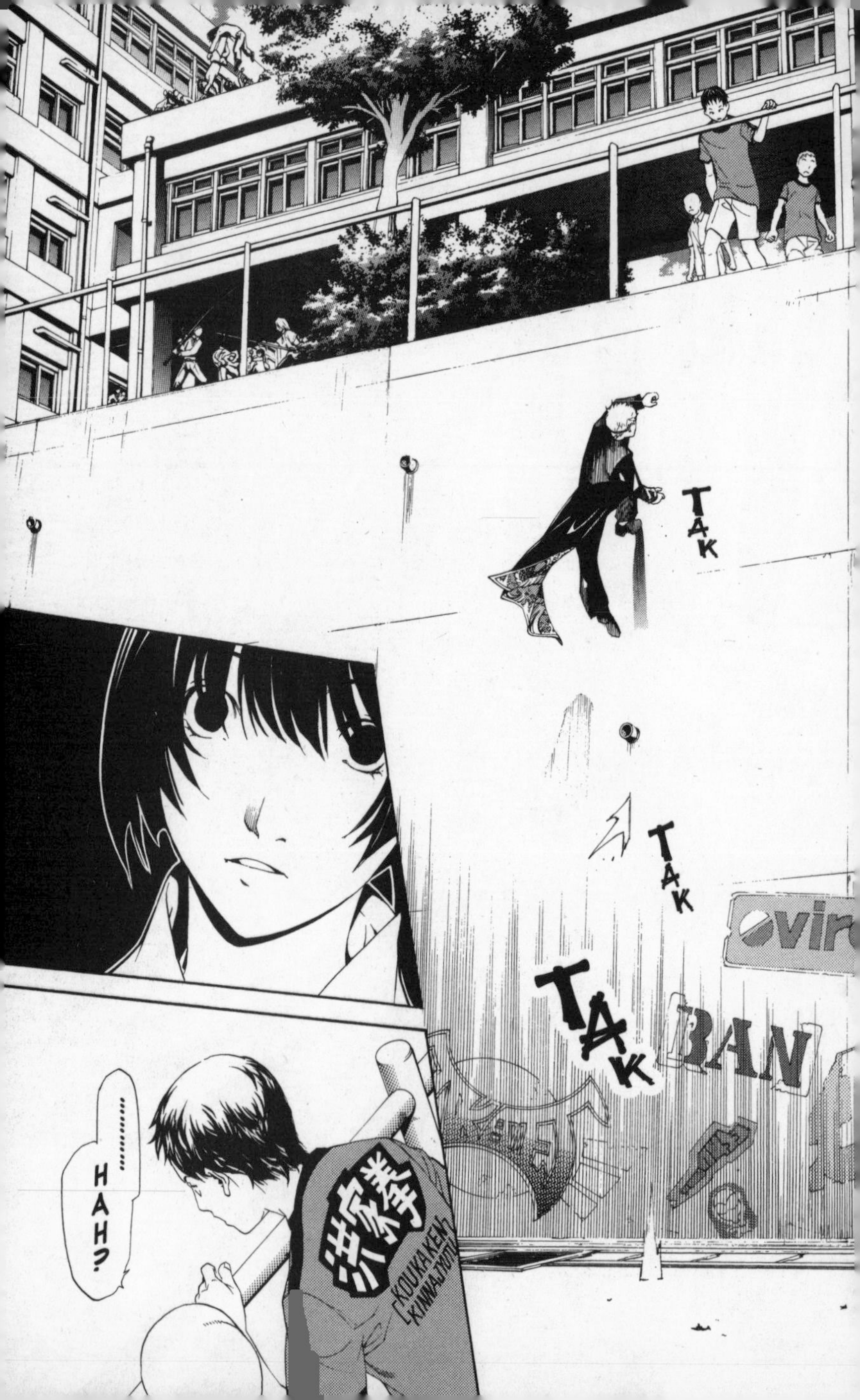
TAK
TAK
TAK
BAN
....
HAH?
洪家拳
[KOUKAKEN]
[KINNAJYOTI]

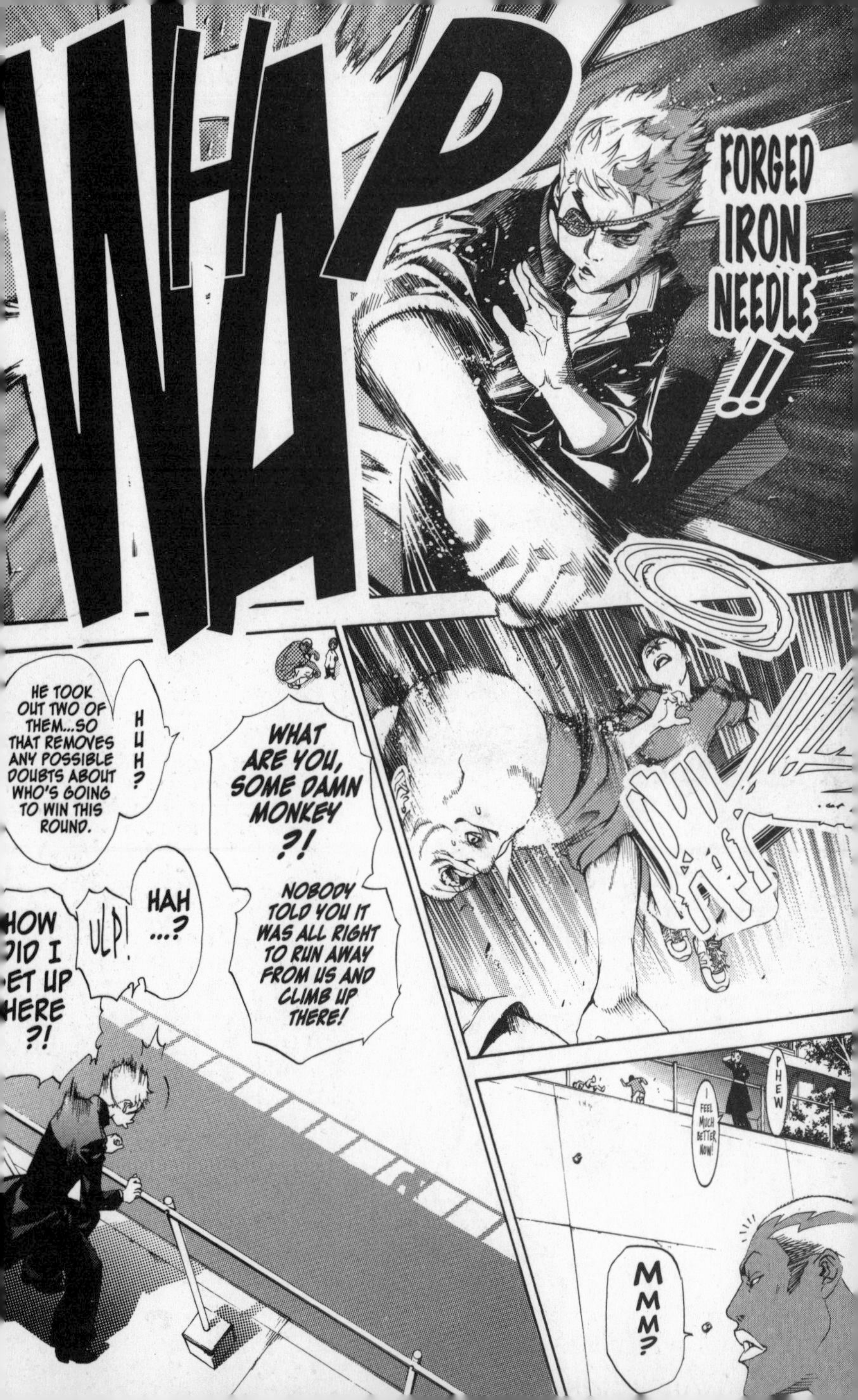
WHAP
FORGED IRON NEEDLE!!
PHEW
I FEEL MUCH BETTER NOW!
MMM?
WHAT ARE YOU, SOME DAMN MONKEY?!
NOBODY TOLD YOU IT WAS ALL RIGHT TO RUN AWAY FROM US AND CLIMB UP THERE!
HUH?
HE TOOK OUT TWO OF THEM...SO THAT REMOVES ANY POSSIBLE DOUBTS ABOUT WHO'S GOING TO WIN THIS ROUND.
HAH...?
ULP!
HOW ID I ET UP HERE ?!

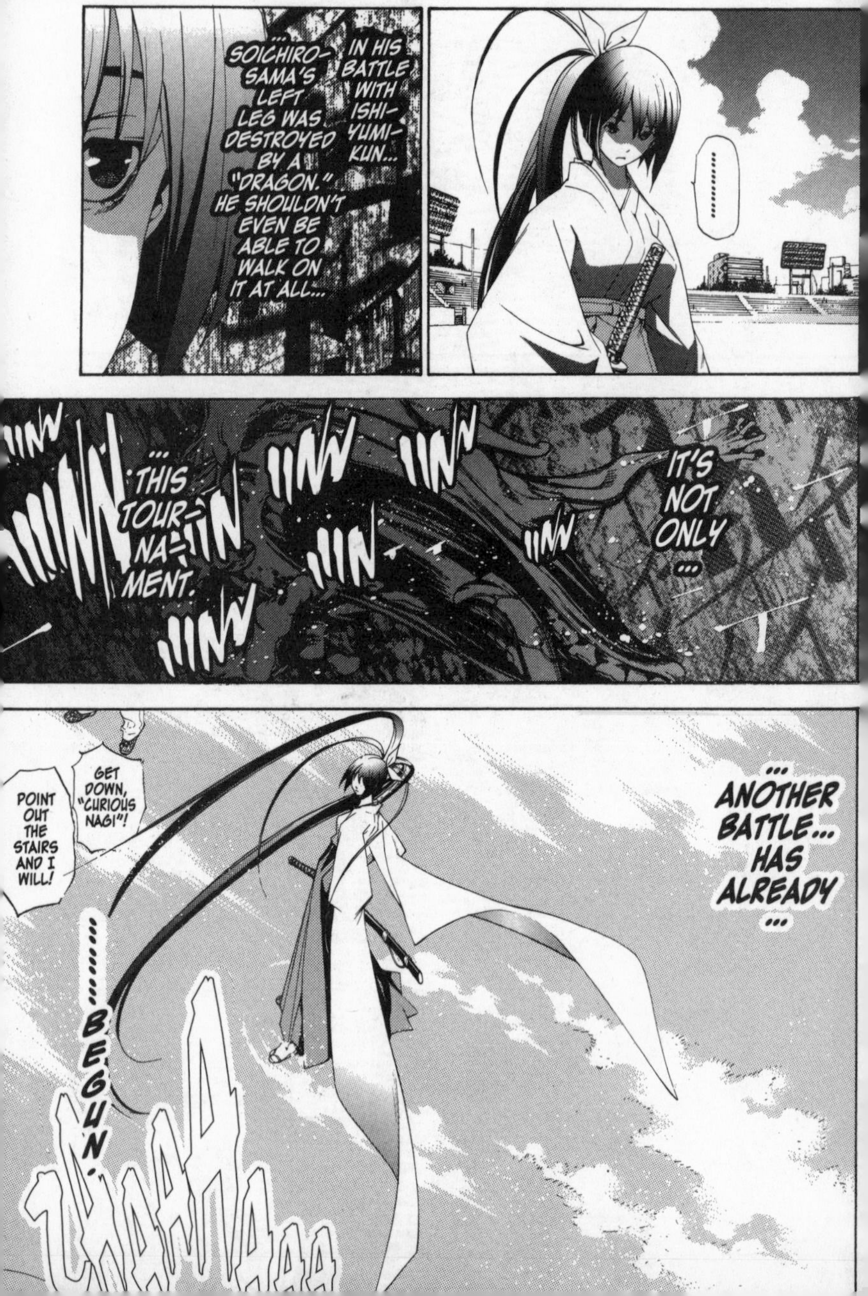
....
IN HIS BATTLE WITH ISHI-YUMI-KUN...
...SOICHIRO-SAMA'S LEFT LEG WAS DESTROYED BY A "DRAGON." HE SHOULDN'T EVEN BE ABLE TO WALK ON IT AT ALL...
IT'S NOT ONLY...
...THIS TOUR-NA-MENT.
...ANOTHER BATTLE... HAS ALREADY...
GET DOWN, "CURIOUS NAGI"!
POINT OUT THE STAIRS AND I WILL!
......BEGUN.

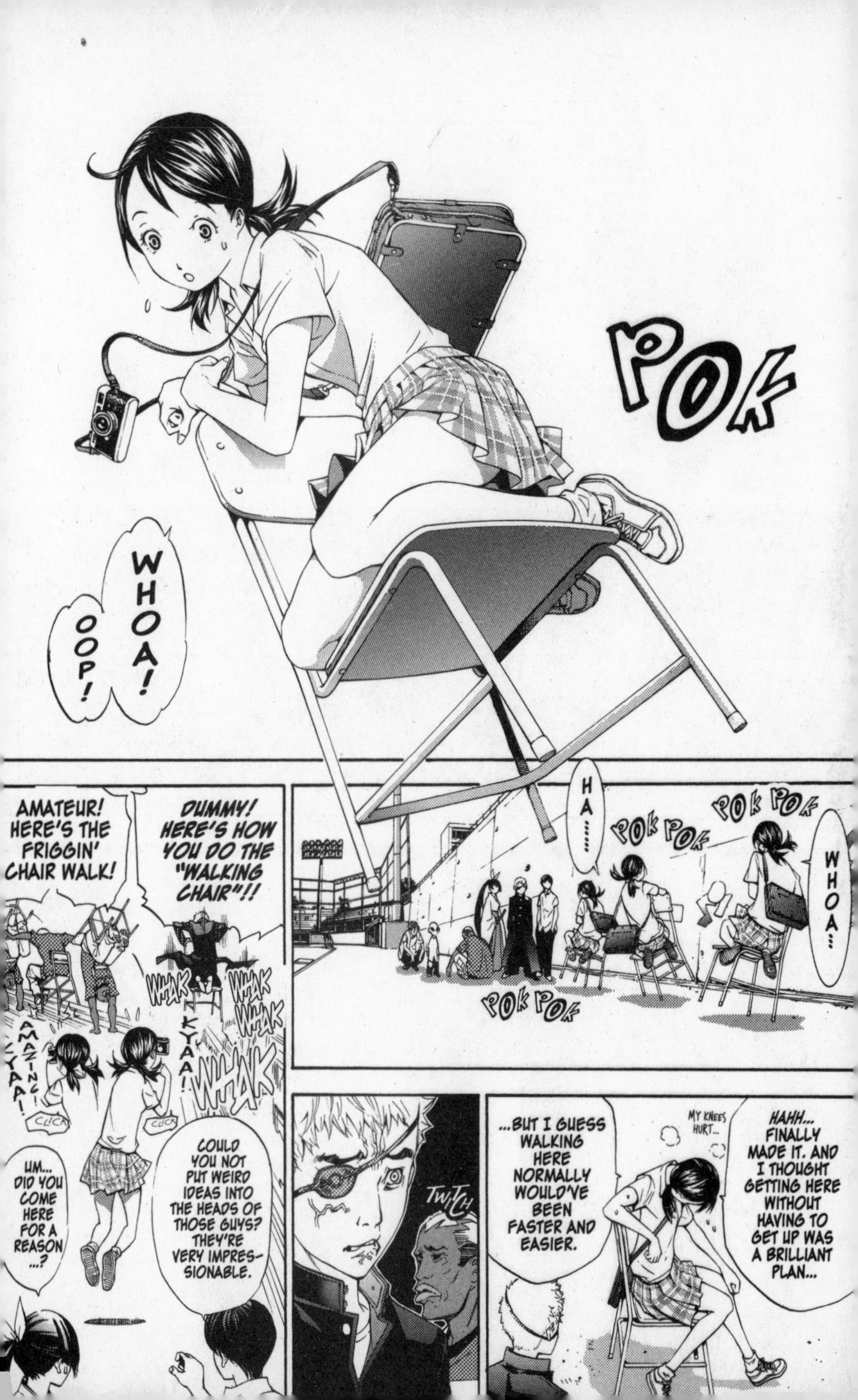
POK
WHOA!
OOP!
WHOA...
POK POK
POK POK
HA.....
POK POK
HAHH... FINALLY MADE IT. AND I THOUGHT GETTING HERE WITHOUT HAVING TO GET UP WAS A BRILLIANT PLAN...
MY KNEES HURT...
...BUT I GUESS WALKING HERE NORMALLY WOULD'VE BEEN FASTER AND EASIER.
TWITCH
DUMMY! HERE'S HOW YOU DO THE "WALKING CHAIR"!!
AMATEUR! HERE'S THE FRIGGIN' CHAIR WALK!
WHAK WHAK WHAK
WHAK
KYAA!
WHAK
AMAZING!
KYAA!
CLICK
CLICK
COULD YOU NOT PUT WEIRD IDEAS INTO THE HEADS OF THOSE GUYS? THEY'RE VERY IMPRESSIONABLE.
UM... DID YOU COME HERE FOR A REASON ...?

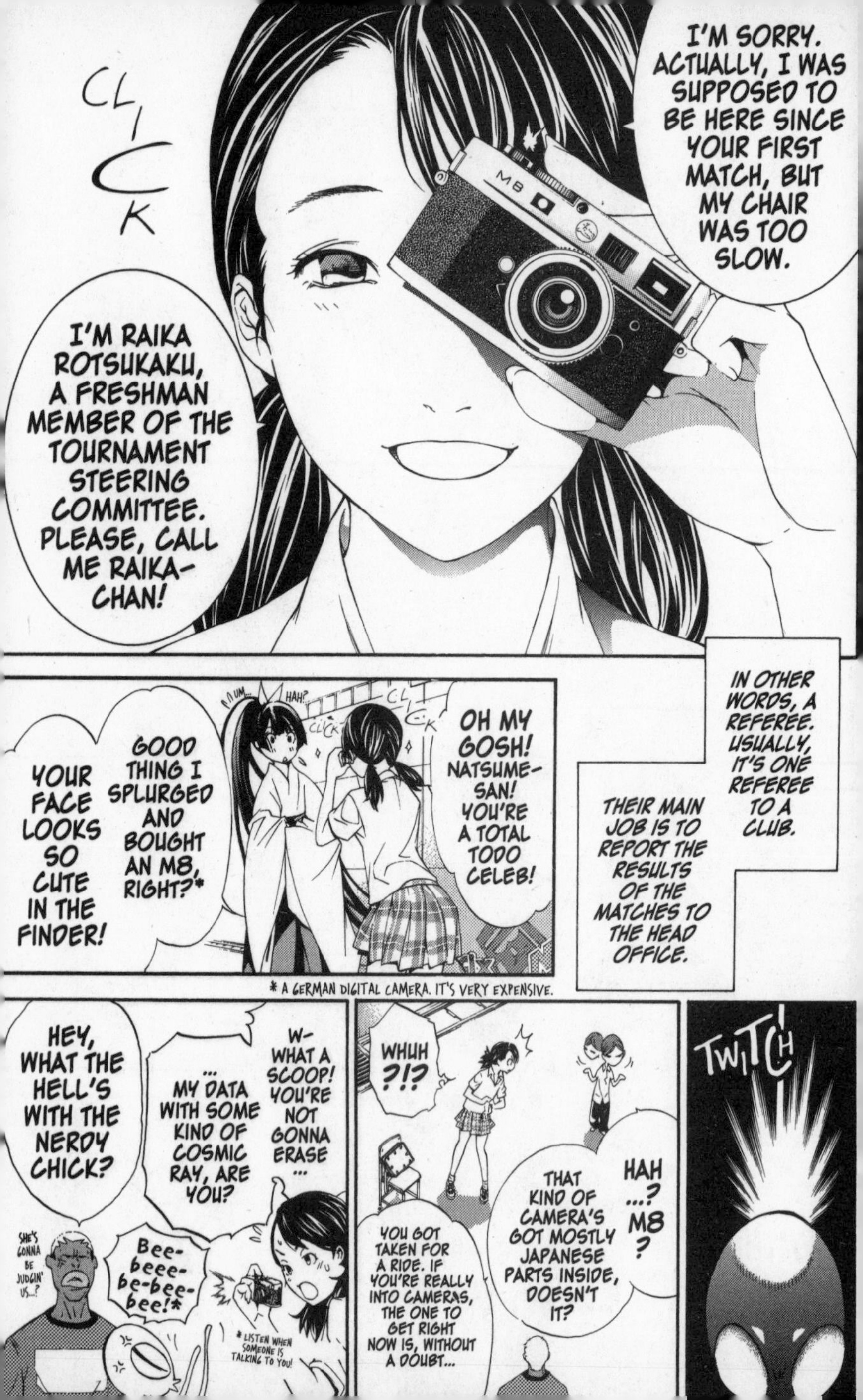
I'M SORRY. ACTUALLY, I WAS SUPPOSED TO BE HERE SINCE YOUR FIRST MATCH, BUT MY CHAIR WAS TOO SLOW.
CLICK
I'M RAIKA ROTSUKAKU, A FRESHMAN MEMBER OF THE TOURNAMENT STEERING COMMITTEE. PLEASE, CALL ME RAIKA-CHAN!
IN OTHER WORDS, A REFEREE. USUALLY, IT'S ONE REFEREE TO A CLUB.
THEIR MAIN JOB IS TO REPORT THE RESULTS OF THE MATCHES TO THE HEAD OFFICE.
OH MY GOSH! NATSUME-SAN! YOU'RE A TOTAL TODO CELEB!
CLICK
HAH?
UM...
CLICK
GOOD THING I SPLURGED AND BOUGHT AN M8, RIGHT?*
YOUR FACE LOOKS SO CUTE IN THE FINDER!
* A GERMAN DIGITAL CAMERA. IT'S VERY EXPENSIVE.
TWITCH
WHUH ?!?
HAH ...? M8 ?
THAT KIND OF CAMERA'S GOT MOSTLY JAPANESE PARTS INSIDE, DOESN'T IT?
YOU GOT TAKEN FOR A RIDE. IF YOU'RE REALLY INTO CAMERAS, THE ONE TO GET RIGHT NOW IS, WITHOUT A DOUBT...
W-WHAT A SCOOP! YOU'RE NOT GONNA ERASE ...
... MY DATA WITH SOME KIND OF COSMIC RAY, ARE YOU?
HEY, WHAT THE HELL'S WITH THE NERDY CHICK?
Bee-beee-be-bee-bee!*
SHE'S GONNA BE JUDGIN' US...?
* LISTEN WHEN SOMEONE IS TALKING TO YOU!

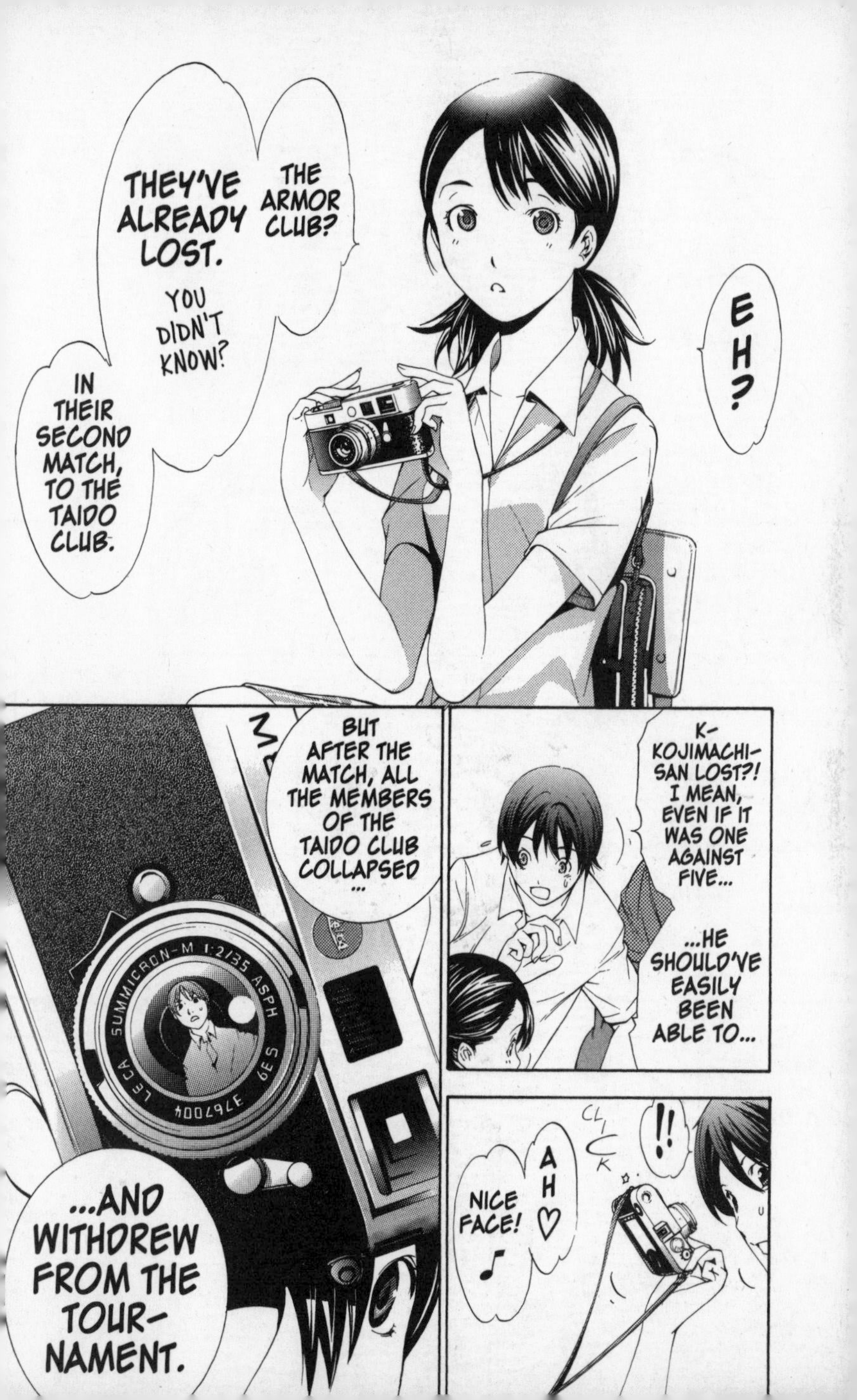
EH?
THE ARMOR CLUB?
THEY'VE ALREADY LOST.
YOU DIDN'T KNOW?
IN THEIR SECOND MATCH, TO THE TAIDO CLUB.
K-KOJIMACHI-SAN LOST?! I MEAN, EVEN IF IT WAS ONE AGAINST FIVE...
...HE SHOULD'VE EASILY BEEN ABLE TO...
CLICK
!!
AH ♡
NICE FACE! ♪
BUT AFTER THE MATCH, ALL THE MEMBERS OF THE TAIDO CLUB COLLAPSED...
LEICA SUMMICRON-M 1:2/35 ASPH
E39 3767004
...AND WITHDREW FROM THE TOUR-NAMENT.

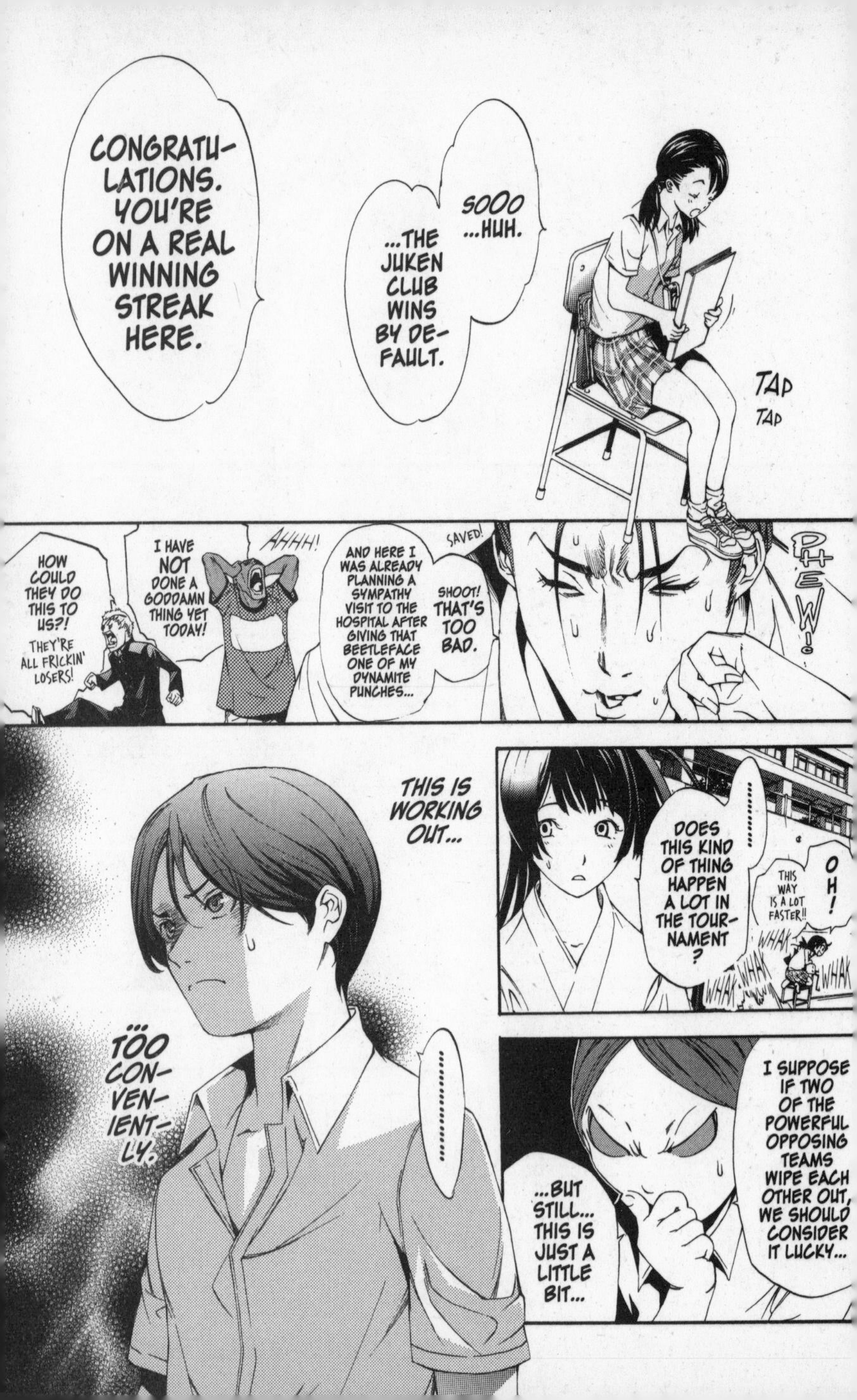
TAP TAP
SOOO ...HUH.
...THE JUKEN CLUB WINS BY DE-FAULT.
CONGRATU-LATIONS. YOU'RE ON A REAL WINNING STREAK HERE.
PHEW!
SAVED!
SHOOT! THAT'S TOO BAD.
AND HERE I WAS ALREADY PLANNING A SYMPATHY VISIT TO THE HOSPITAL AFTER GIVING THAT BEETLEFACE ONE OF MY DYNAMITE PUNCHES...
AHHH!
I HAVE NOT DONE A GODDAMN THING YET TODAY!
HOW COULD THEY DO THIS TO US?!
THEY'RE ALL FRICKIN' LOSERS!
OH!
THIS WAY IS A LOT FASTER!!
WHAK WHAK WHAK WHAK
....
DOES THIS KIND OF THING HAPPEN A LOT IN THE TOUR-NAMENT?
I SUPPOSE IF TWO OF THE POWERFUL OPPOSING TEAMS WIPE EACH OTHER OUT, WE SHOULD CONSIDER IT LUCKY...
...BUT STILL... THIS IS JUST A LITTLE BIT...
THIS IS WORKING OUT...
....
...TÖO CON-VEN-IENT-LY.

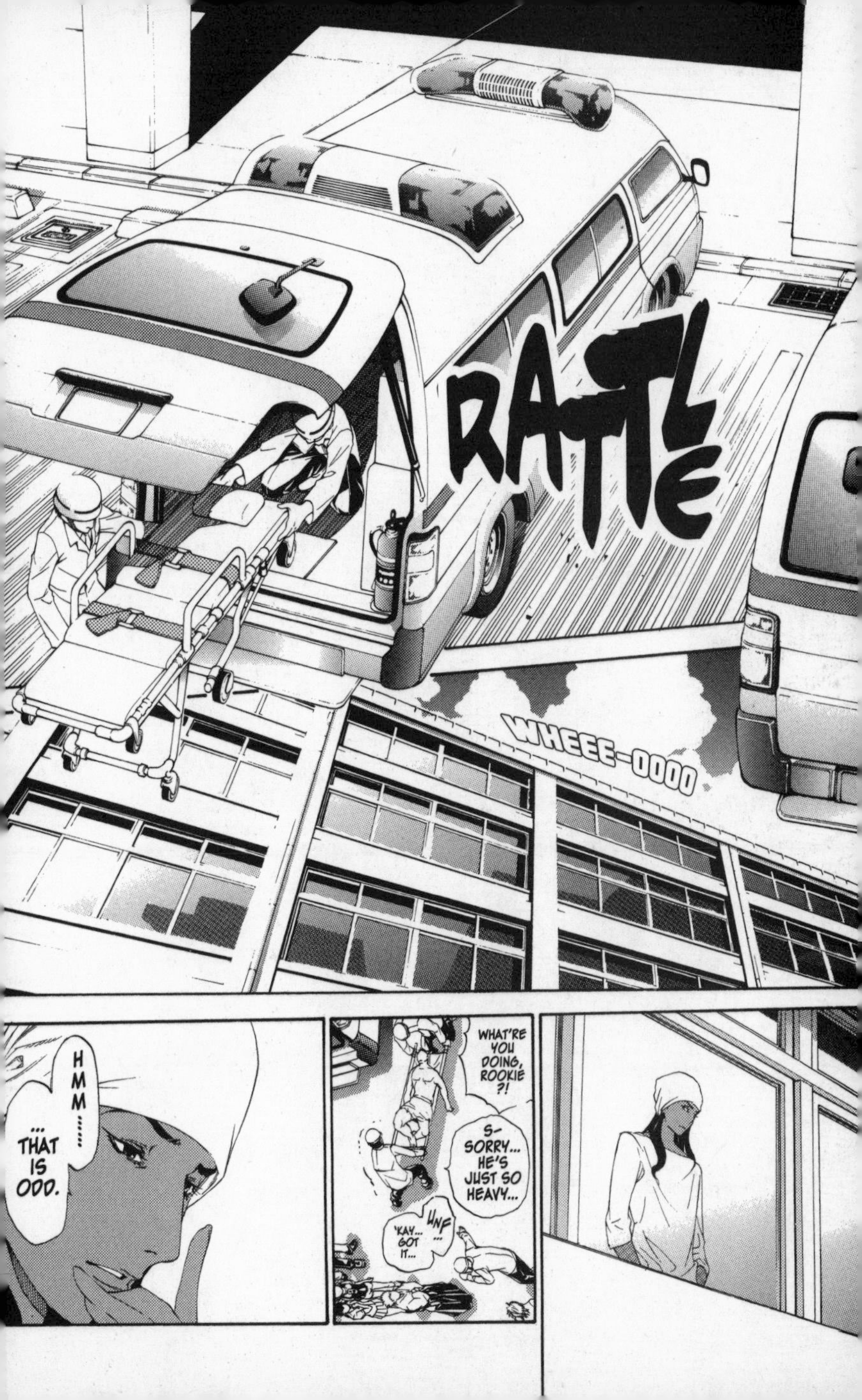
RATTLE
WHEEE-OOOO
WHAT'RE YOU DOING, ROOKIE?!
S-SORRY... HE'S JUST SO HEAVY...
UNF...
'KAY... GOT IT...
HMM.....
... THAT IS ODD.

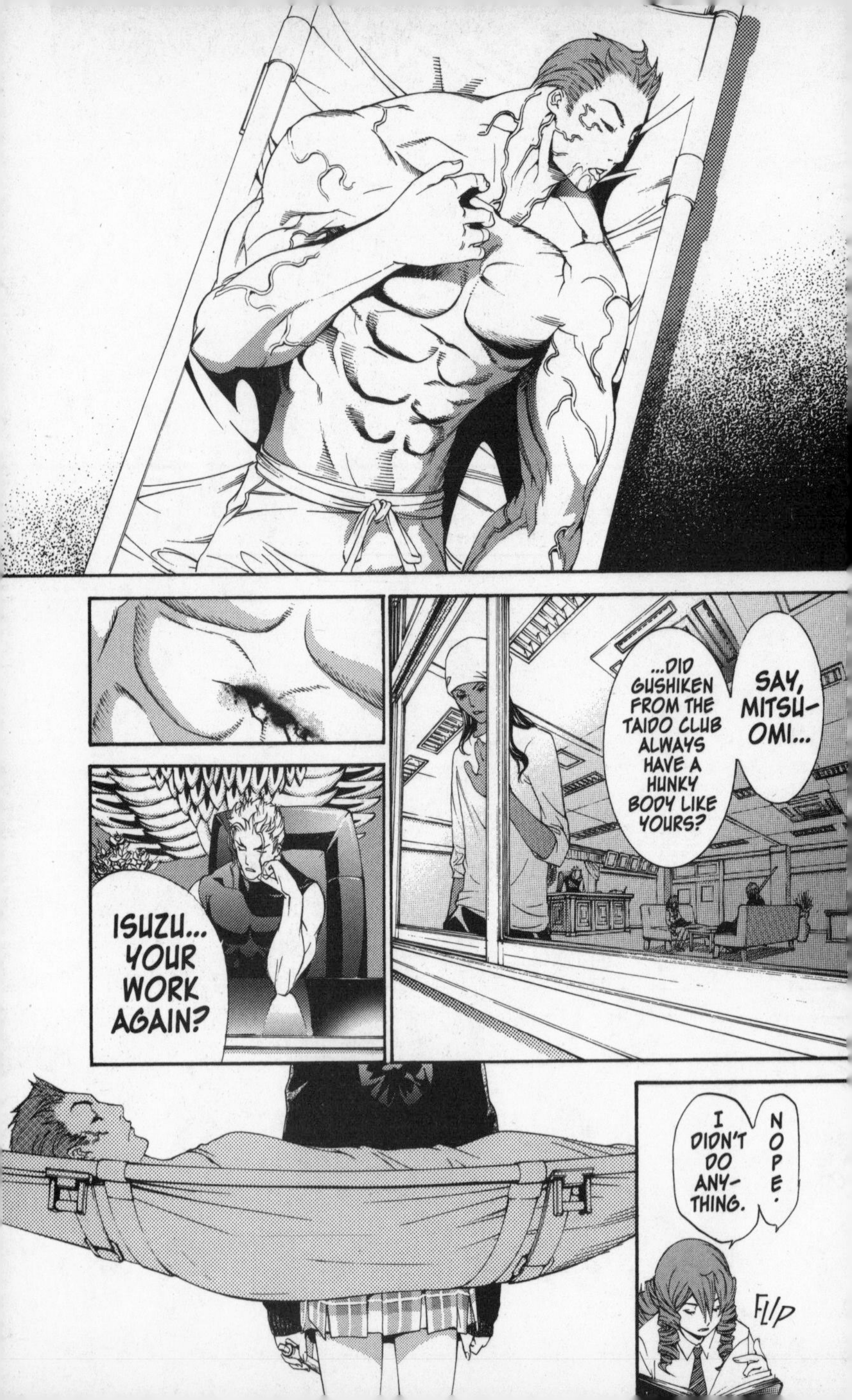
SAY, MITSU-OMI...
...DID GUSHIKEN FROM THE TAIDO CLUB ALWAYS HAVE A HUNKY BODY LIKE YOURS?
ISUZU... YOUR WORK AGAIN?
NOPE.
I DIDN'T DO ANY-THING.
FLIP

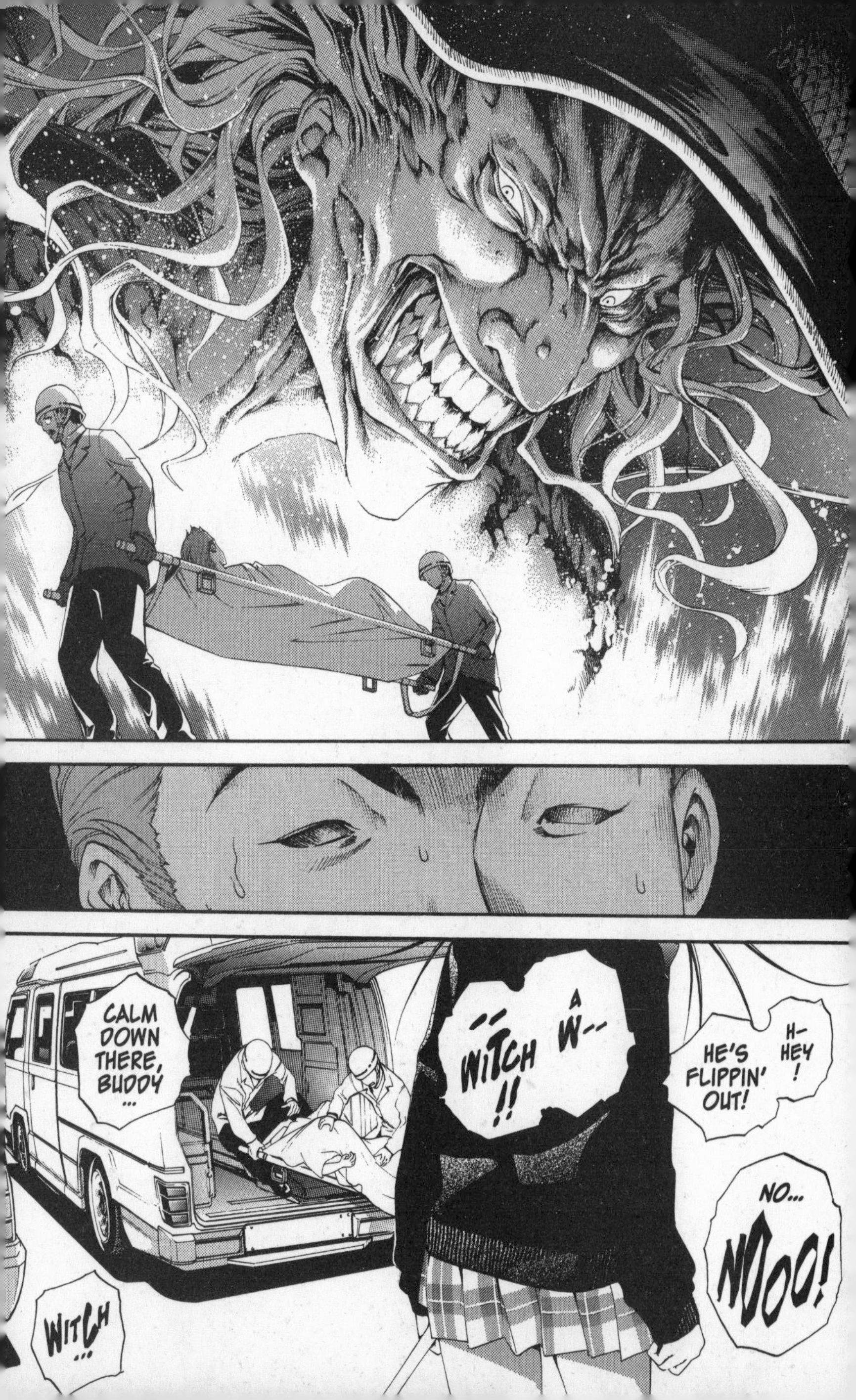
H-HEY!
HE'S FLIPPIN' OUT!
NO... NOOO!
AW--
--WITCH!!
CALM DOWN THERE, BUDDY...
WITCH...

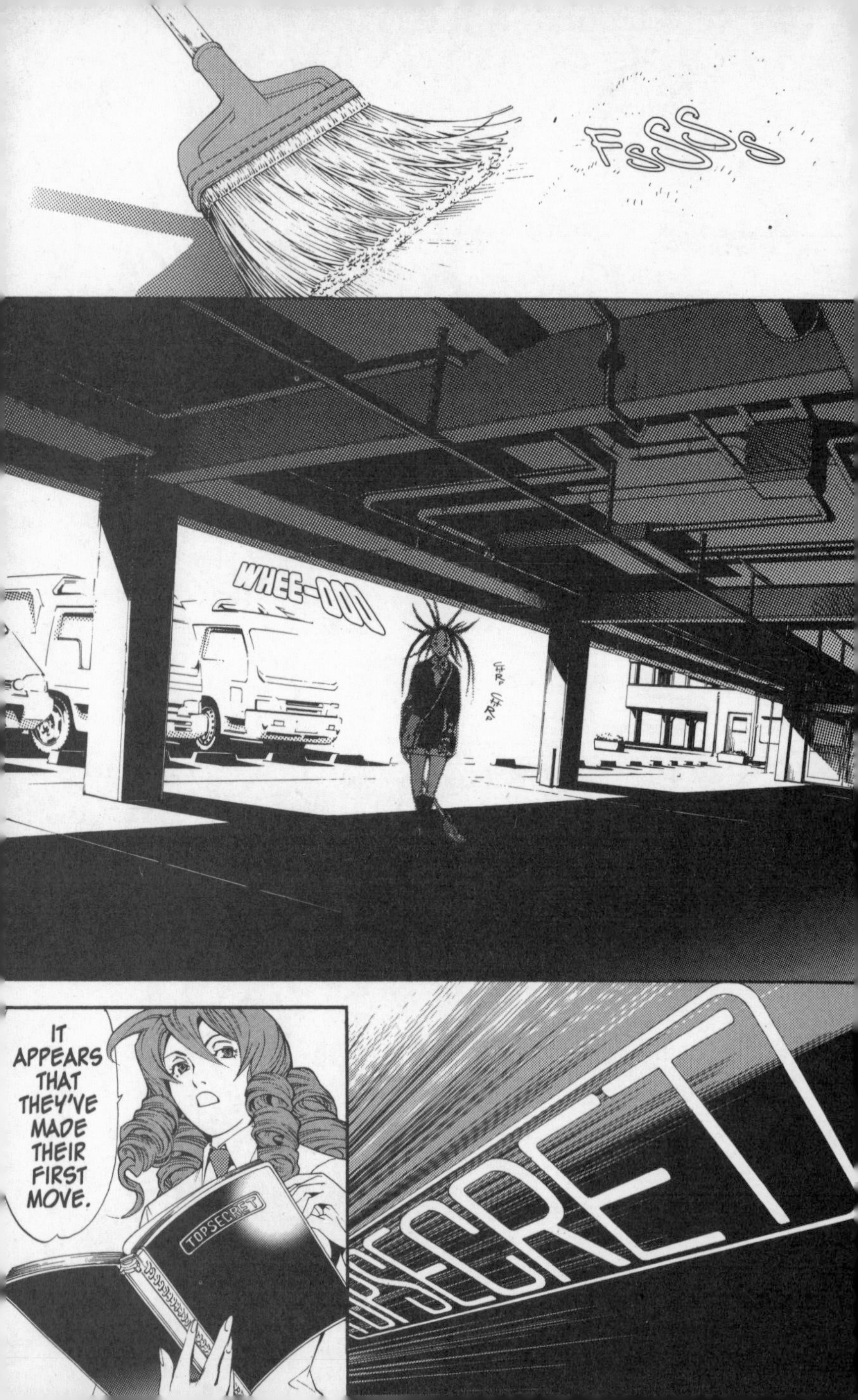
FSSSS
WHEE-OOO
SECRET
IT APPEARS THAT THEY'VE MADE THEIR FIRST MOVE.
TOPSECRET

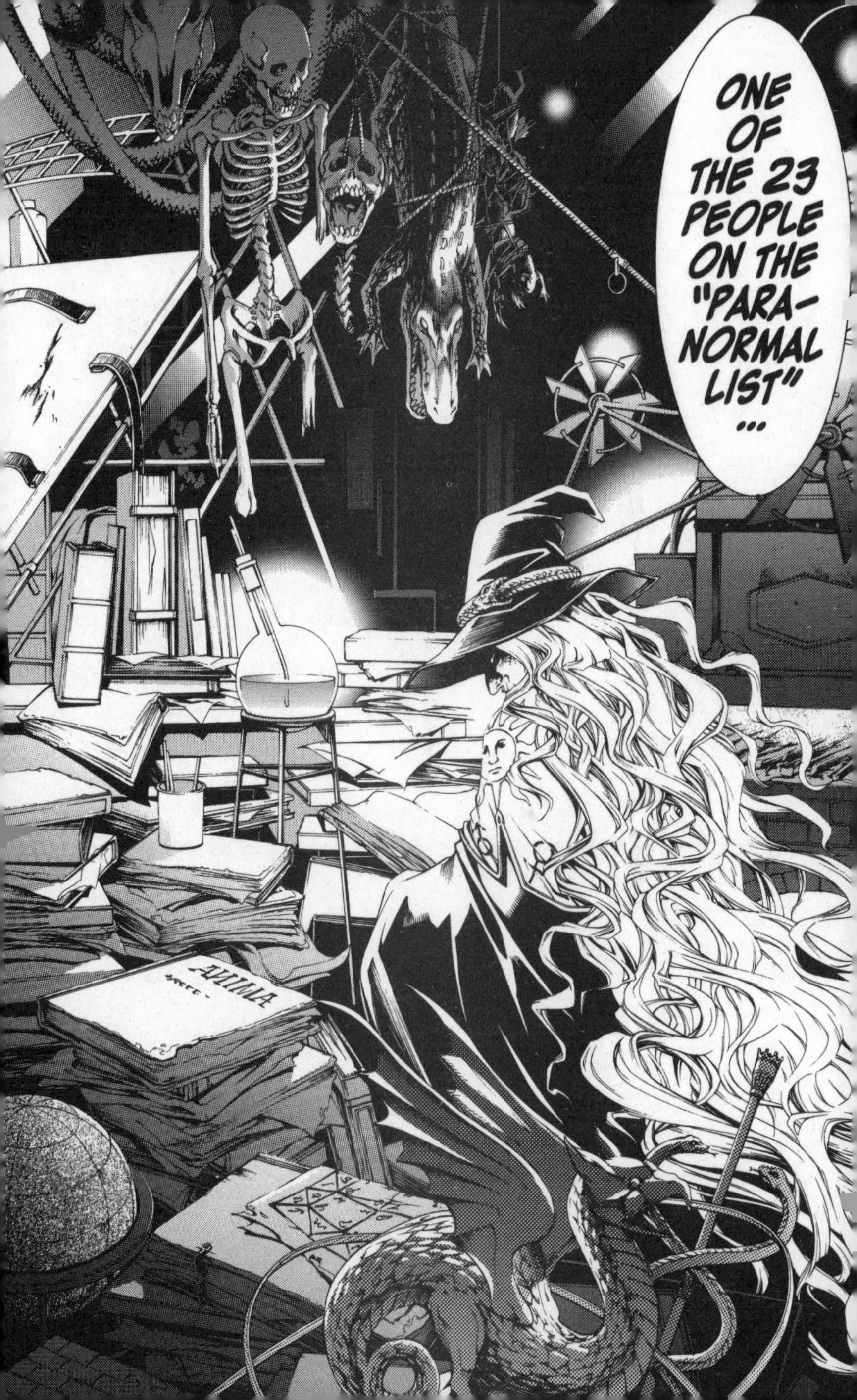
ONE OF THE 23 PEOPLE ON THE "PARA-NORMAL LIST" ...

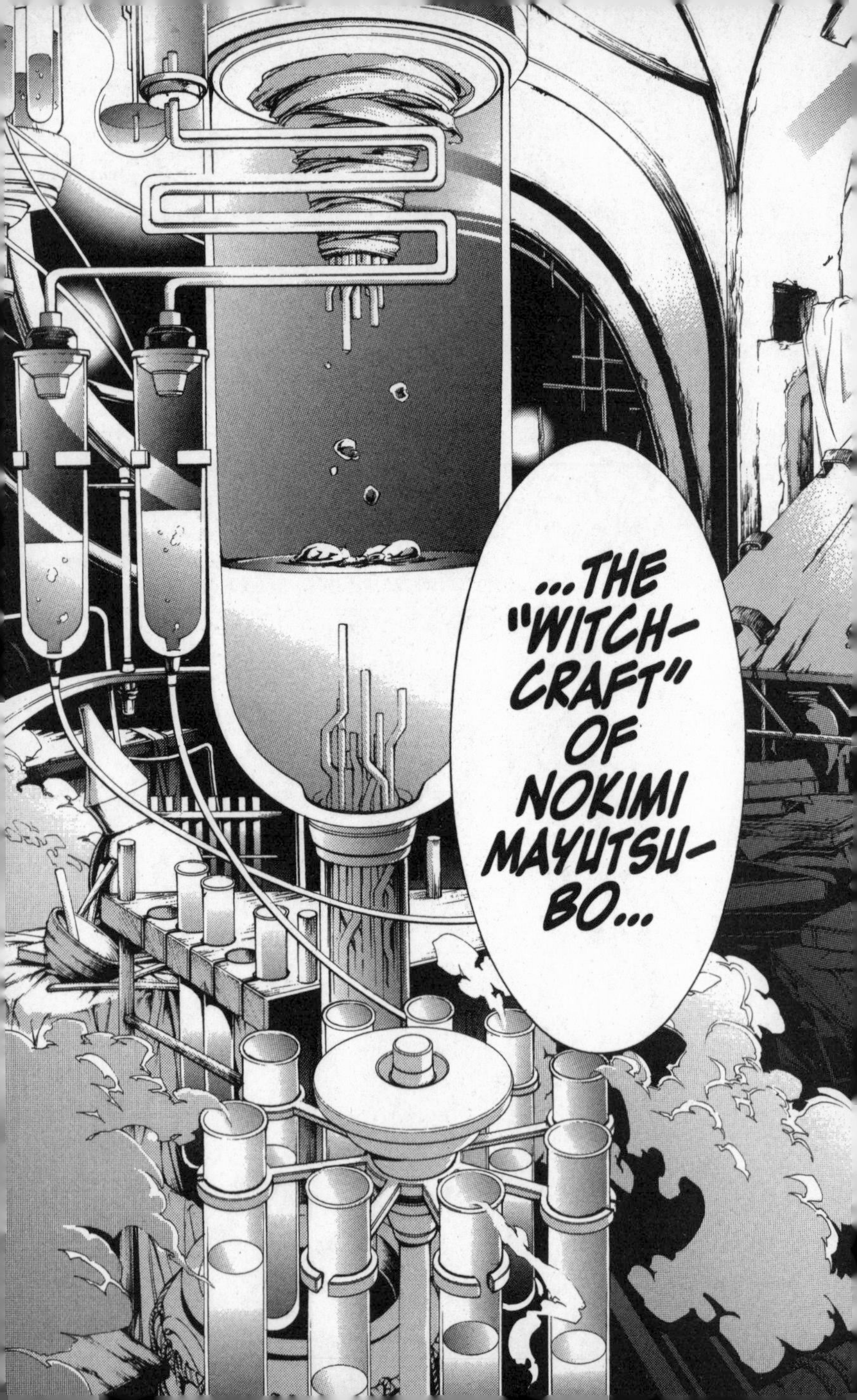
...THE "WITCH-CRAFT" OF NOKIMI MAYUTSU-BO...

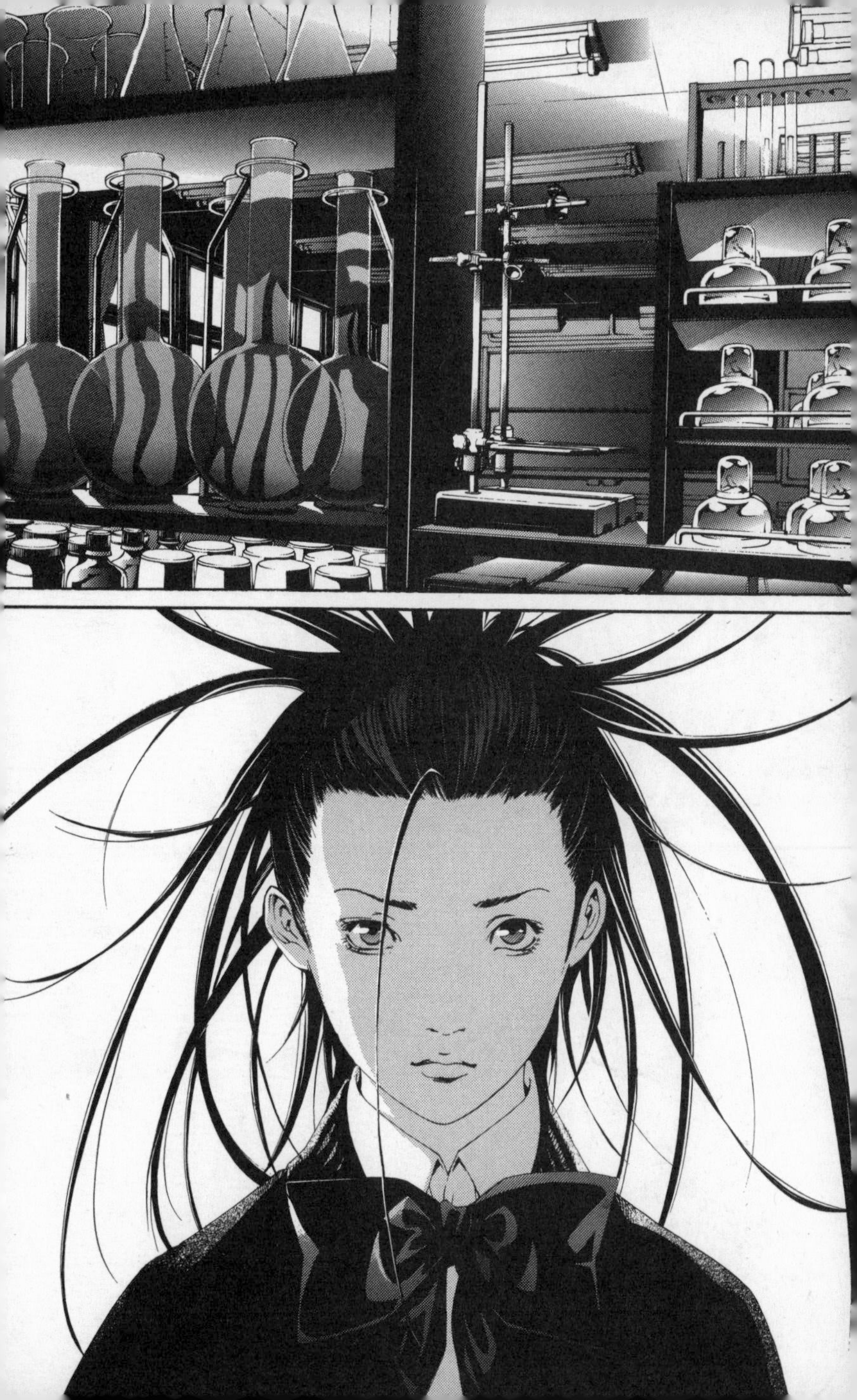

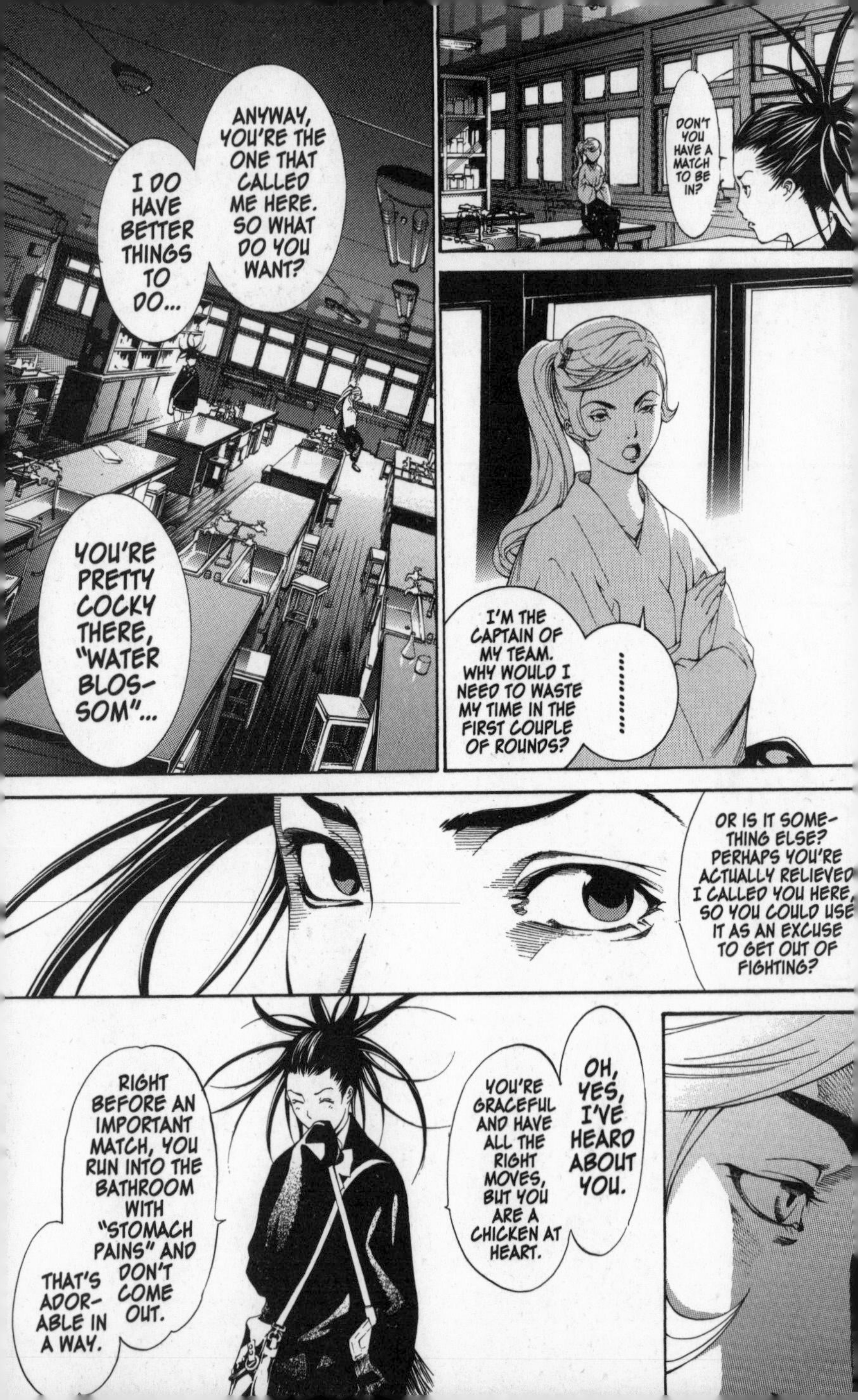
DON'T YOU HAVE A MATCH TO BE IN?
......
I'M THE CAPTAIN OF MY TEAM. WHY WOULD I NEED TO WASTE MY TIME IN THE FIRST COUPLE OF ROUNDS?
ANYWAY, YOU'RE THE ONE THAT CALLED ME HERE. SO WHAT DO YOU WANT?
I DO HAVE BETTER THINGS TO DO...
YOU'RE PRETTY COCKY THERE, "WATER BLOS-SOM"...
OR IS IT SOME-THING ELSE? PERHAPS YOU'RE ACTUALLY RELIEVED I CALLED YOU HERE, SO YOU COULD USE IT AS AN EXCUSE TO GET OUT OF FIGHTING?
OH, YES, I'VE HEARD ABOUT YOU.
YOU'RE GRACEFUL AND HAVE ALL THE RIGHT MOVES, BUT YOU ARE A CHICKEN AT HEART.
RIGHT BEFORE AN IMPORTANT MATCH, YOU RUN INTO THE BATHROOM WITH "STOMACH PAINS" AND DON'T COME OUT.
THAT'S ADOR-ABLE IN A WAY.

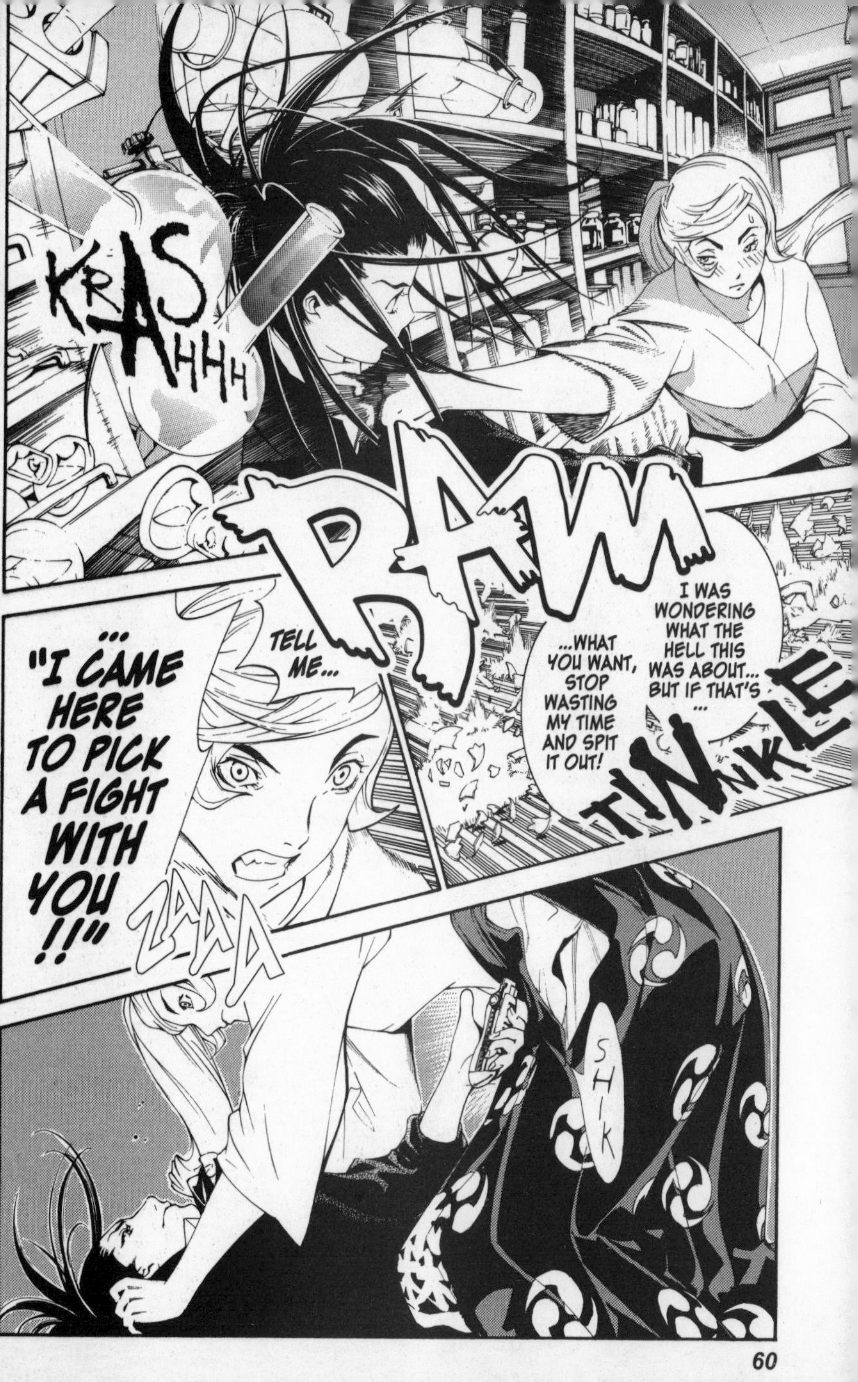
KRASHHH
BAM
I WAS WONDERING WHAT THE HELL THIS WAS ABOUT... BUT IF THAT'S ...
...WHAT YOU WANT, STOP WASTING MY TIME AND SPIT IT OUT!
TINKLE
TELL ME...
..."I CAME HERE TO PICK A FIGHT WITH YOU!!"
ZAAA
SHIK

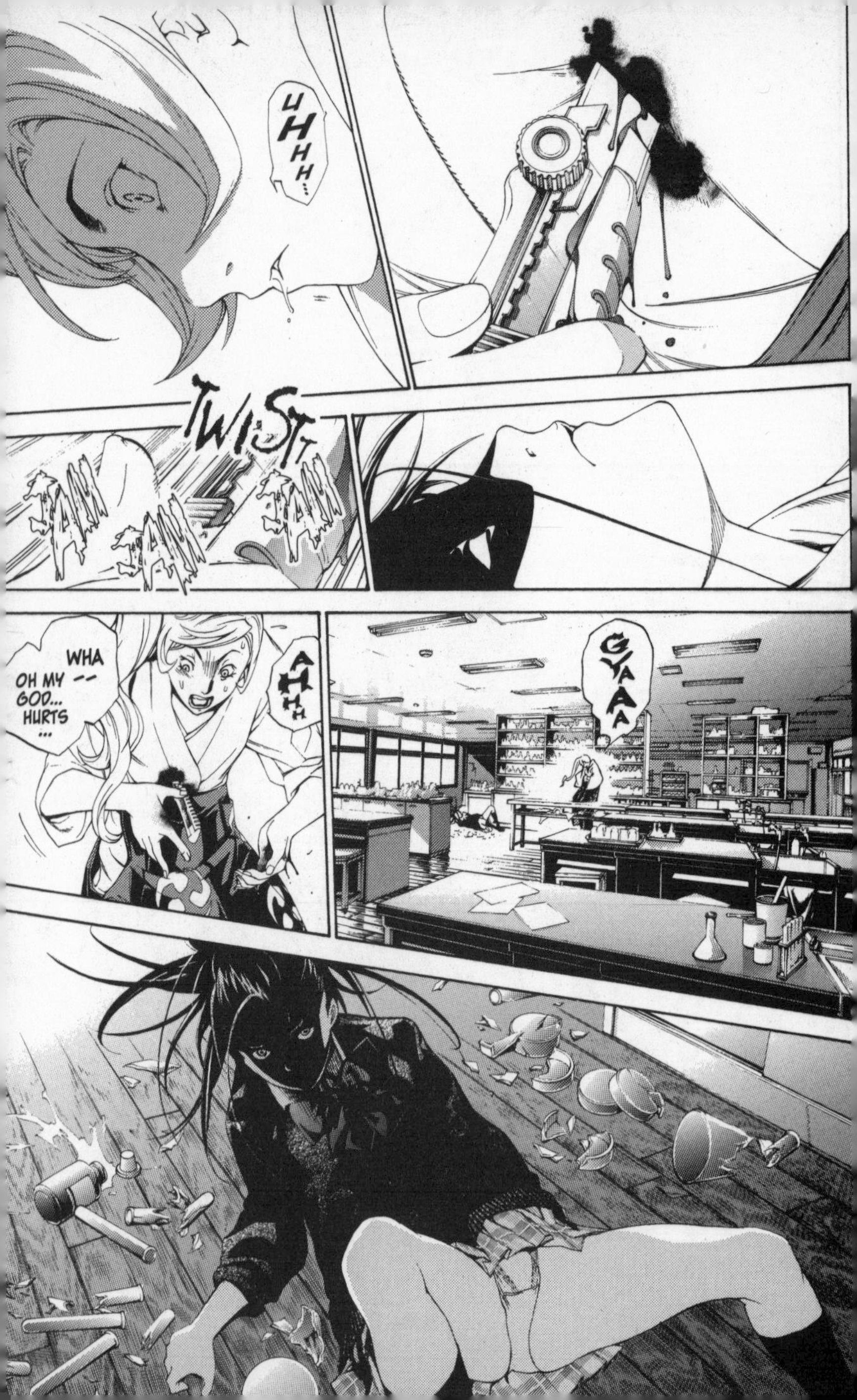
UHHH...
TWIST
GYAAA
AHHH
WHA --
OH MY GOD... HURTS ...

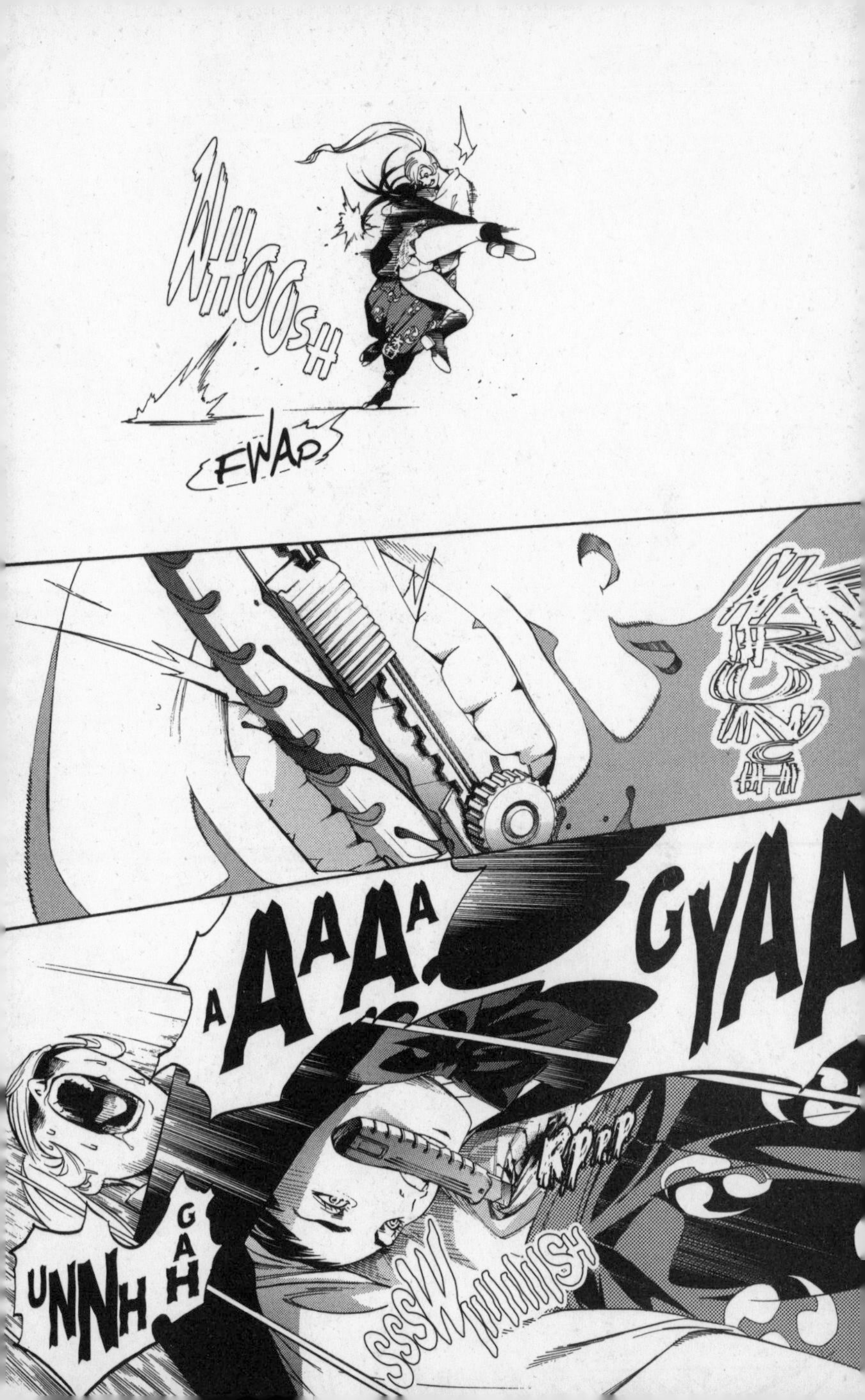
WHOOSH
FWAP
GYAA
AAAAA
RPPP
SSSWIIIISH
GAH
UNNH

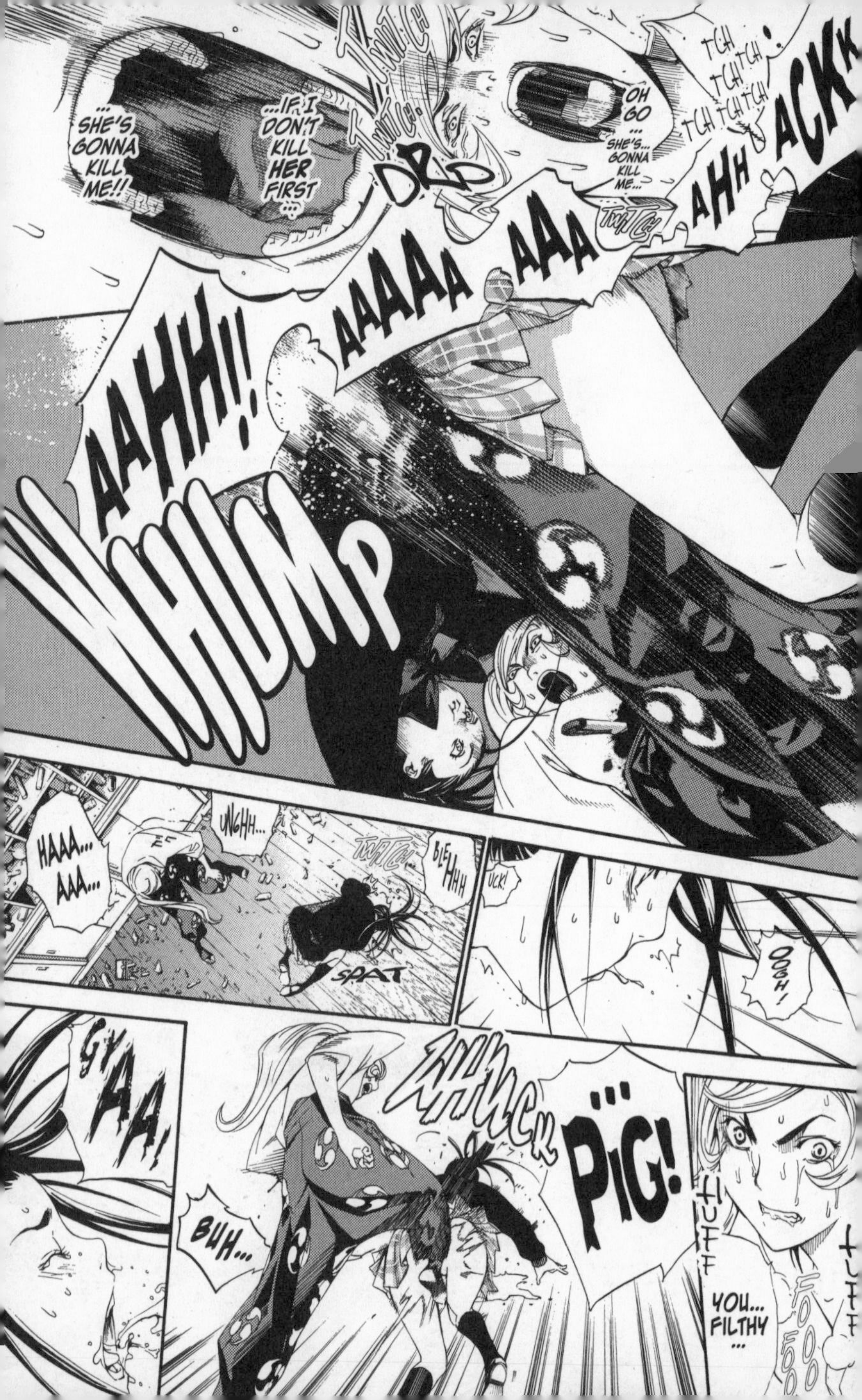
TCH TCH TCH TCH TCH TCH
AHH ACKK
OH GO... SHE'S... GONNA KILL ME...
TWITCH
TWITCH
TWITCH
DRIP
...IF I DON'T KILL HER FIRST...
...SHE'S GONNA KILL ME!!
AAAAA AAA
AAHH!!
WHUMP
UCK!
OOGH!
BLEHHH
TWITCH
UNGHH...
HAAA... AAA...
SPAT
HUFF
HUFF
YOU... FILTHY...
...PIG!
WHUCK
BUH...
GYAA!

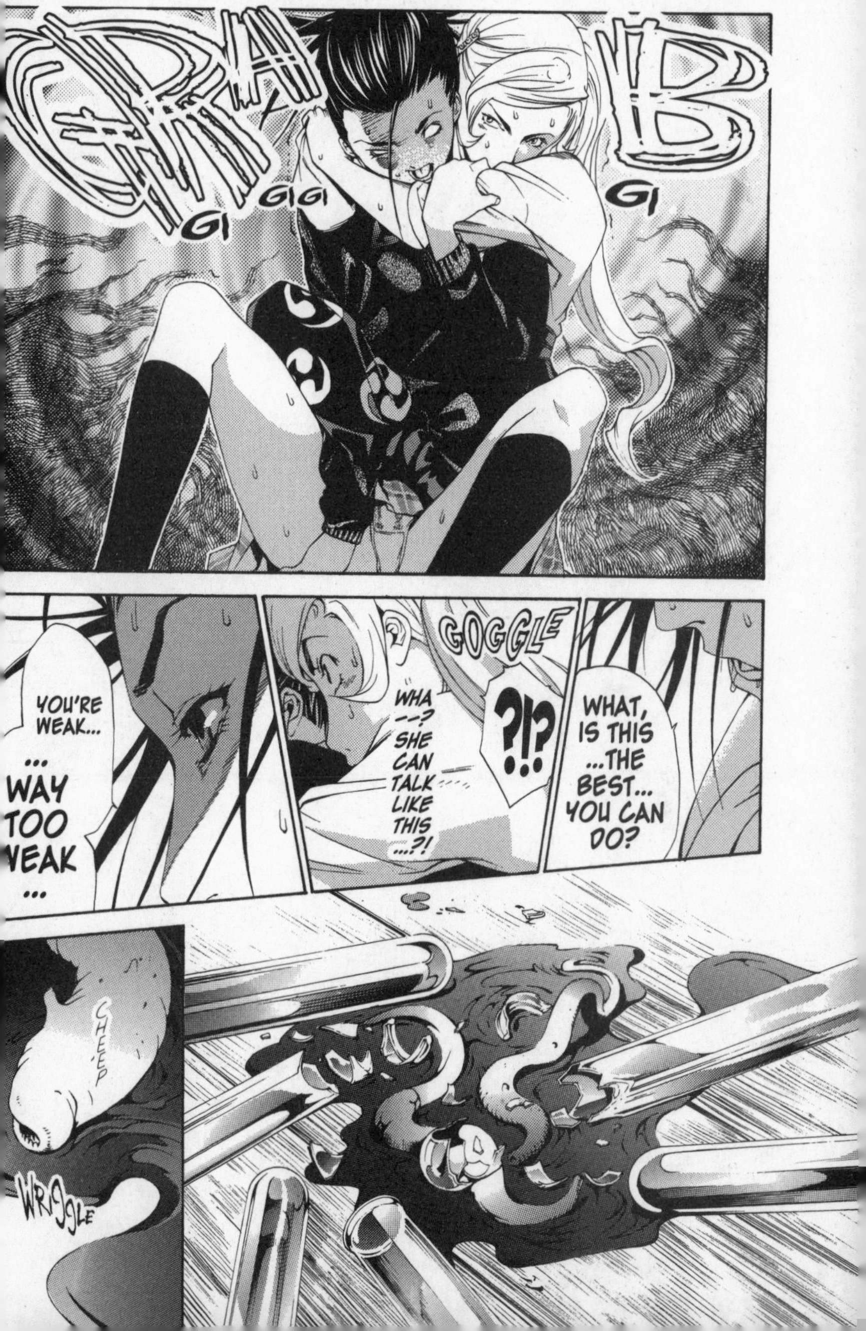
GRAB
GI GIGI GI
WHAT, IS THIS ...THE BEST... YOU CAN DO?
GOGGLE
?!?
WHA--? SHE CAN TALK LIKE THIS ...?!
YOU'RE WEAK...
...WAY TOO WEAK...
CHEEP
WRIGGLE

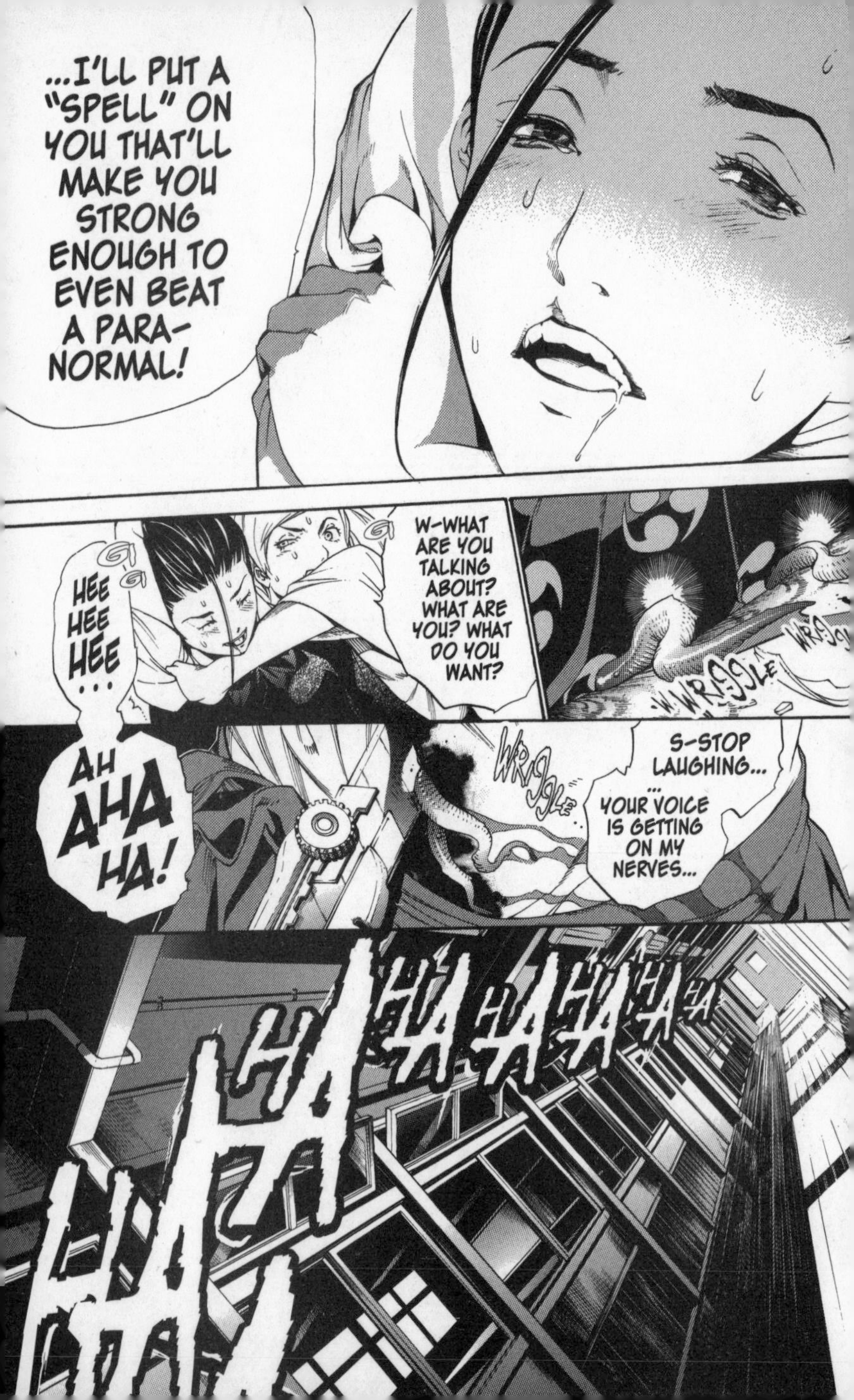
...I'LL PUT A "SPELL" ON YOU THAT'LL MAKE YOU STRONG ENOUGH TO EVEN BEAT A PARA-NORMAL!
WRIGGLE
WRIGGLE
W-WHAT ARE YOU TALKING ABOUT? WHAT ARE YOU? WHAT DO YOU WANT?
HEE HEE HEE...
S-STOP LAUGHING... ...YOUR VOICE IS GETTING ON MY NERVES...
WRIGGLE
AH AHA HA!
HA HA HA HA HA HA

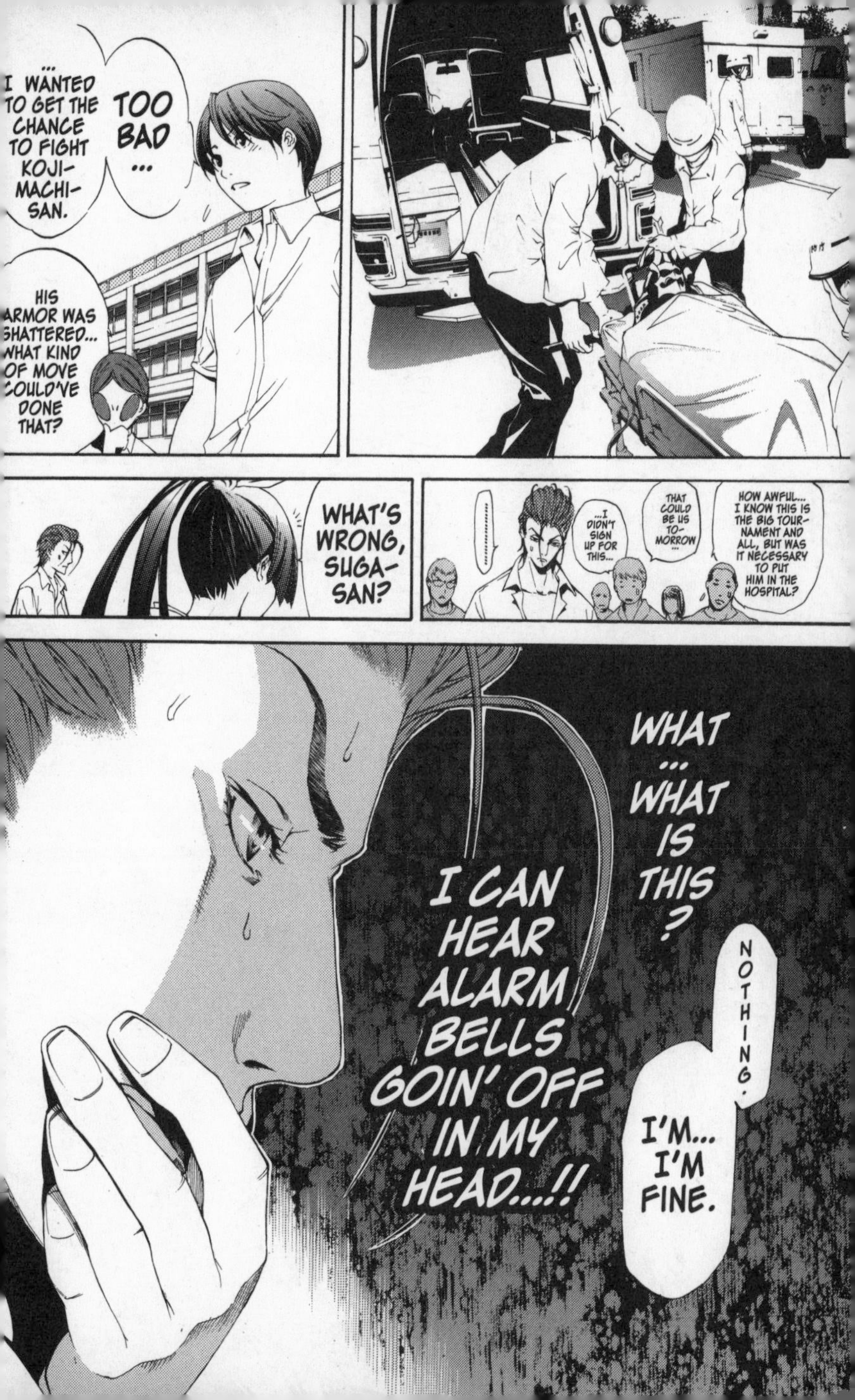
TOO BAD ...
... I WANTED TO GET THE CHANCE TO FIGHT KOJI-MACHI-SAN.
HIS ARMOR WAS SHATTERED... WHAT KIND OF MOVE COULD'VE DONE THAT?
HOW AWFUL... I KNOW THIS IS THE BIG TOUR-NAMENT AND ALL, BUT WAS IT NECESSARY TO PUT HIM IN THE HOSPITAL?
THAT COULD BE US TO-MORROW ...
...I DIDN'T SIGN UP FOR THIS...
......
WHAT'S WRONG, SUGA-SAN?
WHAT ... WHAT IS THIS?
NOTHING.
I'M... I'M FINE.
I CAN HEAR ALARM BELLS GOIN' OFF IN MY HEAD...!!

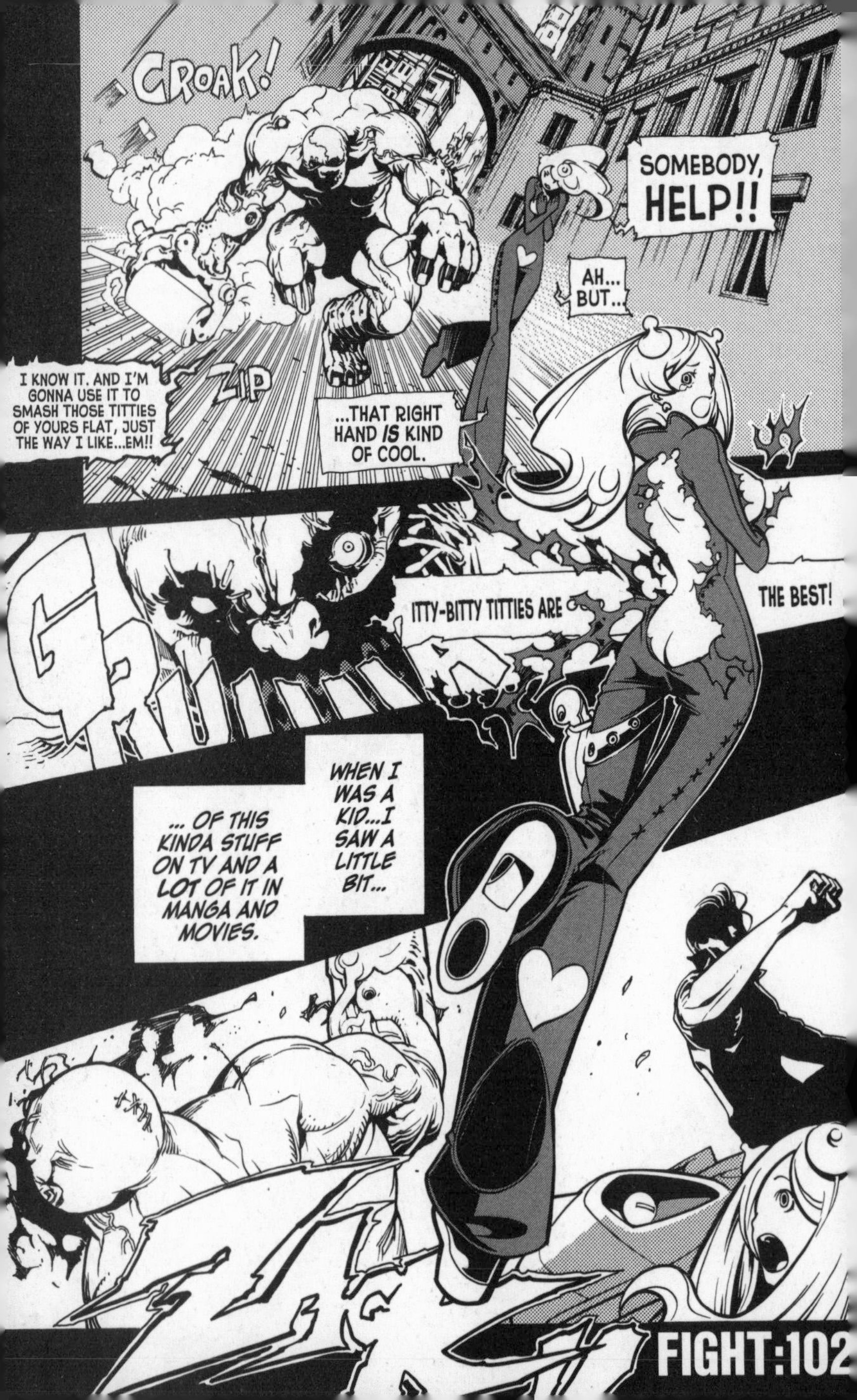
SOMEBODY, HELP!!
CROAK!
AH... BUT...
...THAT RIGHT HAND IS KIND OF COOL.
I KNOW IT. AND I'M GONNA USE IT TO SMASH THOSE TITTIES OF YOURS FLAT, JUST THE WAY I LIKE...EM!!
ZIP
ITTY-BITTY TITTIES ARE
THE BEST!
WHEN I WAS A KID...I SAW A LITTLE BIT...
... OF THIS KINDA STUFF ON TV AND A LOT OF IT IN MANGA AND MOVIES.
FIGHT:102

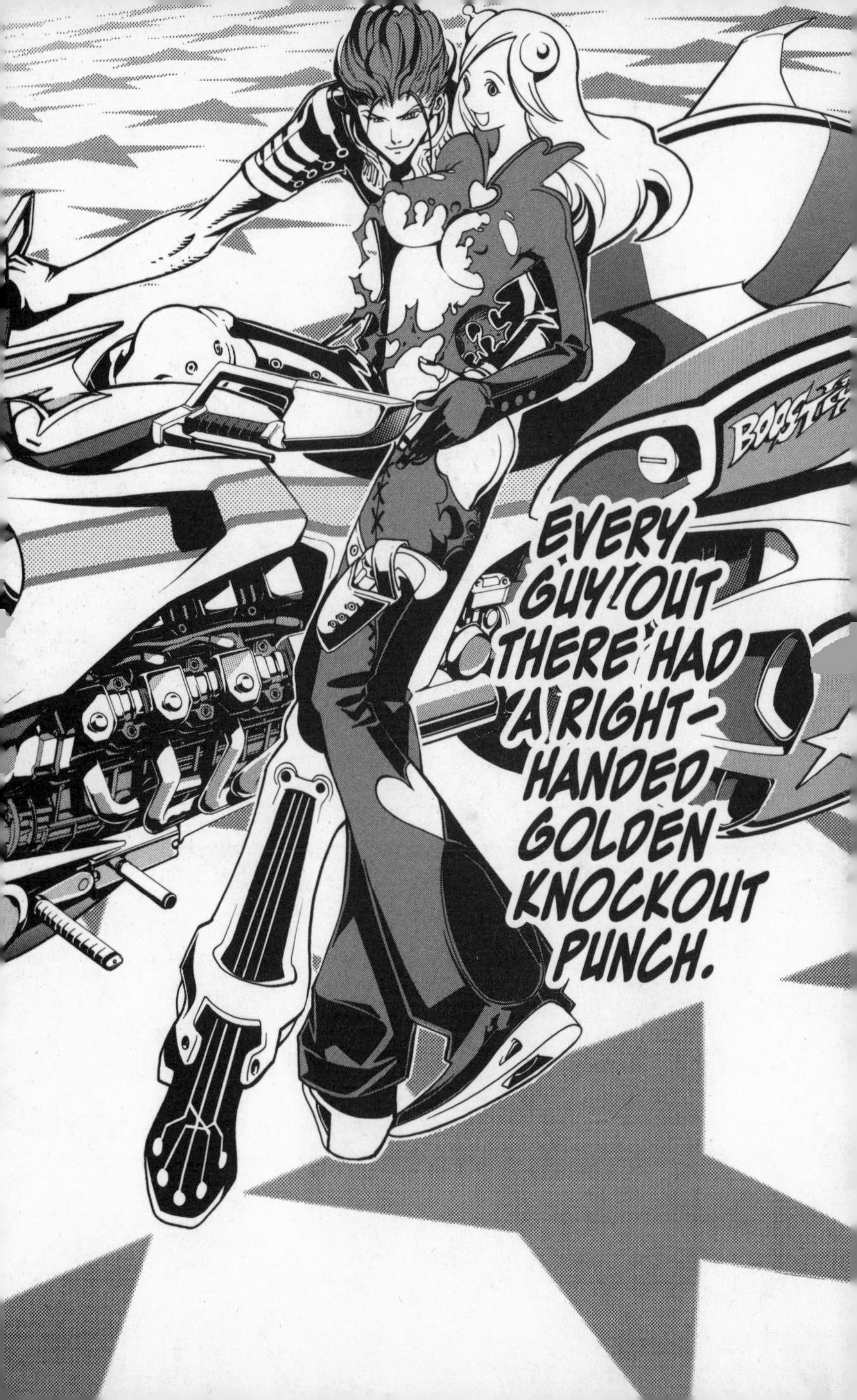
EVERY GUY OUT THERE HAD A RIGHT-HANDED GOLDEN KNOCKOUT PUNCH.

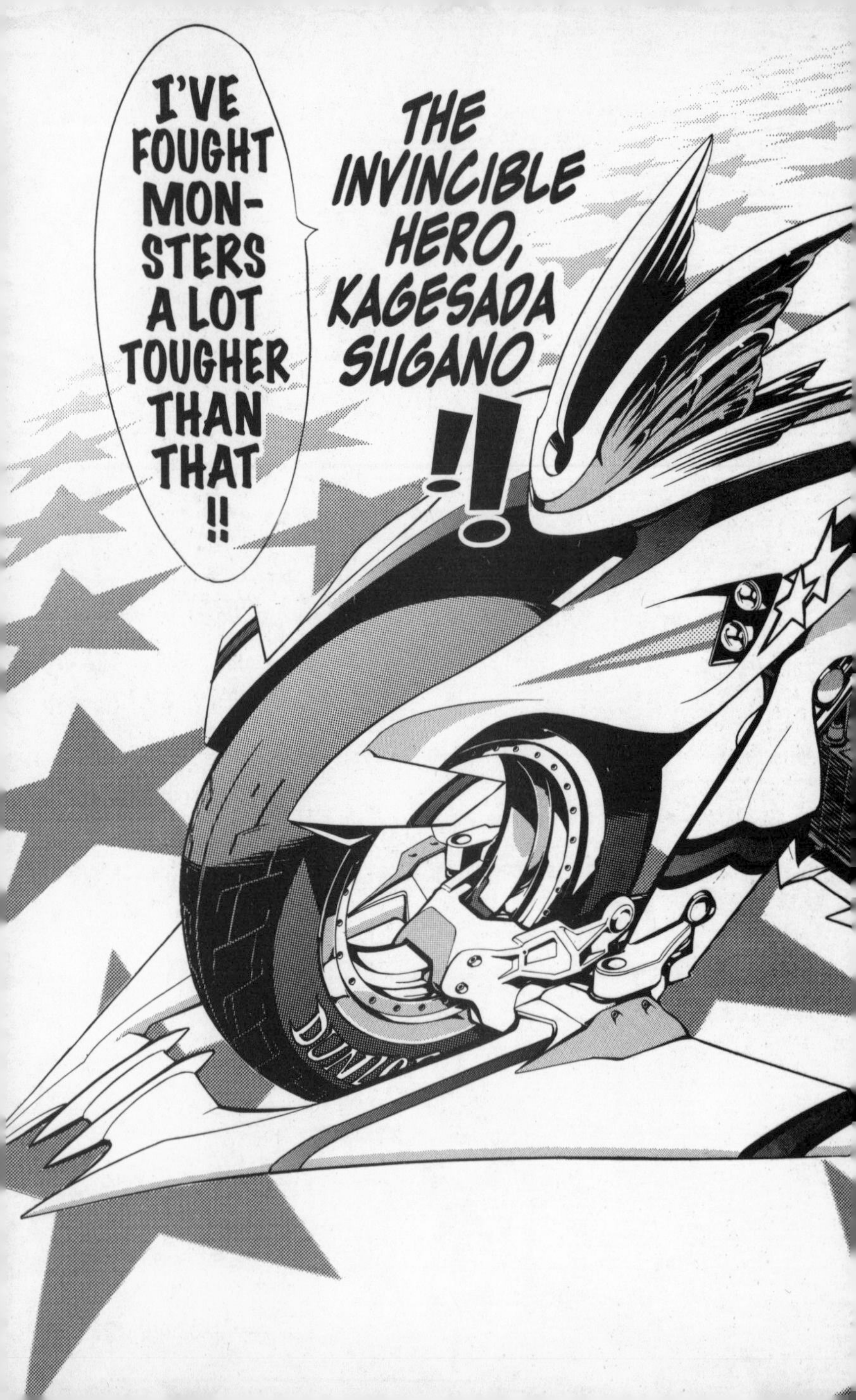
THE INVINCIBLE HERO, KAGESADA SUGANO !!
I'VE FOUGHT MON-STERS A LOT TOUGHER THAN THAT !!

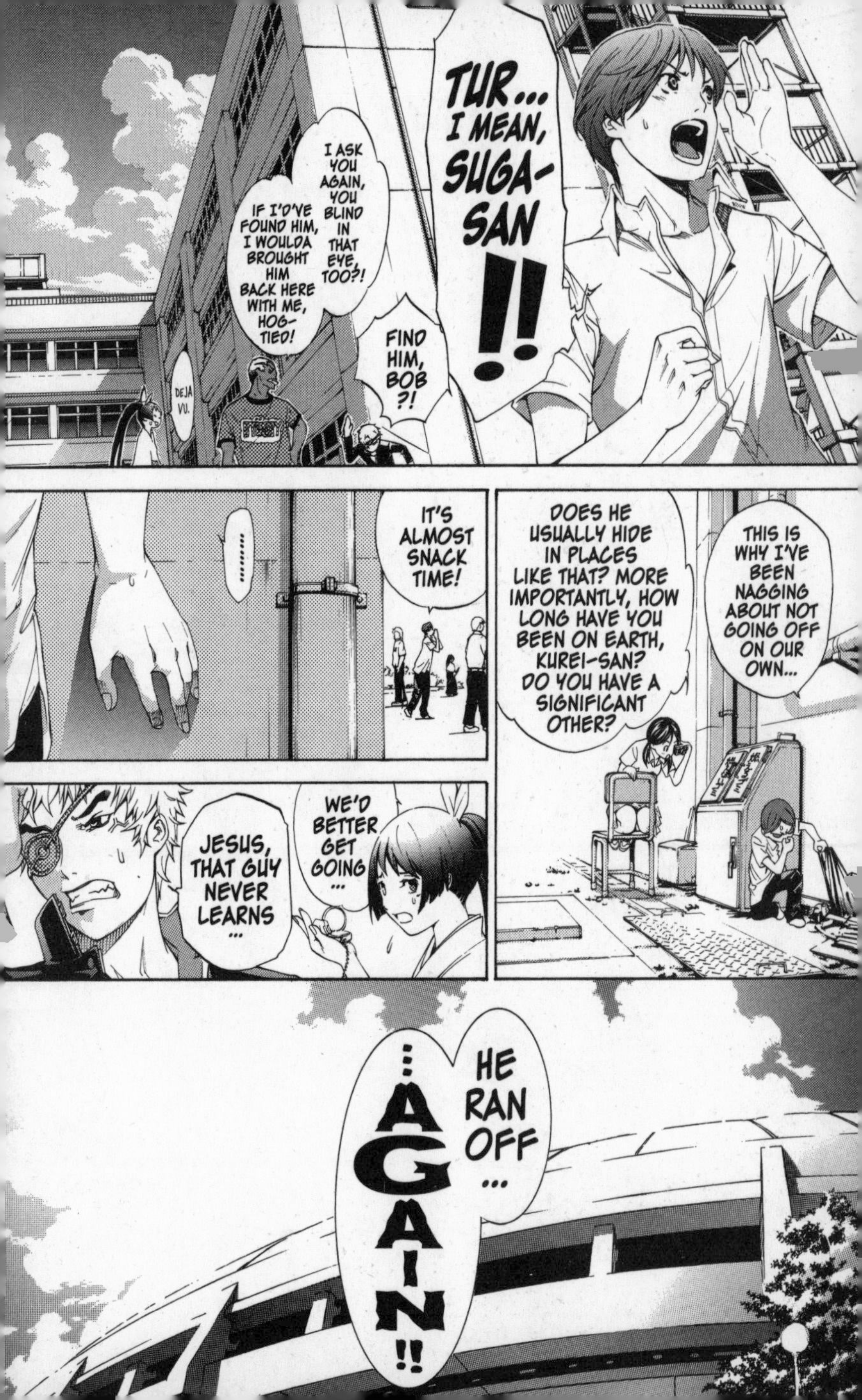
TUR... I MEAN, SUGA-SAN!!
FIND HIM, BOB?!
I ASK YOU AGAIN, YOU BLIND IN THAT EYE, TOO?!
IF I'D'VE FOUND HIM, I WOULDA BROUGHT HIM BACK HERE WITH ME, HOG-TIED!
DEJA VU.
THIS IS WHY I'VE BEEN NAGGING ABOUT NOT GOING OFF ON OUR OWN...
DOES HE USUALLY HIDE IN PLACES LIKE THAT? MORE IMPORTANTLY, HOW LONG HAVE YOU BEEN ON EARTH, KUREI-SAN? DO YOU HAVE A SIGNIFICANT OTHER?
IT'S ALMOST SNACK TIME!
....
WE'D BETTER GET GOING...
JESUS, THAT GUY NEVER LEARNS...
HE RAN OFF... ...AGAIN!!

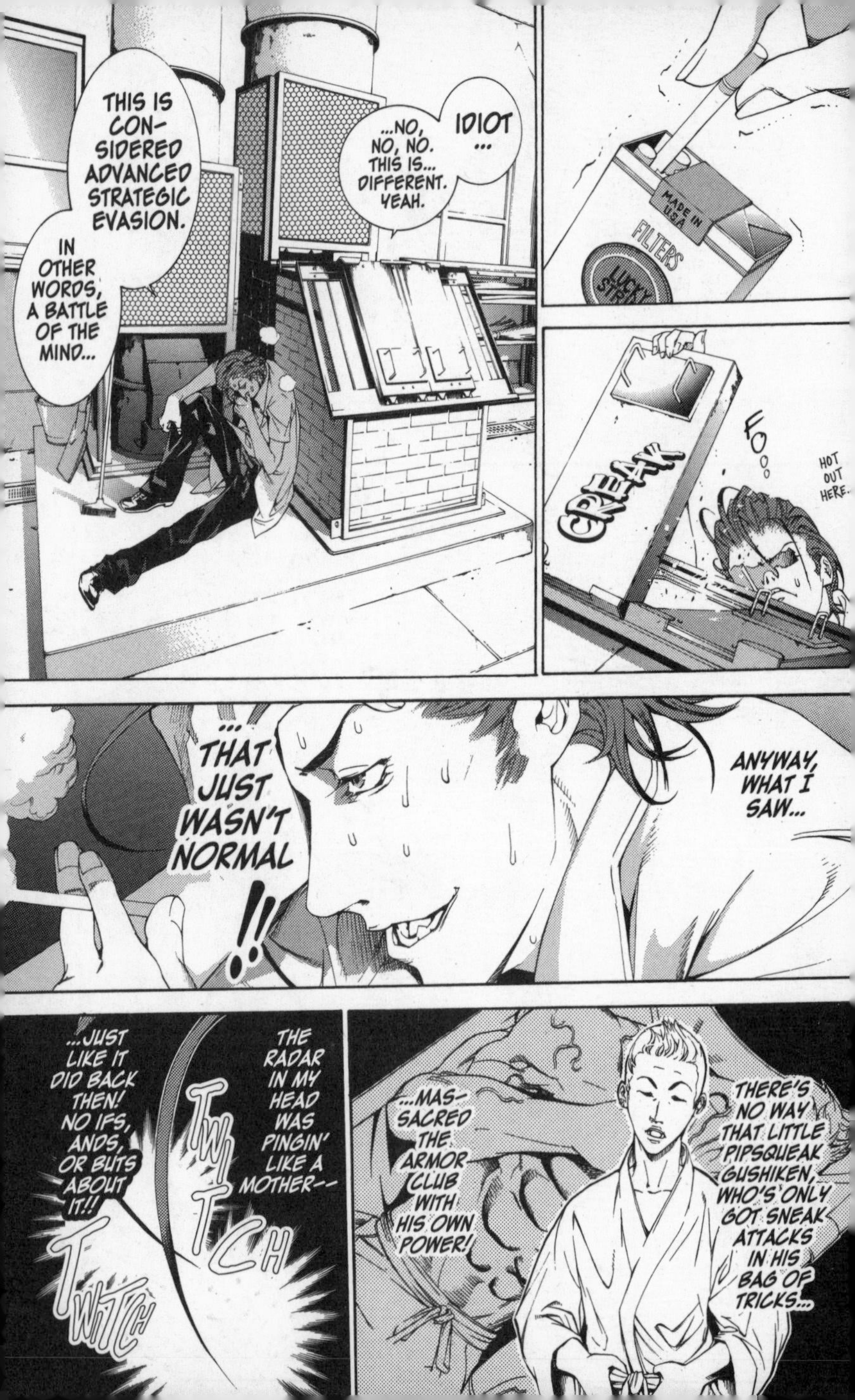
MADE IN USA
FILTERS
CREAK
FOO
HOT OUT HERE.
IDIOT ...
...NO, NO, NO. THIS IS... DIFFERENT. YEAH.
THIS IS CON-SIDERED ADVANCED STRATEGIC EVASION.
IN OTHER WORDS, A BATTLE OF THE MIND...
ANYWAY, WHAT I SAW...
...THAT JUST WASN'T NORMAL!!
THERE'S NO WAY THAT LITTLE PIPSQUEAK GUSHIKEN, WHO'S ONLY GOT SNEAK ATTACKS IN HIS BAG OF TRICKS...
...MAS-SACRED THE ARMOR CLUB WITH HIS OWN POWER!
THE RADAR IN MY HEAD WAS PINGIN' LIKE A MOTHER--
...JUST LIKE IT DID BACK THEN! NO IFS, ANDS, OR BUTS ABOUT IT!!
TWITCH
TWITCH

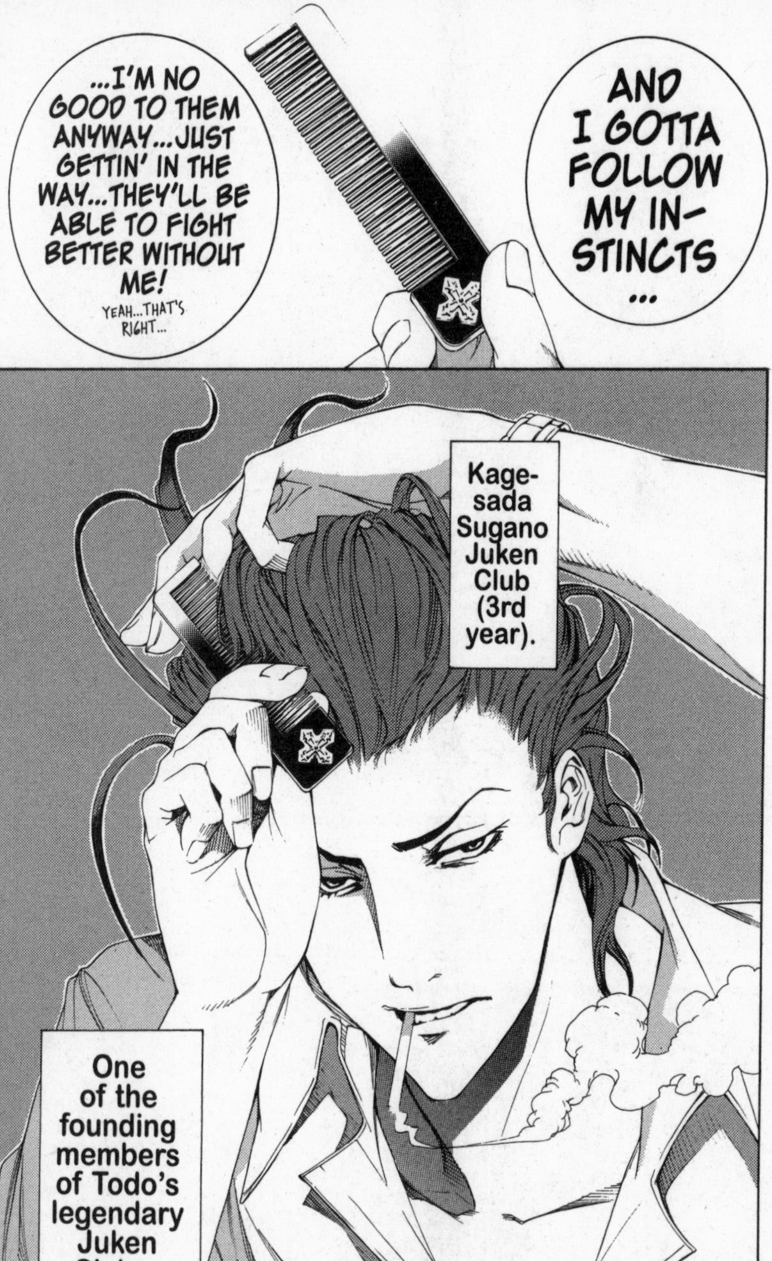
AND I GOTTA FOLLOW MY IN-STINCTS ...
...I'M NO GOOD TO THEM ANYWAY...JUST GETTIN' IN THE WAY...THEY'LL BE ABLE TO FIGHT BETTER WITHOUT ME!
YEAH...THAT'S RIGHT...
Kagesada Sugano Juken Club (3rd year).
One of the founding members of Todo's legendary Juken Club...

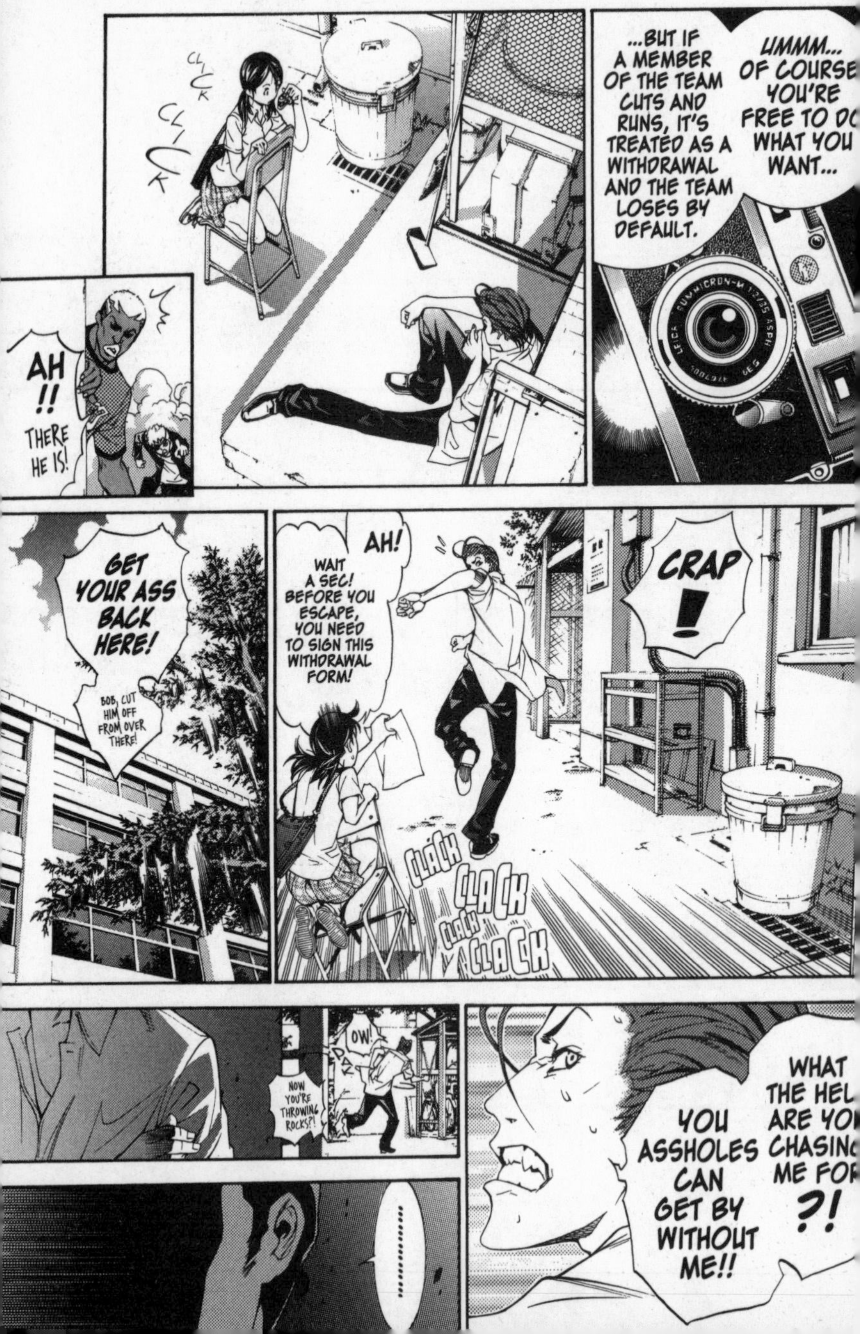
UMMM... OF COURSE YOU'RE FREE TO D WHAT YOU WANT...
...BUT IF A MEMBER OF THE TEAM CUTS AND RUNS, IT'S TREATED AS A WITHDRAWAL AND THE TEAM LOSES BY DEFAULT.
CLICK
CLICK
AH!!
THERE HE IS!
CRAP!
AH!
WAIT A SEC! BEFORE YOU ESCAPE, YOU NEED TO SIGN THIS WITHDRAWAL FORM!
CLACK CLACK CLACK CLACK
GET YOUR ASS BACK HERE!
BOB, CUT HIM OFF FROM OVER THERE!
WHAT THE HEL ARE YO CHASIN ME FO ?!
YOU ASSHOLES CAN GET BY WITHOUT ME!!
OW!
PAK
NOW YOU'RE THROWING ROCKS?!
....

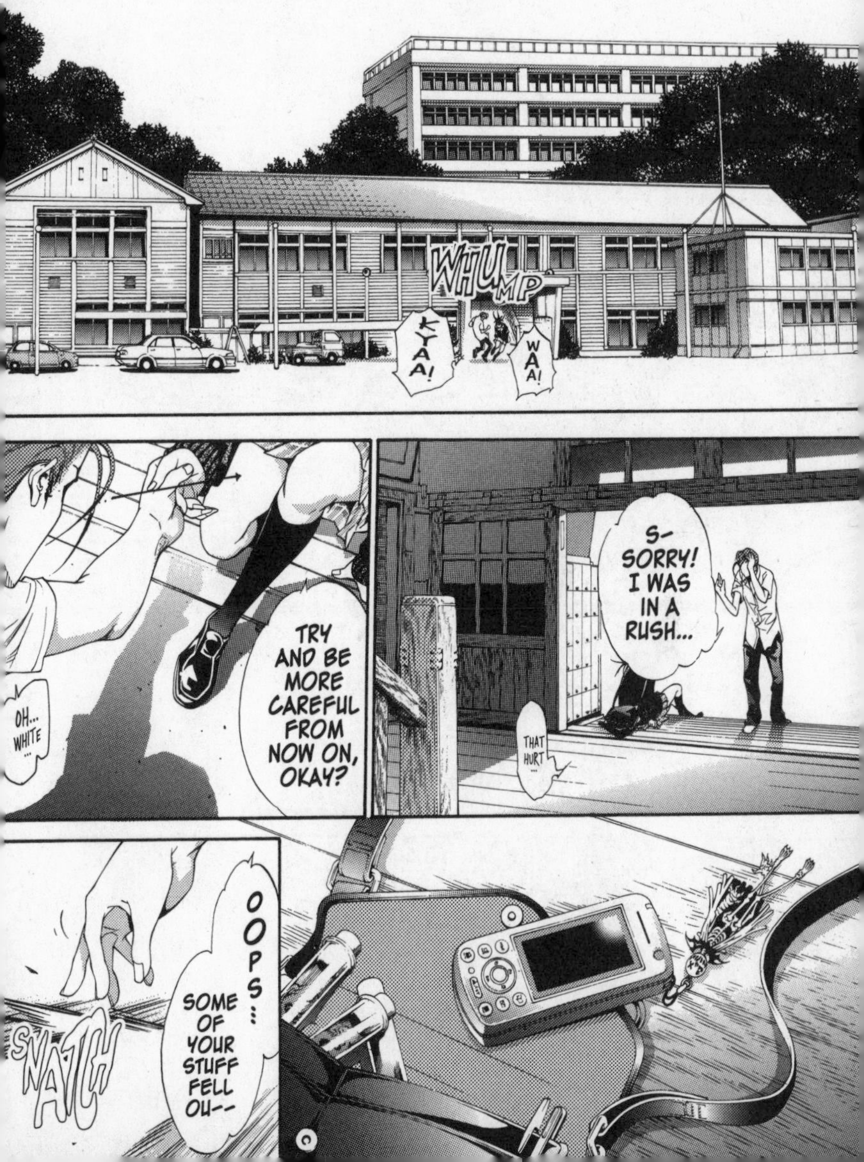
WHUMP
WAA!
KYAA!
S-SORRY! I WAS IN A RUSH...
THAT HURT...
TRY AND BE MORE CAREFUL FROM NOW ON, OKAY?
OH... WHITE...
OOPS... SOME OF YOUR STUFF FELL OU--
SNATCH

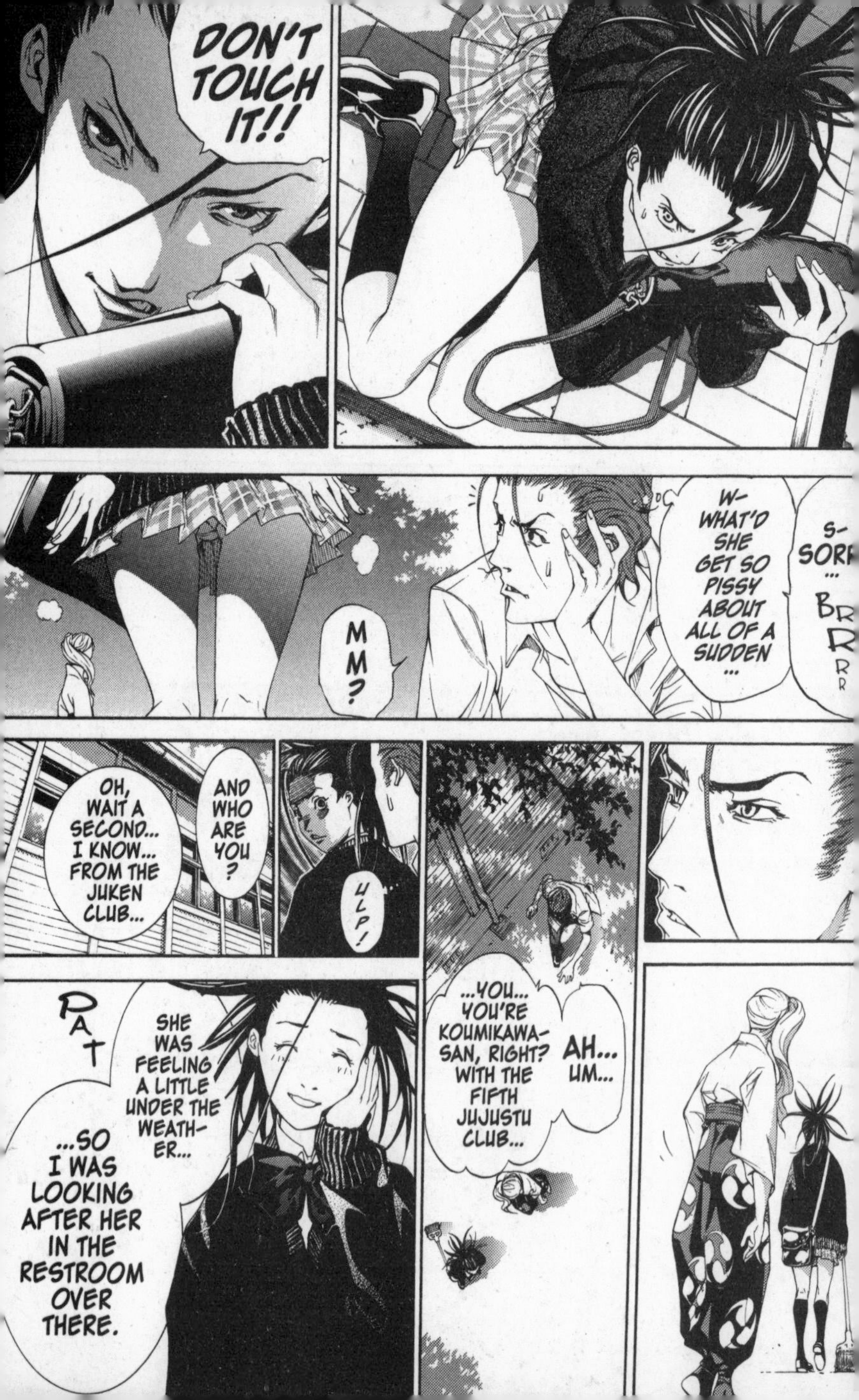
DON'T TOUCH IT!!
S-SORR... BRRR
W-WHAT'D SHE GET SO PISSY ABOUT ALL OF A SUDDEN...
MM?
AND WHO ARE YOU?
ULP!
OH, WAIT A SECOND... I KNOW... FROM THE JUKEN CLUB...
AH... UM...
...YOU... YOU'RE KOUMIKAWA-SAN, RIGHT? WITH THE FIFTH JUJUSTU CLUB...
SHE WAS FEELING A LITTLE UNDER THE WEATHER...
PAT
...SO I WAS LOOKING AFTER HER IN THE RESTROOM OVER THERE.

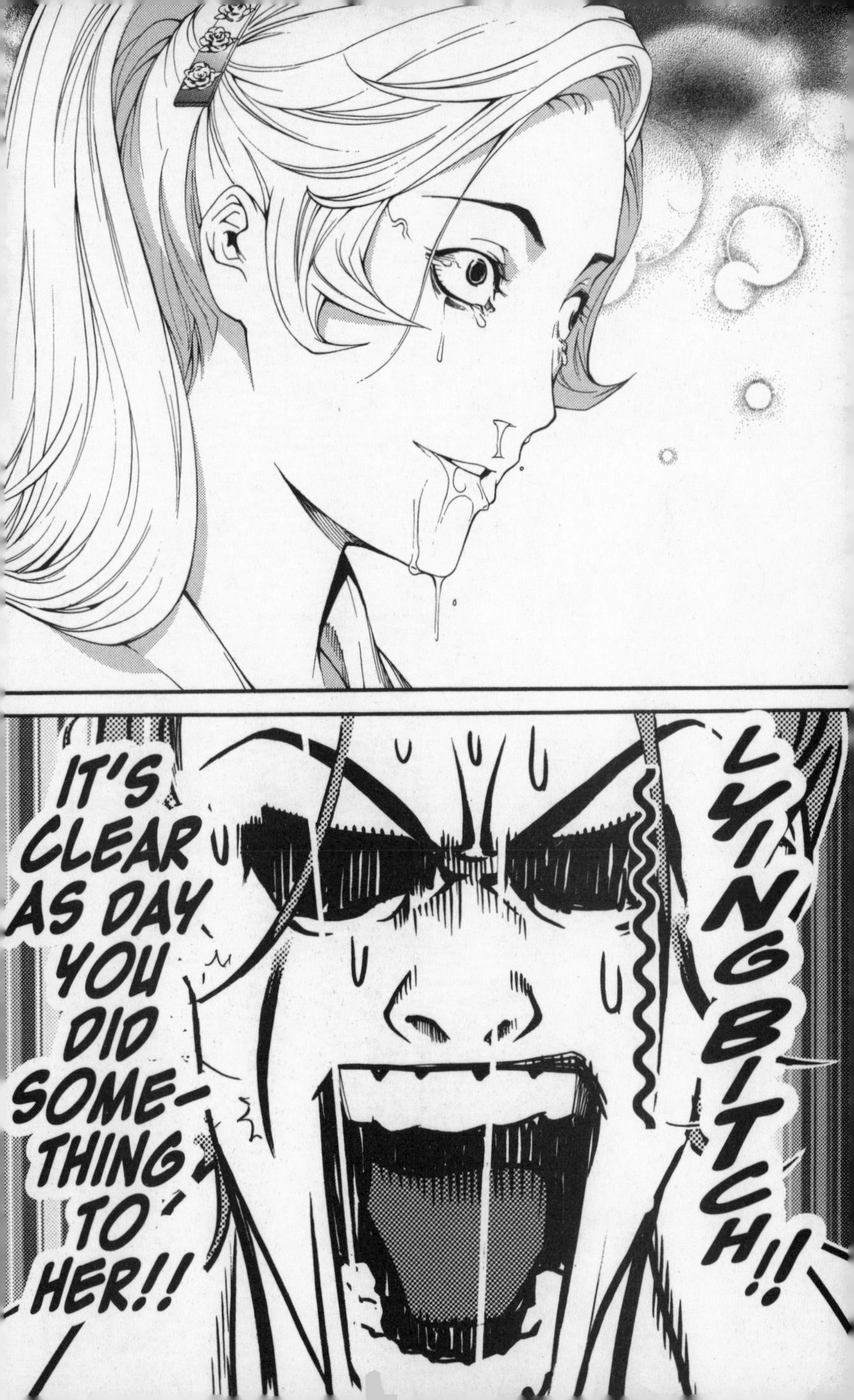
LYING BITCH!!
IT'S CLEAR AS DAY YOU DID SOME-THING TO HER!!

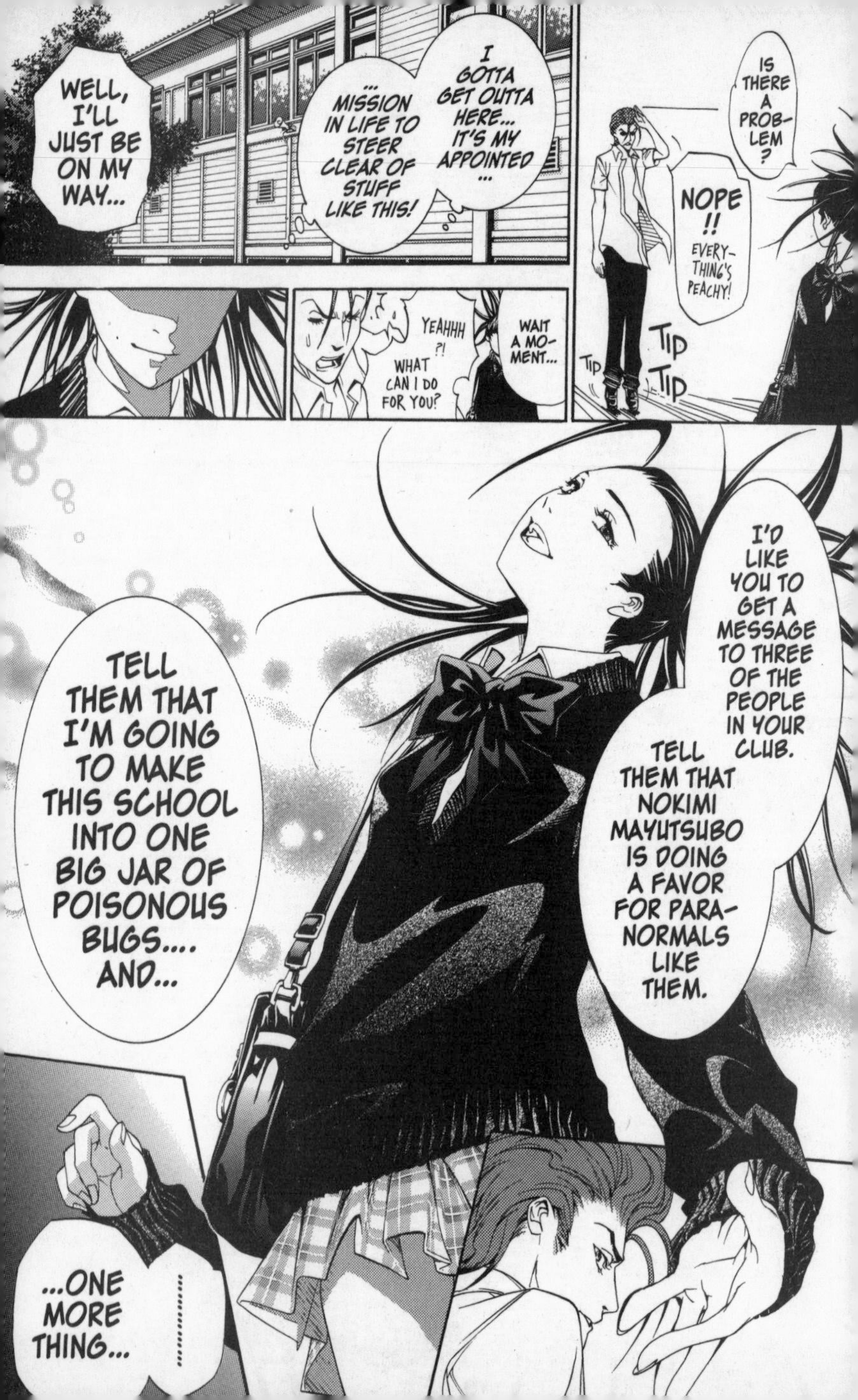
IS THERE A PROBLEM?
NOPE!!
EVERYTHING'S PEACHY!
TIP TIP TIP
I GOTTA GET OUTTA HERE... IT'S MY APPOINTED...
...MISSION IN LIFE TO STEER CLEAR OF STUFF LIKE THIS!
WELL, I'LL JUST BE ON MY WAY...
WAIT A MOMENT...
YEAHHH?!
WHAT CAN I DO FOR YOU?
I'D LIKE YOU TO GET A MESSAGE TO THREE OF THE PEOPLE IN YOUR CLUB.
TELL THEM THAT NOKIMI MAYUTSUBO IS DOING A FAVOR FOR PARANORMALS LIKE THEM.
TELL THEM THAT I'M GOING TO MAKE THIS SCHOOL INTO ONE BIG JAR OF POISONOUS BUGS.... AND...
....
...ONE MORE THING...

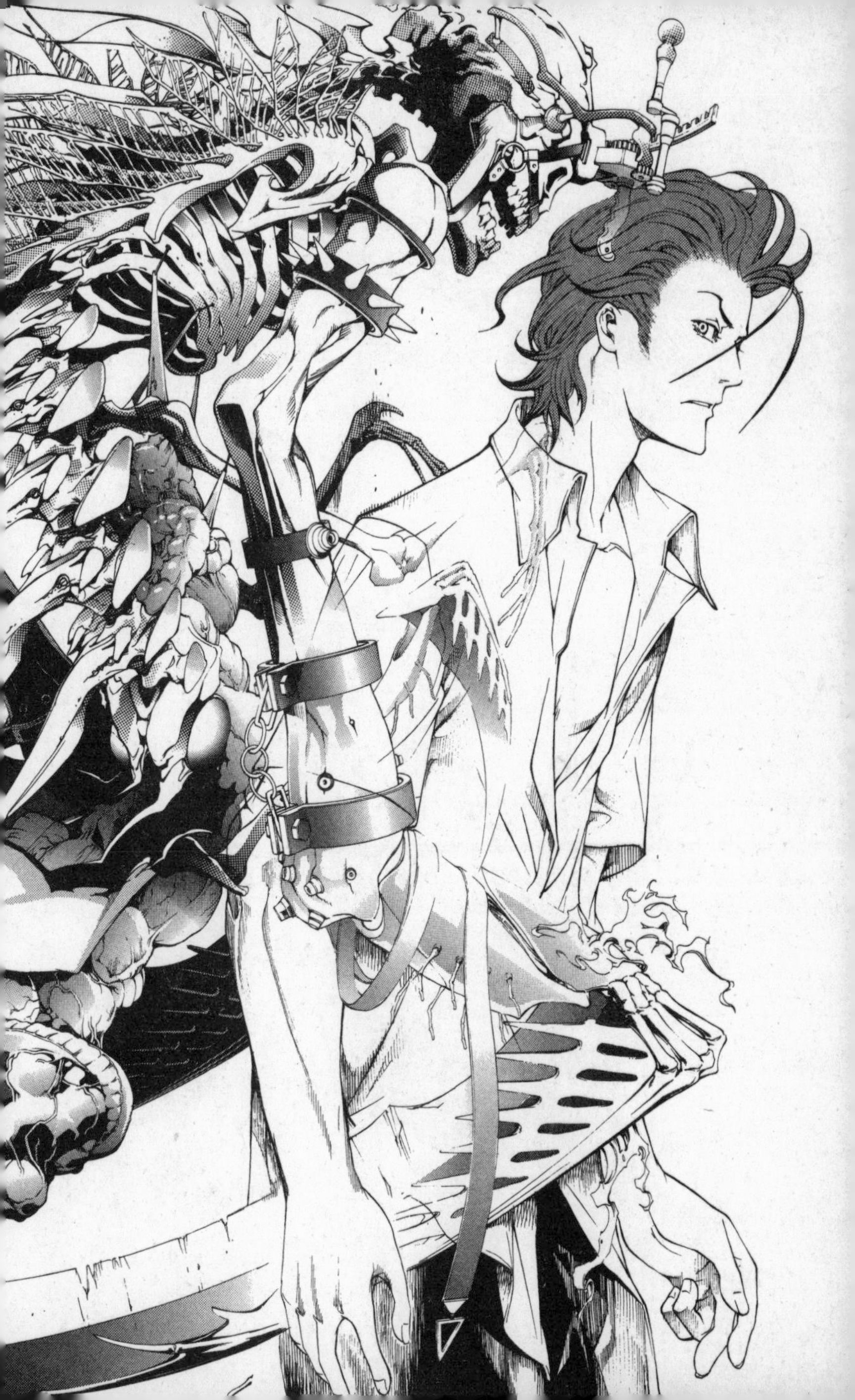

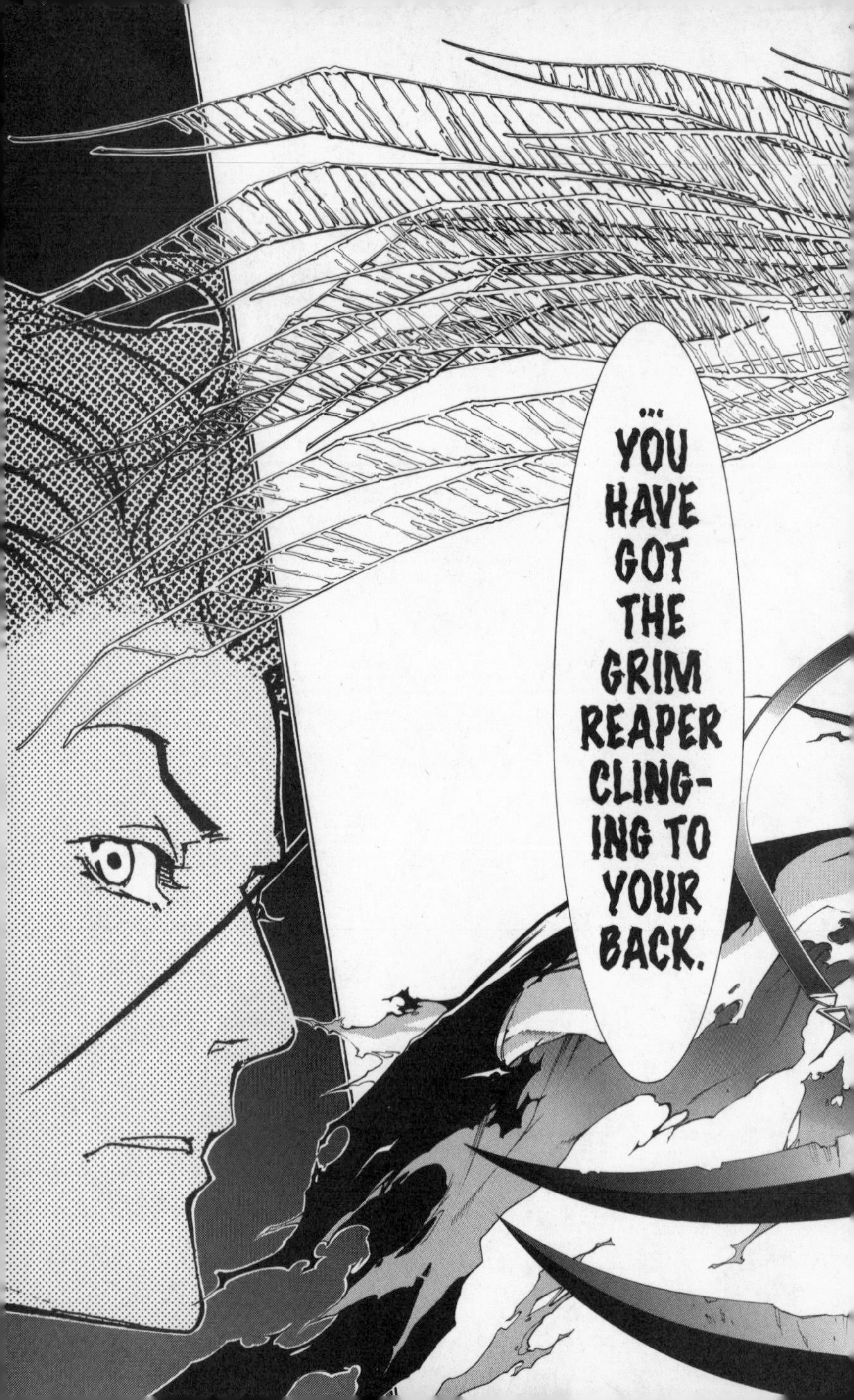
...YOU HAVE GOT THE GRIM REAPER CLING-ING TO YOUR BACK.

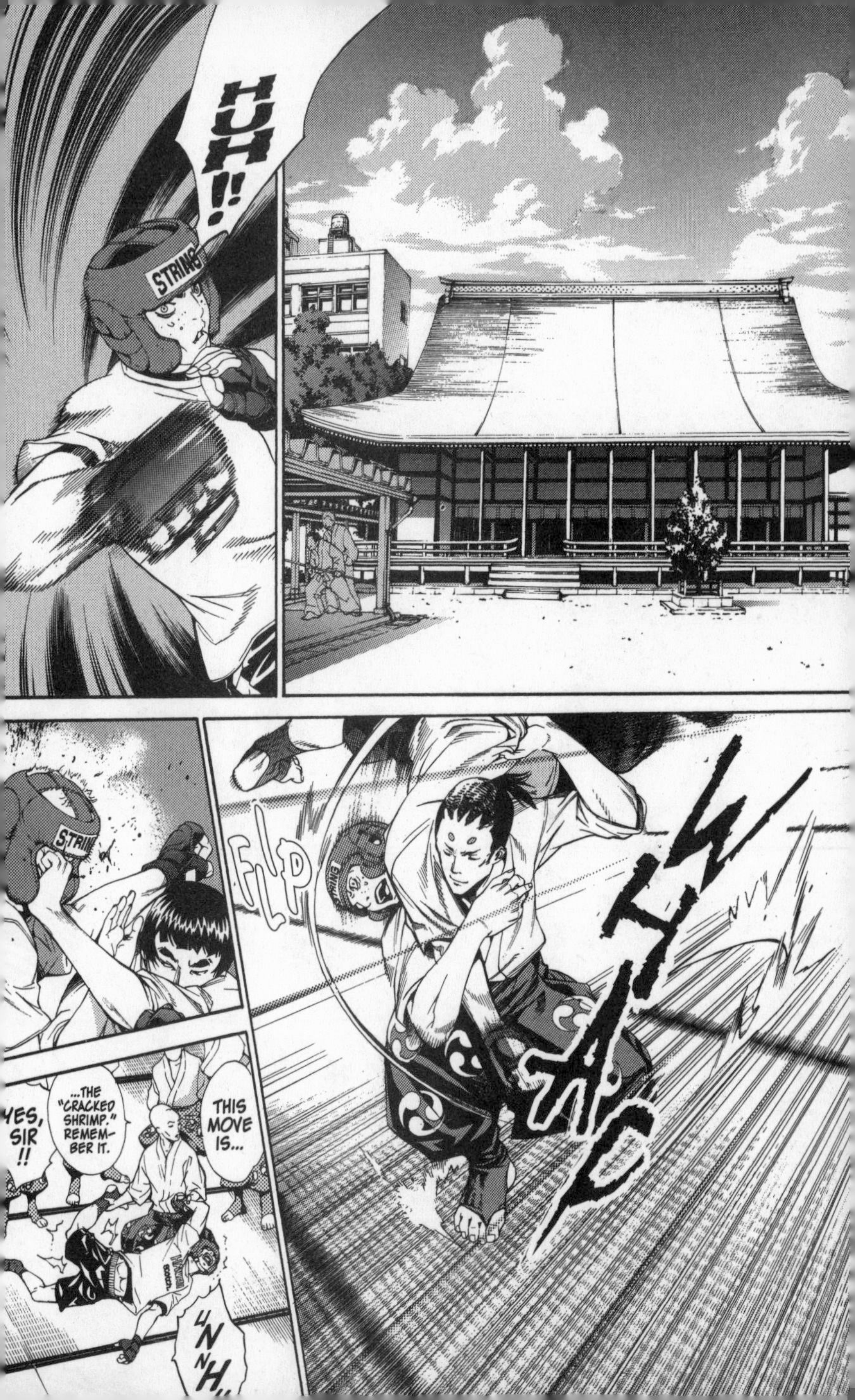
STRING
UH!!
WHAP
FLIP
STRING
THIS MOVE IS...
...THE "CRACKED SHRIMP." REMEMBER IT.
YES, SIR!!
UNNH..

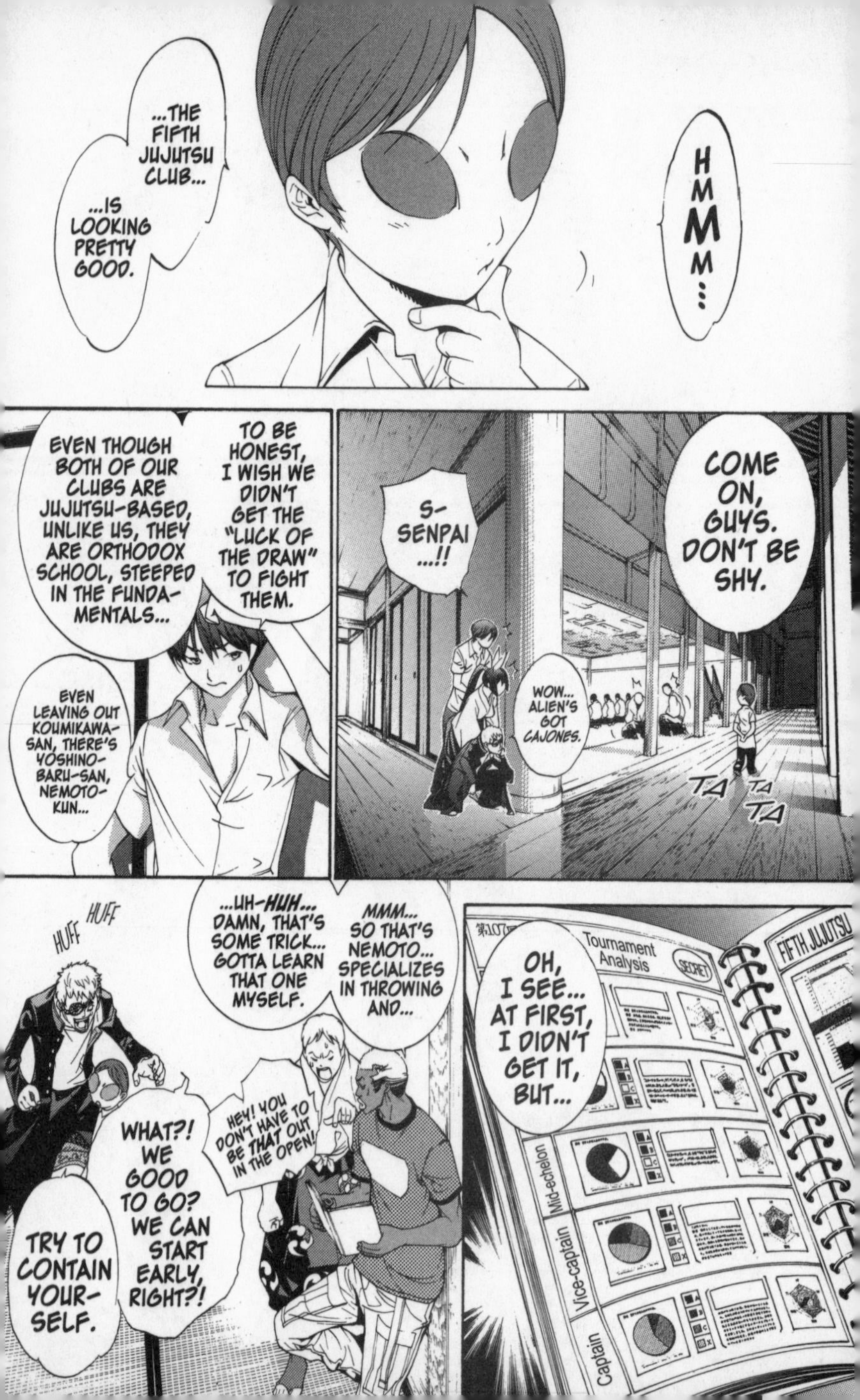
HMMM...
...THE FIFTH JUJUTSU CLUB...
...IS LOOKING PRETTY GOOD.
COME ON, GUYS. DON'T BE SHY.
S-SENPAI ...!!
WOW... ALIEN'S GOT CAJONES.
TA TA TA TA
TO BE HONEST, I WISH WE DIDN'T GET THE "LUCK OF THE DRAW" TO FIGHT THEM.
EVEN THOUGH BOTH OF OUR CLUBS ARE JUJUTSU-BASED, UNLIKE US, THEY ARE ORTHODOX SCHOOL, STEEPED IN THE FUNDA-MENTALS...
EVEN LEAVING OUT KOUMIKAWA-SAN, THERE'S YOSHINO-BARU-SAN, NEMOTO-KUN...
Tournament Analysis
SECRET
FIFTH JUJUTSU
Mid-echelon
Vice-captain
Captain
OH, I SEE... AT FIRST, I DIDN'T GET IT, BUT...
MMM... SO THAT'S NEMOTO... SPECIALIZES IN THROWING AND...
...UH-*HUH*... DAMN, THAT'S SOME TRICK... GOTTA LEARN THAT ONE MYSELF.
HEY! YOU DON'T HAVE TO BE *THAT* OUT IN THE OPEN!
WHAT?! WE GOOD TO GO? WE CAN START EARLY, RIGHT?!
TRY TO CONTAIN YOUR-SELF.
HUFF HUFF

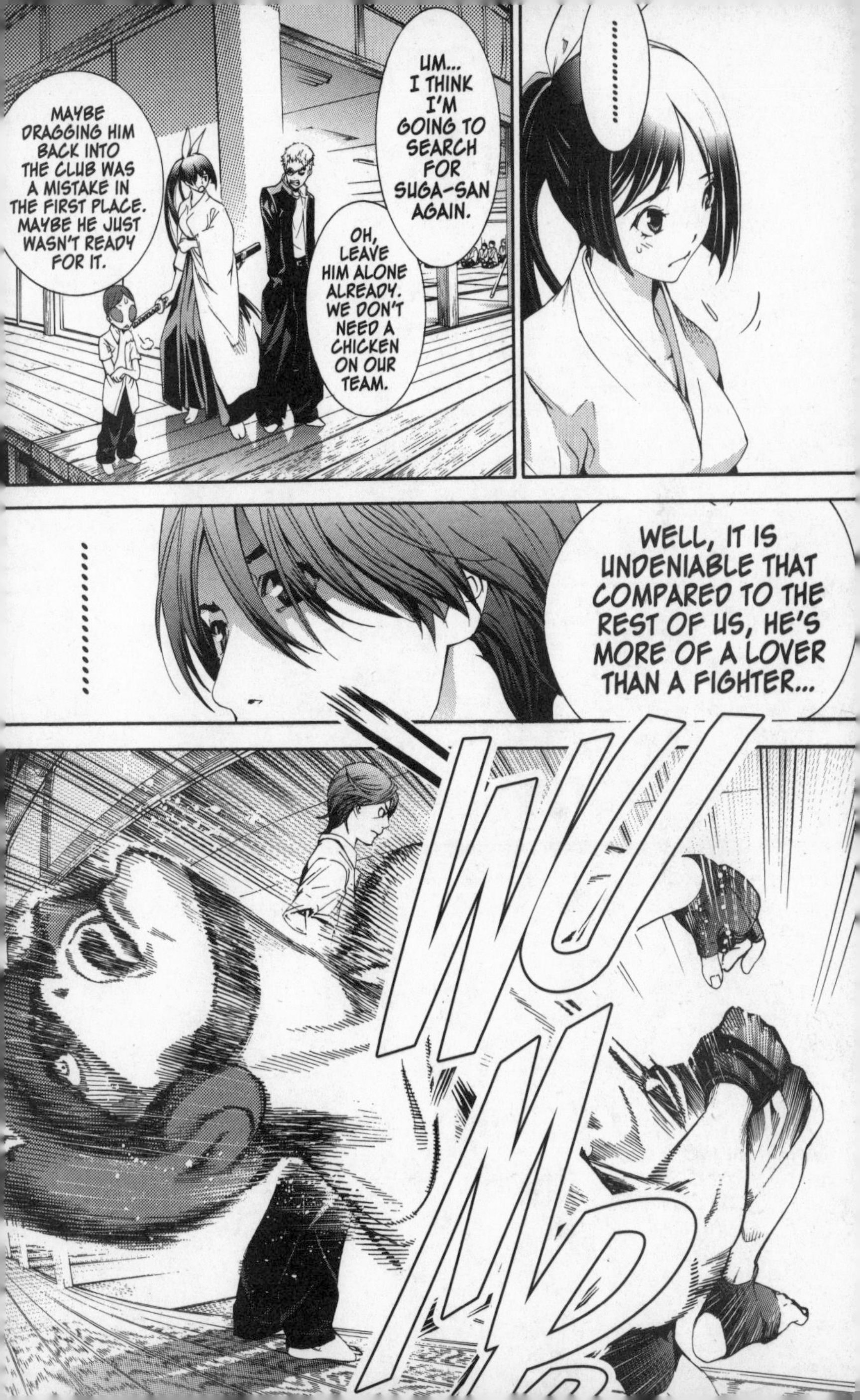
......
UM... I THINK I'M GOING TO SEARCH FOR SUGA-SAN AGAIN.
OH, LEAVE HIM ALONE ALREADY. WE DON'T NEED A CHICKEN ON OUR TEAM.
MAYBE DRAGGING HIM BACK INTO THE CLUB WAS A MISTAKE IN THE FIRST PLACE. MAYBE HE JUST WASN'T READY FOR IT.
WELL, IT IS UNDENIABLE THAT COMPARED TO THE REST OF US, HE'S MORE OF A LOVER THAN A FIGHTER...
....
WUMP

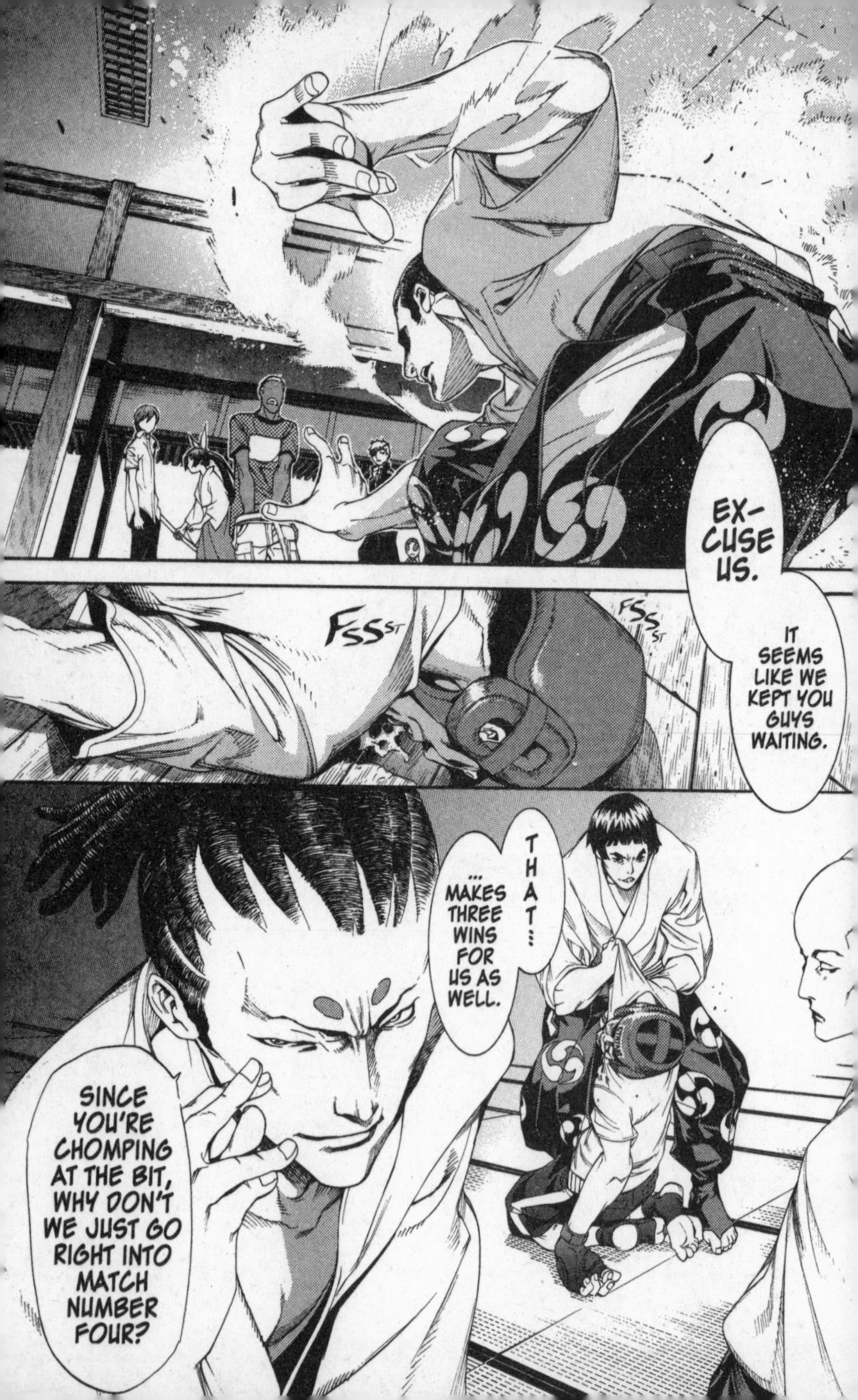
EX-CUSE US.
FSSST
FSSST
IT SEEMS LIKE WE KEPT YOU GUYS WAITING.
THAT...
...MAKES THREE WINS FOR US AS WELL.
SINCE YOU'RE CHOMPING AT THE BIT, WHY DON'T WE JUST GO RIGHT INTO MATCH NUMBER FOUR?

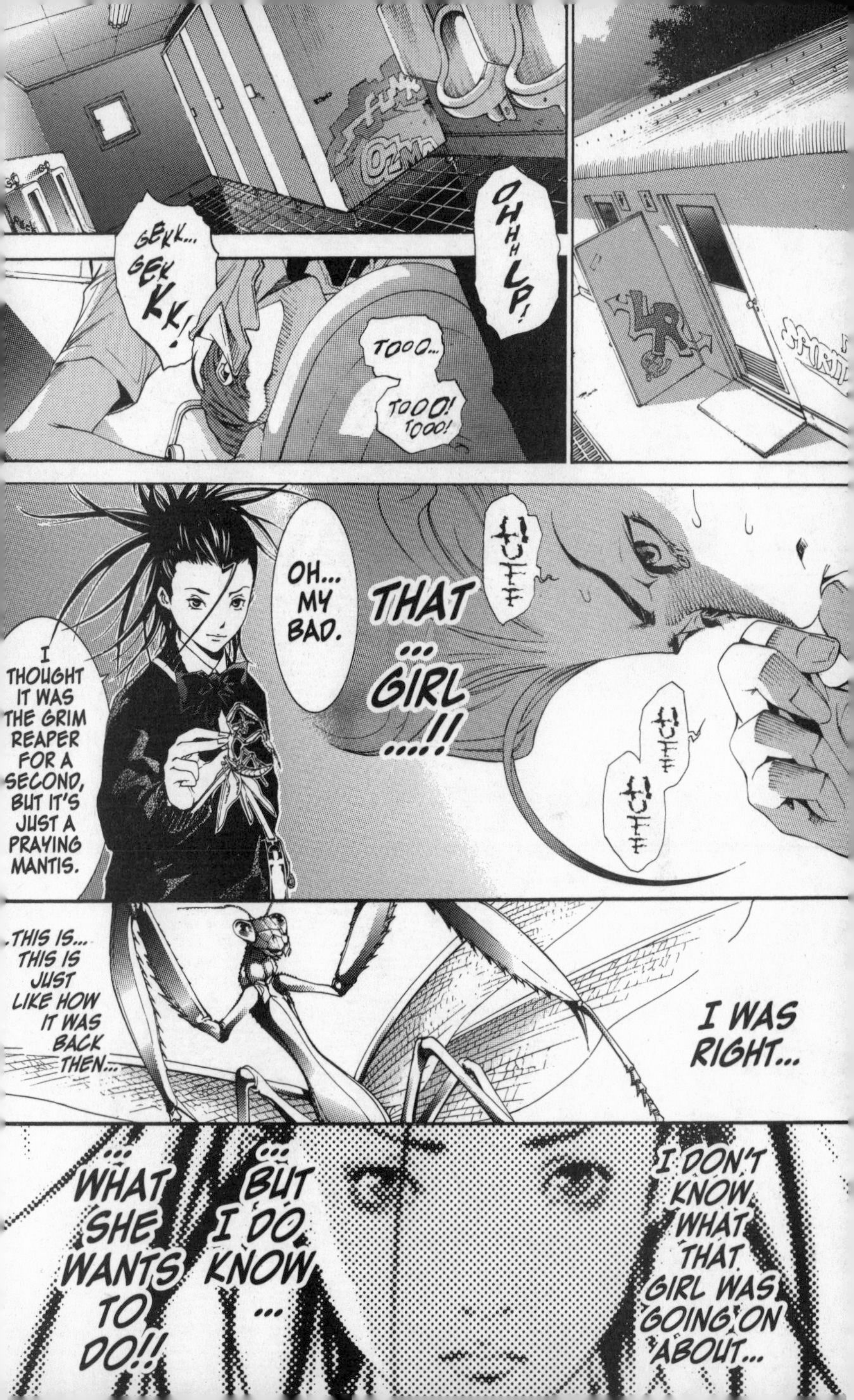
OHHHHLP!
TOOO...
TOOO! TOOO!
GEKK... GEKK KK!
HUFF
THAT... GIRL...!!
HUFF HUFF
OH... MY BAD.
I THOUGHT IT WAS THE GRIM REAPER FOR A SECOND, BUT IT'S JUST A PRAYING MANTIS.
I WAS RIGHT...
THIS IS... THIS IS JUST LIKE HOW IT WAS BACK THEN...
I DON'T KNOW WHAT THAT GIRL WAS GOING ON ABOUT...
...BUT I DO KNOW...
...WHAT SHE WANTS TO DO!!

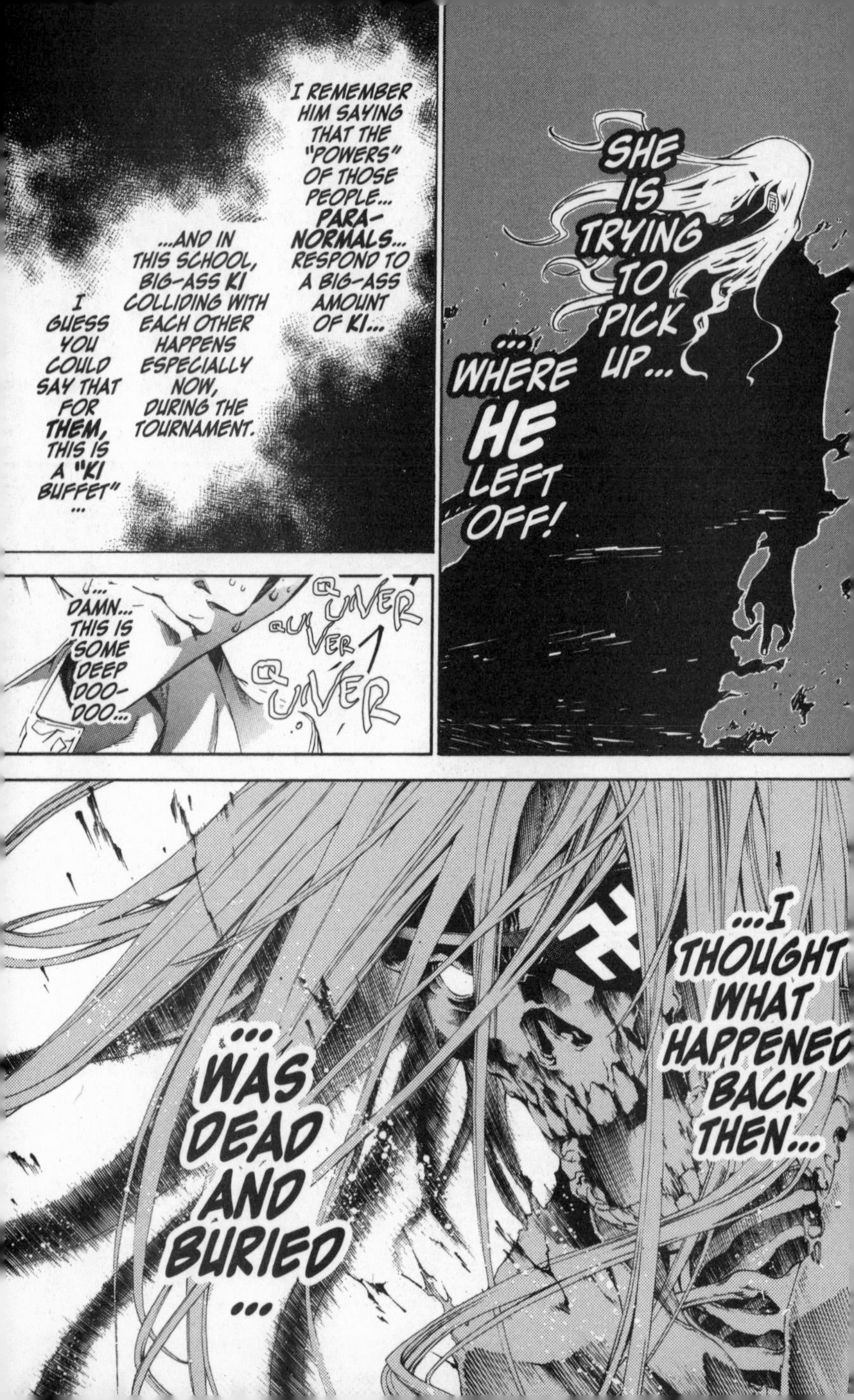
SHE IS TRYING TO PICK UP...
...WHERE HE LEFT OFF!
I REMEMBER HIM SAYING THAT THE "POWERS" OF THOSE PEOPLE... PARA-NORMALS... RESPOND TO A BIG-ASS AMOUNT OF KI...
...AND IN THIS SCHOOL, BIG-ASS KI COLLIDING WITH EACH OTHER HAPPENS ESPECIALLY NOW, DURING THE TOURNAMENT.
I GUESS YOU COULD SAY THAT FOR THEM, THIS IS A "KI BUFFET"...
QUIVER QUIVER QUIVER
DAMN... THIS IS SOME DEEP DOO-DOO...
...I THOUGHT WHAT HAPPENED BACK THEN...
...WAS DEAD AND BURIED...

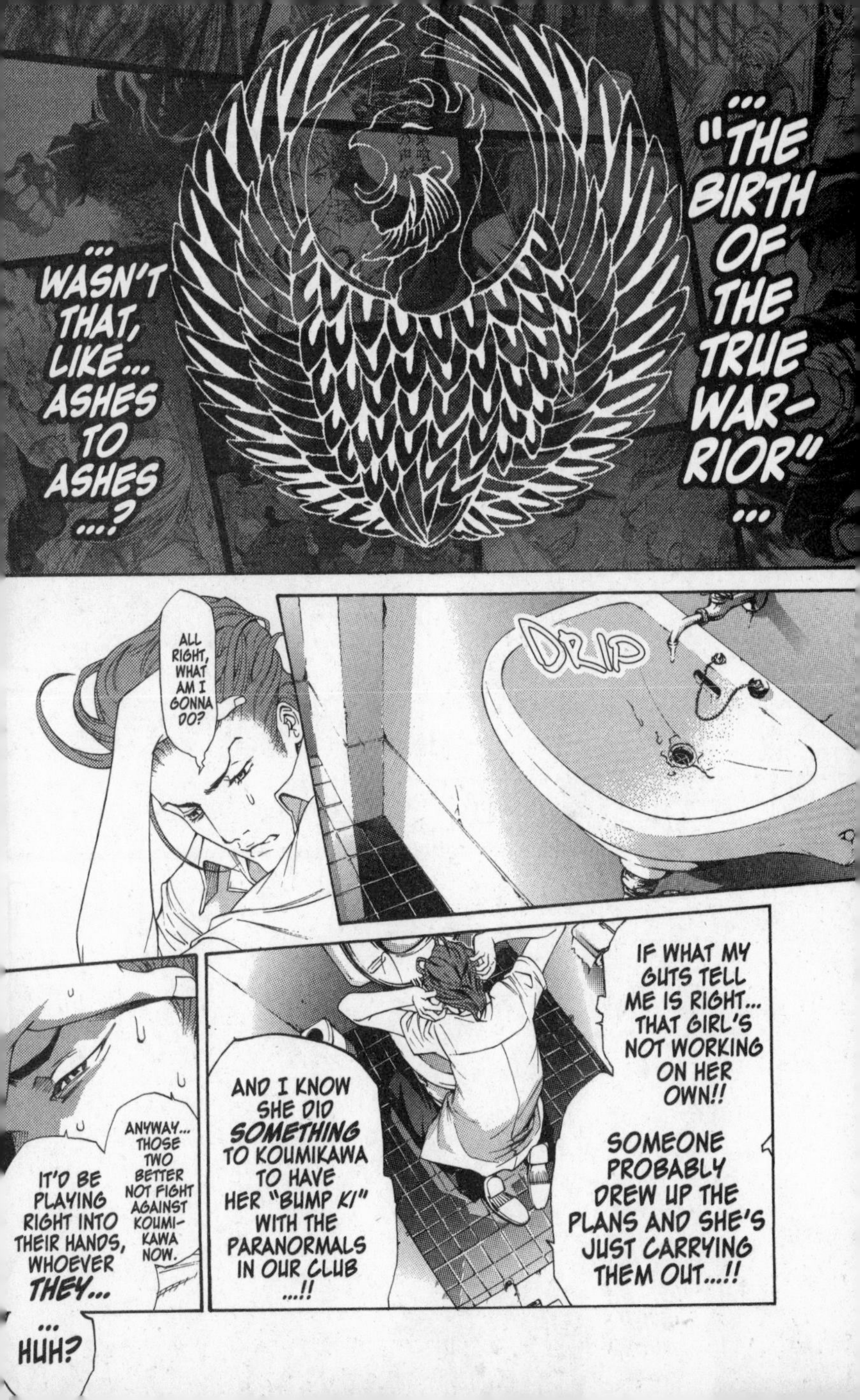
..."THE BIRTH OF THE TRUE WAR-RIOR"...
...WASN'T THAT, LIKE... ASHES TO ASHES ...?
DRIP
ALL RIGHT, WHAT AM I GONNA DO?
IF WHAT MY GUTS TELL ME IS RIGHT... THAT GIRL'S NOT WORKING ON HER OWN!!
SOMEONE PROBABLY DREW UP THE PLANS AND SHE'S JUST CARRYING THEM OUT...!!
AND I KNOW SHE DID *SOMETHING* TO KOUMIKAWA TO HAVE HER "BUMP KI" WITH THE PARANORMALS IN OUR CLUB ...!!
ANYWAY... THOSE TWO BETTER NOT FIGHT AGAINST KOUMI-KAWA NOW.
IT'D BE PLAYING RIGHT INTO THEIR HANDS, WHOEVER *THEY*...
... HUH?

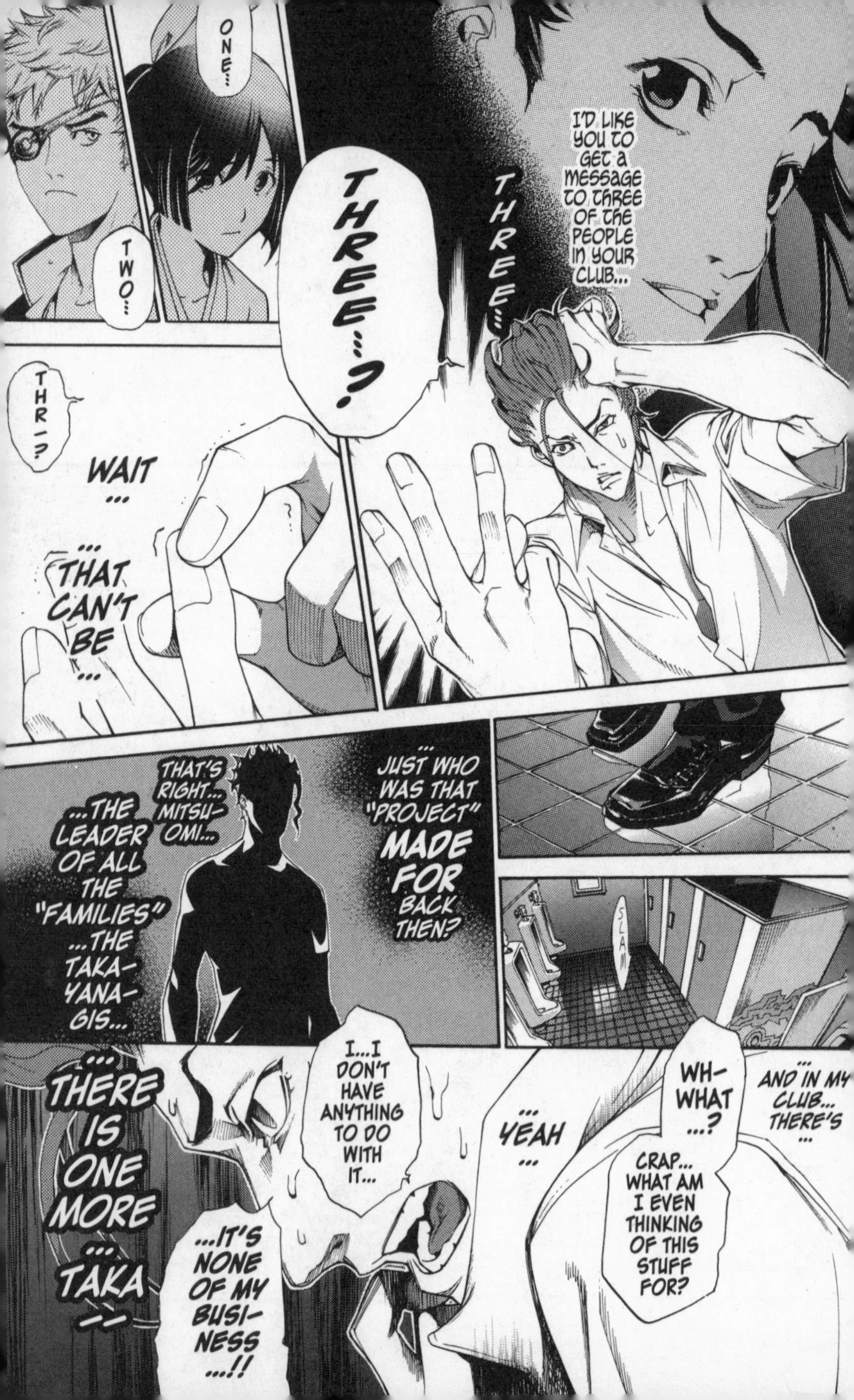
I'D LIKE YOU TO GET A MESSAGE TO THREE OF THE PEOPLE IN YOUR CLUB...
THREE...
ONE...
TWO...
THREE...?
THR—?
WAIT...
...THAT CAN'T BE...
SLAM
...JUST WHO WAS THAT "PROJECT" MADE FOR BACK THEN?
THAT'S RIGHT... MITSU-OMI...
...THE LEADER OF ALL THE "FAMILIES" ...THE TAKA-YANA-GIS...
...AND IN MY CLUB... THERE'S...
WH-WHAT...?
CRAP... WHAT AM I EVEN THINKING OF THIS STUFF FOR?
...YEAH...
I...I DON'T HAVE ANYTHING TO DO WITH IT...
...IT'S NONE OF MY BUSI-NESS...!!
...THERE IS ONE MORE... TAKA—

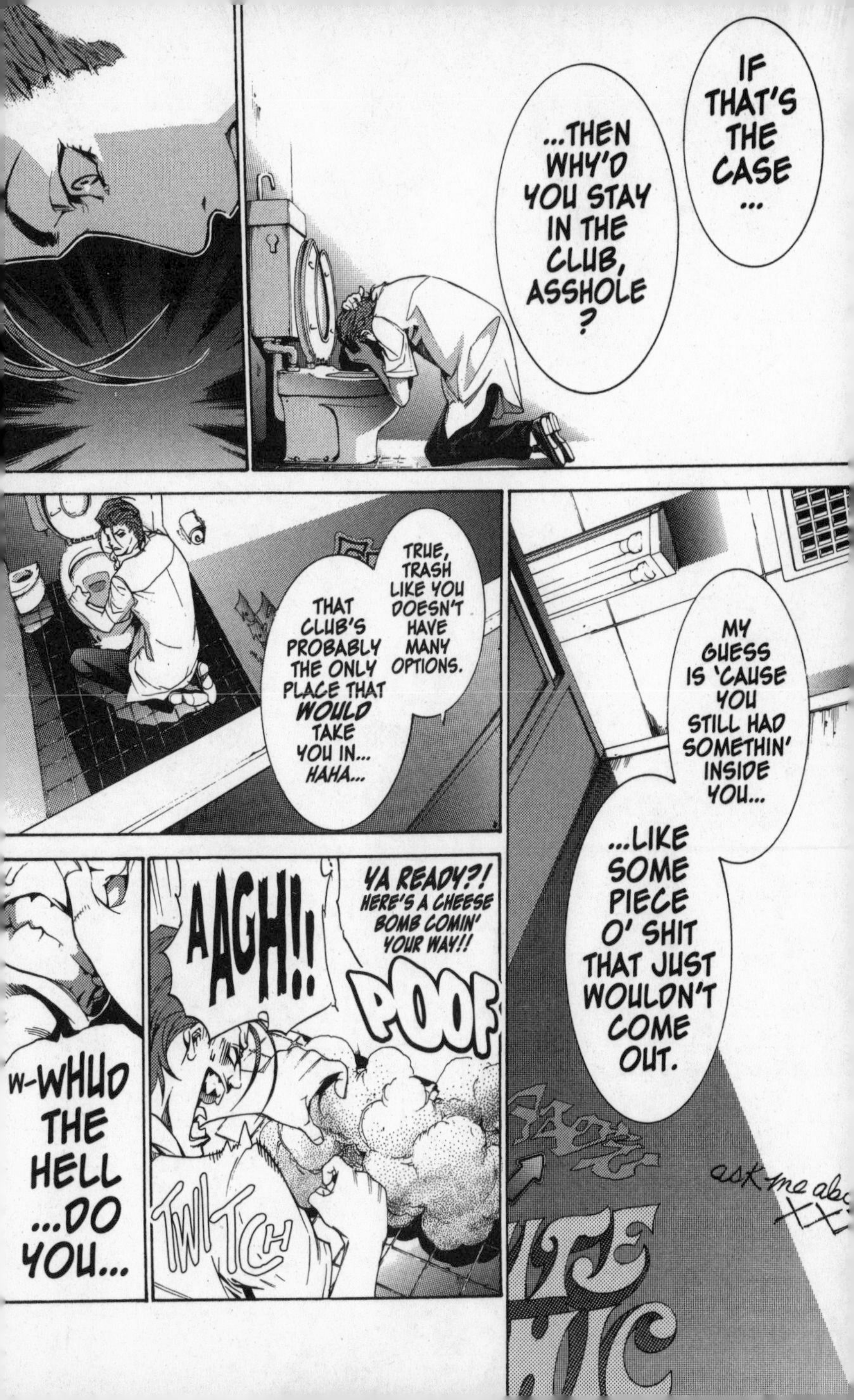
IF THAT'S THE CASE...
...THEN WHY'D YOU STAY IN THE CLUB, ASSHOLE?
MY GUESS IS 'CAUSE YOU STILL HAD SOMETHIN' INSIDE YOU...
...LIKE SOME PIECE O' SHIT THAT JUST WOULDN'T COME OUT.
TRUE, TRASH LIKE YOU DOESN'T HAVE MANY OPTIONS.
THAT CLUB'S PROBABLY THE ONLY PLACE THAT *WOULD* TAKE YOU IN... *HAHA...*
YA READY?! HERE'S A CHEESE BOMB COMIN' YOUR WAY!!
AAGH!!
POOF
TWITCH
W-WHUD THE HELL ...DO YOU...

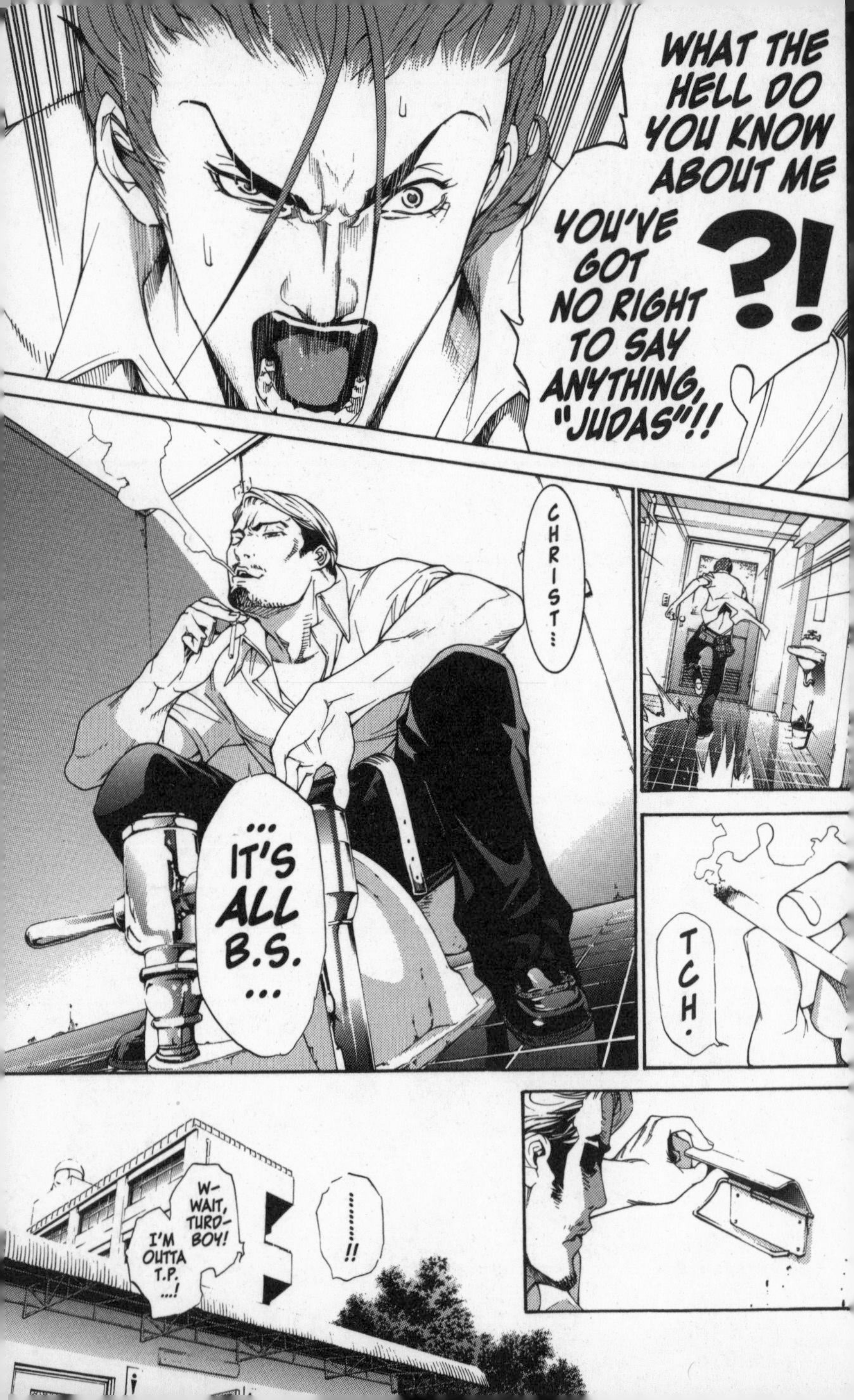
WHAT THE HELL DO YOU KNOW ABOUT ME ?!
YOU'VE GOT NO RIGHT TO SAY ANYTHING, "JUDAS"!!
TCH.
CHRIST...
...IT'S ALL B.S. ...
........!!
W-WAIT, TURD-BOY!
I'M OUTTA T.P. ...!

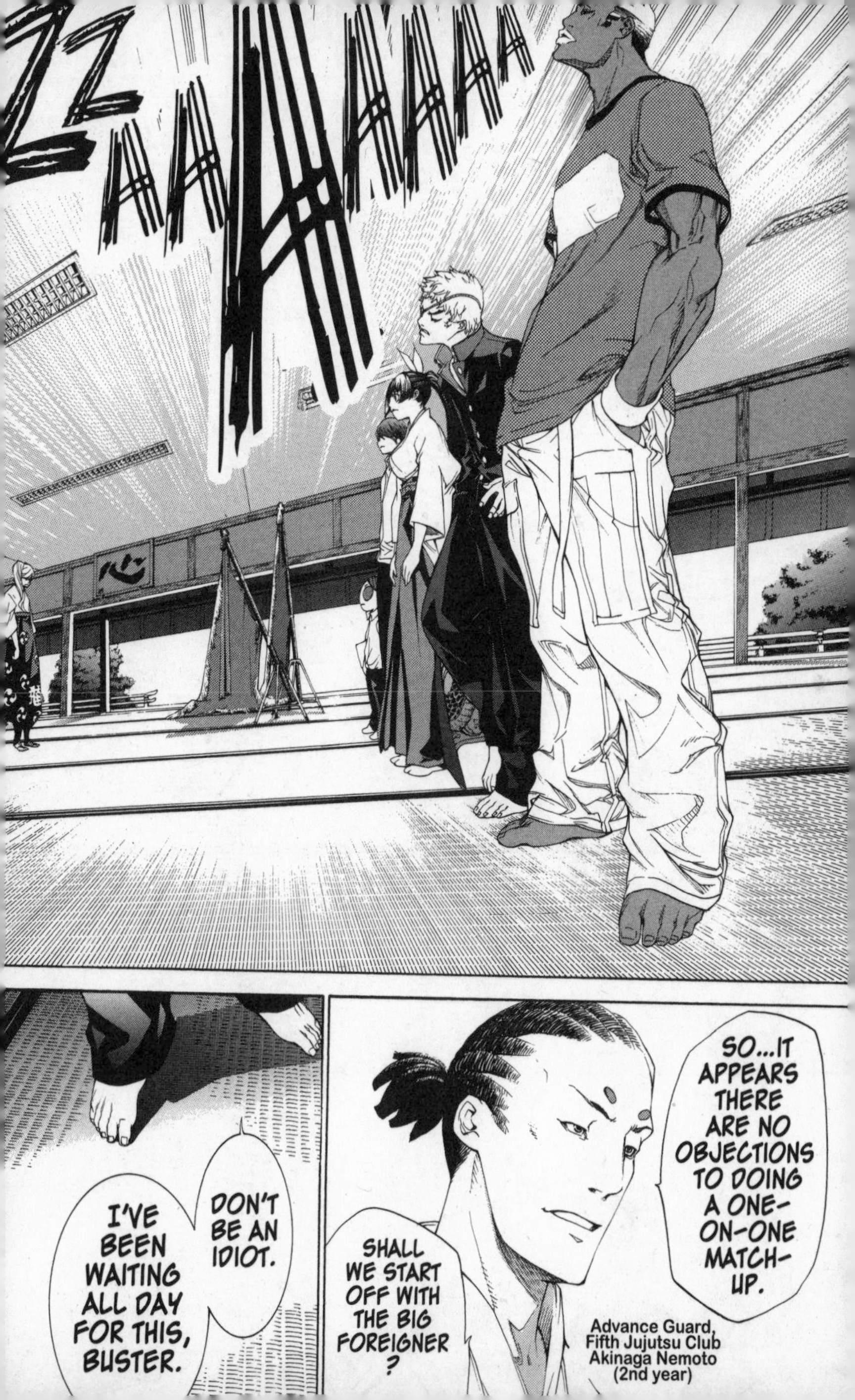
ZZAAAAAAA
SO...IT APPEARS THERE ARE NO OBJECTIONS TO DOING A ONE-ON-ONE MATCH-UP.
SHALL WE START OFF WITH THE BIG FOREIGNER?
Advance Guard, Fifth Jujutsu Club Akinaga Nemoto (2nd year)
DON'T BE AN IDIOT.
I'VE BEEN WAITING ALL DAY FOR THIS, BUSTER.

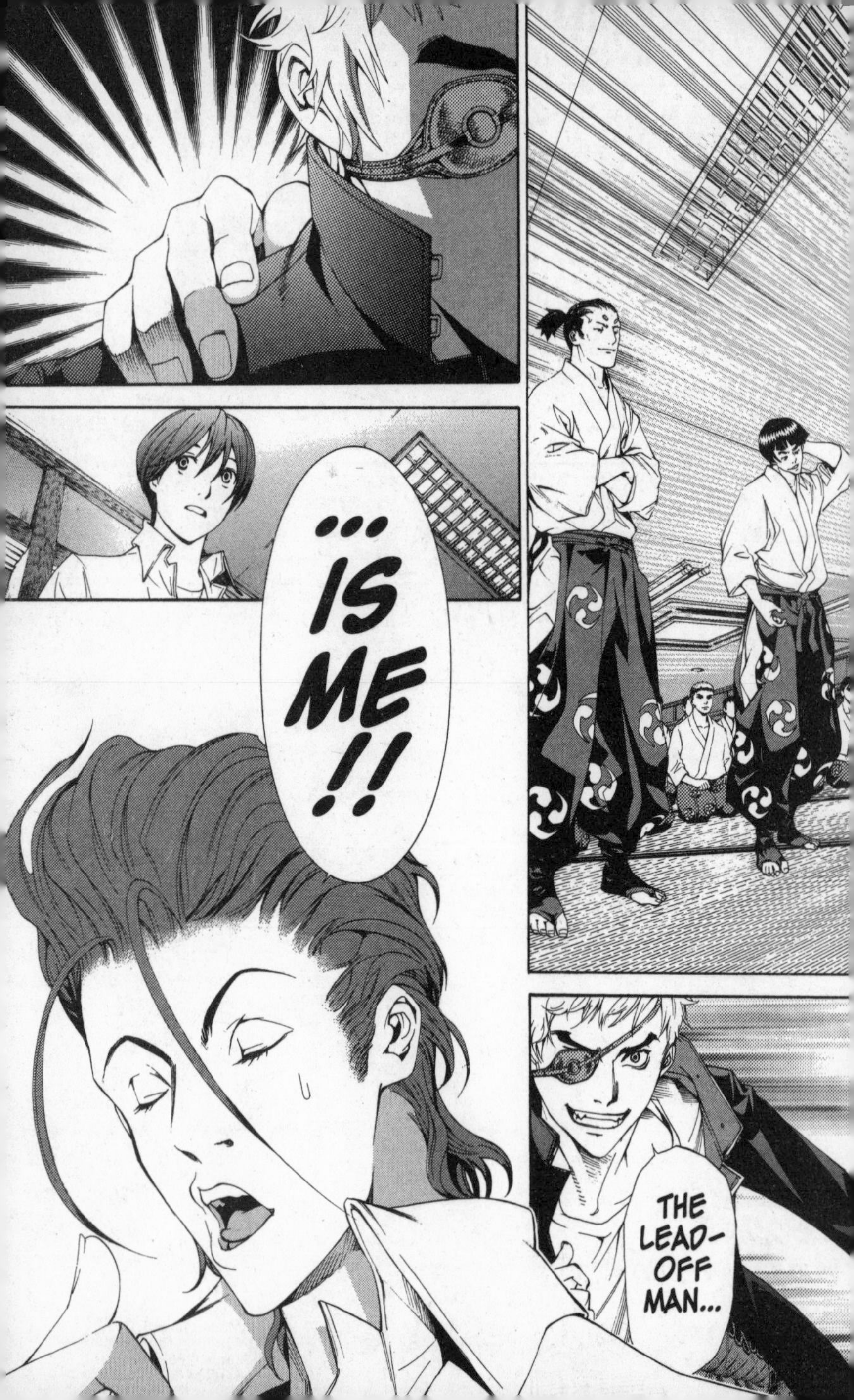
THE LEAD-OFF MAN...
...IS ME!!

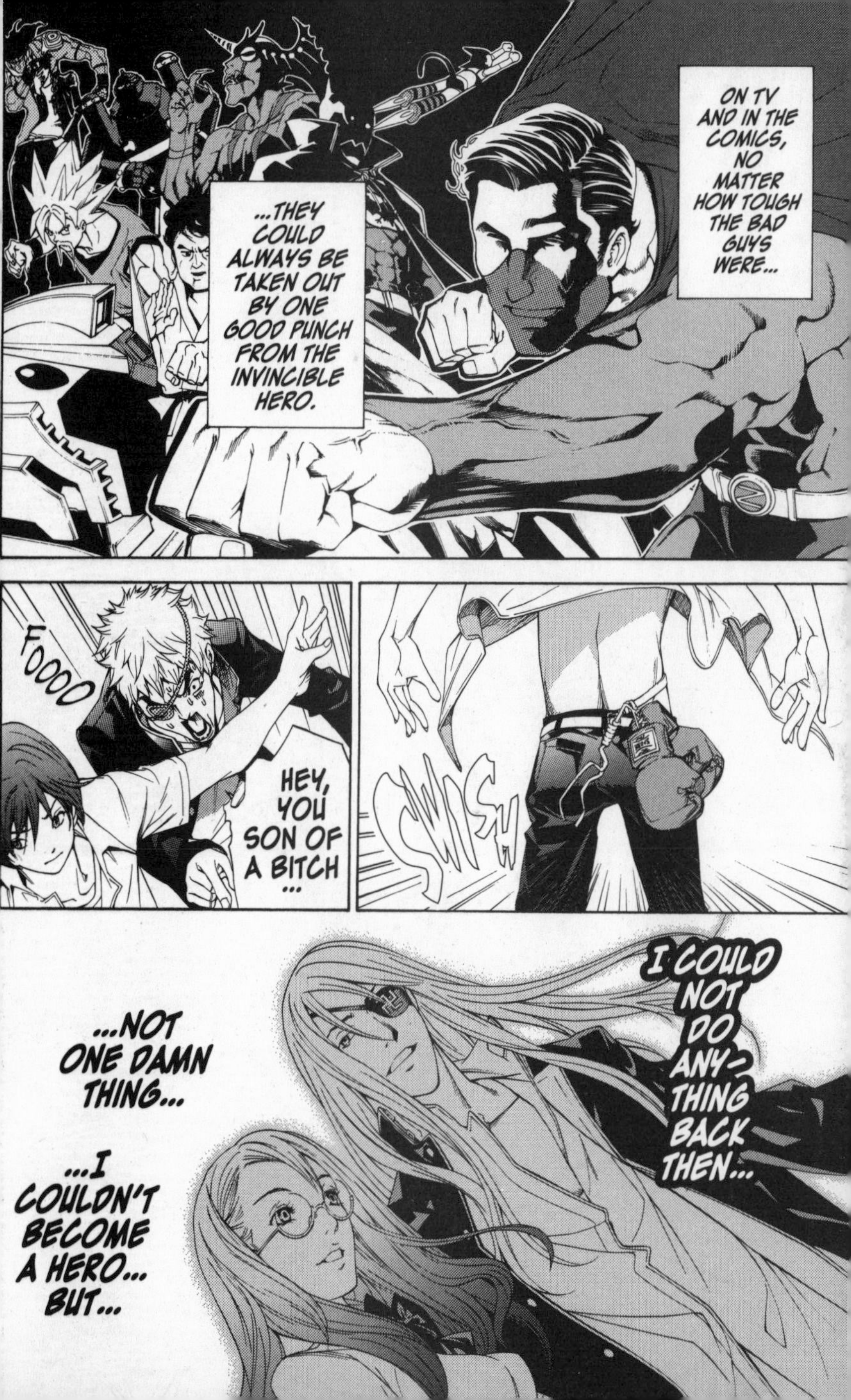
ON TV AND IN THE COMICS, NO MATTER HOW TOUGH THE BAD GUYS WERE...
...THEY COULD ALWAYS BE TAKEN OUT BY ONE GOOD PUNCH FROM THE INVINCIBLE HERO.
SWISH
FOOOO
HEY, YOU SON OF A BITCH ...
I COULD NOT DO ANYTHING BACK THEN...
...NOT ONE DAMN THING...
...I COULDN'T BECOME A HERO... BUT...

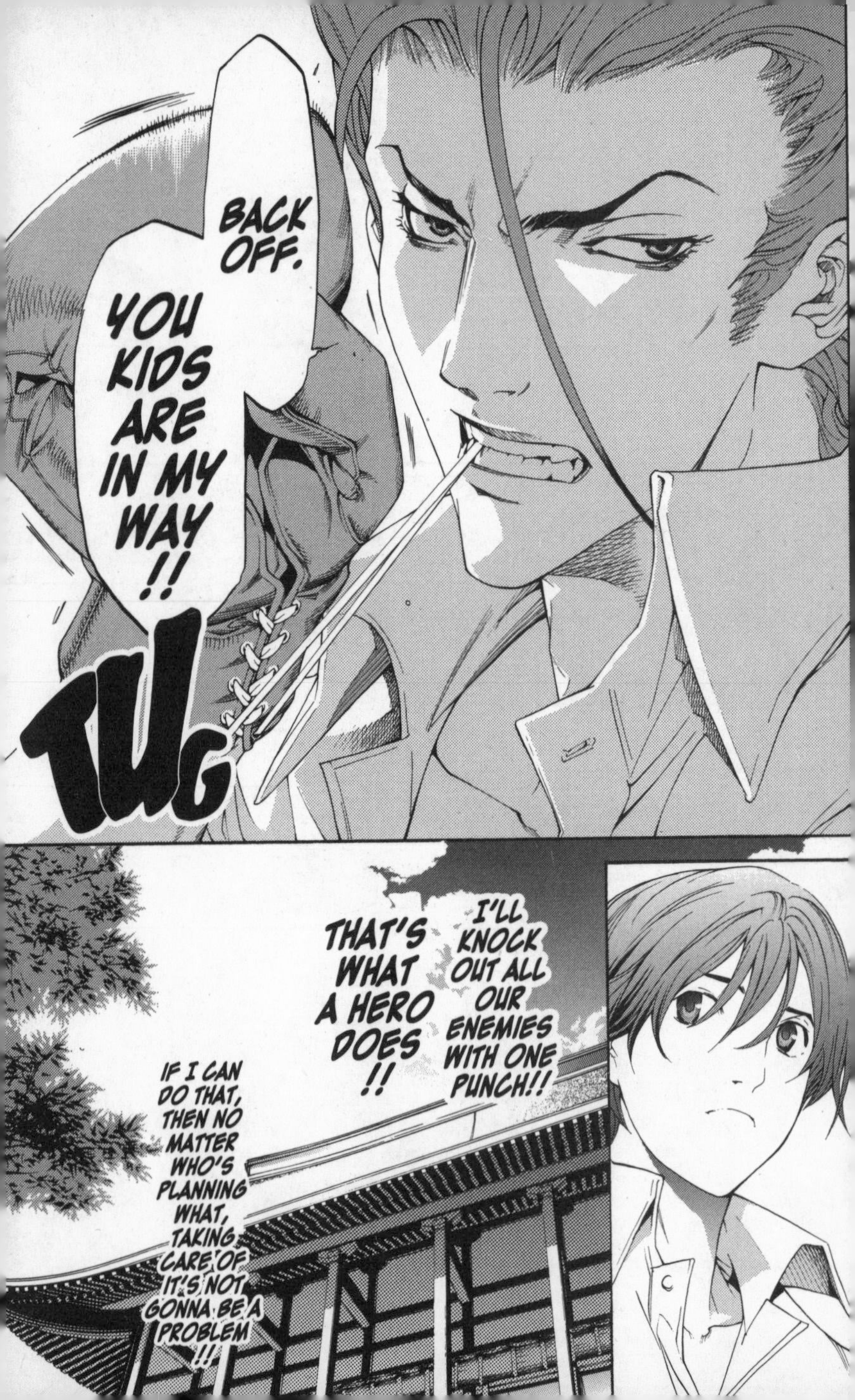
BACK OFF.
YOU KIDS ARE IN MY WAY!!
TUG
I'LL KNOCK OUT ALL OUR ENEMIES WITH ONE PUNCH!!
THAT'S WHAT A HERO DOES!!
IF I CAN DO THAT, THEN NO MATTER WHO'S PLANNING WHAT, TAKING CARE OF IT'S NOT GONNA BE A PROBLEM!!

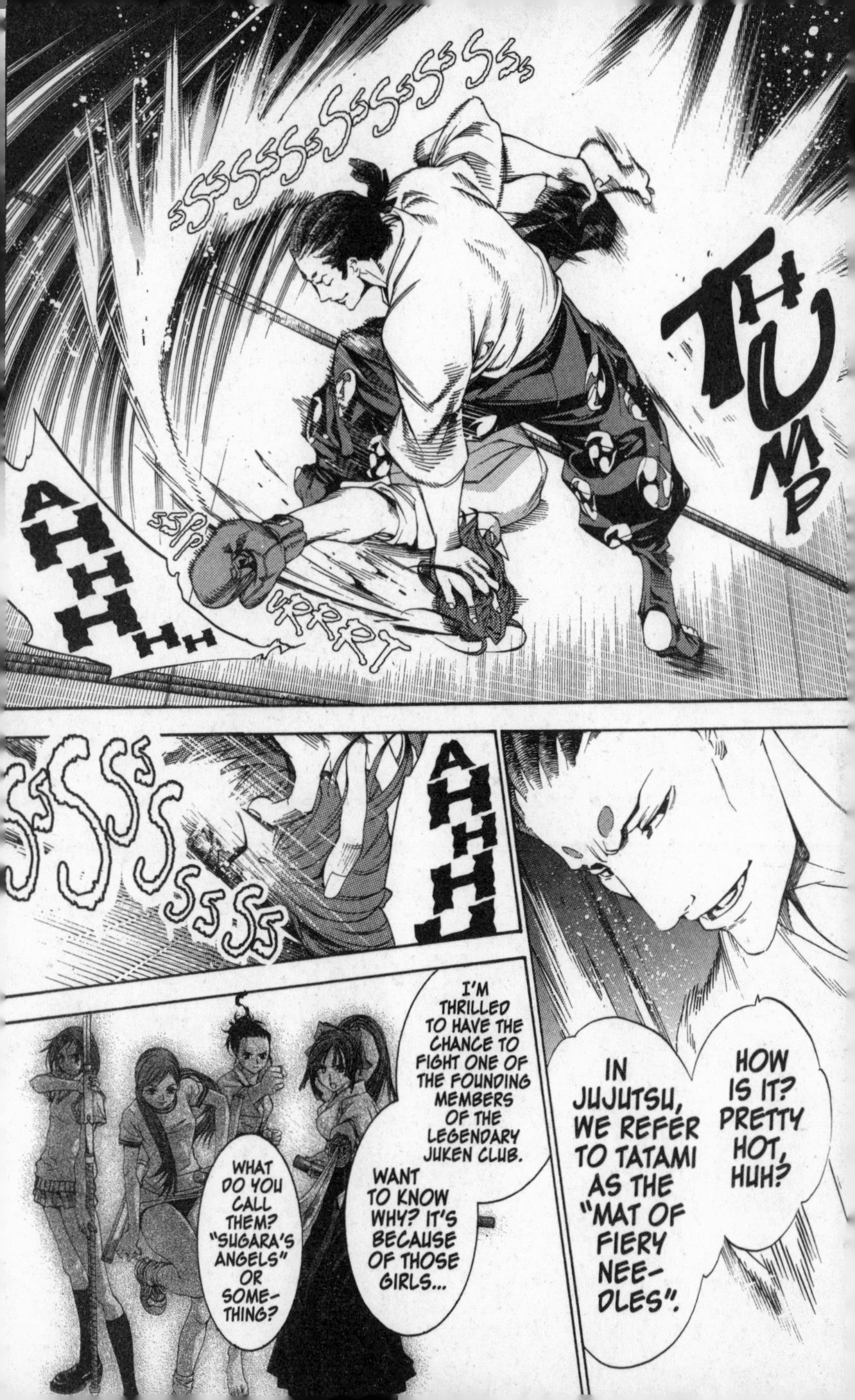
SSSSSSSSSSSSSSSS
THUMP
SSPP
URRRT
AHHHHHH
HOW IS IT? PRETTY HOT, HUH?
IN JUJUTSU, WE REFER TO TATAMI AS THE "MAT OF FIERY NEE-DLES".
SSSSSSSSS
AHHH
I'M THRILLED TO HAVE THE CHANCE TO FIGHT ONE OF THE FOUNDING MEMBERS OF THE LEGENDARY JUKEN CLUB.
WANT TO KNOW WHY? IT'S BECAUSE OF THOSE GIRLS...
WHAT DO YOU CALL THEM? "SUGARA'S ANGELS" OR SOME-THING?

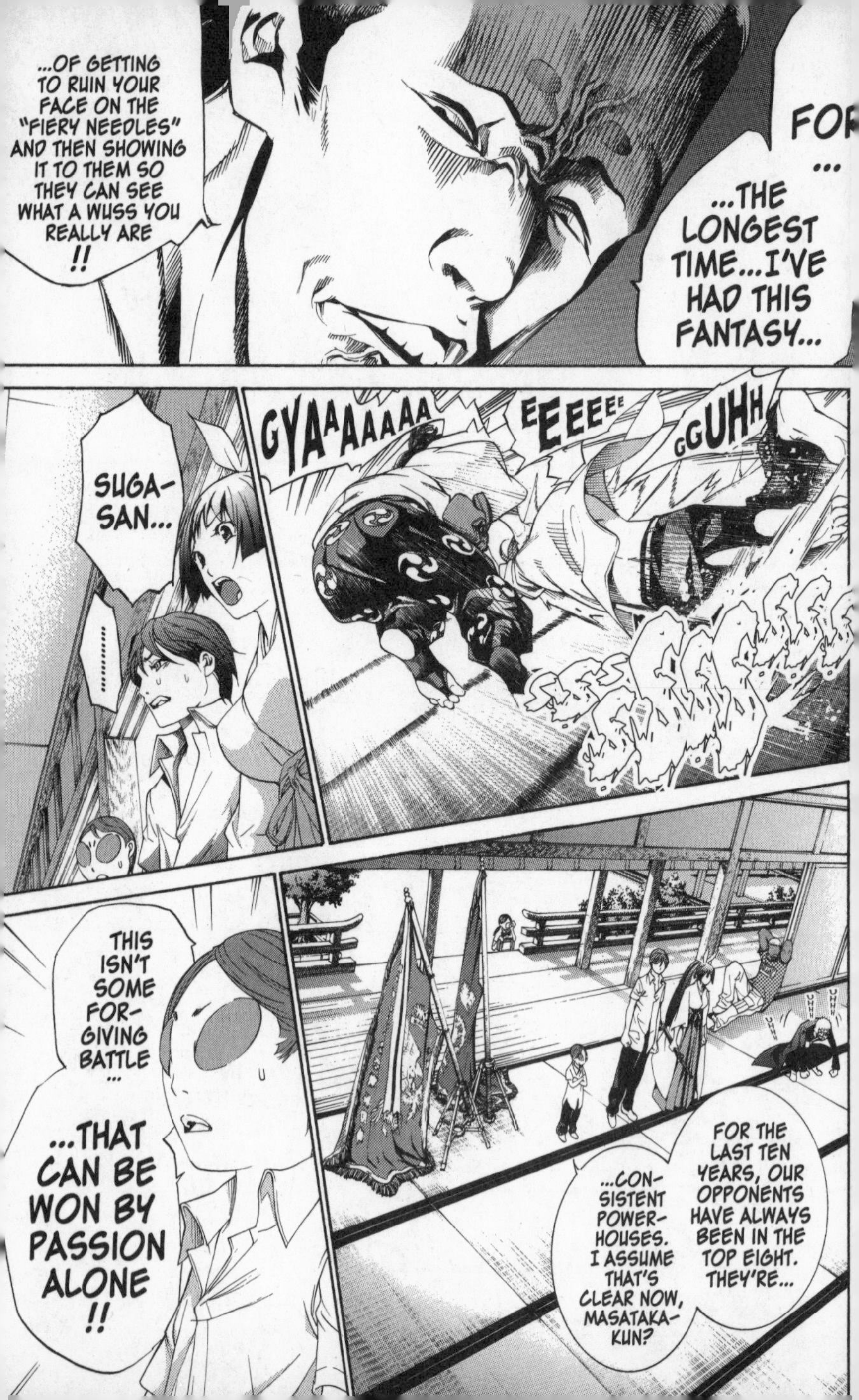
FOR...
...THE LONGEST TIME...I'VE HAD THIS FANTASY...
...OF GETTING TO RUIN YOUR FACE ON THE "FIERY NEEDLES" AND THEN SHOWING IT TO THEM SO THEY CAN SEE WHAT A WUSS YOU REALLY ARE!!
GYAAAAAAA
EEEEE
GGUHH
SUGA-SAN...
......
FOR THE LAST TEN YEARS, OUR OPPONENTS HAVE ALWAYS BEEN IN THE TOP EIGHT. THEY'RE...
...CONSISTENT POWERHOUSES. I ASSUME THAT'S CLEAR NOW, MASATAKA-KUN?
THIS ISN'T SOME FORGIVING BATTLE...
...THAT CAN BE WON BY PASSION ALONE!!

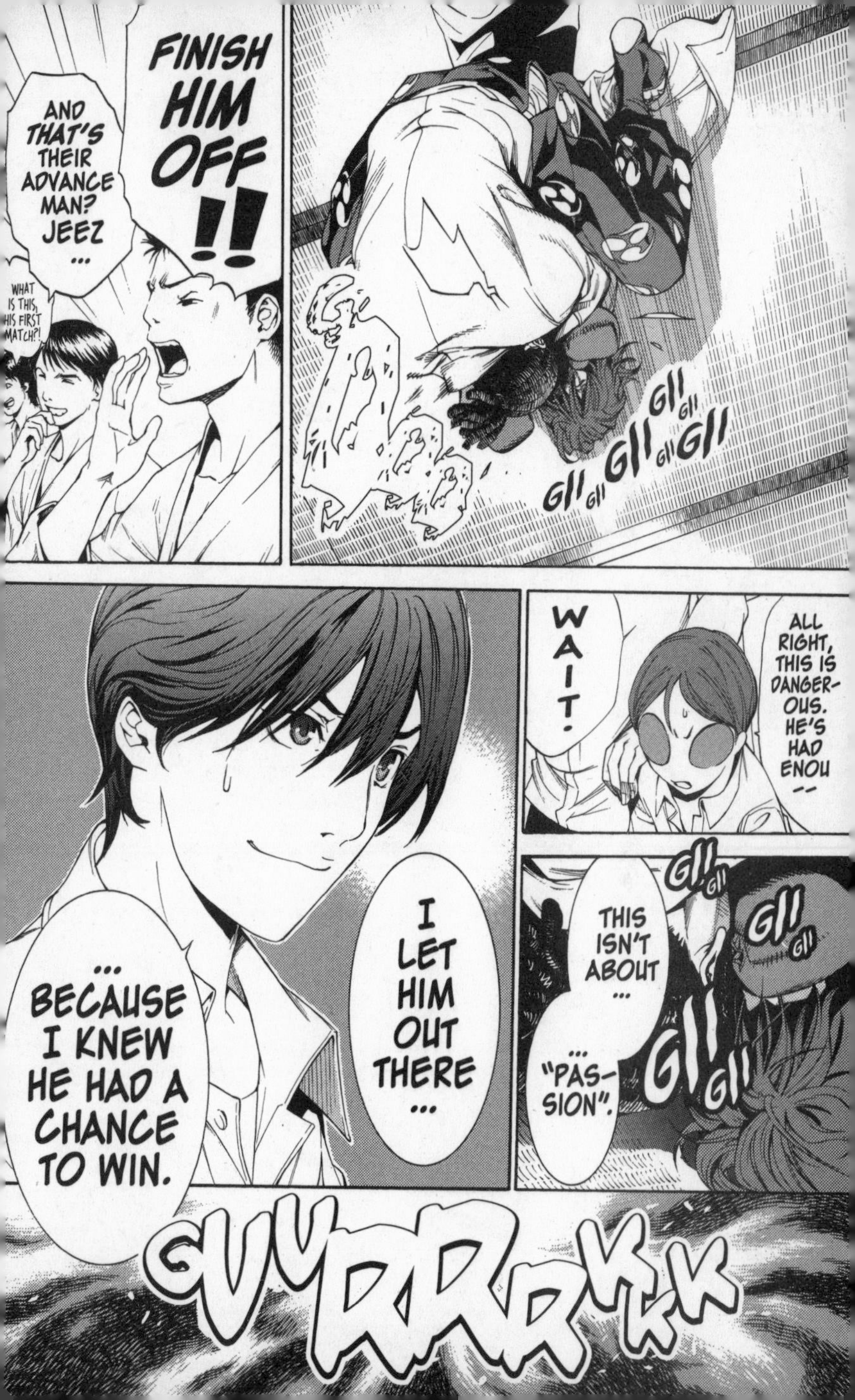
GII GII GII GII GII GII GII
FINISH HIM OFF!!
AND THAT'S THEIR ADVANCE MAN? JEEZ ...
WHAT IS THIS, HIS FIRST MATCH?!
ALL RIGHT, THIS IS DANGER-OUS. HE'S HAD ENOU --
WAIT!
THIS ISN'T ABOUT ...
... "PAS-SION".
GII GII GII GII GII GII
I LET HIM OUT THERE ...
... BECAUSE I KNEW HE HAD A CHANCE TO WIN.

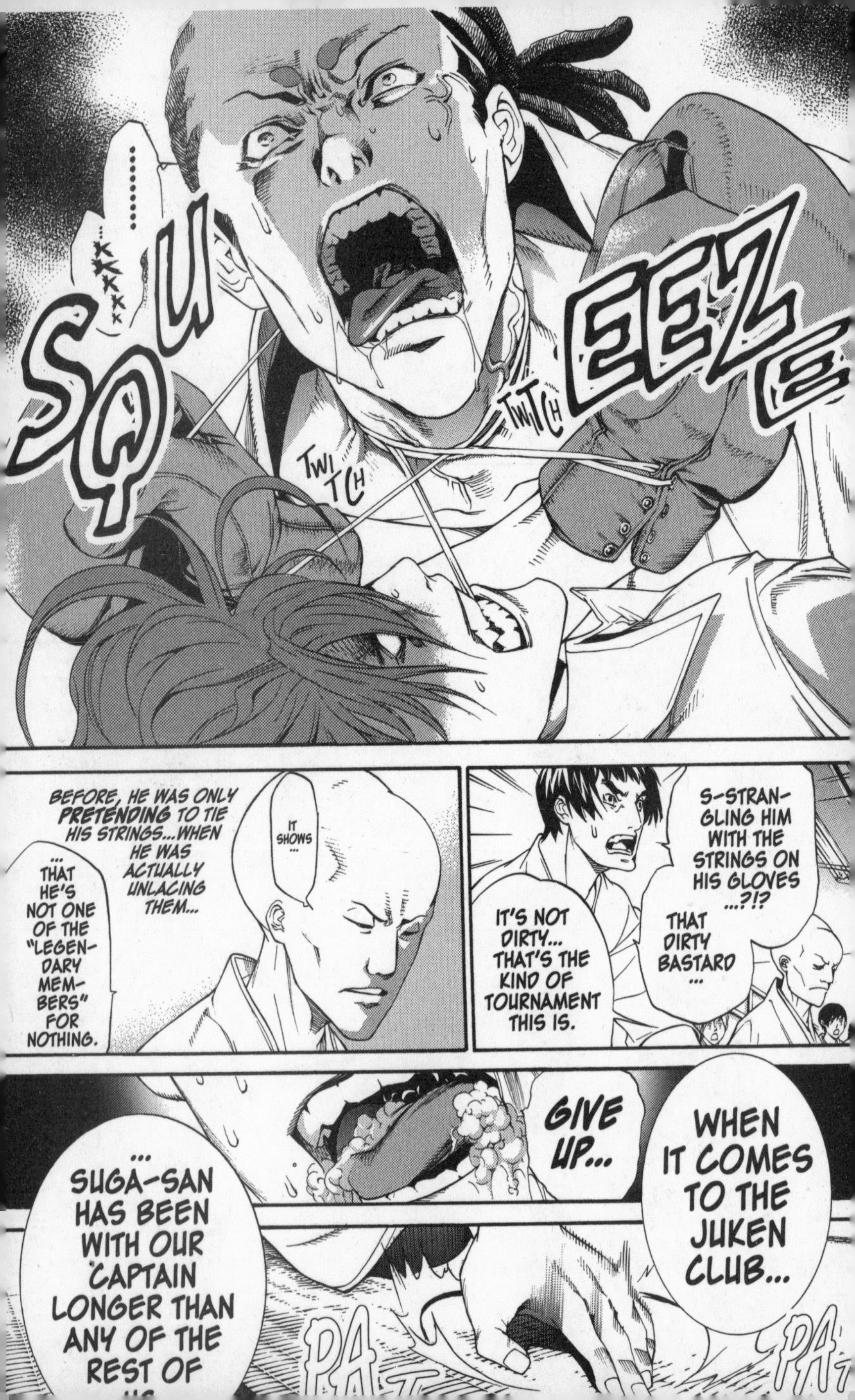

......KKKKK...
SQUEEZE
TWITCH
TWITCH
S-STRANGLING HIM WITH THE STRINGS ON HIS GLOVES...?!?
THAT DIRTY BASTARD...
IT'S NOT DIRTY... THAT'S THE KIND OF TOURNAMENT THIS IS.
IT SHOWS...
BEFORE, HE WAS ONLY PRETENDING TO TIE HIS STRINGS...WHEN HE WAS ACTUALLY UNLACING THEM...
...THAT HE'S NOT ONE OF THE "LEGENDARY MEMBERS" FOR NOTHING.
GIVE UP...
WHEN IT COMES TO THE JUKEN CLUB...
...SUGA-SAN HAS BEEN WITH OUR CAPTAIN LONGER THAN ANY OF THE REST OF
PA
PA

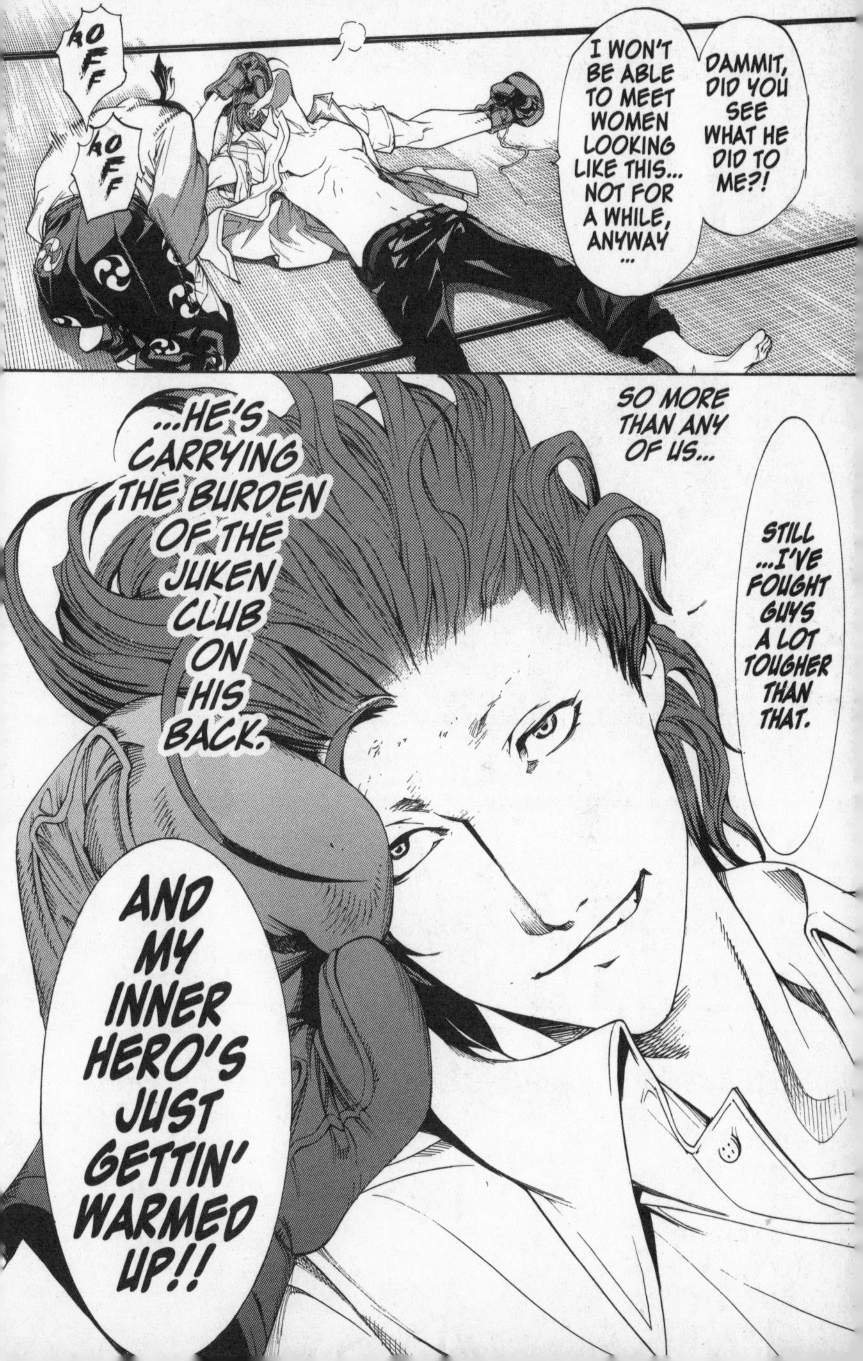
DAMMIT, DID YOU SEE WHAT HE DID TO ME?!
I WON'T BE ABLE TO MEET WOMEN LOOKING LIKE THIS... NOT FOR A WHILE, ANYWAY...
KOFF
KOFF
SO MORE THAN ANY OF US...
...HE'S CARRYING THE BURDEN OF THE JUKEN CLUB ON HIS BACK.
STILL ...I'VE FOUGHT GUYS A LOT TOUGHER THAN THAT.
AND MY INNER HERO'S JUST GETTIN' WARMED UP!!

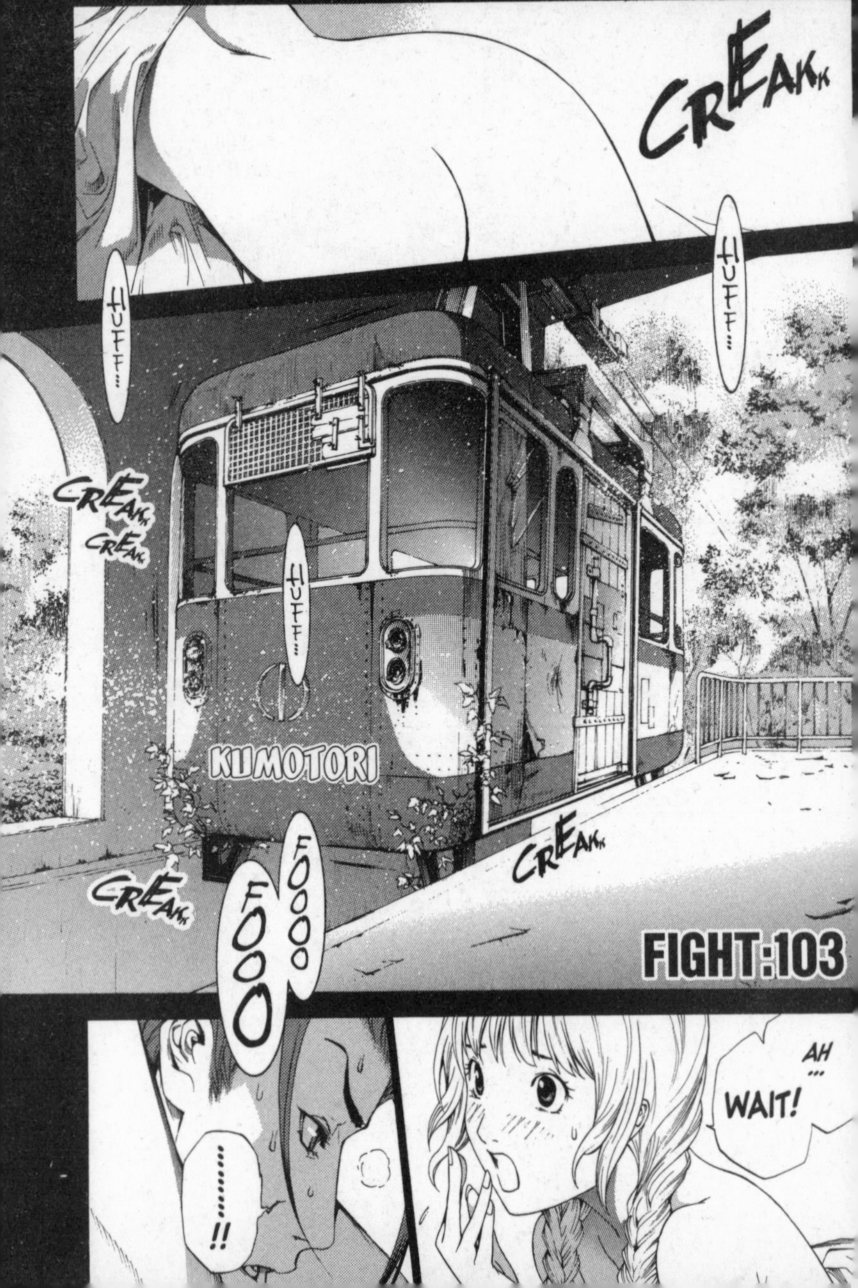
CREAKK
HUFF...
HUFF...
HUFF...
CREAKK
CREAKK
KUMOTORI
CREAKK
CREAKK
FOOOO
FOOOO
FIGHT:103
AH... WAIT!
......!!

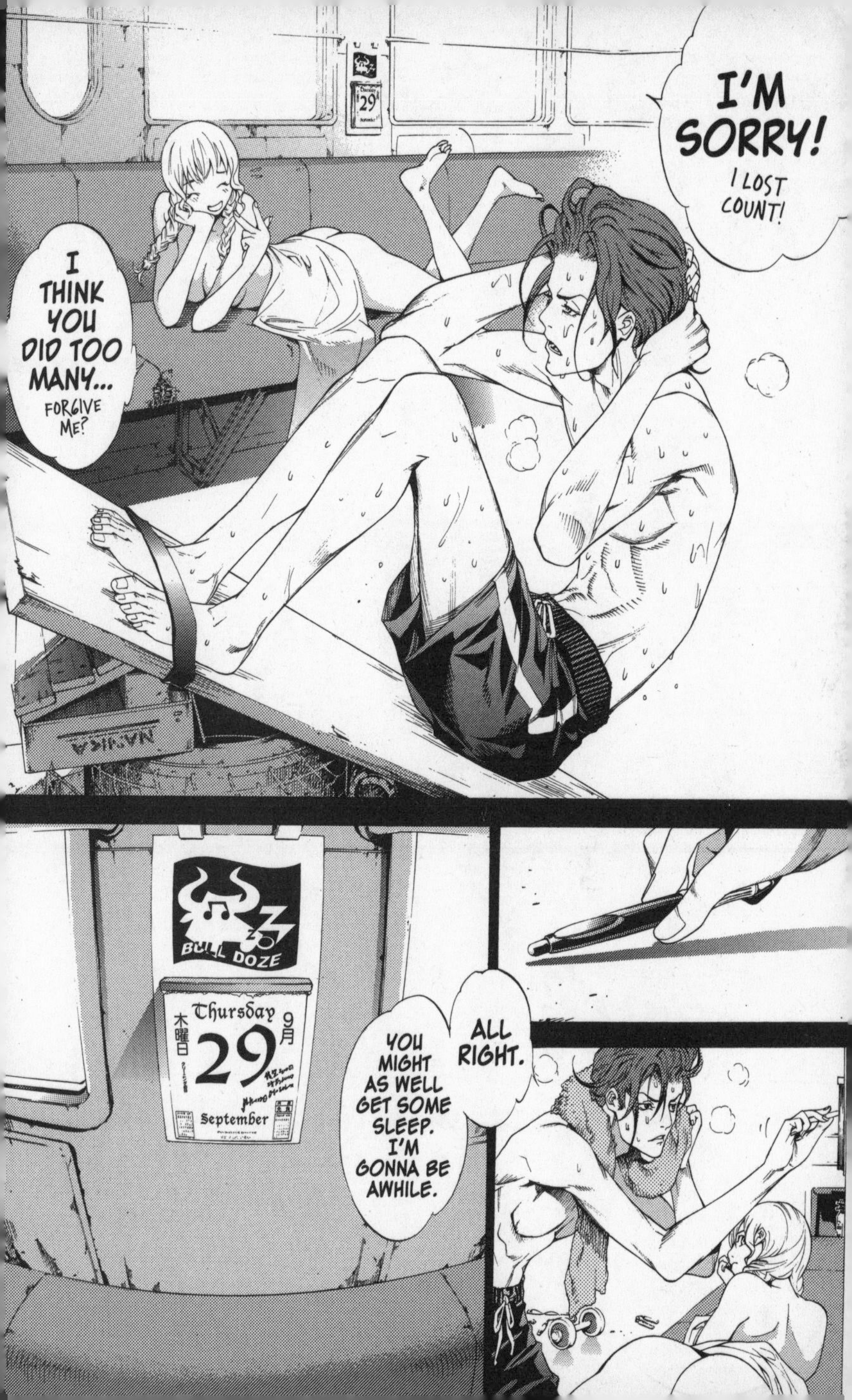
I'M SORRY!
I LOST COUNT!
I THINK YOU DID TOO MANY...
FORGIVE ME?
ALL RIGHT.
YOU MIGHT AS WELL GET SOME SLEEP. I'M GONNA BE AWHILE.
BULL DOZE
Thursday
木曜日
29
9月
September

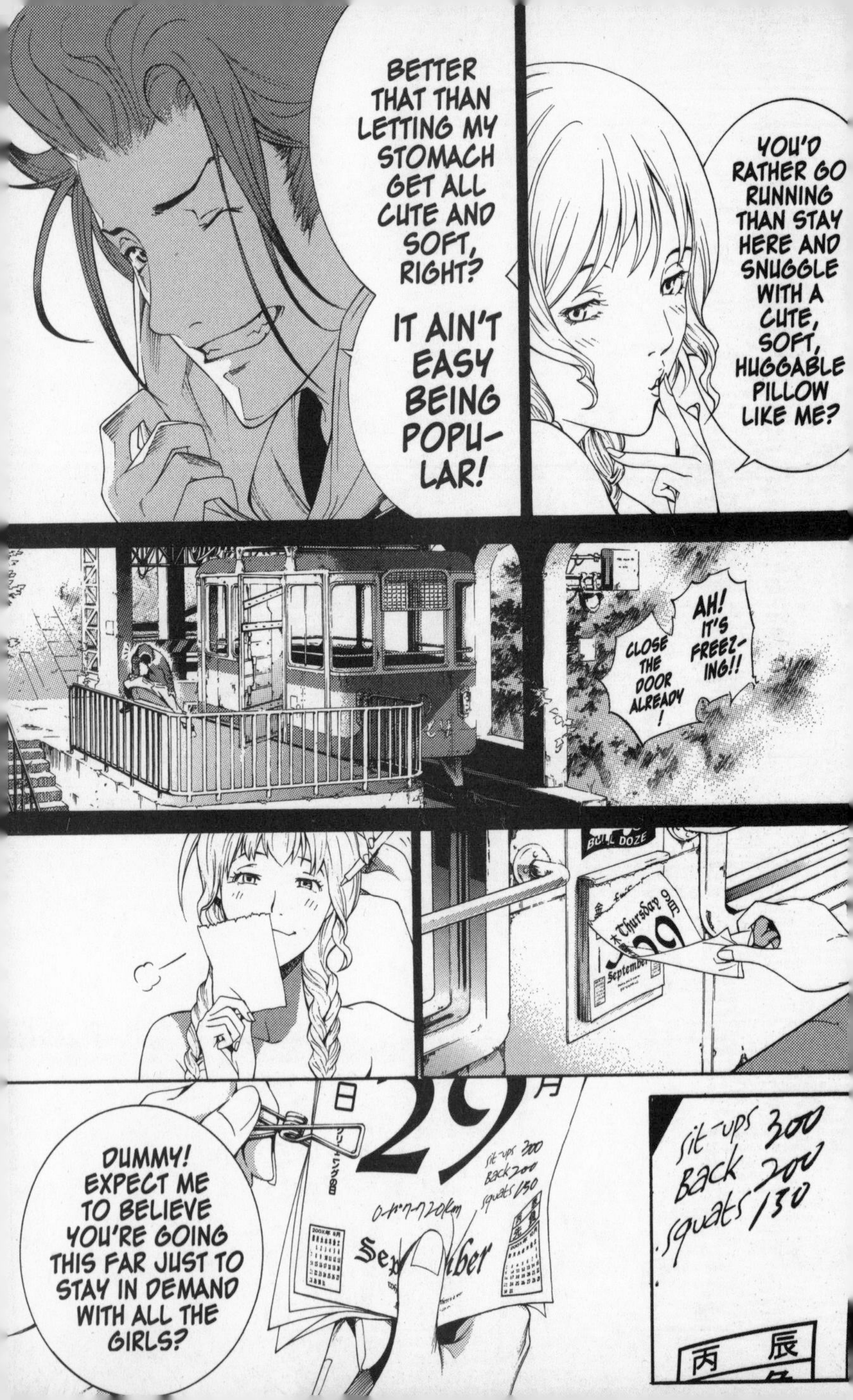
YOU'D RATHER GO RUNNING THAN STAY HERE AND SNUGGLE WITH A CUTE, SOFT, HUGGABLE PILLOW LIKE ME?
BETTER THAT THAN LETTING MY STOMACH GET ALL CUTE AND SOFT, RIGHT?
IT AIN'T EASY BEING POPU-LAR!
AH! IT'S FREEZ-ING!!
CLOSE THE DOOR ALREADY!
BULL DOZE
Thursday
29
September
sit-ups 300
Back 200
squats 130
29
DUMMY! EXPECT ME TO BELIEVE YOU'RE GOING THIS FAR JUST TO STAY IN DEMAND WITH ALL THE GIRLS?

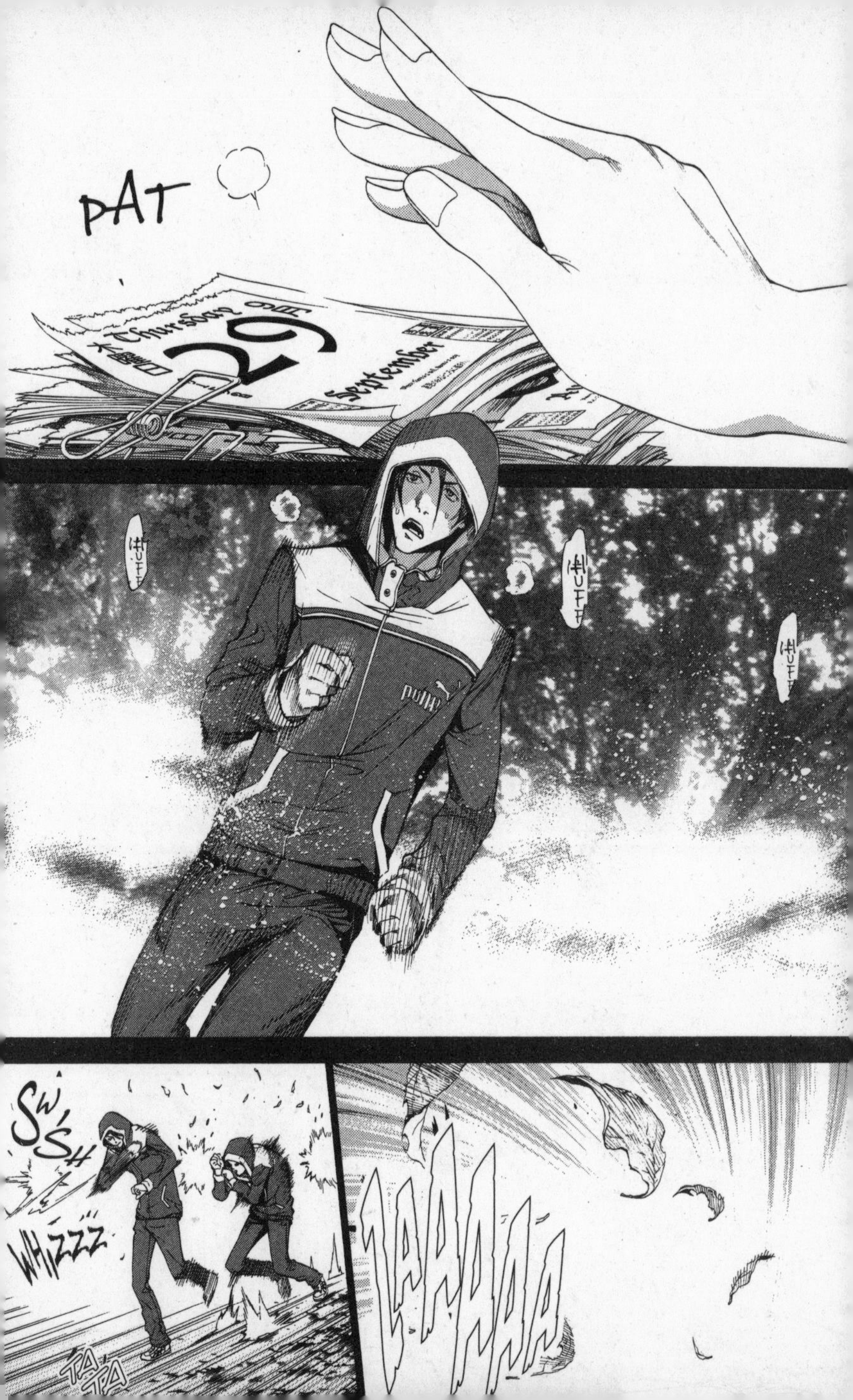
PAT
Thursday
29
September
HUFF
HUFF
HUFF
TAPAPAPA
SWISH
WHIZZZ
TA TA

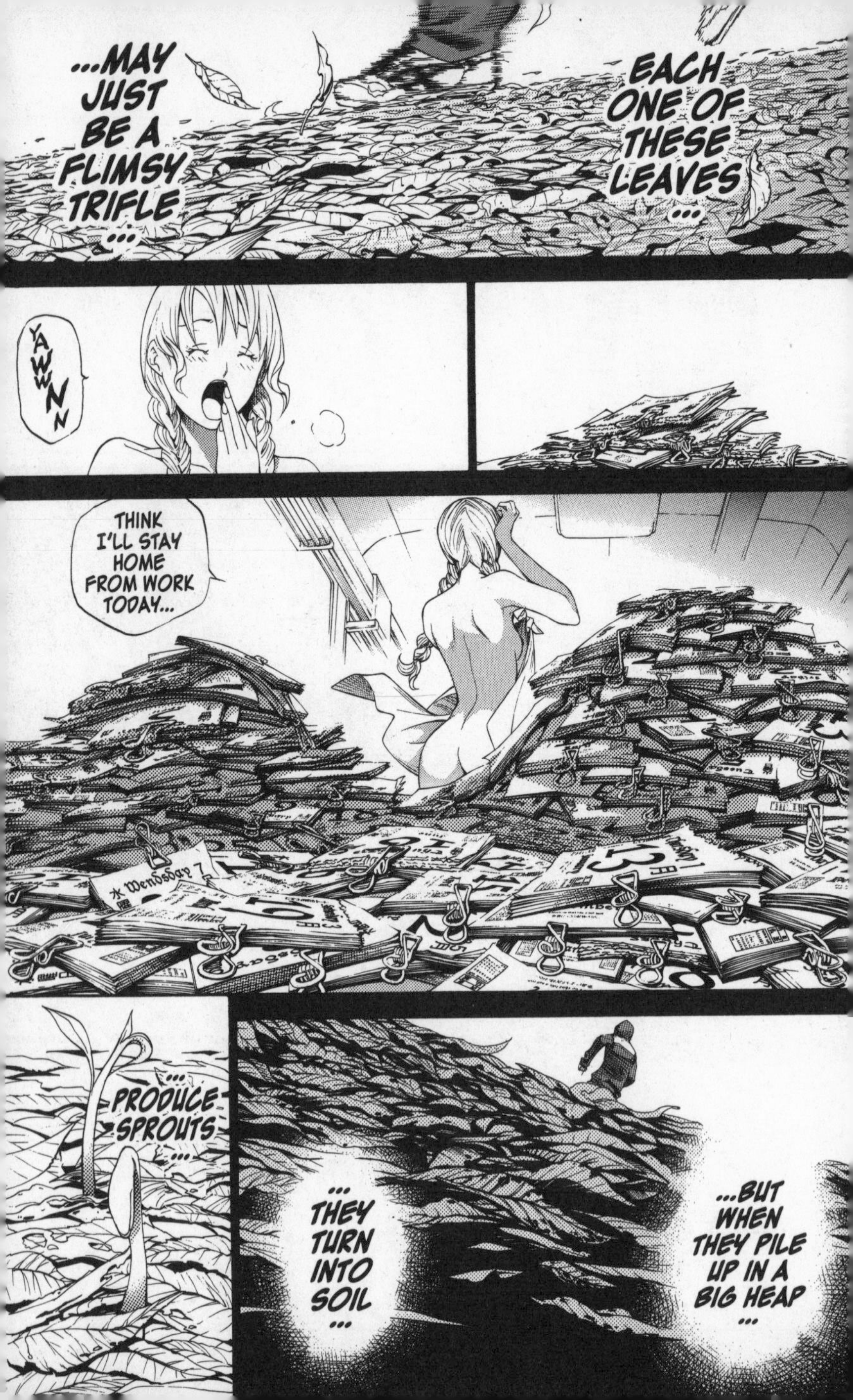
EACH ONE OF THESE LEAVES...
...MAY JUST BE A FLIMSY TRIFLE...
YAWWNN
THINK I'LL STAY HOME FROM WORK TODAY...
...BUT WHEN THEY PILE UP IN A BIG HEAP...
...THEY TURN INTO SOIL...
...PRODUCE SPROUTS...

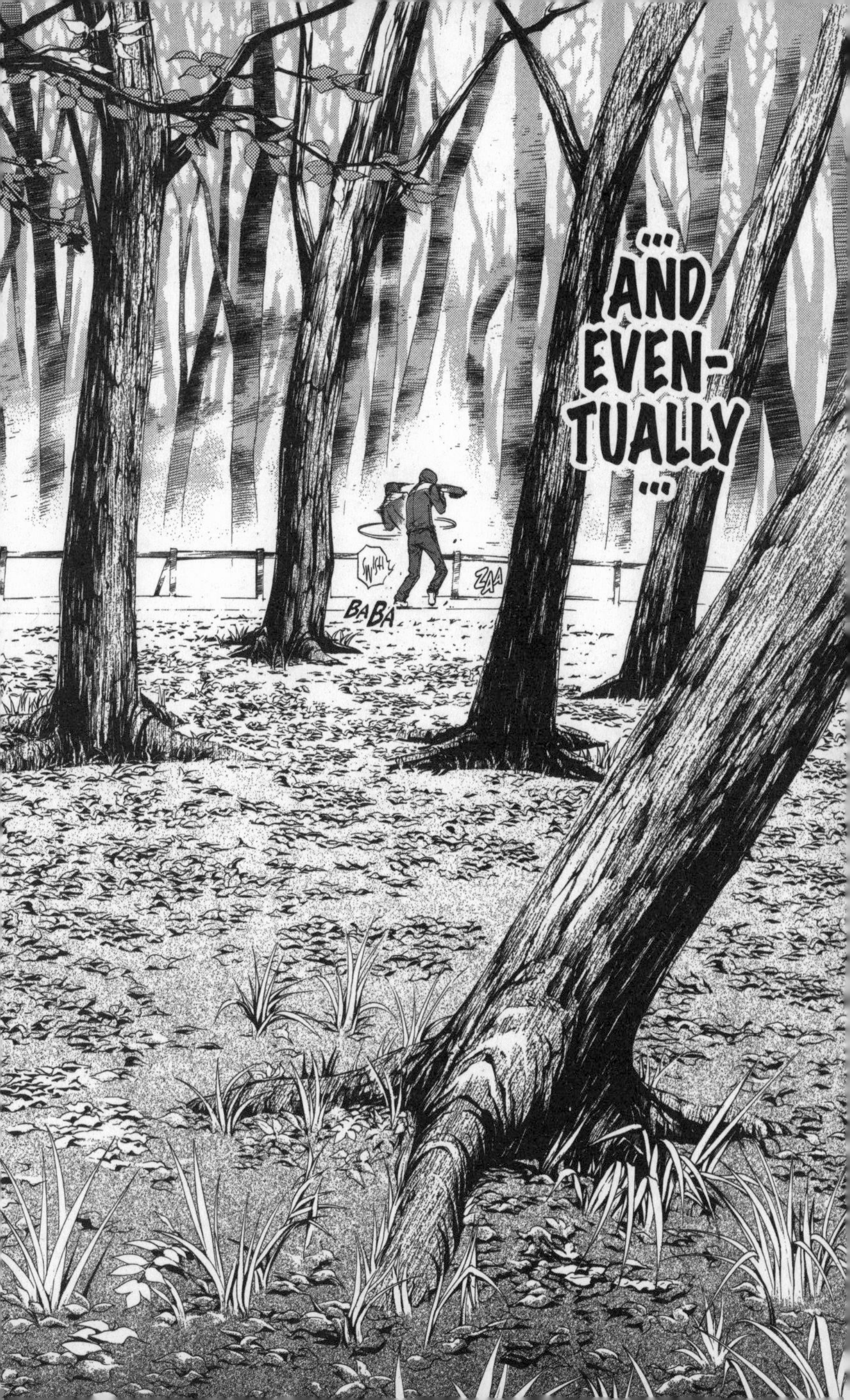
...AND EVEN-TUALLY...
SWISH
ZAA
BABA

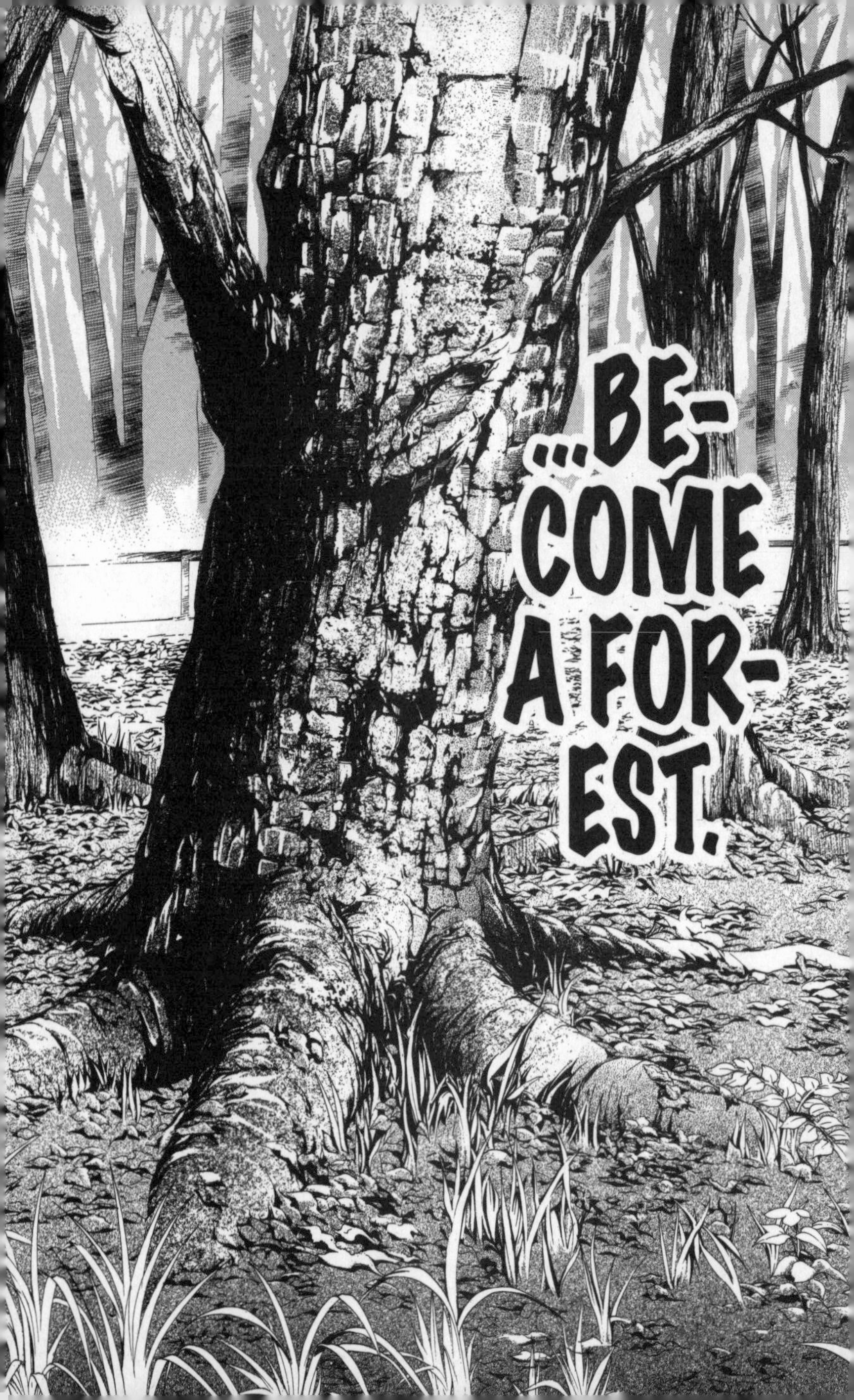
...BE-
COME
A FOR-
EST.

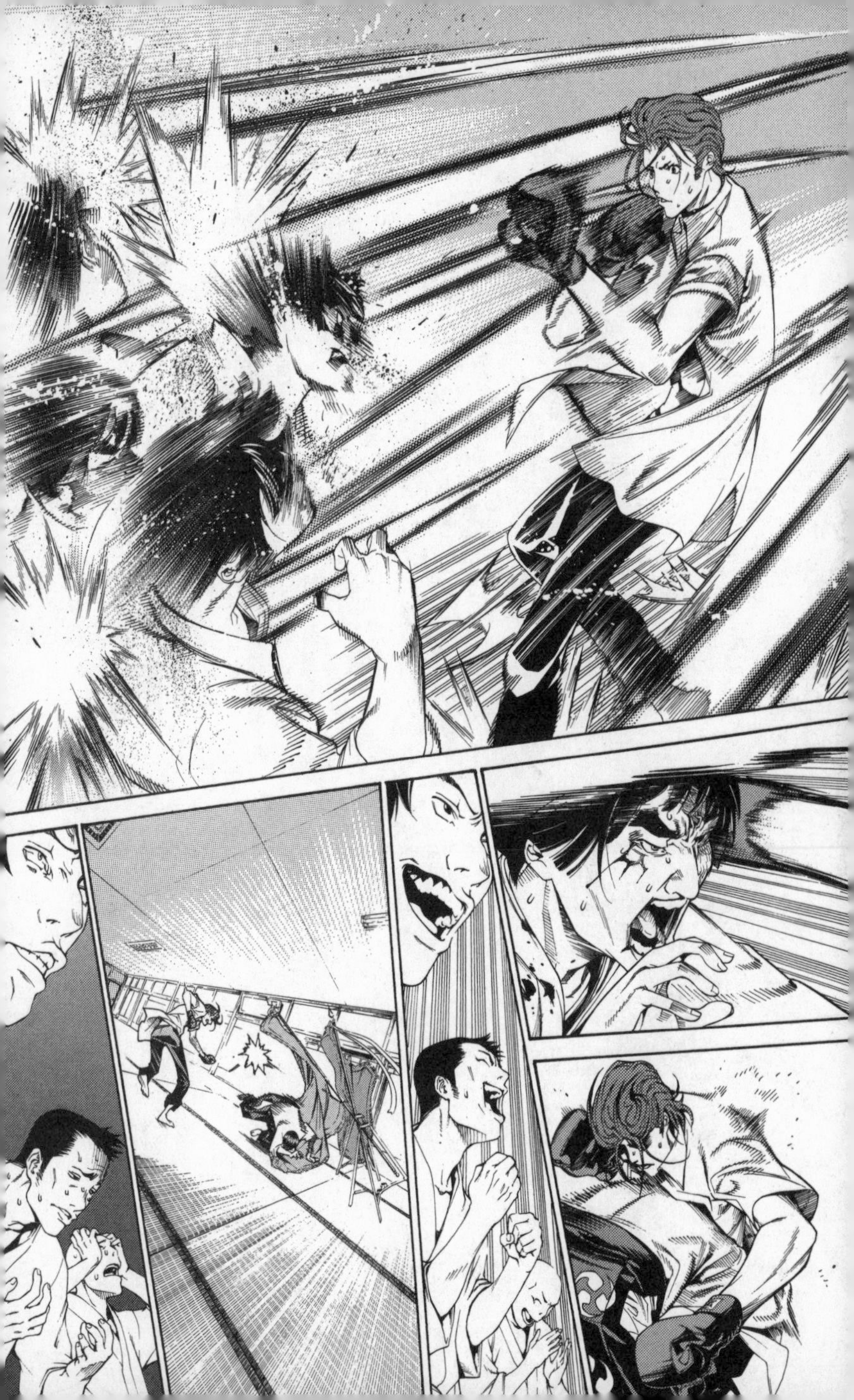

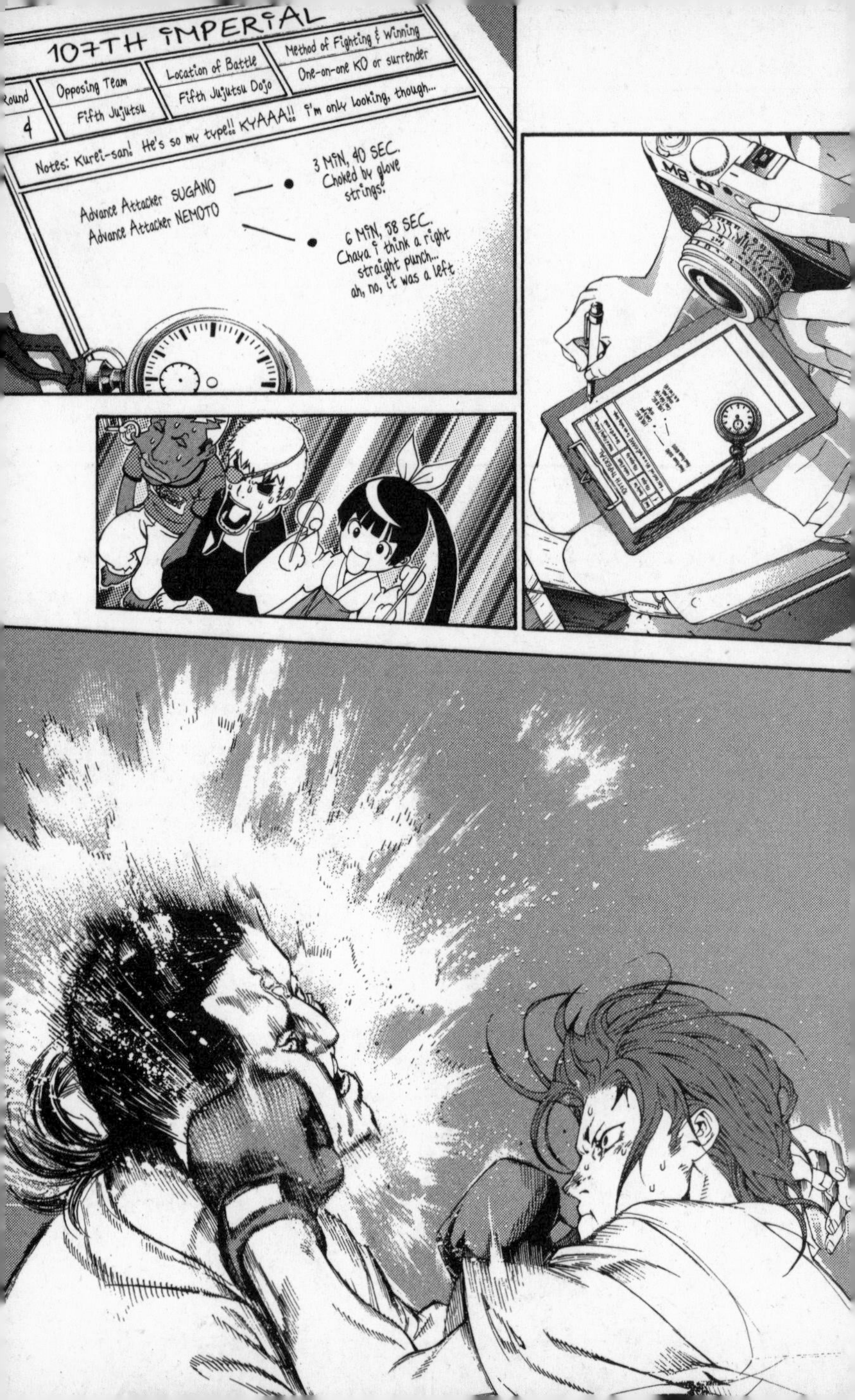
107TH IMPERIAL
Round
4
Opposing Team
Fifth Jujutsu
Location of Battle
Fifth Jujutsu Dojo
Method of Fighting & Winning
One-on-one KO or surrender
Notes: Kurei-san! He's so my type!! KYAAA!! I'm only looking, though...
Advance Attacker SUGANO
3 MIN, 40 SEC. Choked by glove strings!
Advance Attacker NEMOTO
6 MIN, 58 SEC. Chaya I think a right straight punch... ah, no, it was a left

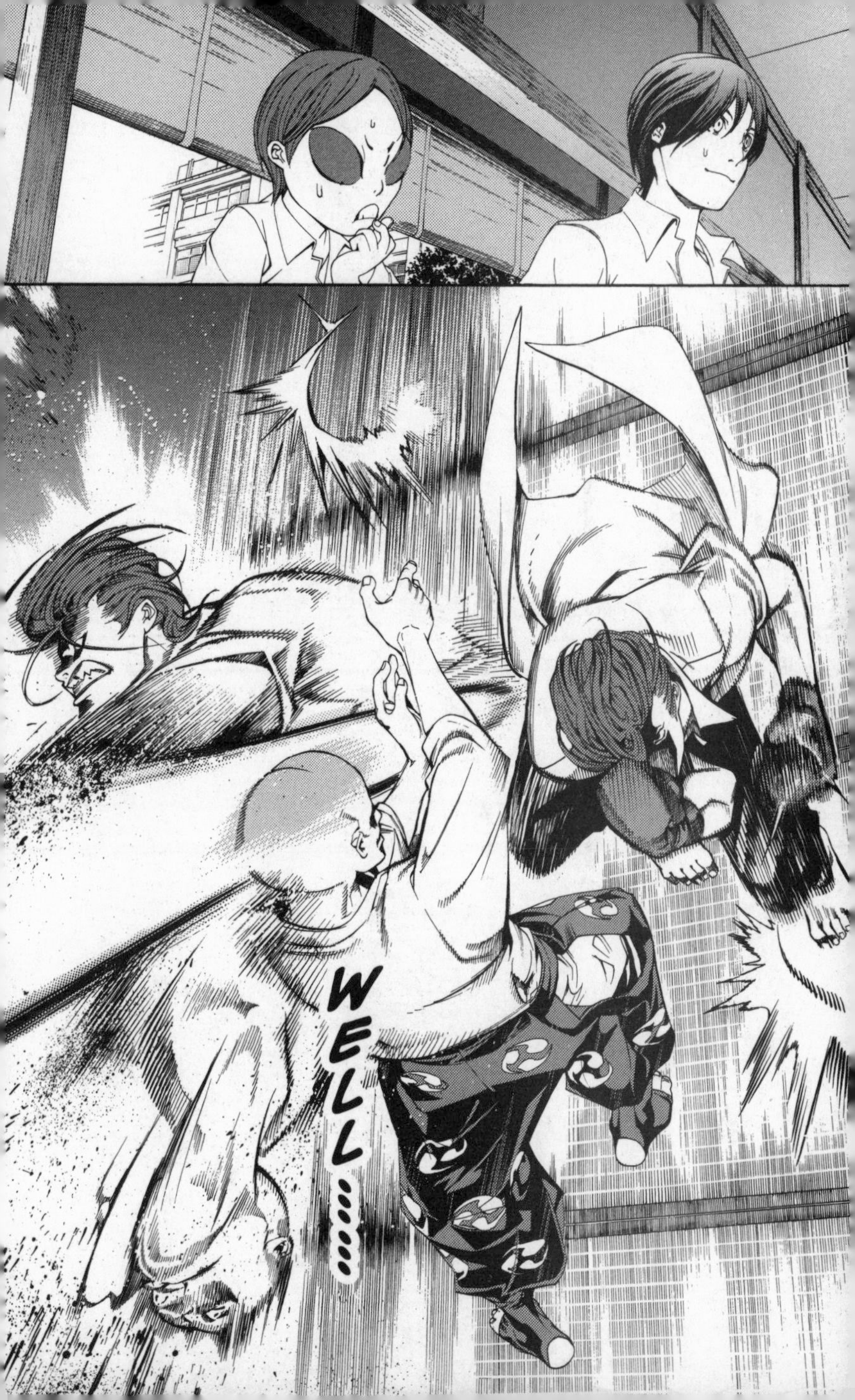
WELL......

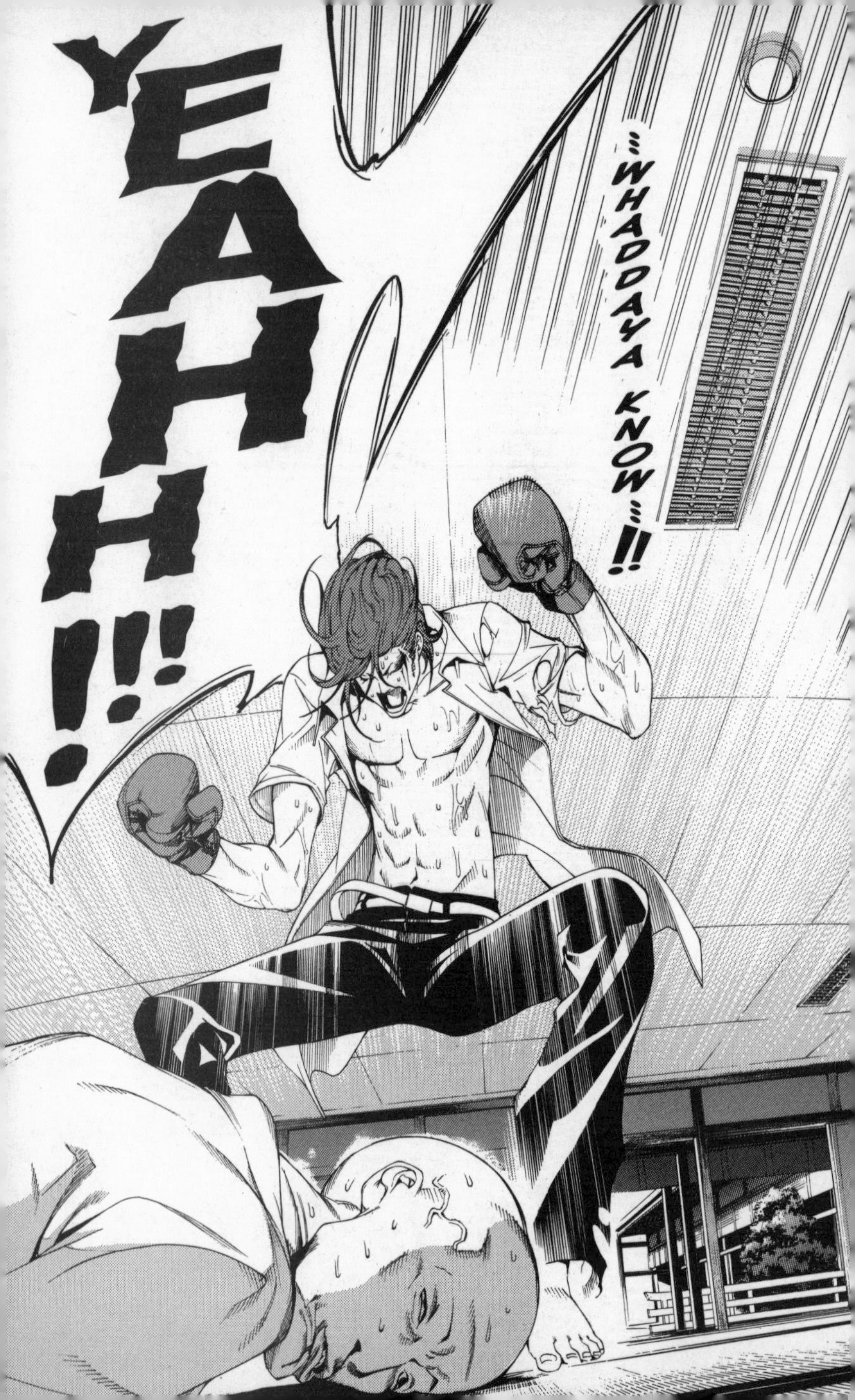
...WHADDAYA KNOW...!!
YEAHH!!!

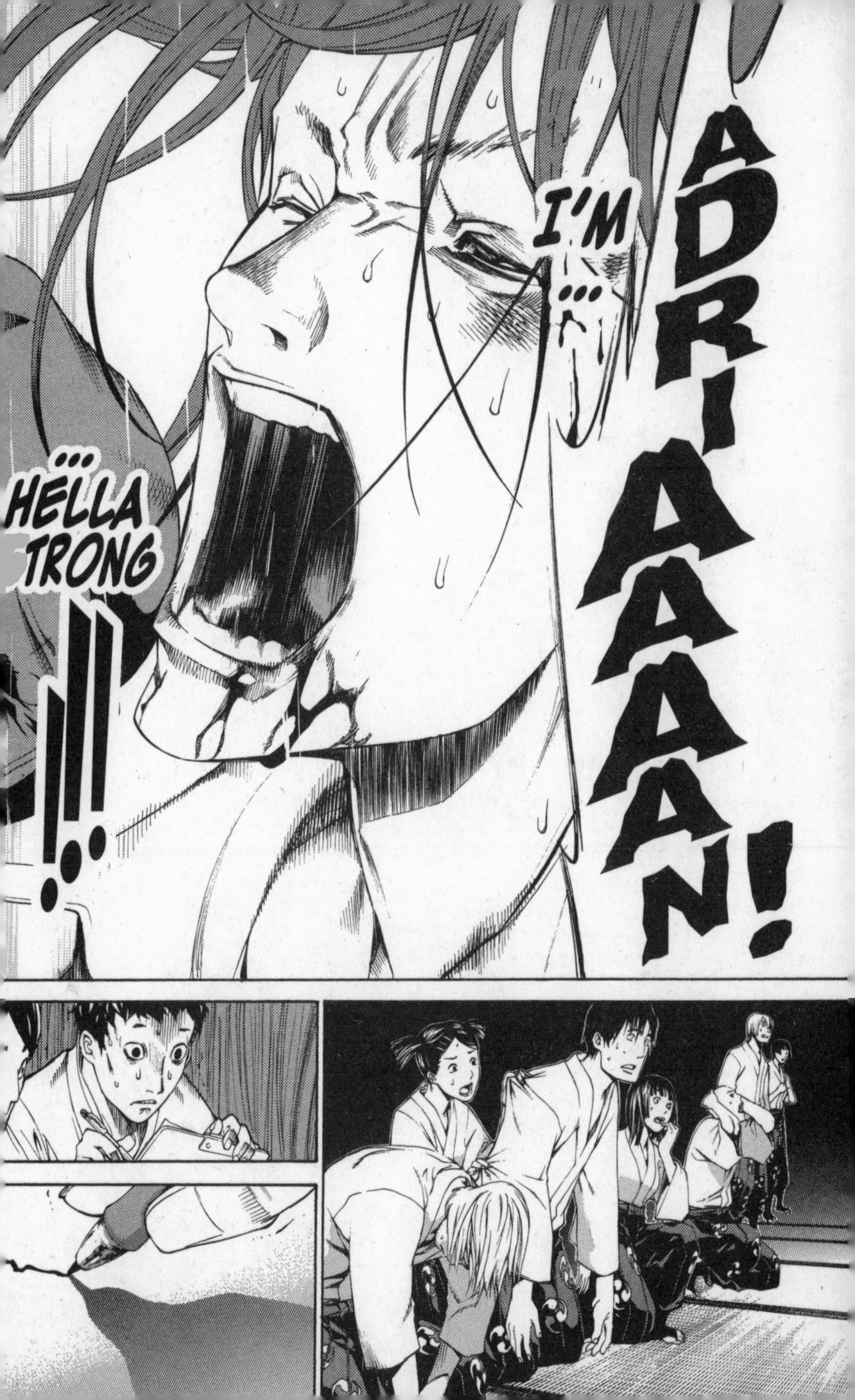
ADRIAAAAN!
I'M ...
... HELLA
TRONG
!!...

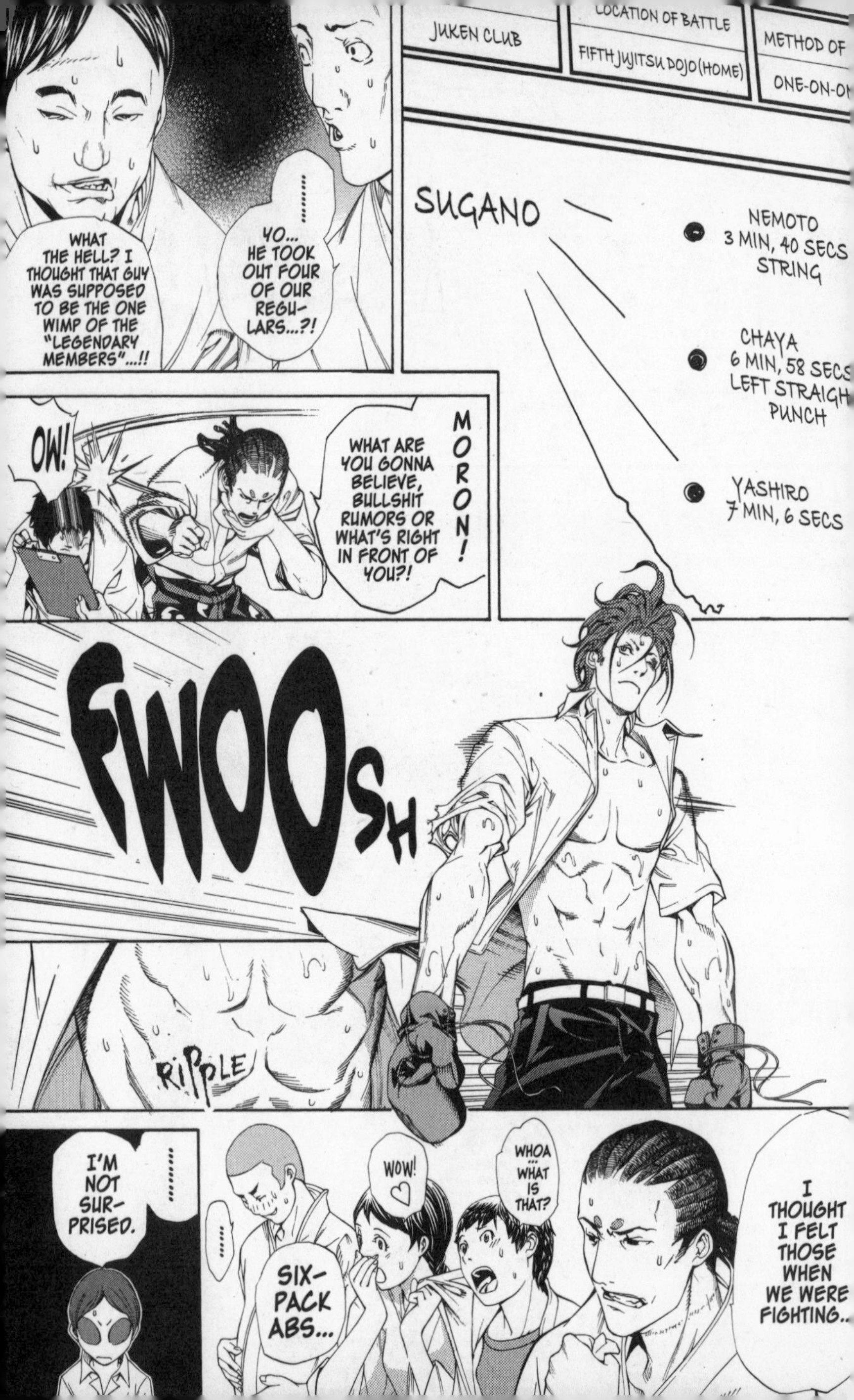

LOCATION OF BATTLE
METHOD OF
JUKEN CLUB
FIFTH JUJITSU DOJO (HOME)
ONE-ON-ON
SUGANO
NEMOTO 3 MIN, 40 SECS STRING
CHAYA 6 MIN, 58 SECS LEFT STRAIGH PUNCH
YASHIRO 7 MIN, 6 SECS
......
YO... HE TOOK OUT FOUR OF OUR REGU-LARS...?!
WHAT THE HELL? I THOUGHT THAT GUY WAS SUPPOSED TO BE THE ONE WIMP OF THE "LEGENDARY MEMBERS"...!!
MORON!
WHAT ARE YOU GONNA BELIEVE, BULLSHIT RUMORS OR WHAT'S RIGHT IN FRONT OF YOU?!
OW!
FWOOSH
RIPPLE
I THOUGHT I FELT THOSE WHEN WE WERE FIGHTING...
WHOA... WHAT IS THAT?
WOW! ♡
......
SIX-PACK ABS...
......
I'M NOT SUR-PRISED.

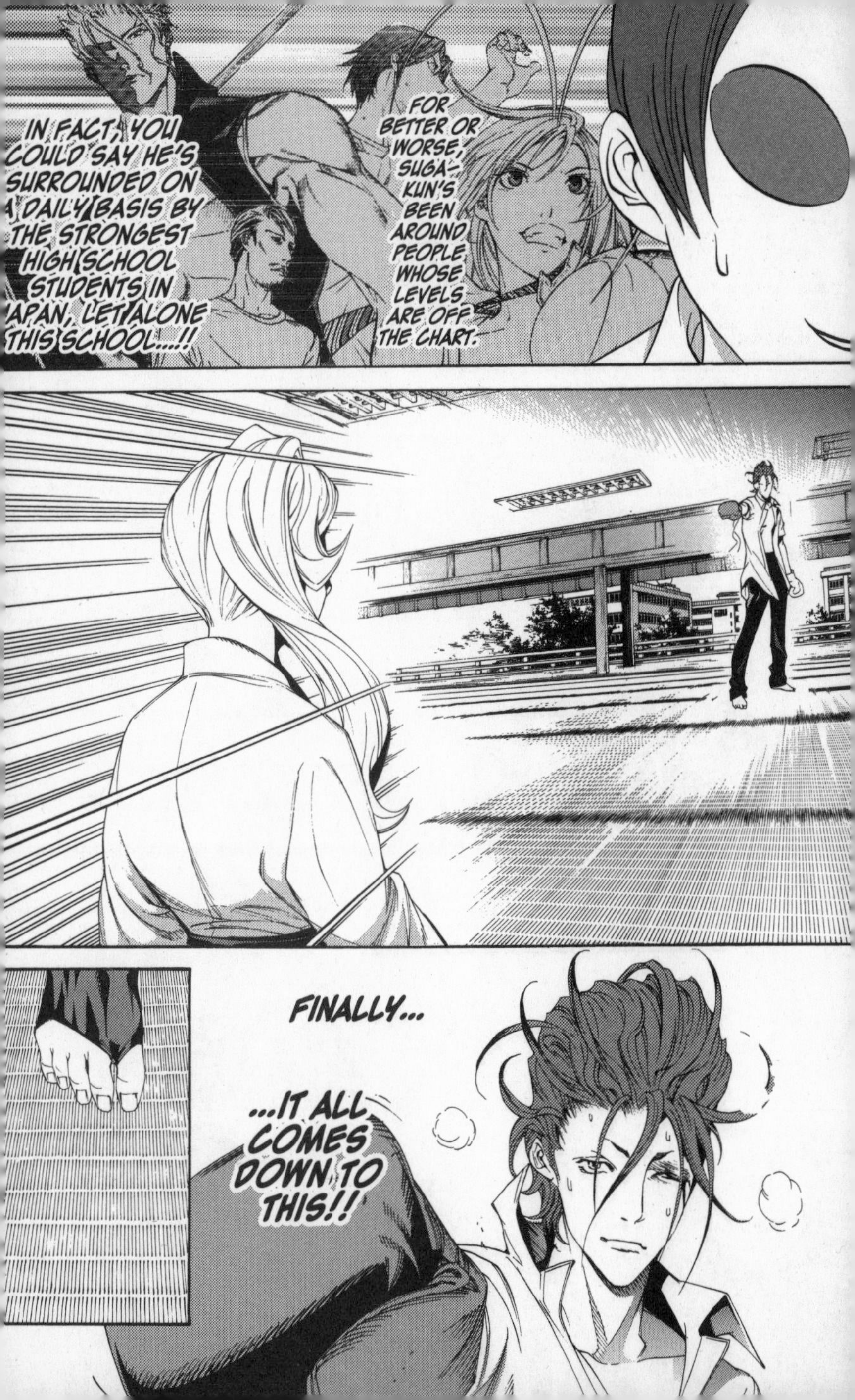
FOR BETTER OR WORSE, SUGA-KUN'S BEEN AROUND PEOPLE WHOSE LEVELS ARE OFF THE CHART.
IN FACT, YOU COULD SAY HE'S SURROUNDED ON A DAILY BASIS BY THE STRONGEST HIGH SCHOOL STUDENTS IN JAPAN, LET ALONE THIS SCHOOL...!!
FINALLY...
...IT ALL COMES DOWN TO THIS!!

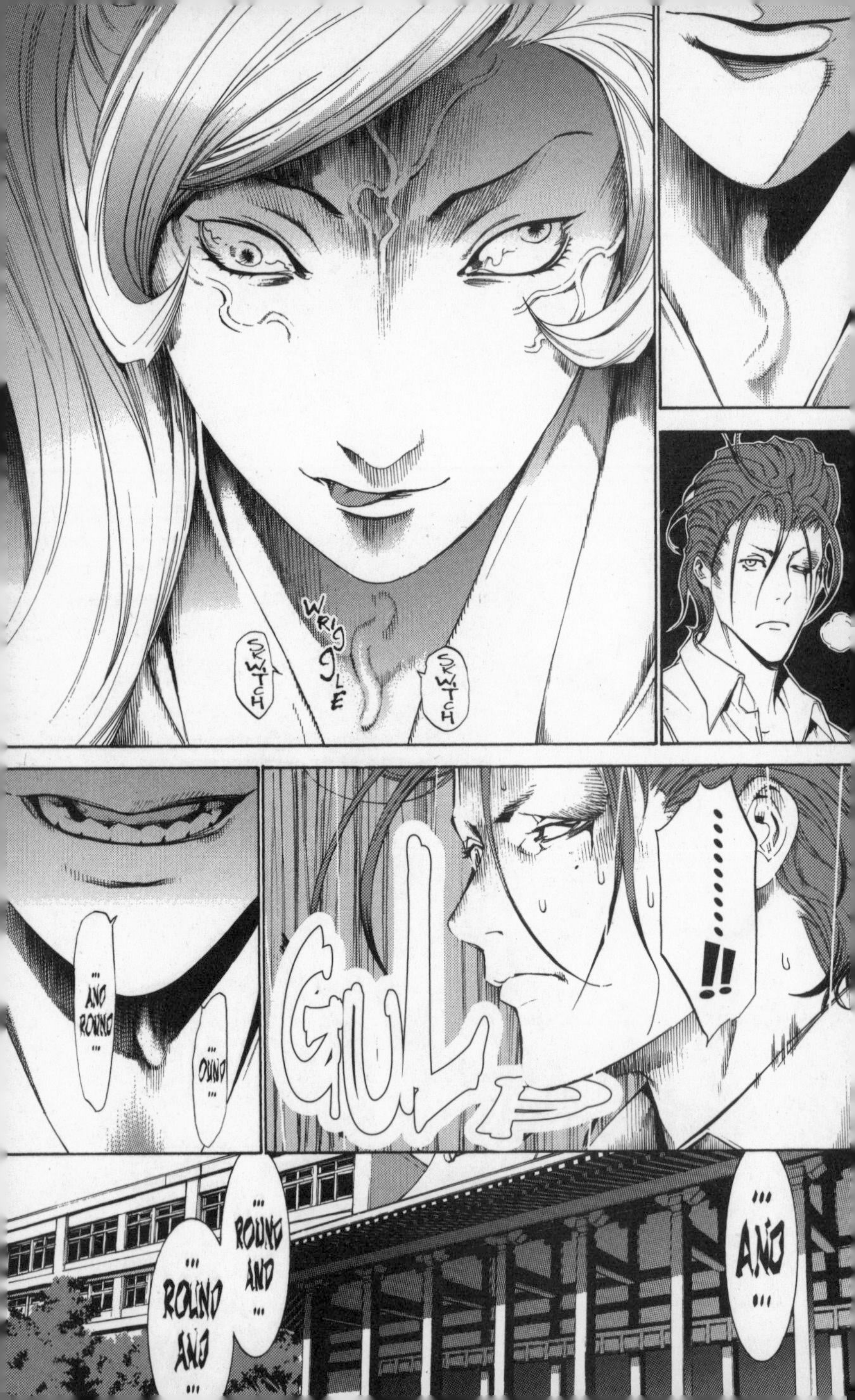
SKWITCH
WRIGGLE
SKWITCH
......!!
GULP
...AND ROUND...
...OUND...
...AND...
...ROUND AND...
...ROUND AND...

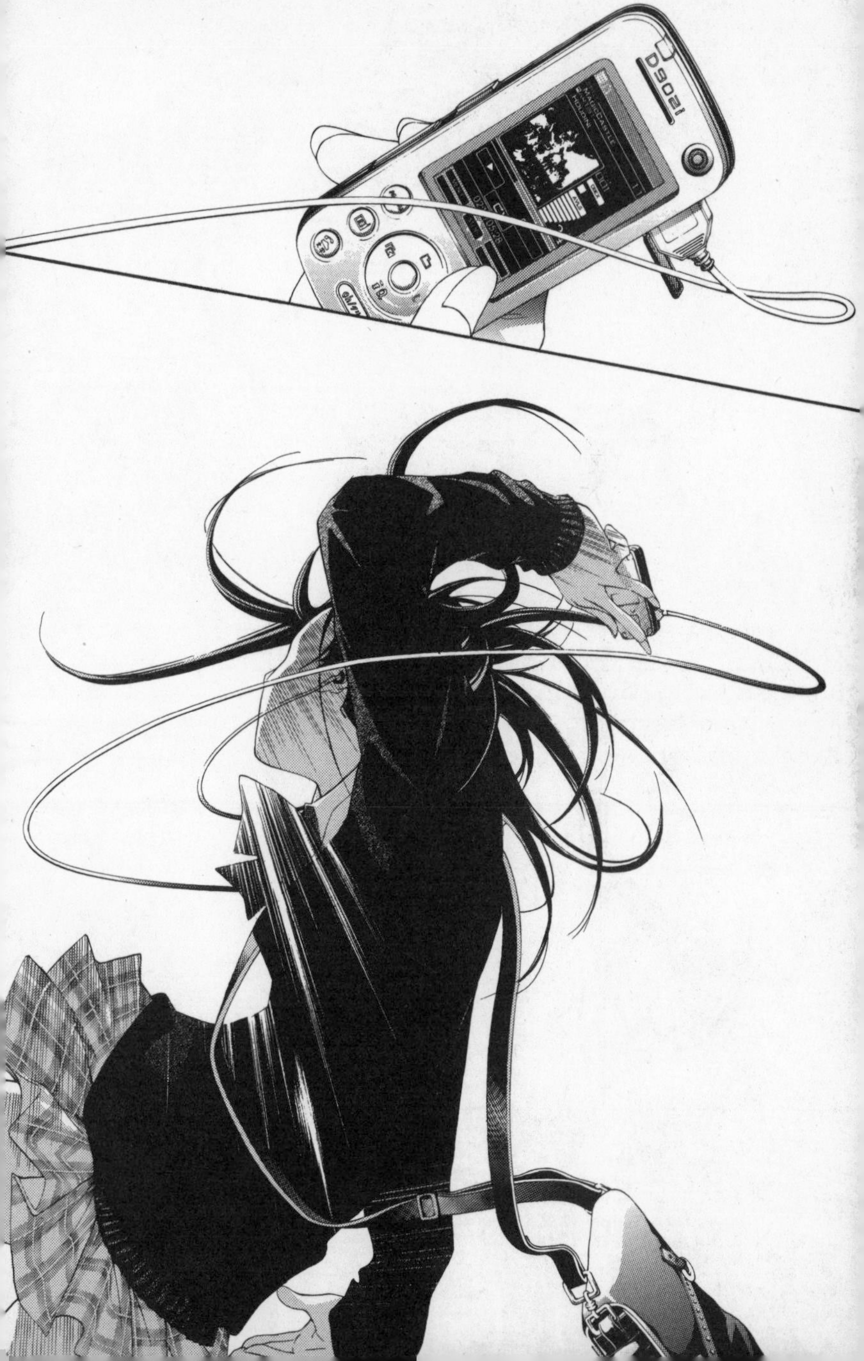

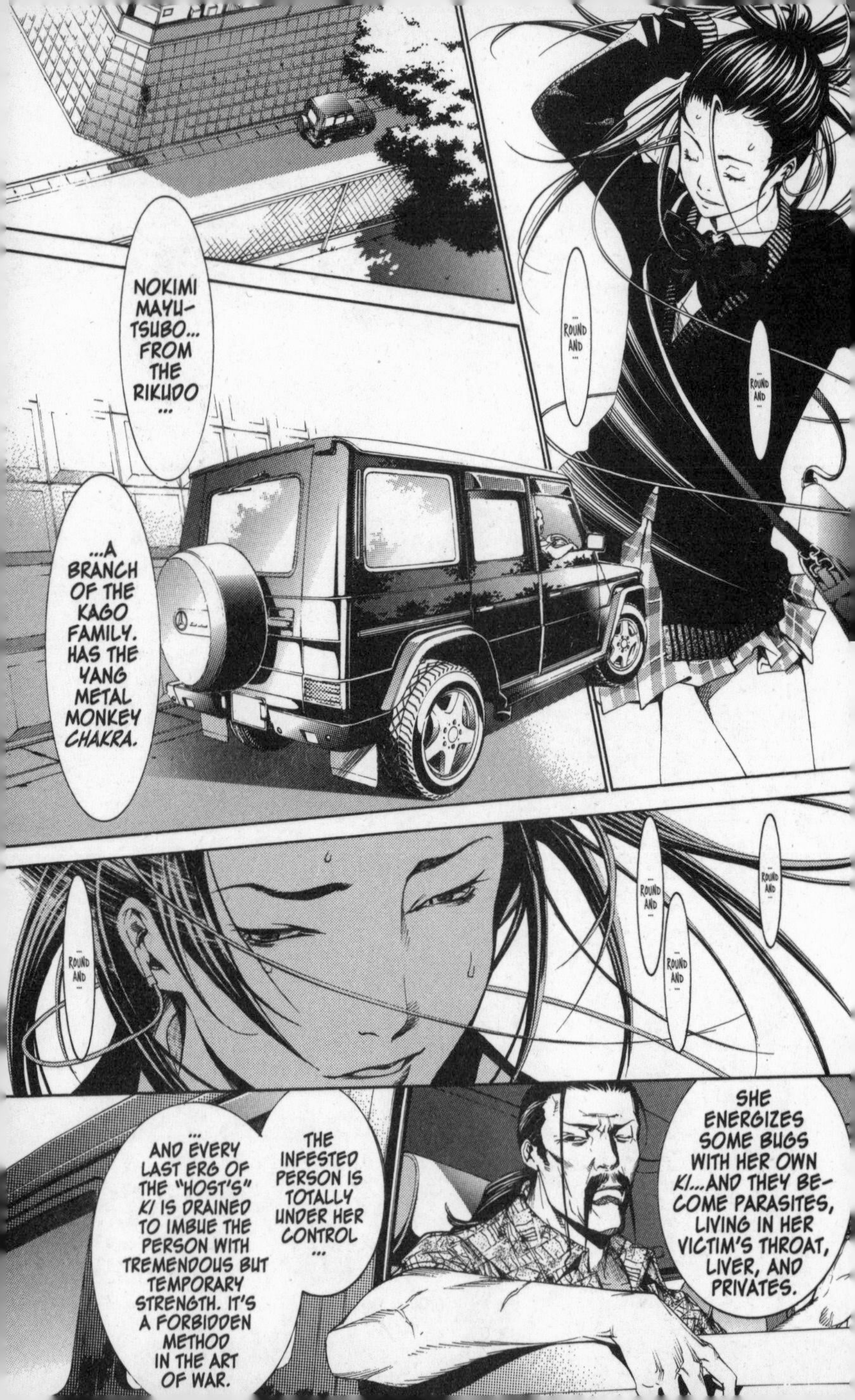
...ROUND AND...
...ROUND AND...
NOKIMI MAYU-TSUBO... FROM THE RIKUDO...
...A BRANCH OF THE KAGO FAMILY. HAS THE YANG METAL MONKEY CHAKRA.
...ROUND AND...
...ROUND AND...
...ROUND AND...
...ROUND AND...
SHE ENERGIZES SOME BUGS WITH HER OWN KI...AND THEY BE-COME PARASITES, LIVING IN HER VICTIM'S THROAT, LIVER, AND PRIVATES.
THE INFESTED PERSON IS TOTALLY UNDER HER CONTROL...
...AND EVERY LAST ERG OF THE "HOST'S" KI IS DRAINED TO IMBUE THE PERSON WITH TREMENDOUS BUT TEMPORARY STRENGTH. IT'S A FORBIDDEN METHOD IN THE ART OF WAR.

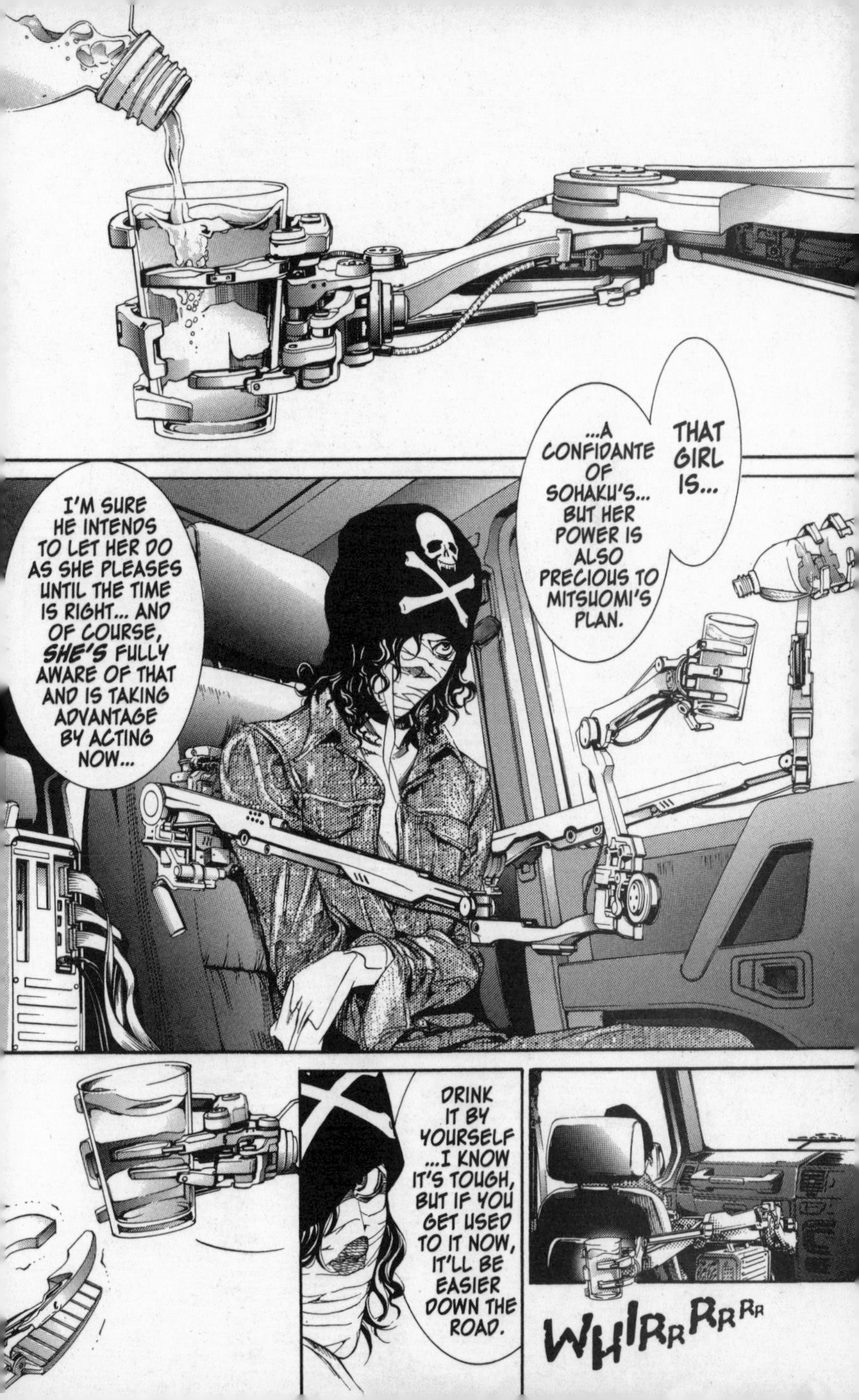
THAT GIRL IS...
...A CONFIDANTE OF SOHAKU'S... BUT HER POWER IS ALSO PRECIOUS TO MITSUOMI'S PLAN.
I'M SURE HE INTENDS TO LET HER DO AS SHE PLEASES UNTIL THE TIME IS RIGHT... AND OF COURSE, *SHE'S* FULLY AWARE OF THAT AND IS TAKING ADVANTAGE BY ACTING NOW...
WHIRRRRR
DRINK IT BY YOURSELF ...I KNOW IT'S TOUGH, BUT IF YOU GET USED TO IT NOW, IT'LL BE EASIER DOWN THE ROAD.

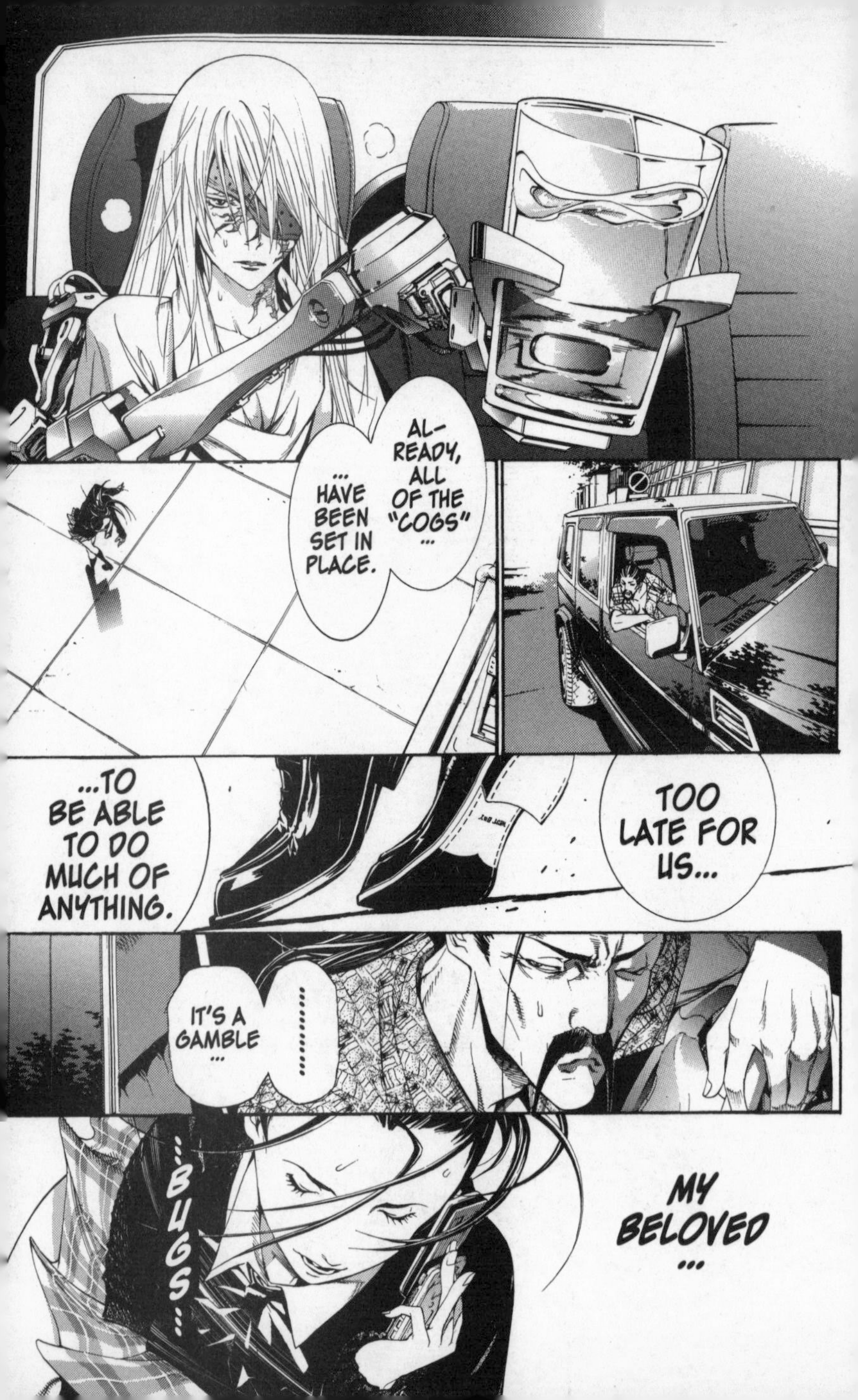
ALREADY, ALL OF THE "COGS"...
...HAVE BEEN SET IN PLACE.
TOO LATE FOR US...
...TO BE ABLE TO DO MUCH OF ANYTHING.
....
IT'S A GAMBLE...
MY BELOVED...
...BUGS...

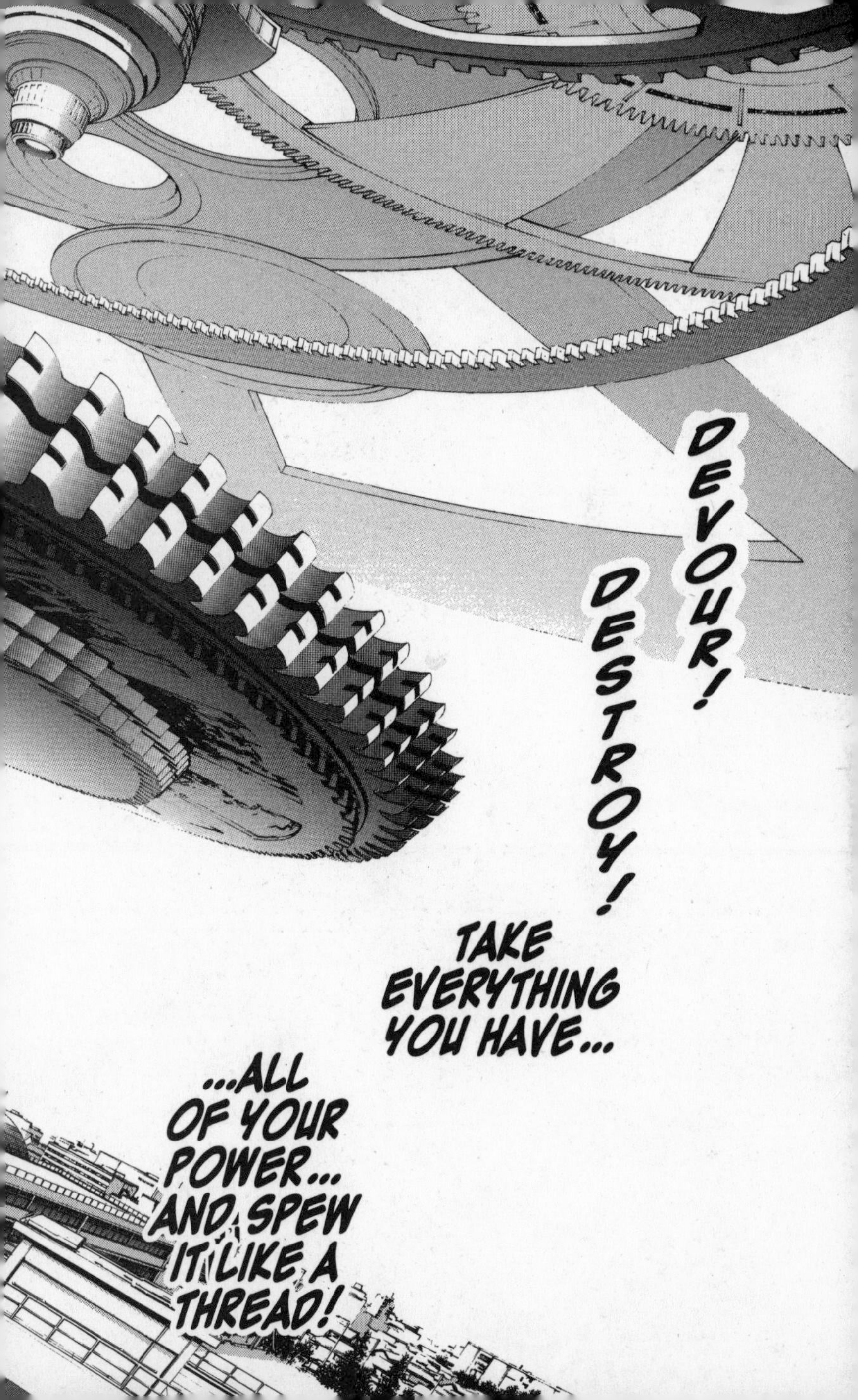
DEVOUR!
DESTROY!
TAKE EVERYTHING YOU HAVE...
...ALL OF YOUR POWER... AND SPEW IT LIKE A THREAD!

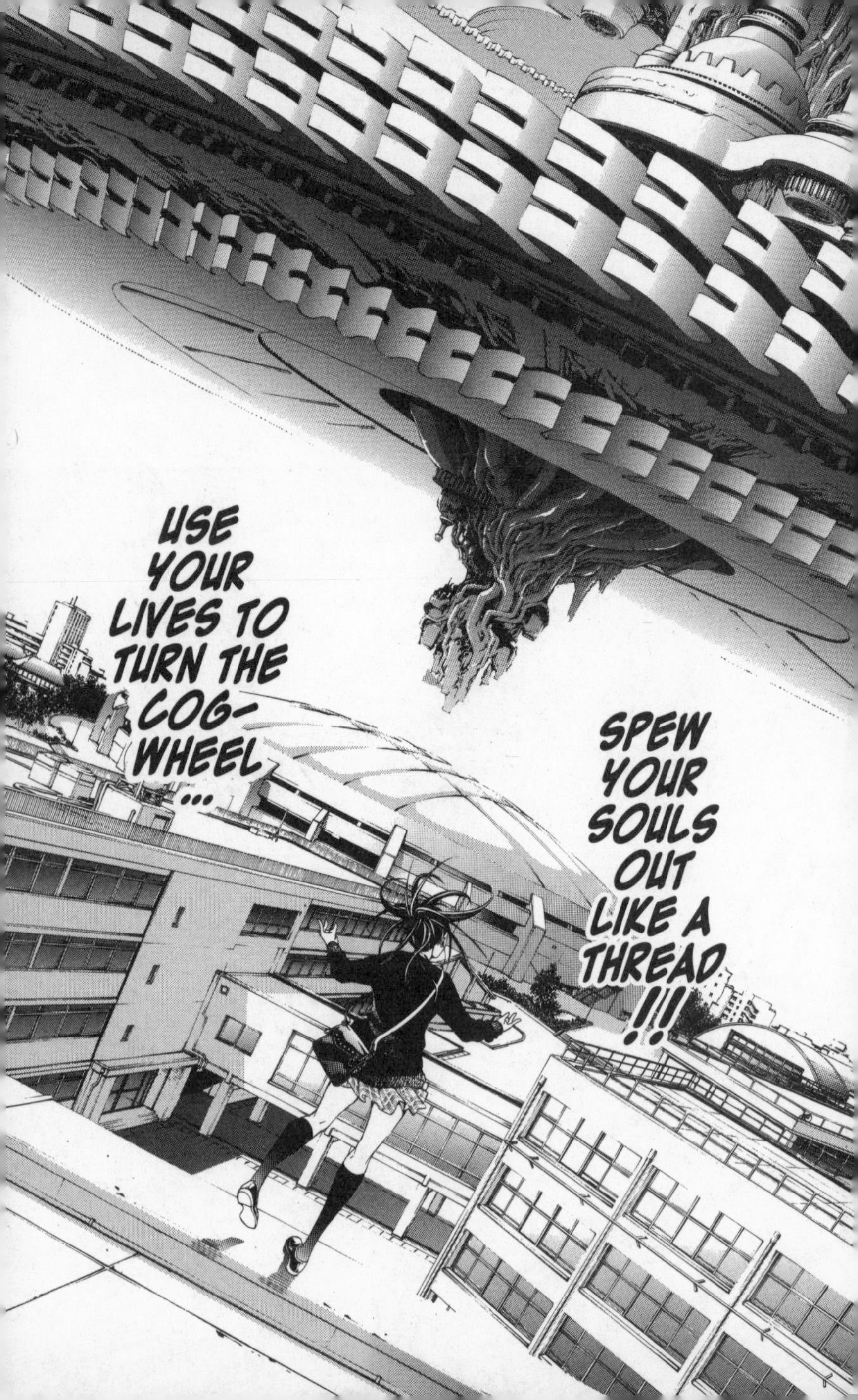
USE YOUR LIVES TO TURN THE COG-WHEEL...
SPEW YOUR SOULS OUT LIKE A THREAD!!

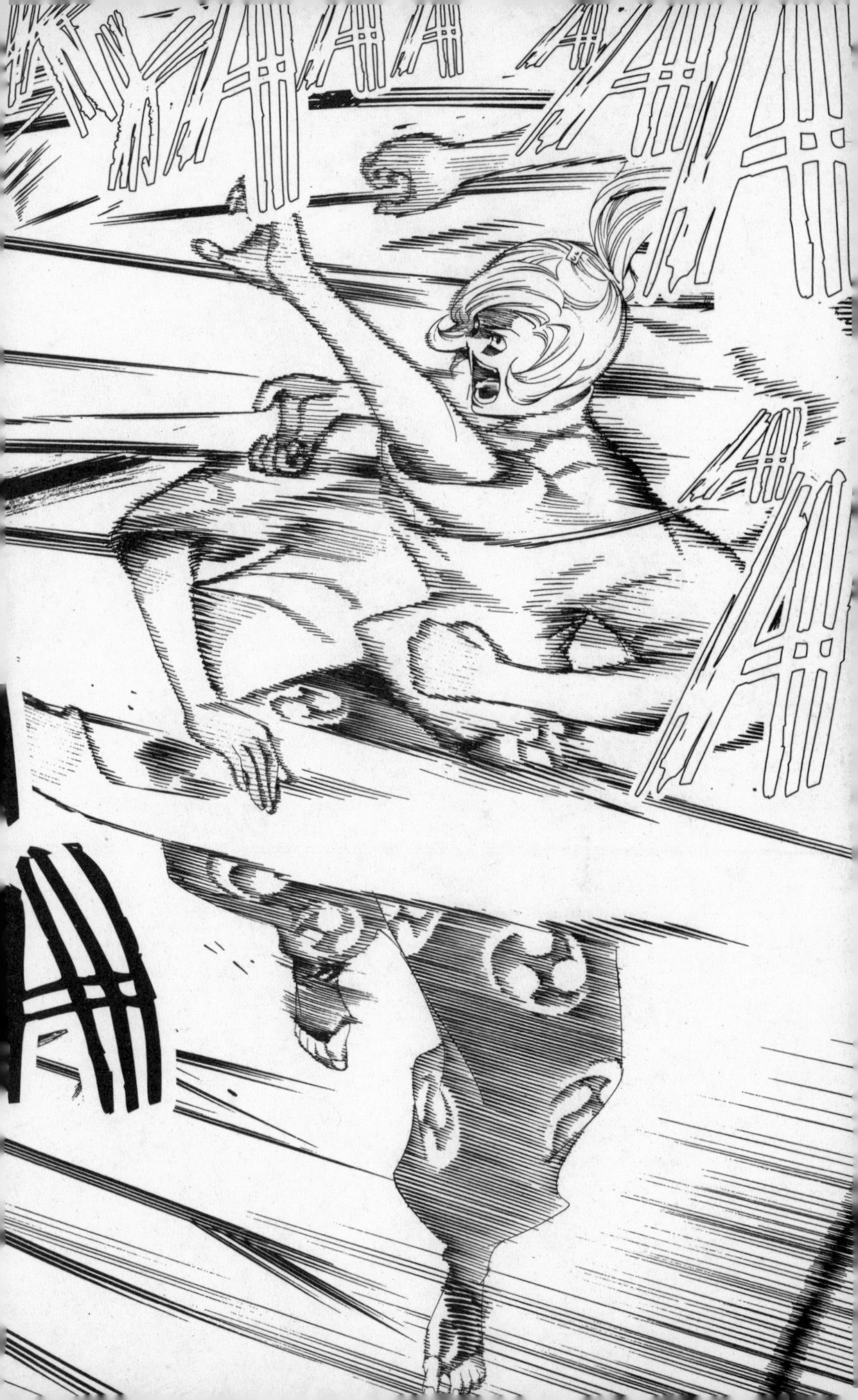
KYAAAA AAAAAAA!!

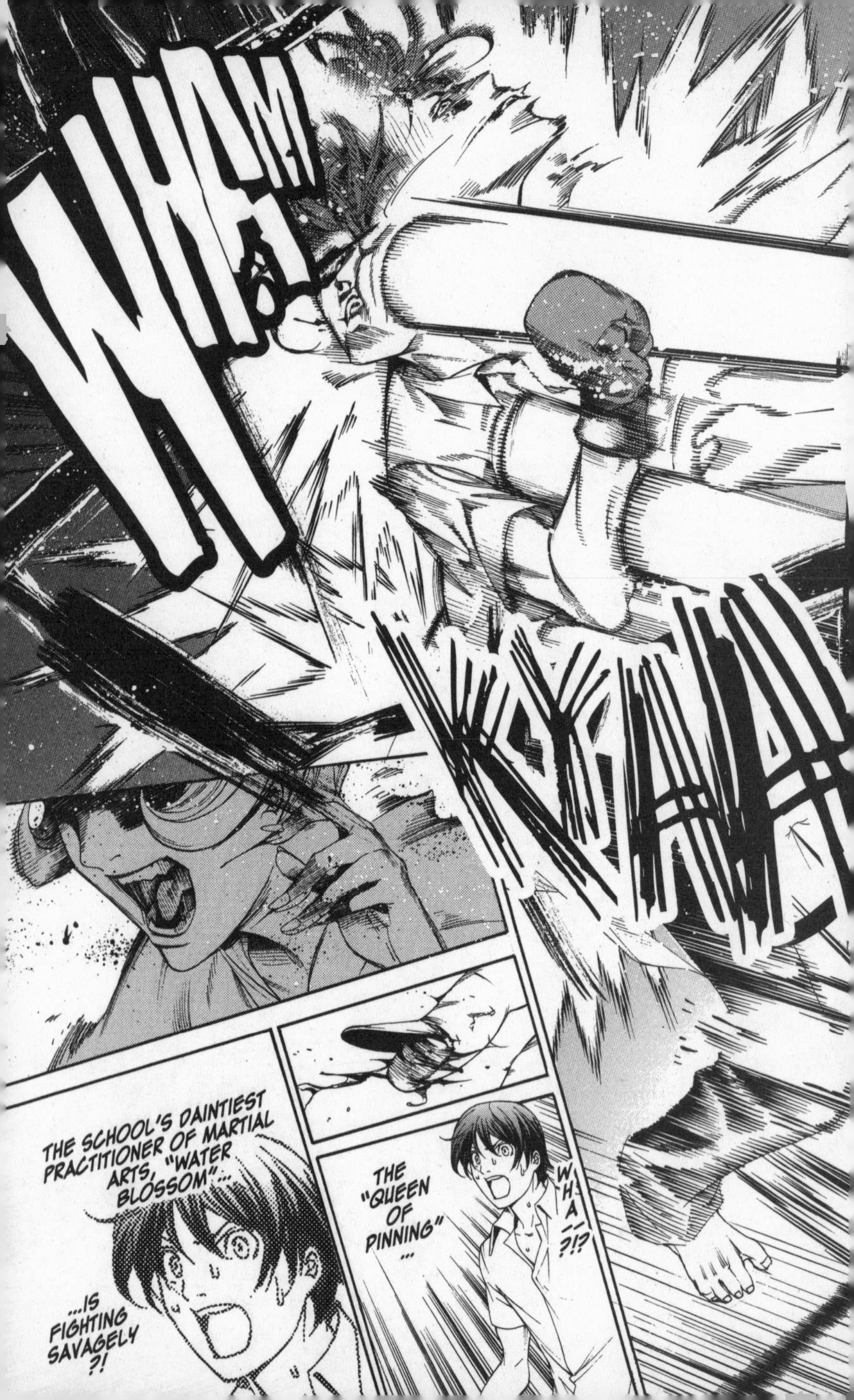
WHAM
WHA--?!?
THE "QUEEN OF PINNING"...
THE SCHOOL'S DAINTIEST PRACTITIONER OF MARTIAL ARTS, "WATER BLOSSOM"...
...IS FIGHTING SAVAGELY?!

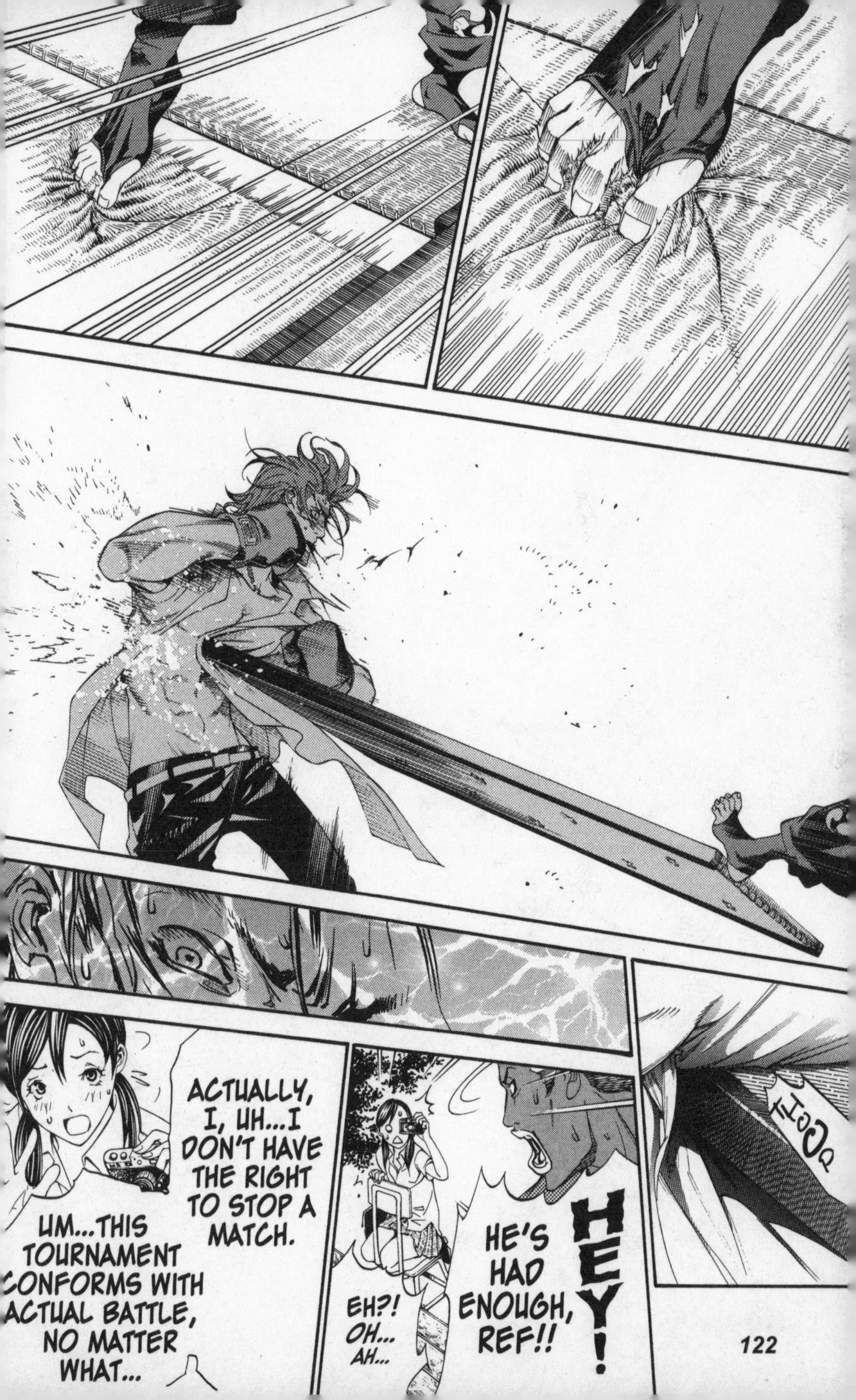
HEY!
HE'S HAD ENOUGH, REF!!
EH?! OH... AH...
ACTUALLY, I, UH...I DON'T HAVE THE RIGHT TO STOP A MATCH.
UM...THIS TOURNAMENT CONFORMS WITH ACTUAL BATTLE, NO MATTER WHAT...

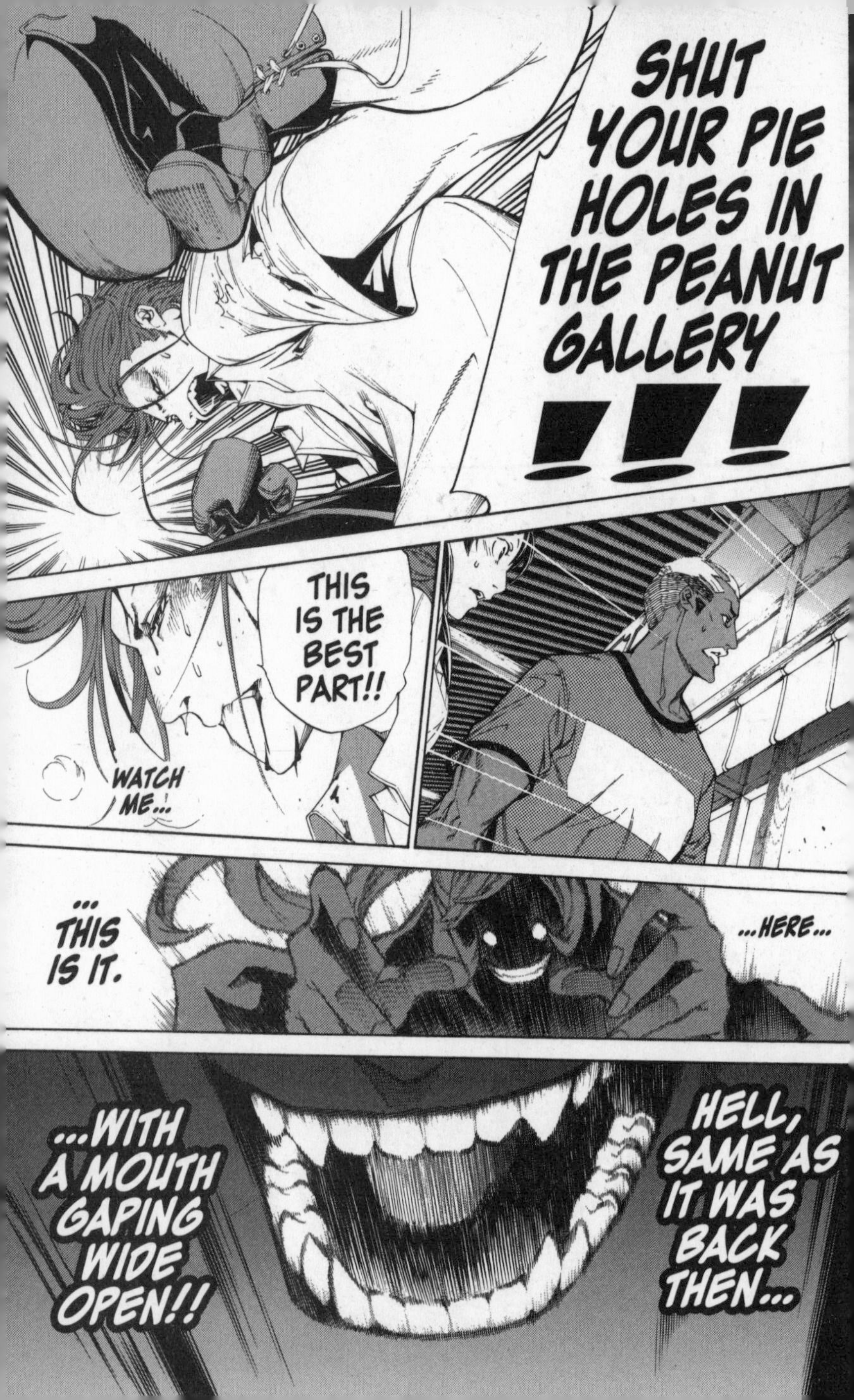
SHUT YOUR PIE HOLES IN THE PEANUT GALLERY!!!
THIS IS THE BEST PART!!
WATCH ME...
...HERE...
...THIS IS IT.
HELL, SAME AS IT WAS BACK THEN...
...WITH A MOUTH GAPING WIDE OPEN!!

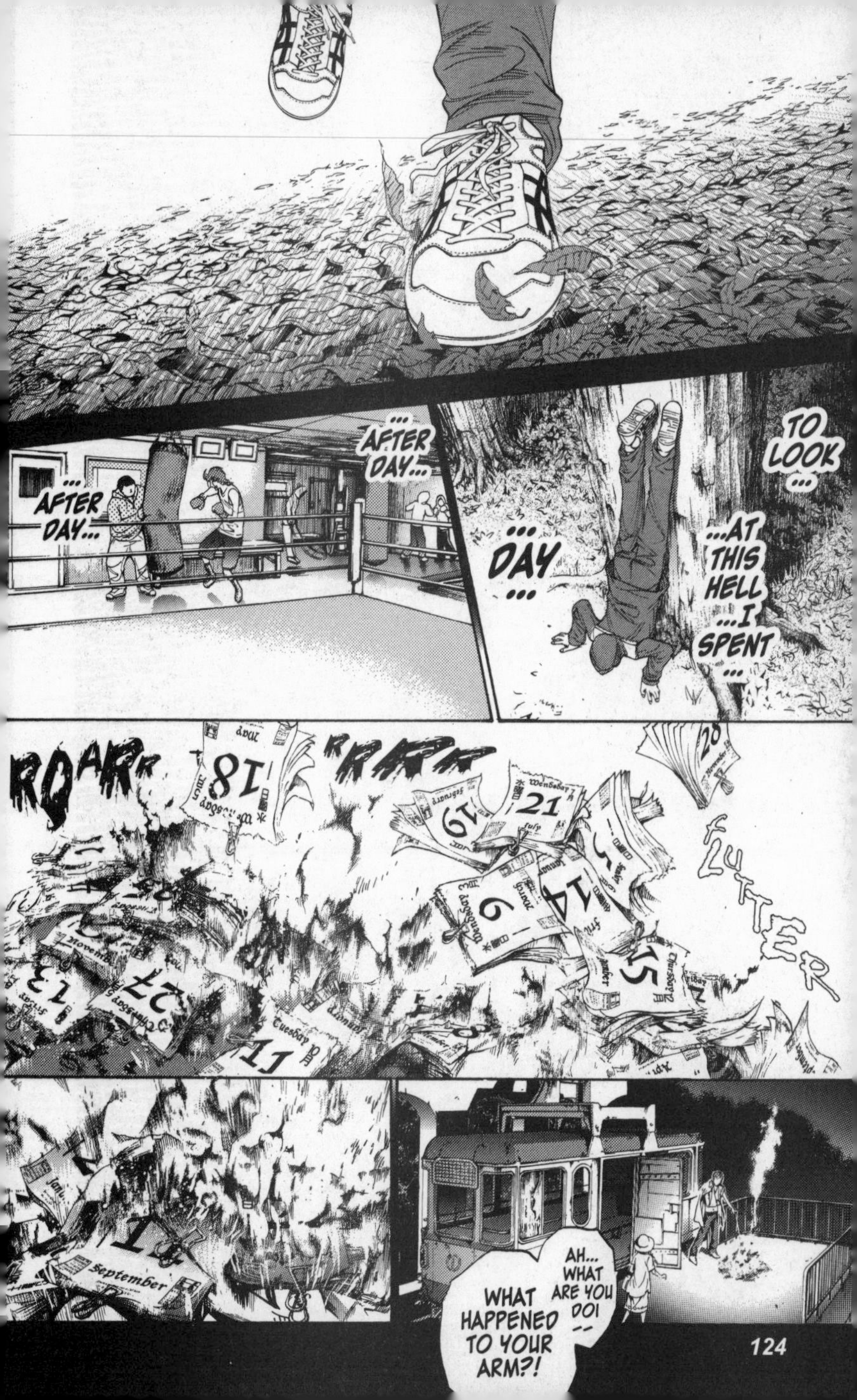
TO LOOK ...
...AT THIS HELL ...I SPENT ...
...DAY ...
...AFTER DAY...
...AFTER DAY...
FLUTTER
RRARR
ROARR
AH... WHAT ARE YOU DOI --
WHAT HAPPENED TO YOUR ARM?!

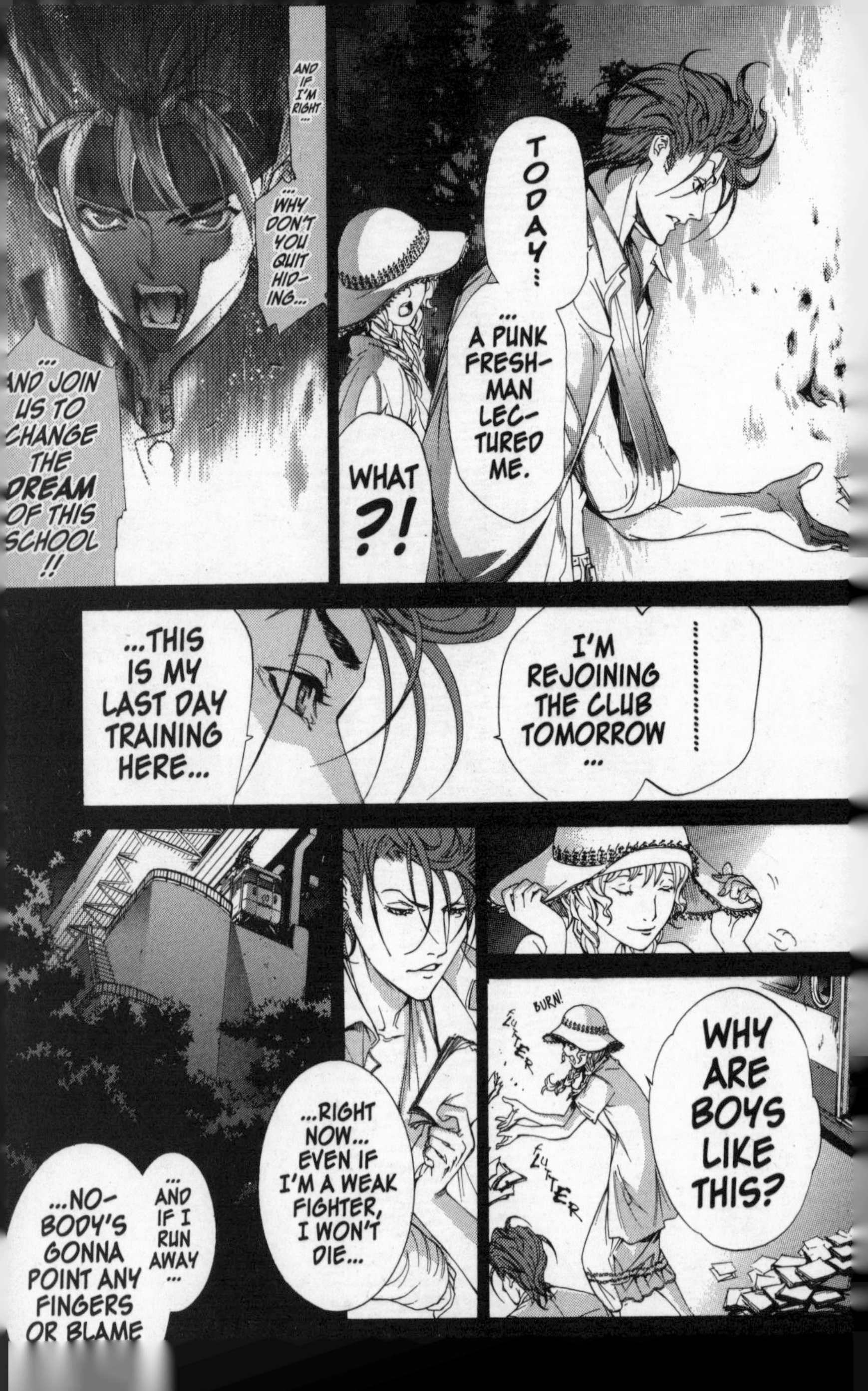
TODAY...
...A PUNK FRESHMAN LECTURED ME.
WHAT ?!
AND IF I'M RIGHT...
...WHY DON'T YOU QUIT HIDING...
...AND JOIN US TO CHANGE THE DREAM OF THIS SCHOOL!!
......
I'M REJOINING THE CLUB TOMORROW...
...THIS IS MY LAST DAY TRAINING HERE...
BURN!
FLUTTER
WHY ARE BOYS LIKE THIS?
FLUTTER
...RIGHT NOW... EVEN IF I'M A WEAK FIGHTER, I WON'T DIE...
...AND IF I RUN AWAY...
...NOBODY'S GONNA POINT ANY FINGERS OR BLAME

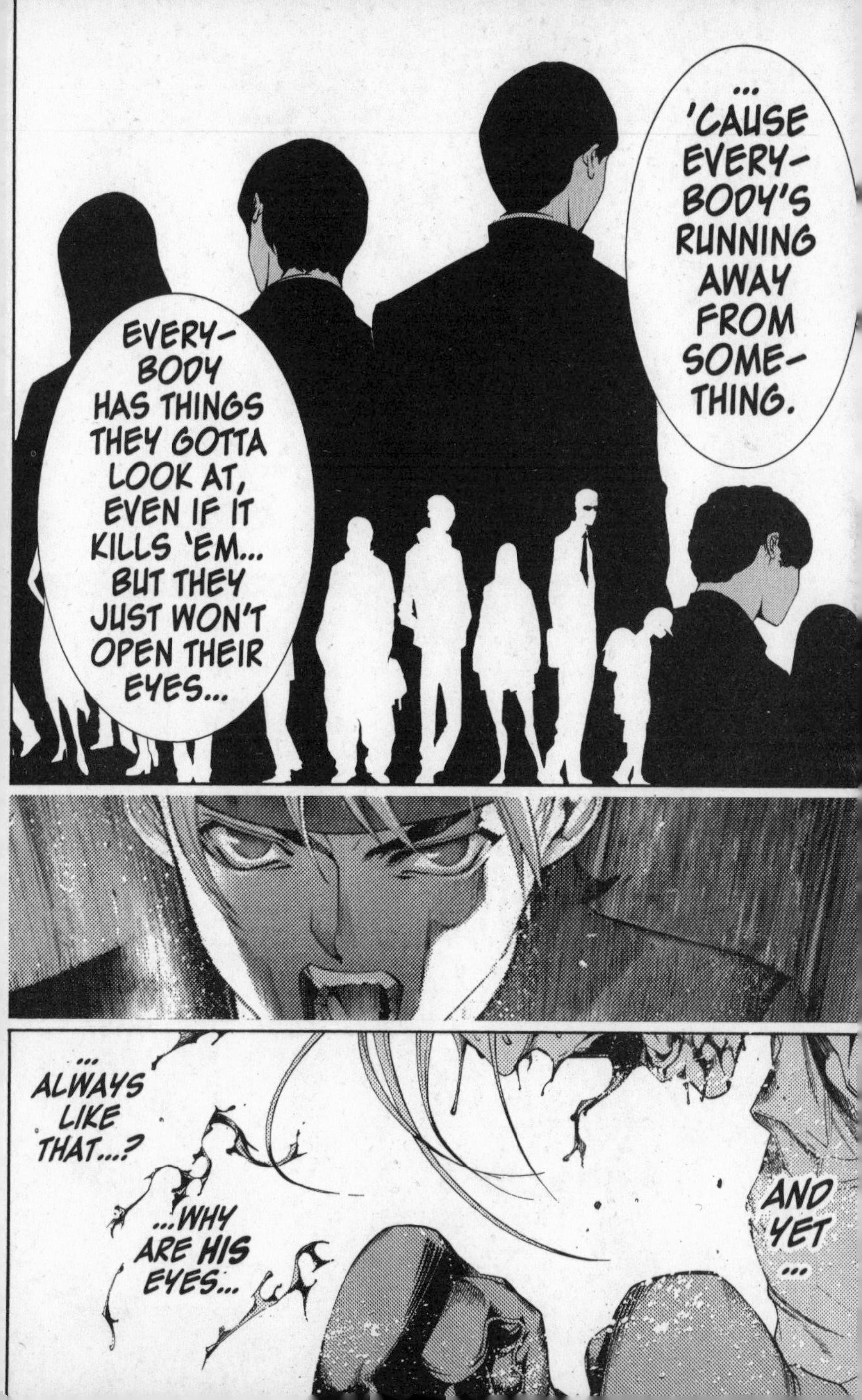
...'CAUSE EVERYBODY'S RUNNING AWAY FROM SOMETHING.
EVERYBODY HAS THINGS THEY GOTTA LOOK AT, EVEN IF IT KILLS 'EM... BUT THEY JUST WON'T OPEN THEIR EYES...
AND YET...
...WHY ARE HIS EYES...
...ALWAYS LIKE THAT...?

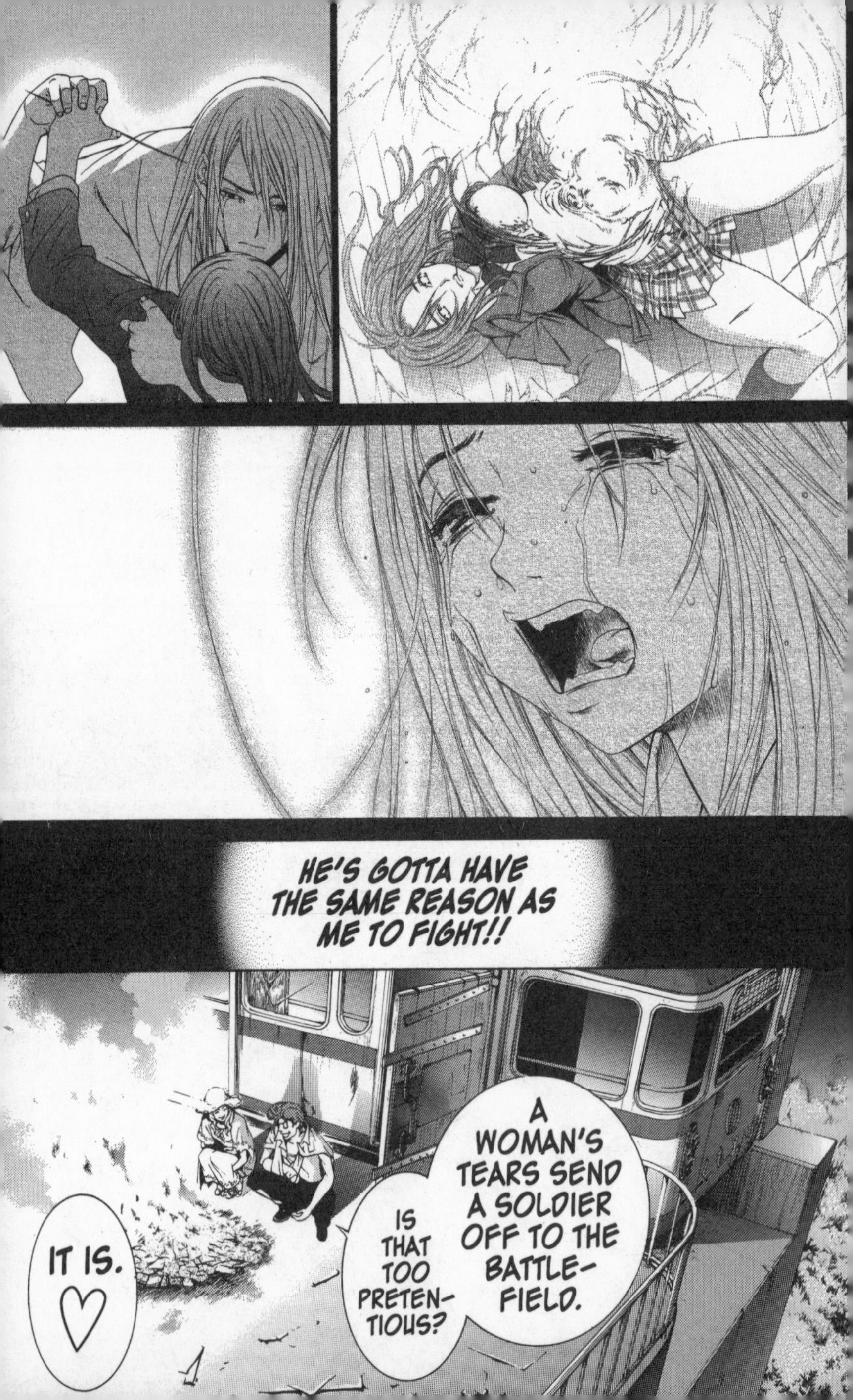
HE'S GOTTA HAVE THE SAME REASON AS ME TO FIGHT!!
A WOMAN'S TEARS SEND A SOLDIER OFF TO THE BATTLE-FIELD.
IS THAT TOO PRETEN-TIOUS?
IT IS. ♡

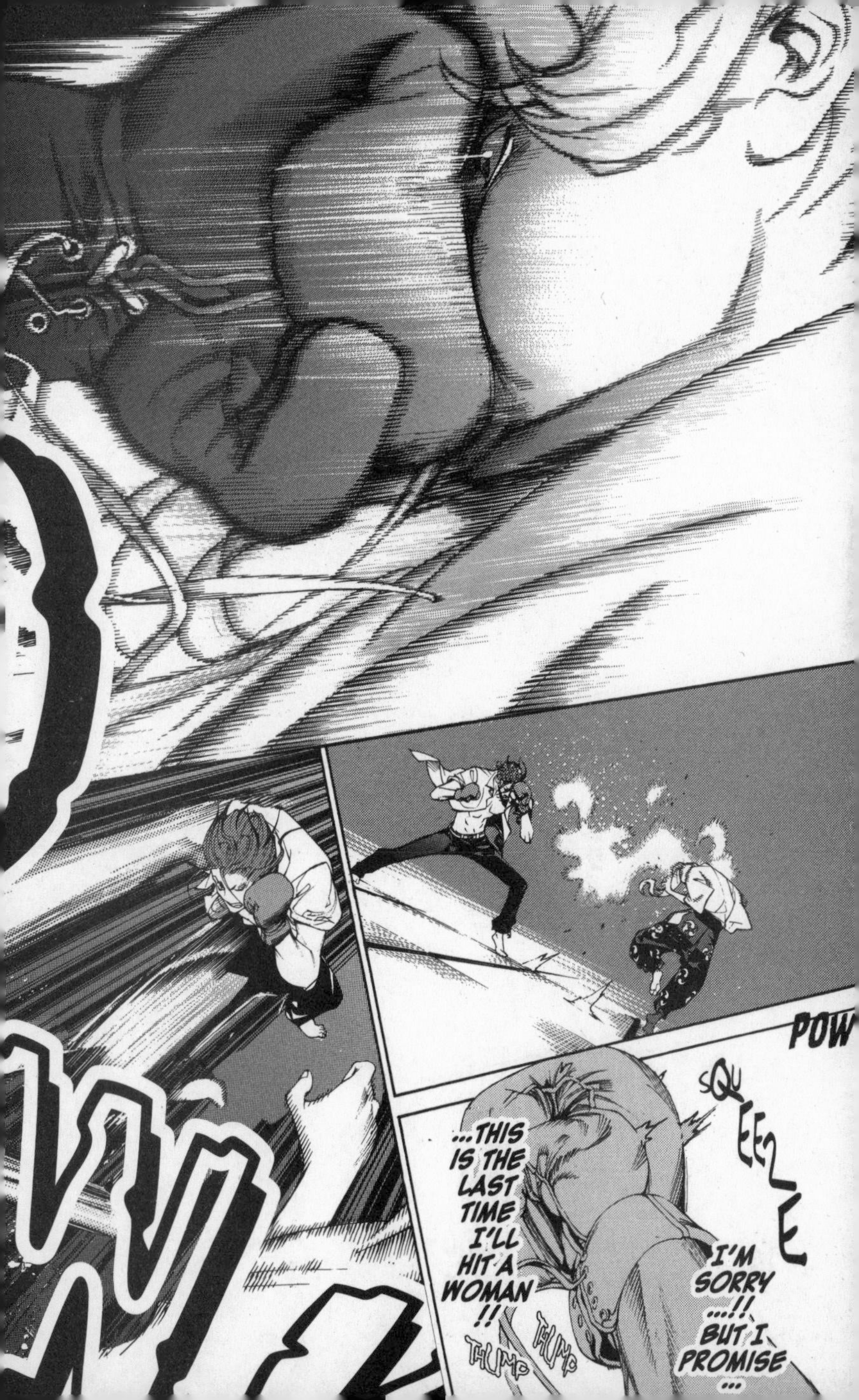
POW
SQUEEZE
I'M SORRY ...!! BUT I PROMISE ...
...THIS IS THE LAST TIME I'LL HIT A WOMAN !!
THUMP
THUMP

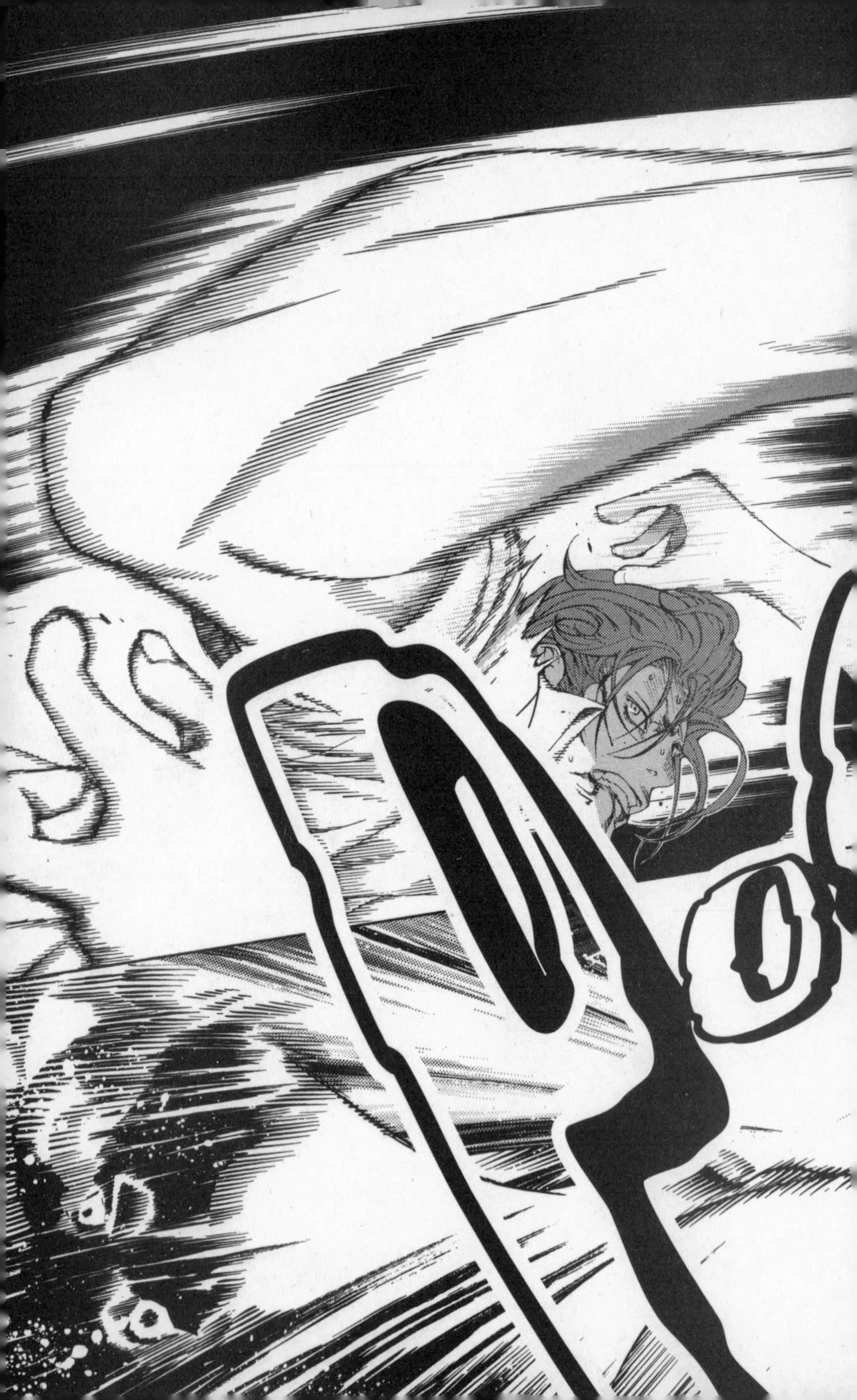

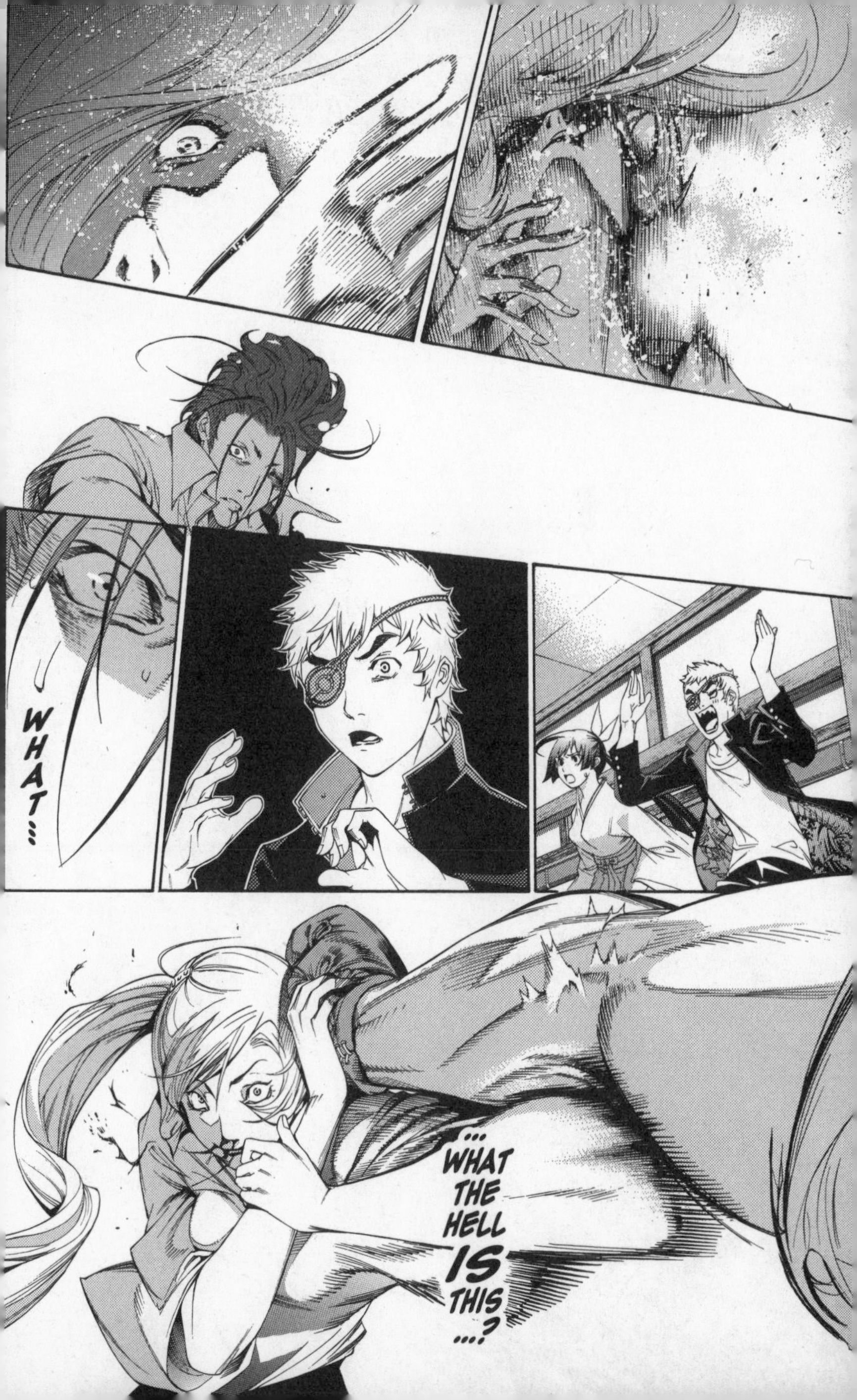
WHAT...!?
...WHAT THE HELL IS THIS...?

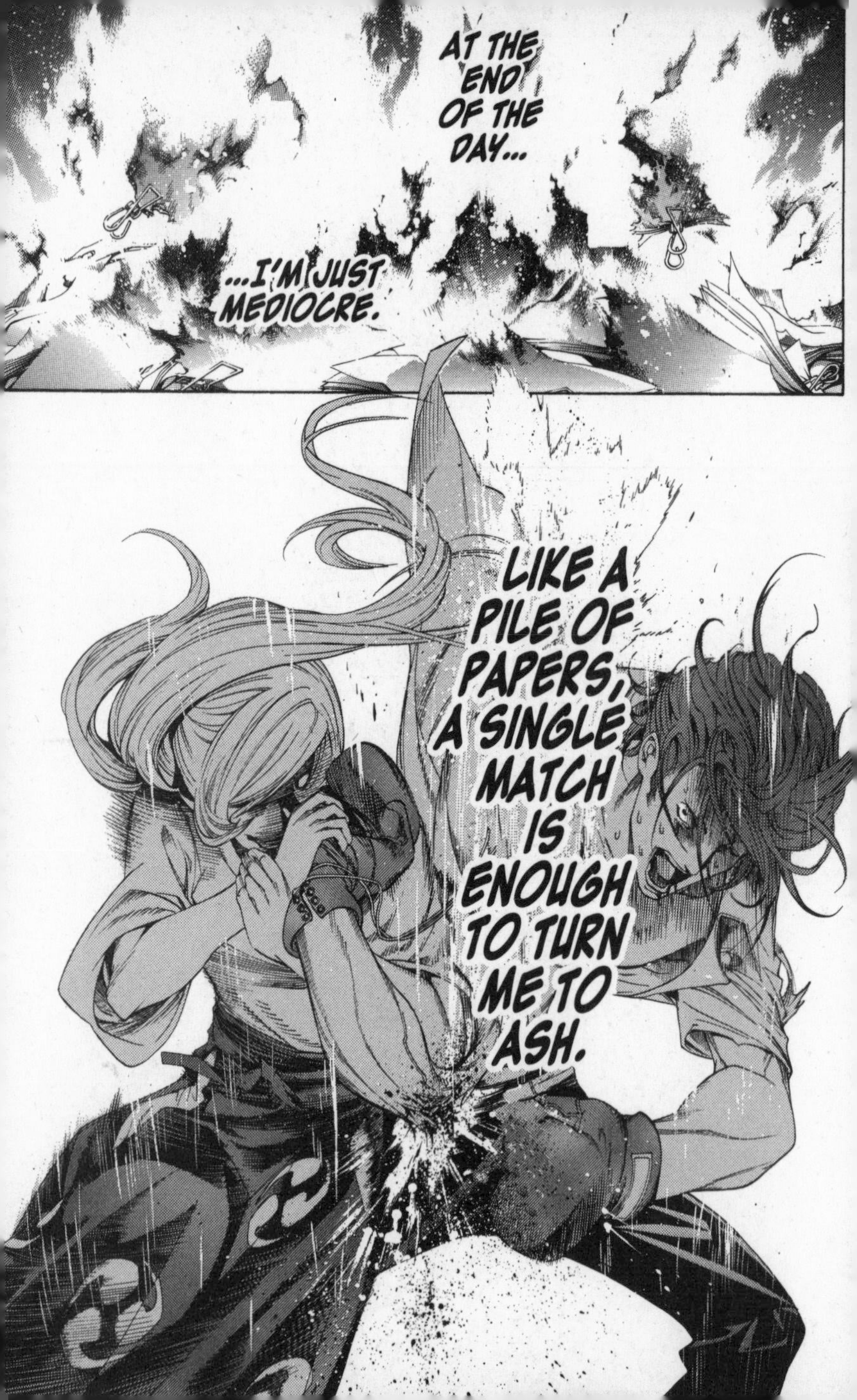
AT THE END OF THE DAY...
...I'M JUST MEDIOCRE.
LIKE A PILE OF PAPERS, A SINGLE MATCH IS ENOUGH TO TURN ME TO ASH.

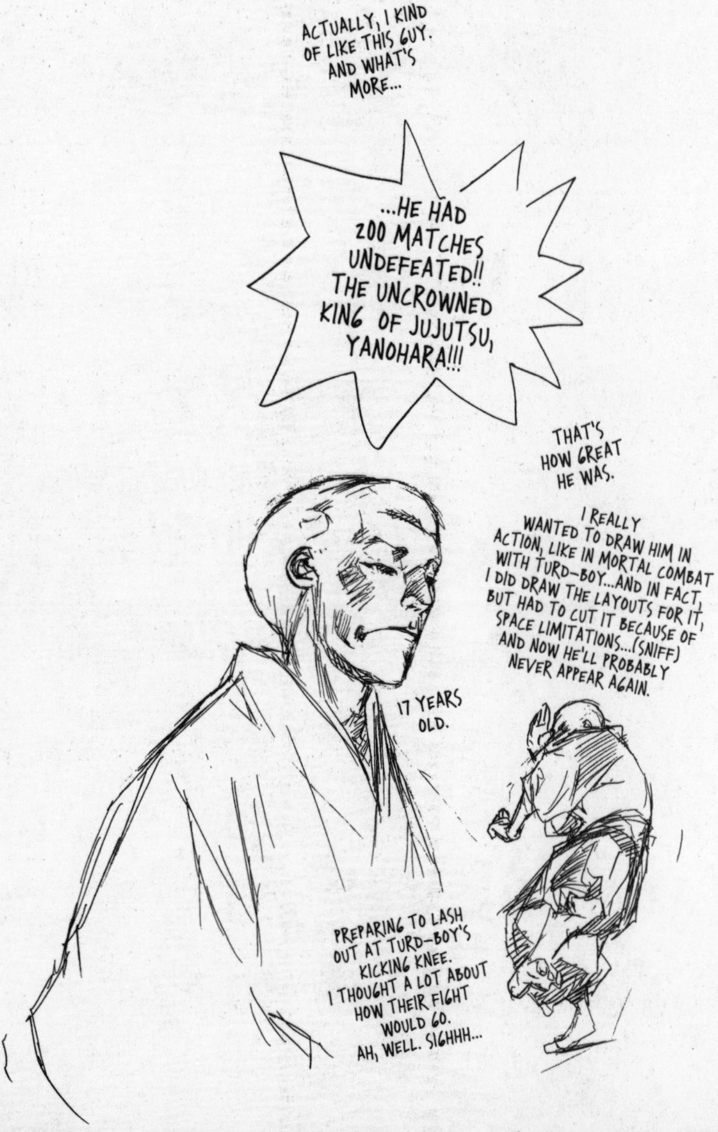
ACTUALLY, I KIND OF LIKE THIS GUY. AND WHAT'S MORE...
...HE HAD 200 MATCHES UNDEFEATED!! THE UNCROWNED KING OF JUJUTSU, YANOHARA!!!
THAT'S HOW GREAT HE WAS.
I REALLY WANTED TO DRAW HIM IN ACTION, LIKE IN MORTAL COMBAT WITH TURD-BOY...AND IN FACT, I DID DRAW THE LAYOUTS FOR IT, BUT HAD TO CUT IT BECAUSE OF SPACE LIMITATIONS...(SNIFF) AND NOW HE'LL PROBABLY NEVER APPEAR AGAIN.
17 YEARS OLD.
PREPARING TO LASH OUT AT TURD-BOY'S KICKING KNEE. I THOUGHT A LOT ABOUT HOW THEIR FIGHT WOULD GO. AH, WELL. SIGHHH...

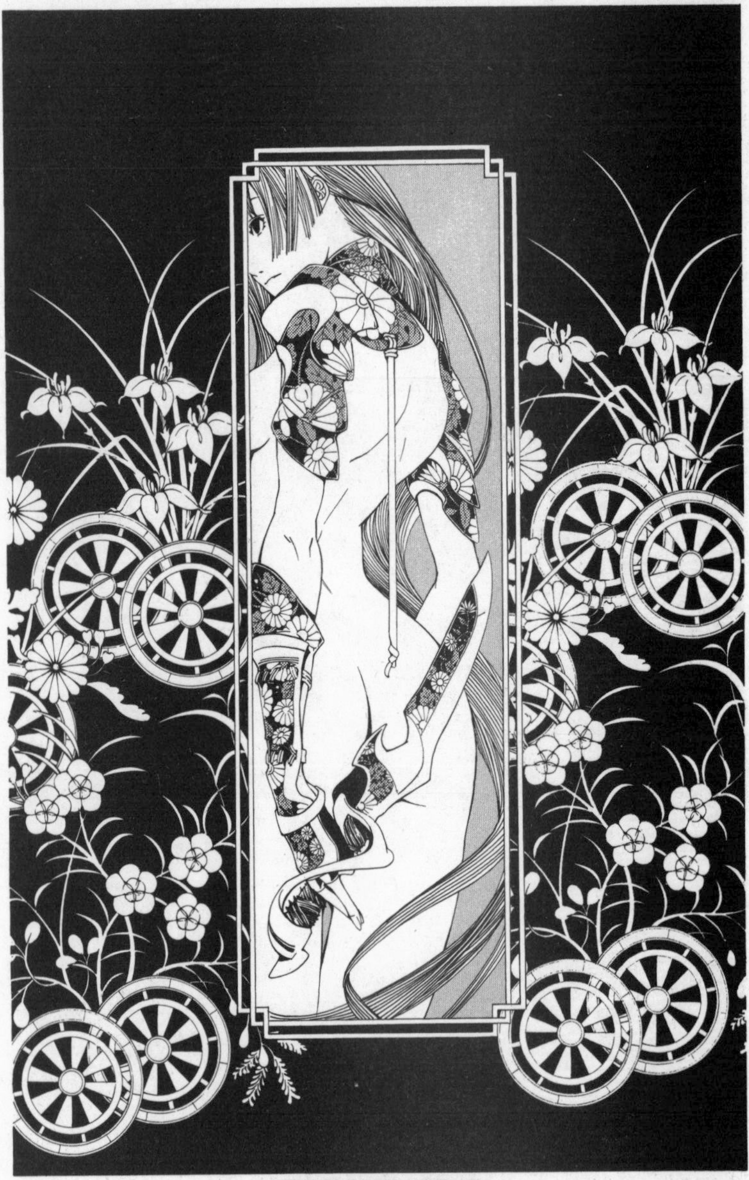

FIGHT:104

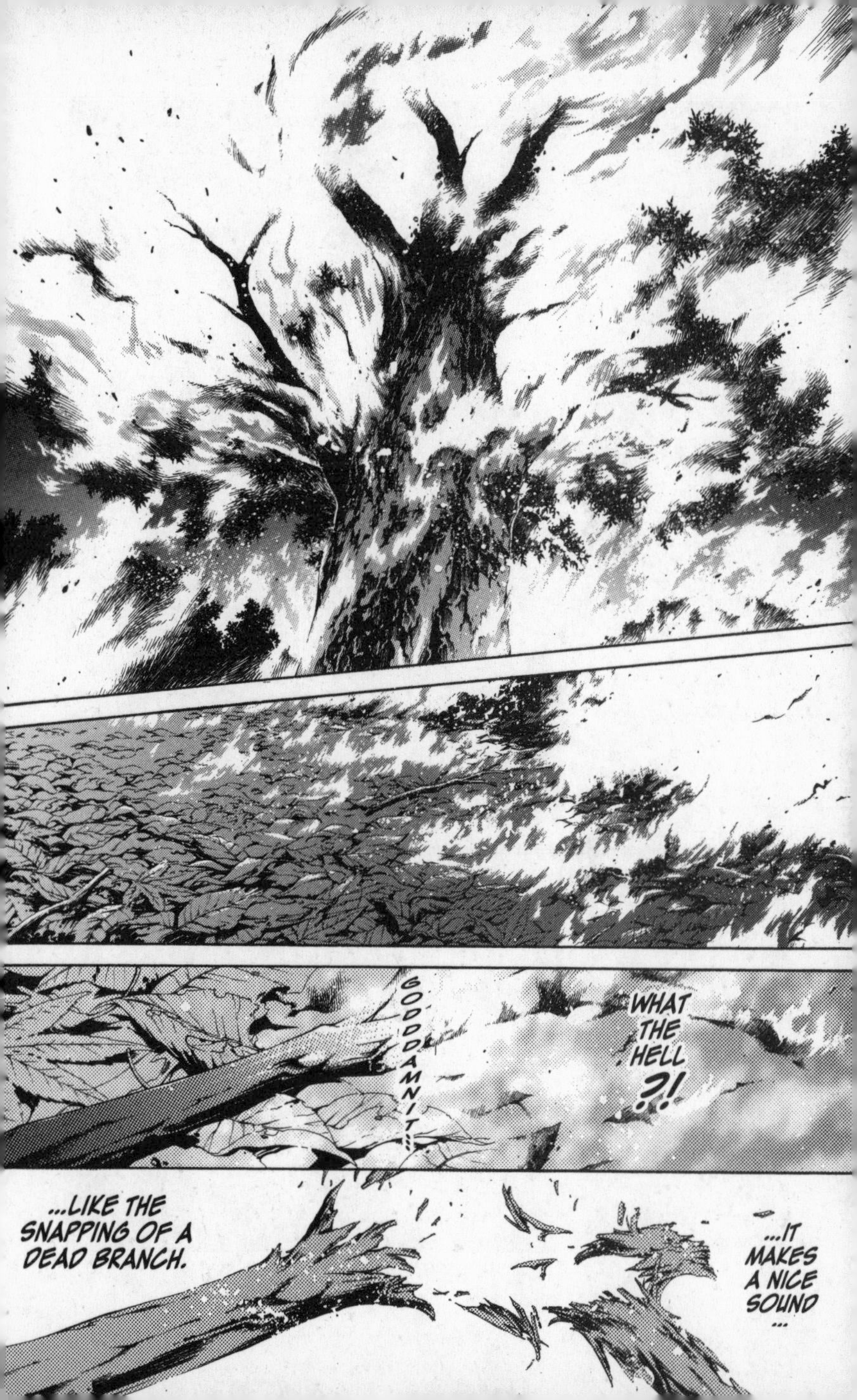
WHAT THE HELL ?!
GODDDAMNIT!!
...IT MAKES A NICE SOUND ...
...LIKE THE SNAPPING OF A DEAD BRANCH.

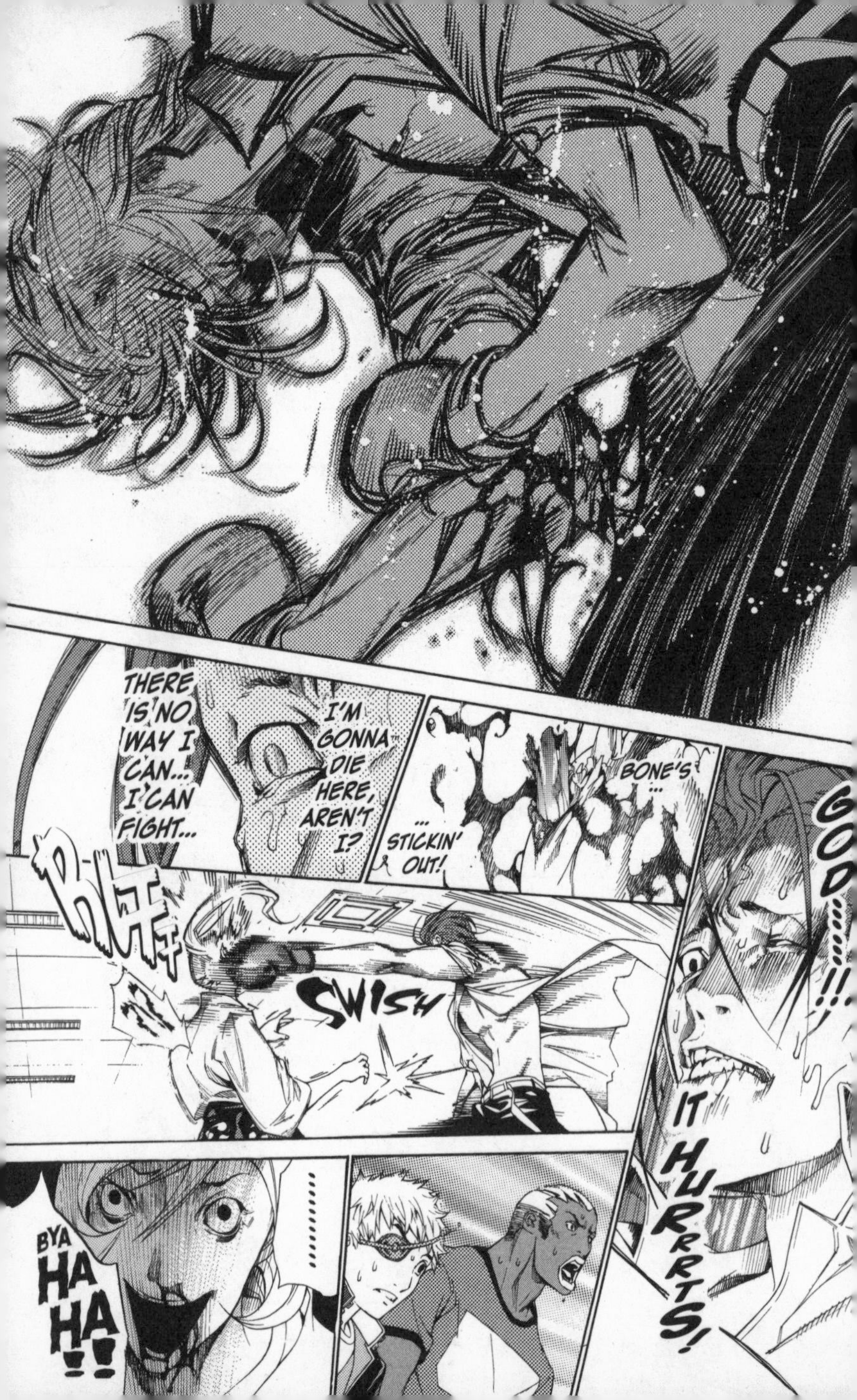
GOD.....!!
IT HURRRTS!
BONE'S...
...STICKIN' OUT!
I'M GONNA DIE HERE, AREN'T I?
THERE IS NO WAY I CAN... I CAN FIGHT...
SWISH
PAFF
......
BYA HAHAHA!!

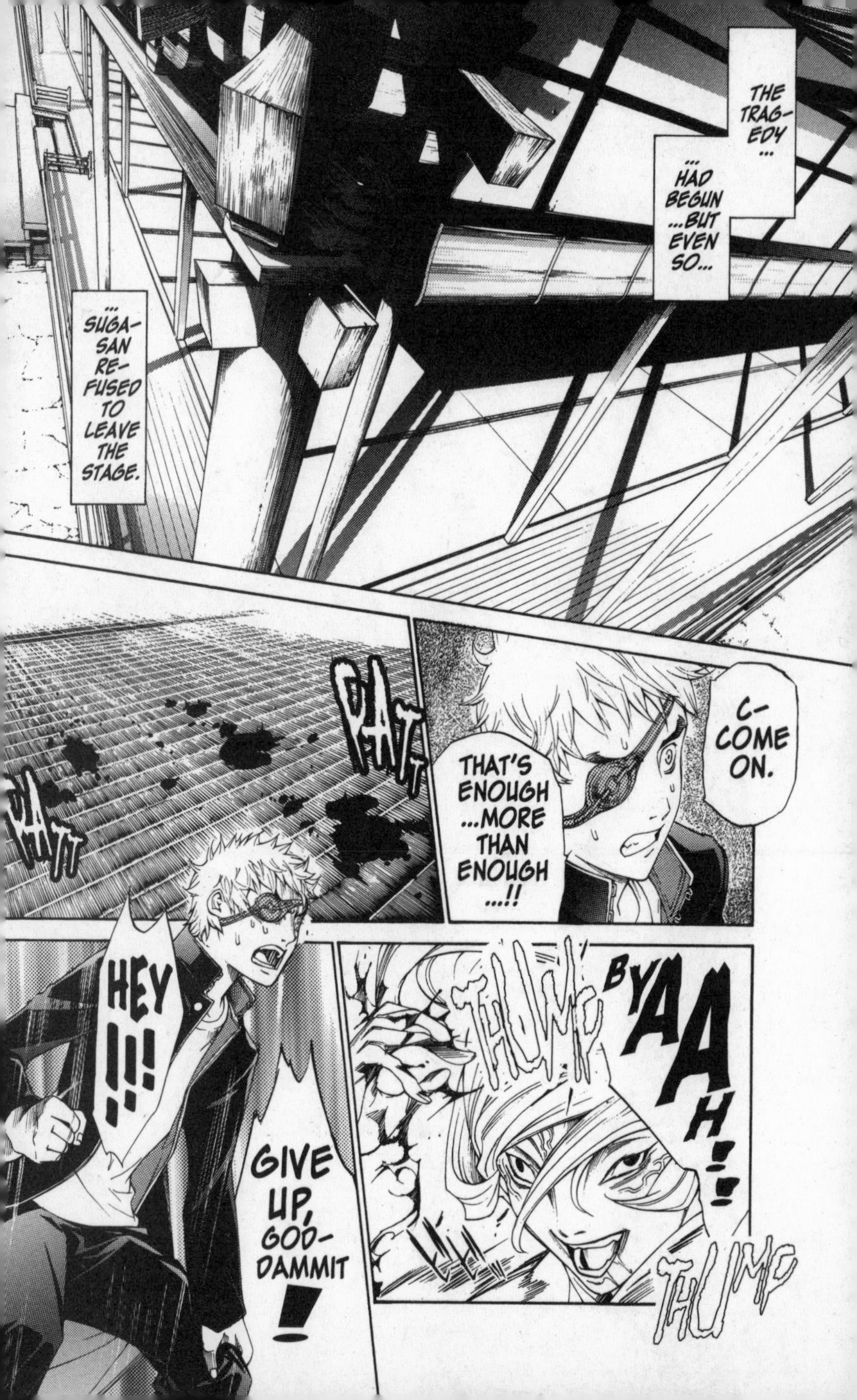
THE TRAG-EDY ...
...HAD BEGUN ...BUT EVEN SO...
...SUGA-SAN RE-FUSED TO LEAVE THE STAGE.
C-COME ON.
THAT'S ENOUGH ...MORE THAN ENOUGH ...!!
BYAAH!!
THUMP
THUMP
HEY!!!
GIVE UP, GOD-DAMMIT!

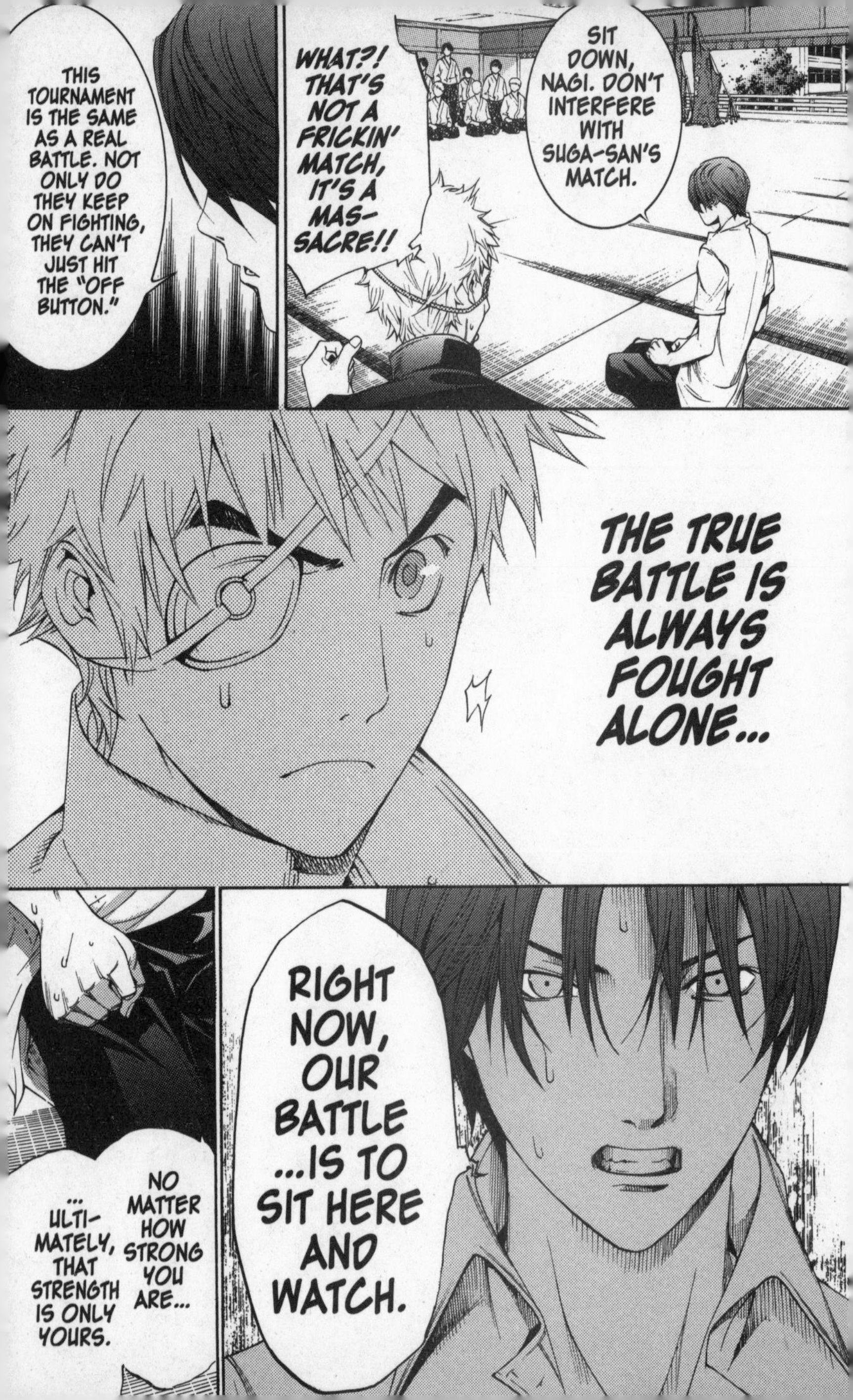
SIT DOWN, NAGI. DON'T INTERFERE WITH SUGA-SAN'S MATCH.
WHAT?! THAT'S NOT A FRICKIN' MATCH, IT'S A MAS-SACRE!!
THIS TOURNAMENT IS THE SAME AS A REAL BATTLE. NOT ONLY DO THEY KEEP ON FIGHTING, THEY CAN'T JUST HIT THE "OFF BUTTON."
THE TRUE BATTLE IS ALWAYS FOUGHT ALONE...
RIGHT NOW, OUR BATTLE ...IS TO SIT HERE AND WATCH.
NO MATTER HOW STRONG YOU ARE...
...ULTI-MATELY, THAT STRENGTH IS ONLY YOURS.

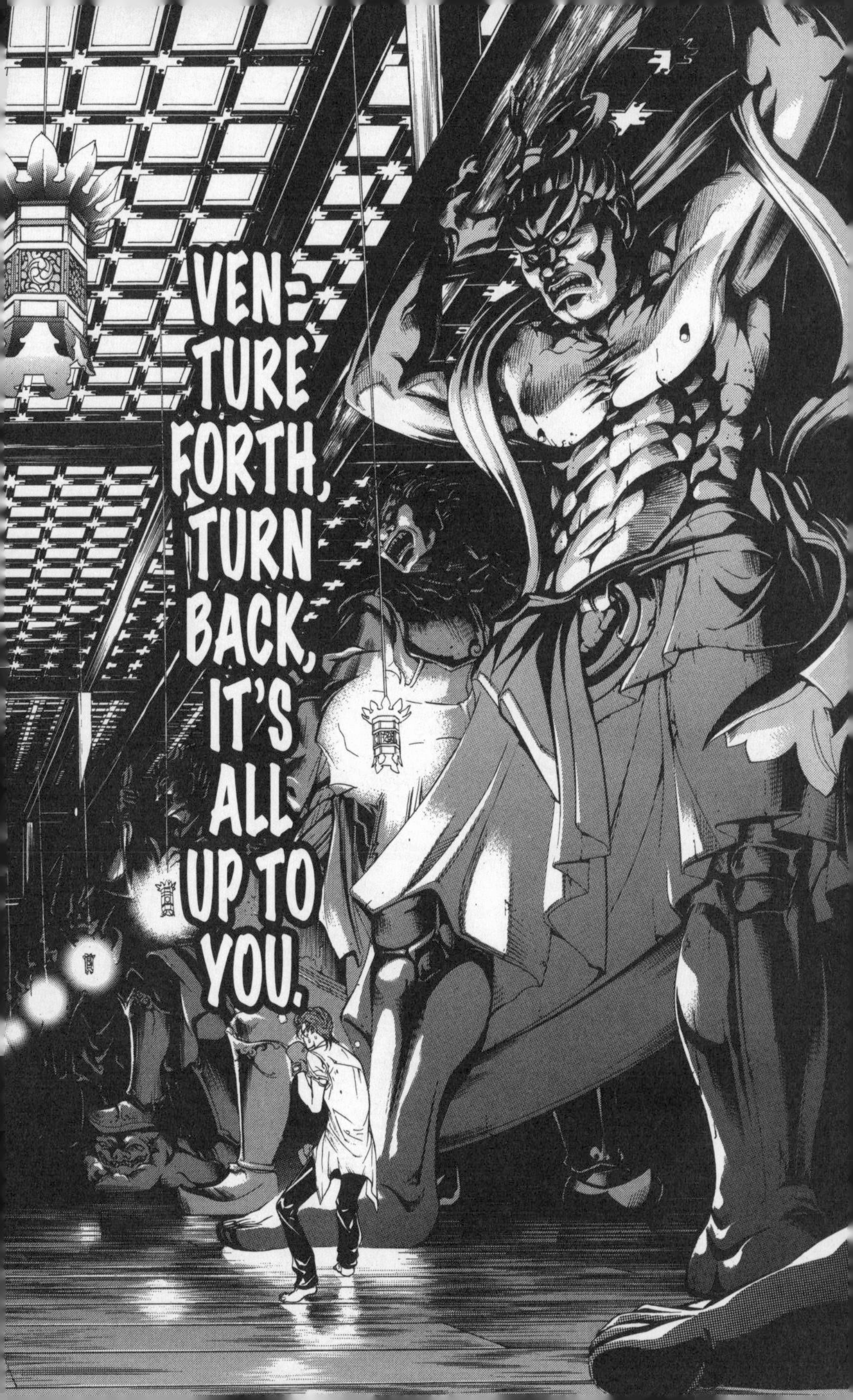
VEN-
TURE
FORTH,
TURN
BACK,
IT'S
ALL
UP TO
YOU.

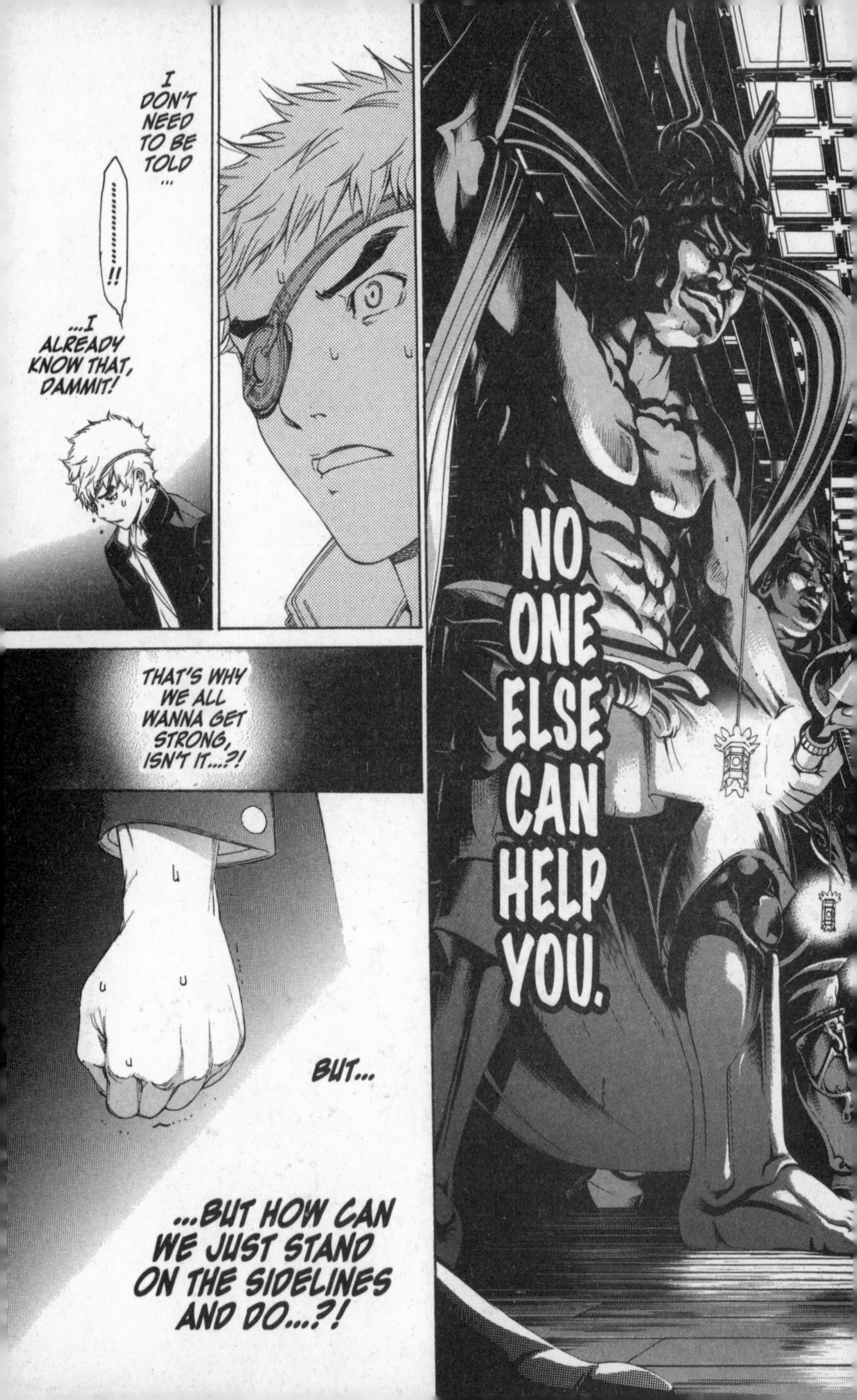
NO ONE ELSE CAN HELP YOU.
I DON'T NEED TO BE TOLD ...
.........!!
...I ALREADY KNOW THAT, DAMMIT!
THAT'S WHY WE ALL WANNA GET STRONG, ISN'T IT...?!
BUT...
...BUT HOW CAN WE JUST STAND ON THE SIDELINES AND DO...?!

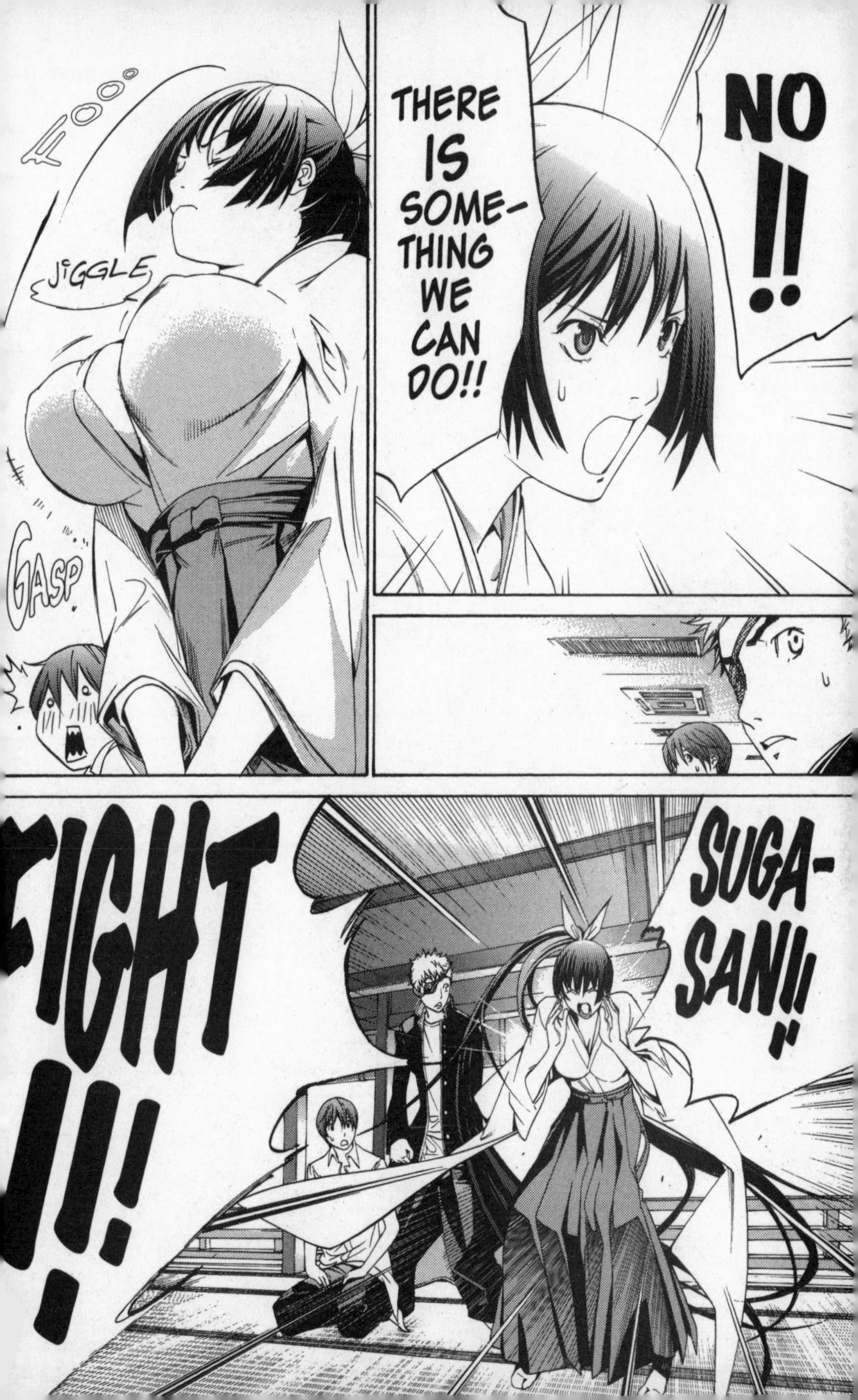
NO!!
THERE IS SOMETHING WE CAN DO!!
FOOO
JIGGLE
GASP
SUGA-SAN!!
FIGHT!!!

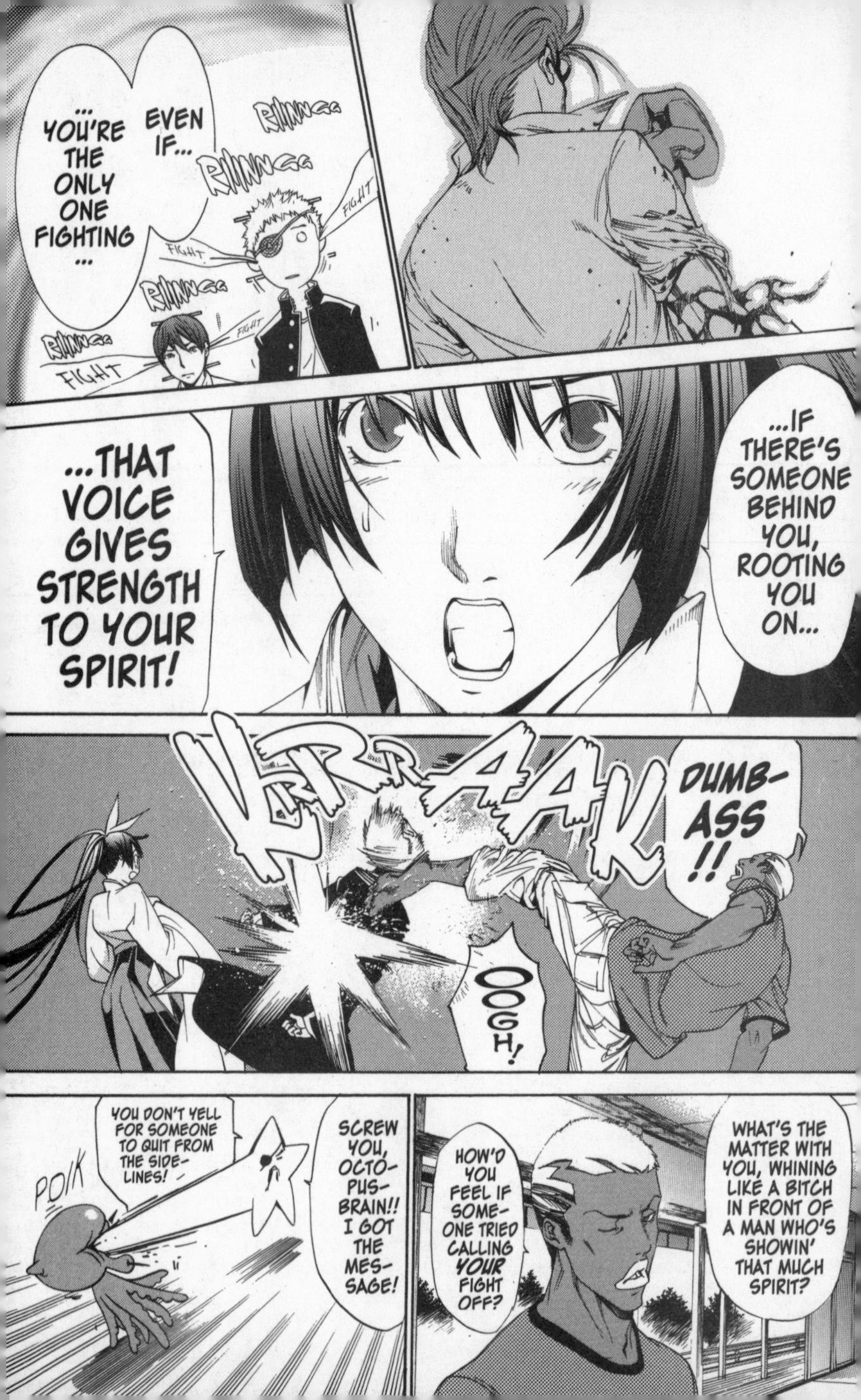
EVEN IF...
... YOU'RE THE ONLY ONE FIGHTING ...
RIIINNGG
RIIINNGG
FIGHT
FIGHT
RIIINNGG
FIGHT
RIIINNGG
FIGHT
...IF THERE'S SOMEONE BEHIND YOU, ROOTING YOU ON...
...THAT VOICE GIVES STRENGTH TO YOUR SPIRIT!
DUMB-ASS !!
VRRRAAK
OOGH!
WHAT'S THE MATTER WITH YOU, WHINING LIKE A BITCH IN FRONT OF A MAN WHO'S SHOWIN' THAT MUCH SPIRIT?
HOW'D YOU FEEL IF SOME-ONE TRIED CALLING *YOUR* FIGHT OFF?
SCREW YOU, OCTO-PUS-BRAIN!! I GOT THE MES-SAGE!
YOU DON'T YELL FOR SOMEONE TO QUIT FROM THE SIDE-LINES!
POIK

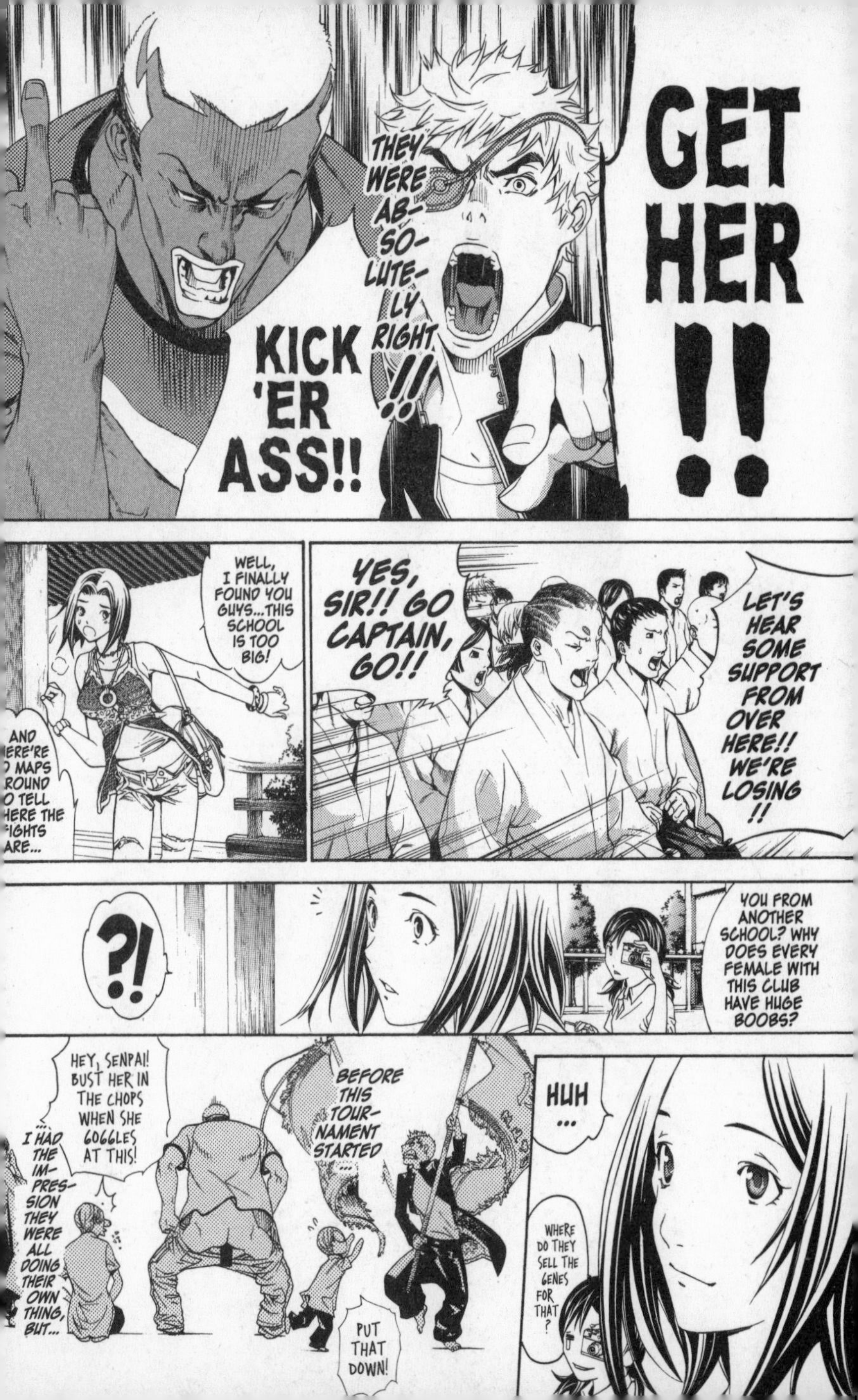
GET HER!!
THEY WERE AB-SO-LUTE-LY RIGHT!!
KICK 'ER ASS!!
LET'S HEAR SOME SUPPORT FROM OVER HERE!! WE'RE LOSING!!
YES, SIR!! GO CAPTAIN, GO!!
WELL, I FINALLY FOUND YOU GUYS...THIS SCHOOL IS TOO BIG!
AND ERE'RE O MAPS ROUND O TELL HERE THE IGHTS ARE...
YOU FROM ANOTHER SCHOOL? WHY DOES EVERY FEMALE WITH THIS CLUB HAVE HUGE BOOBS?
?!
HUH...
WHERE DO THEY SELL THE GENES FOR THAT?
BEFORE THIS TOUR-NAMENT STARTED...
HEY, SENPAI! BUST HER IN THE CHOPS WHEN SHE GOGGLES AT THIS!
...I HAD THE IM-PRES-SION THEY WERE ALL DOING THEIR OWN THING, BUT...
PUT THAT DOWN!

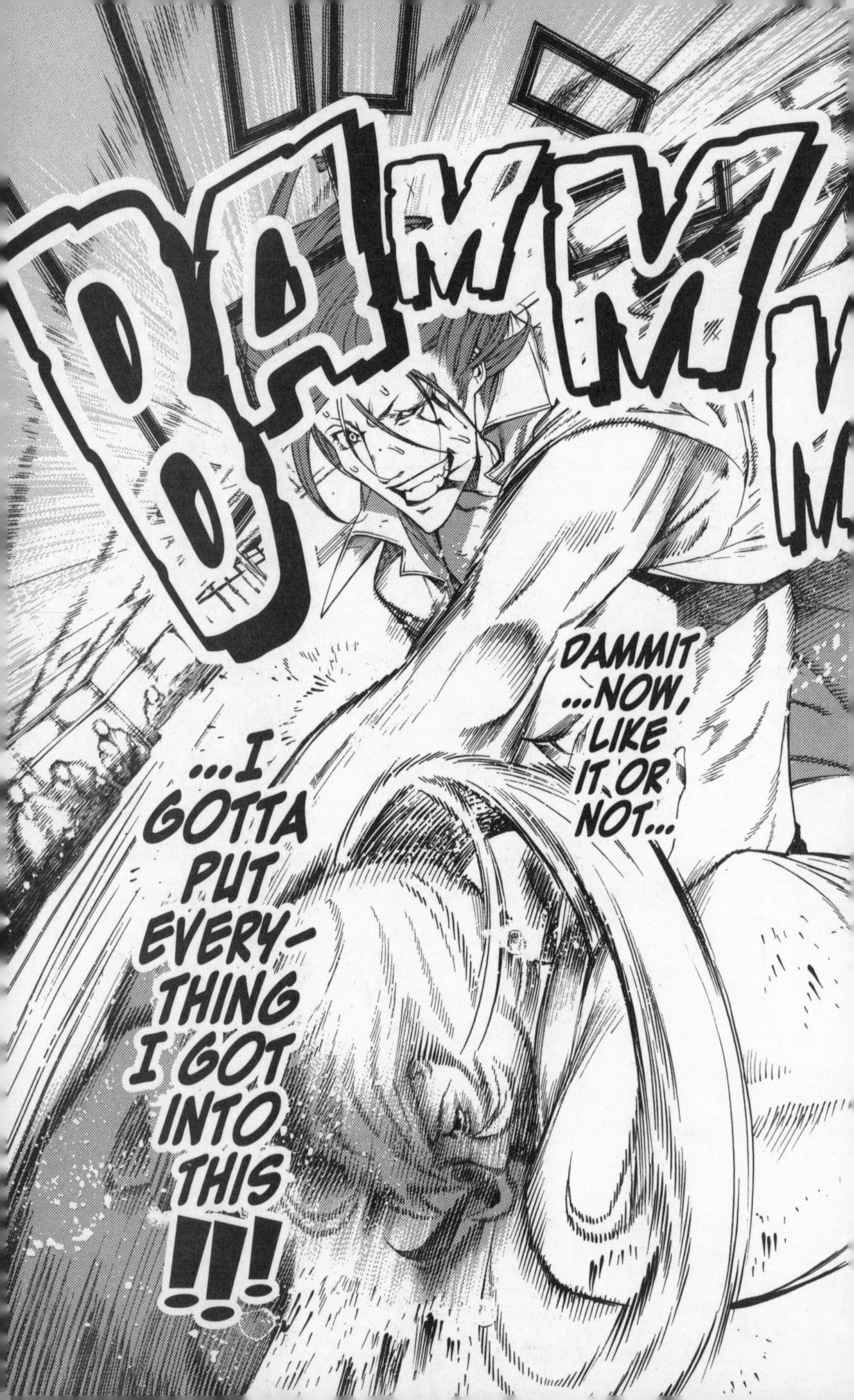
BAMMM
DAMMIT ...NOW, LIKE IT OR NOT...
...I GOTTA PUT EVERY-THING I GOT INTO THIS!!!

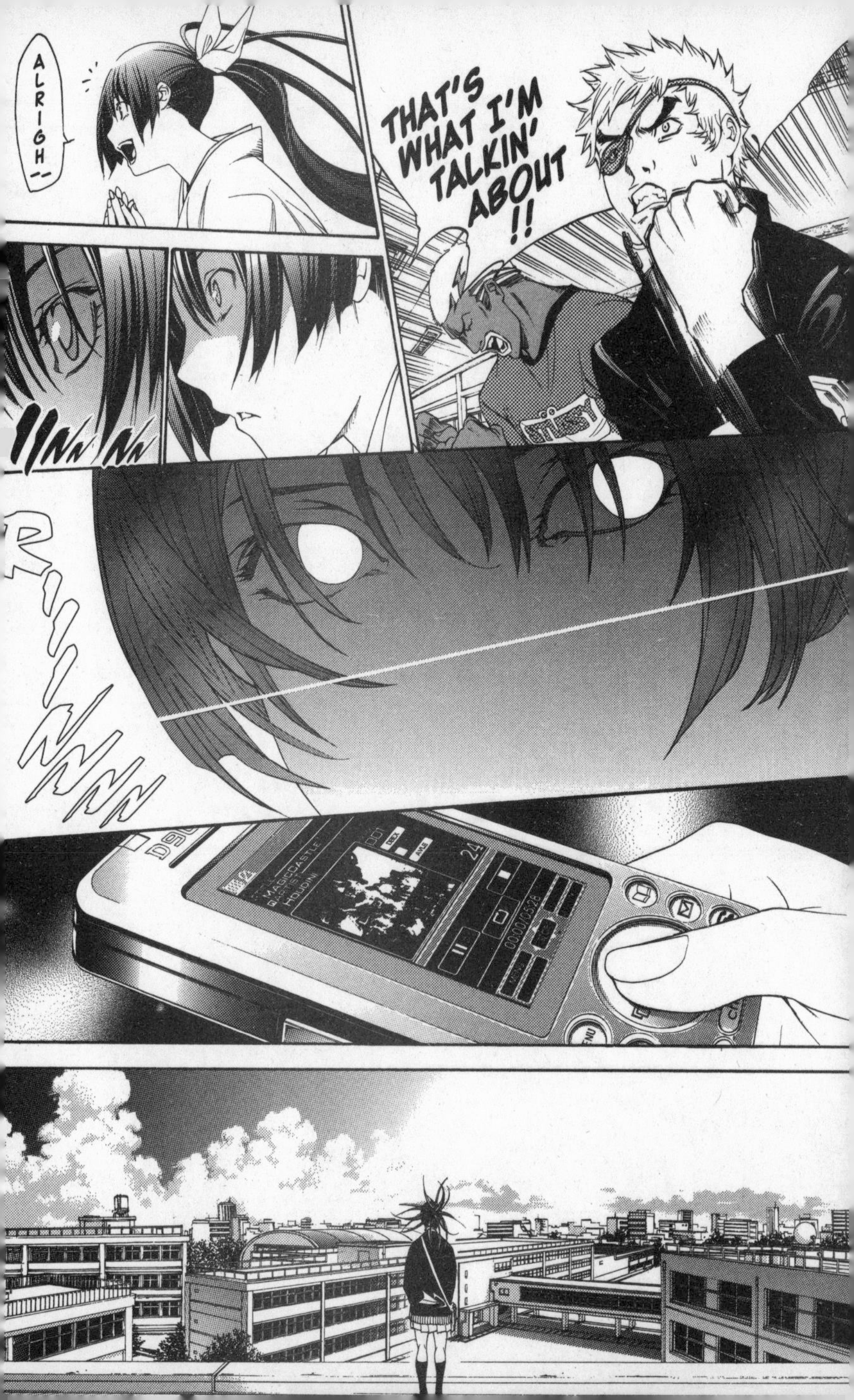
THAT'S WHAT I'M TALKIN' ABOUT!!
ALRIGH—
RIIINNNNN
MAGICCASTLE
HOUDINI

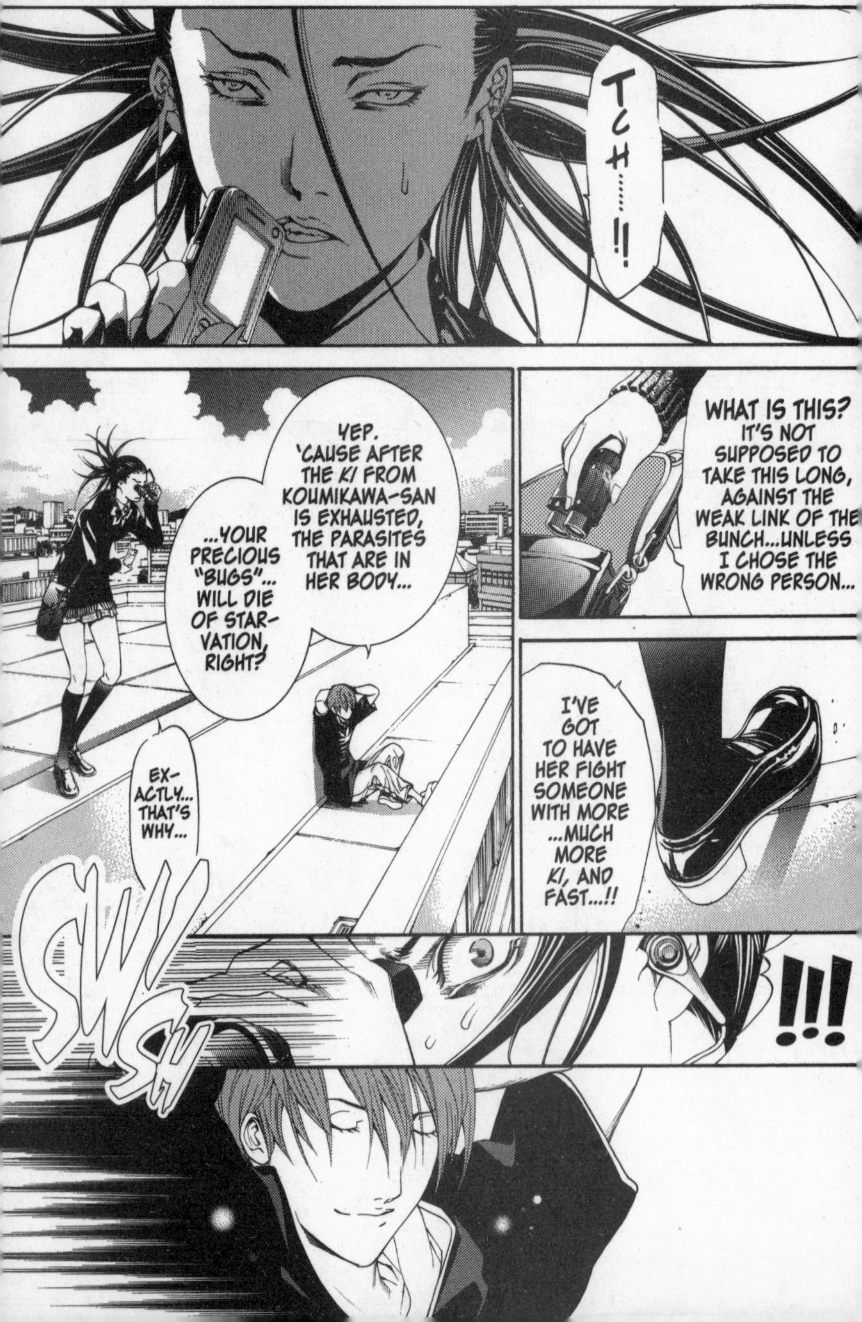
TCH.....!!
WHAT IS THIS? IT'S NOT SUPPOSED TO TAKE THIS LONG, AGAINST THE WEAK LINK OF THE BUNCH...UNLESS I CHOSE THE WRONG PERSON...
I'VE GOT TO HAVE HER FIGHT SOMEONE WITH MORE ...MUCH MORE KI, AND FAST...!!
YEP. 'CAUSE AFTER THE KI FROM KOUMIKAWA-SAN IS EXHAUSTED, THE PARASITES THAT ARE IN HER BODY...
...YOUR PRECIOUS "BUGS"... WILL DIE OF STAR-VATION, RIGHT?
EX-ACTLY... THAT'S WHY...
!!!
SWISH

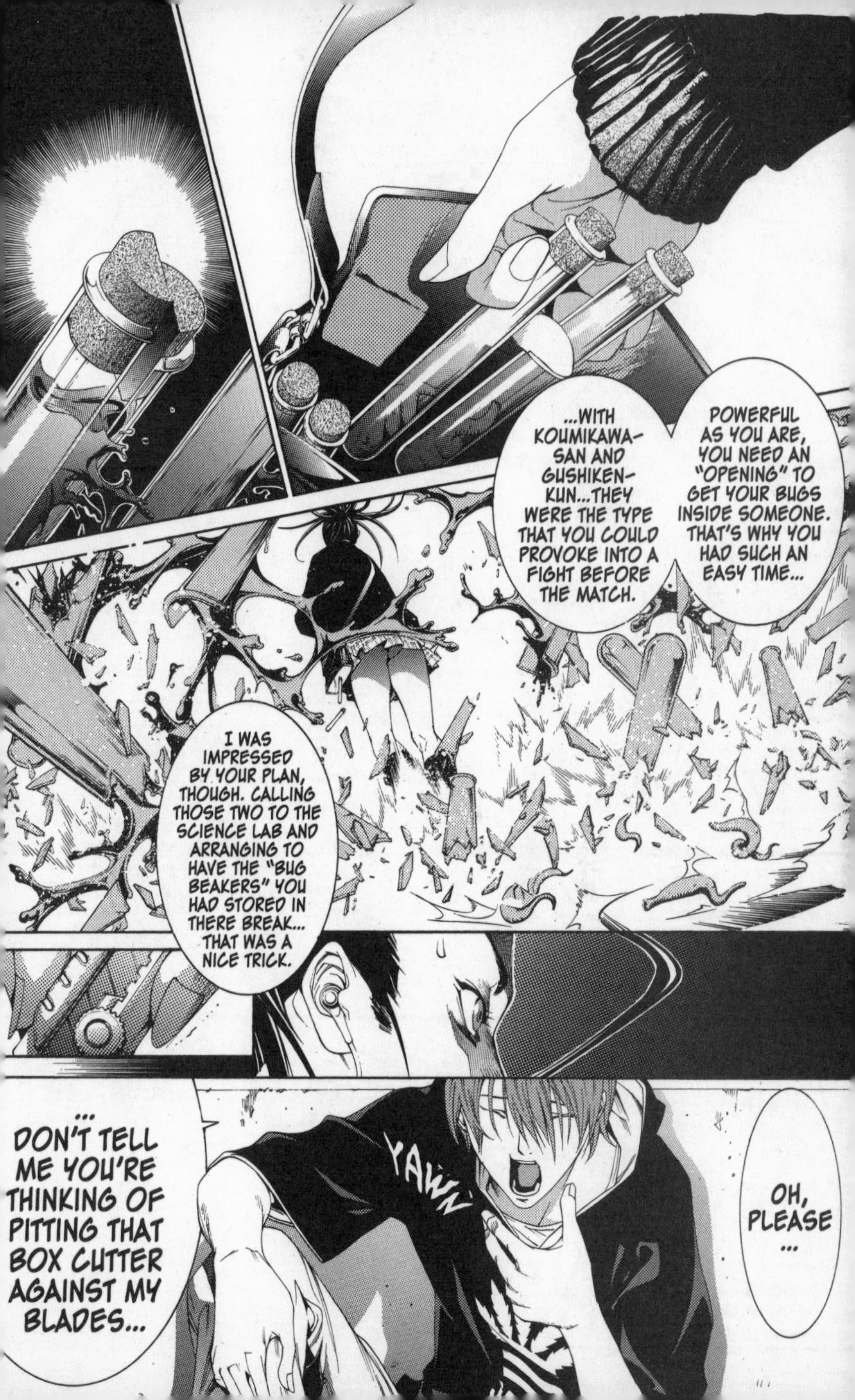
POWERFUL AS YOU ARE, YOU NEED AN "OPENING" TO GET YOUR BUGS INSIDE SOMEONE. THAT'S WHY YOU HAD SUCH AN EASY TIME...
...WITH KOUMIKAWA-SAN AND GUSHIKEN-KUN...THEY WERE THE TYPE THAT YOU COULD PROVOKE INTO A FIGHT BEFORE THE MATCH.
I WAS IMPRESSED BY YOUR PLAN, THOUGH. CALLING THOSE TWO TO THE SCIENCE LAB AND ARRANGING TO HAVE THE "BUG BEAKERS" YOU HAD STORED IN THERE BREAK... THAT WAS A NICE TRICK.
YAWN
OH, PLEASE ...
... DON'T TELL ME YOU'RE THINKING OF PITTING THAT BOX CUTTER AGAINST MY BLADES...

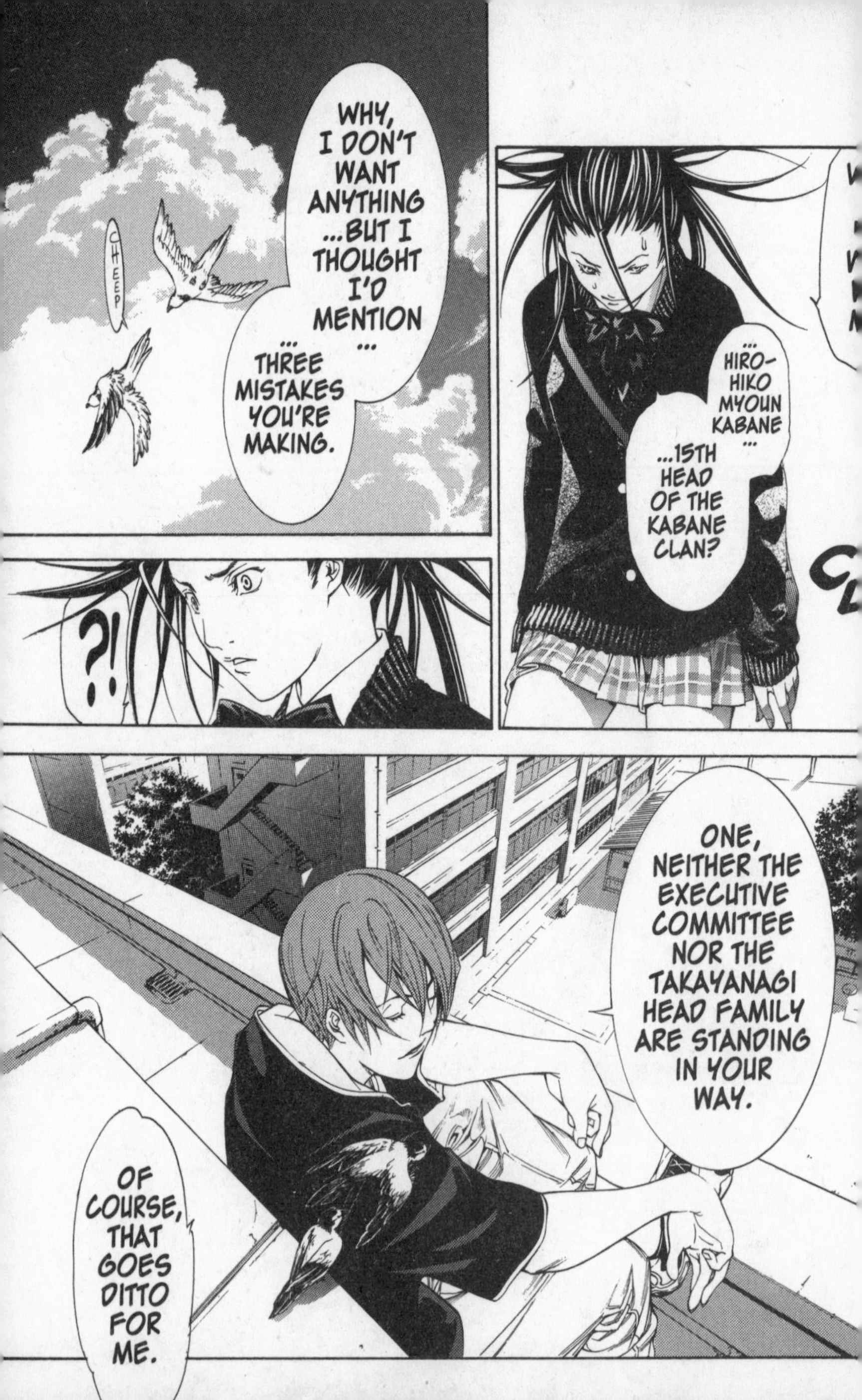
...HIRO-HIKO MYOUN KABANE ...
...15TH HEAD OF THE KABANE CLAN?
WHY, I DON'T WANT ANYTHING ...BUT I THOUGHT I'D MENTION ...
... THREE MISTAKES YOU'RE MAKING.
CHEEP
?!
ONE, NEITHER THE EXECUTIVE COMMITTEE NOR THE TAKAYANAGI HEAD FAMILY ARE STANDING IN YOUR WAY.
OF COURSE, THAT GOES DITTO FOR ME.

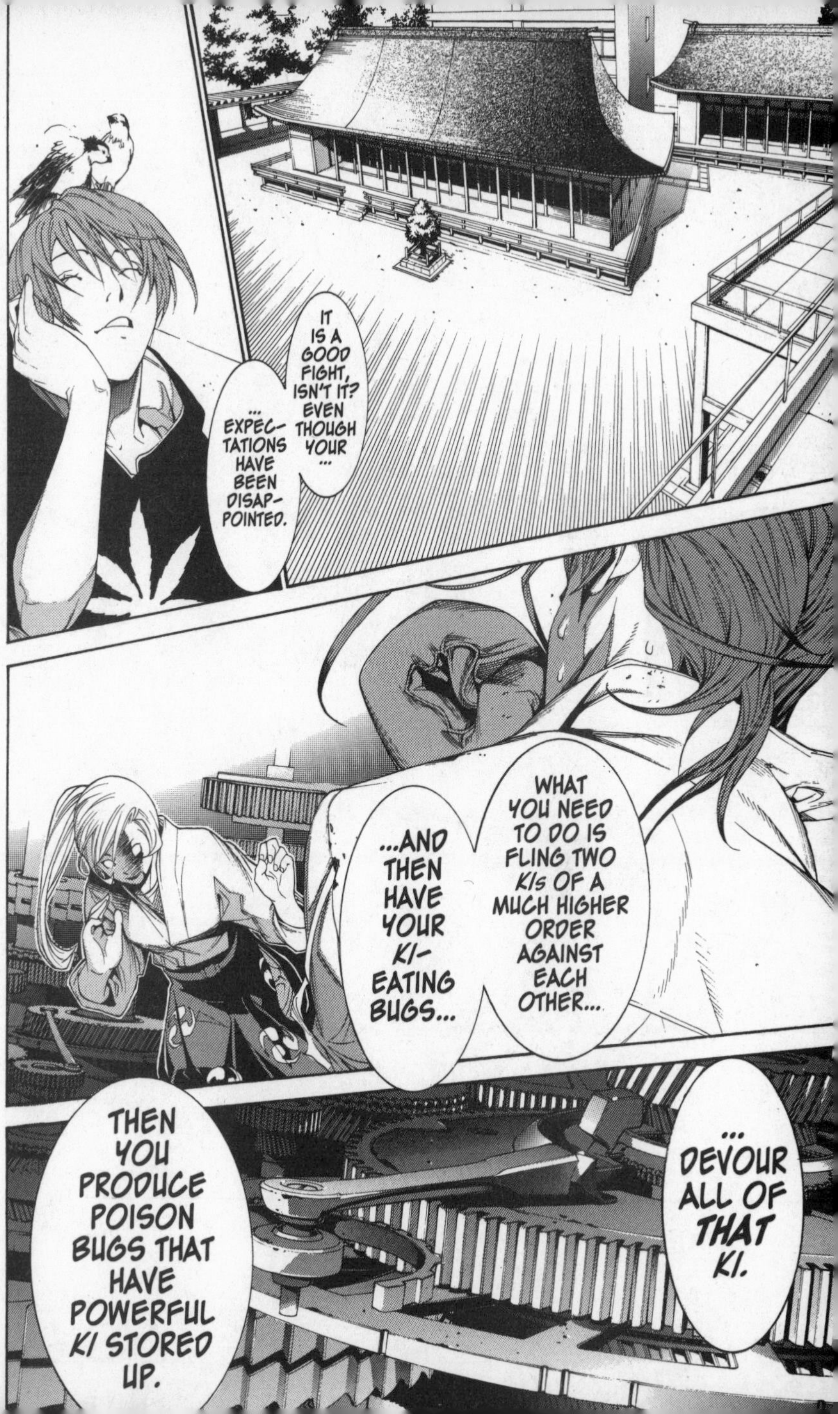
IT IS A GOOD FIGHT, ISN'T IT? EVEN THOUGH YOUR ...
... EXPECTATIONS HAVE BEEN DISAPPOINTED.
WHAT YOU NEED TO DO IS FLING TWO KIs OF A MUCH HIGHER ORDER AGAINST EACH OTHER...
...AND THEN HAVE YOUR KI-EATING BUGS...
... DEVOUR ALL OF THAT KI.
THEN YOU PRODUCE POISON BUGS THAT HAVE POWERFUL KI STORED UP.

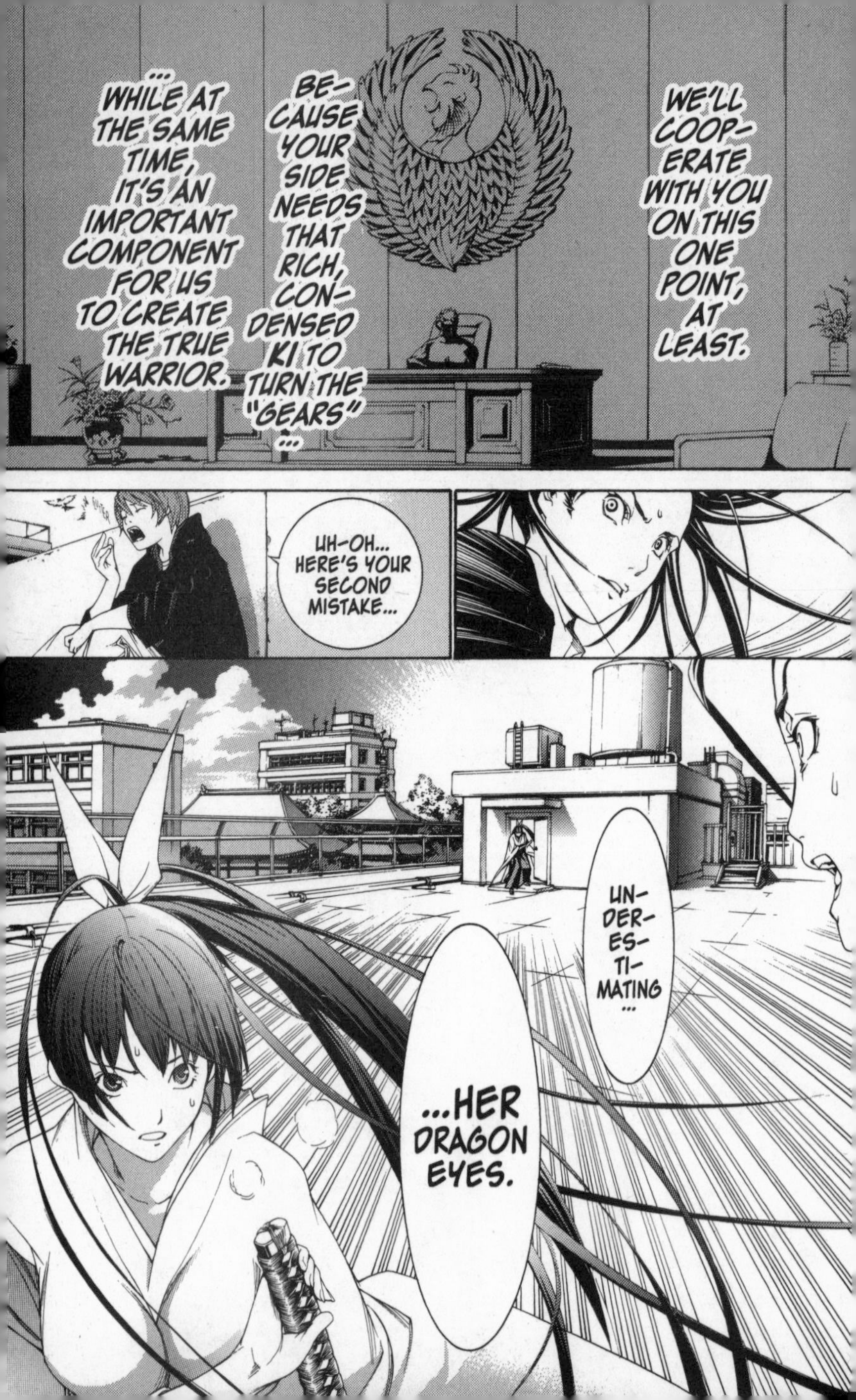
WE'LL COOPERATE WITH YOU ON THIS ONE POINT, AT LEAST.
BECAUSE YOUR SIDE NEEDS THAT RICH, CONDENSED KI TO TURN THE "GEARS"...
...WHILE AT THE SAME TIME, IT'S AN IMPORTANT COMPONENT FOR US TO CREATE THE TRUE WARRIOR.
UH-OH... HERE'S YOUR SECOND MISTAKE...
UNDERESTIMATING...
...HER DRAGON EYES.

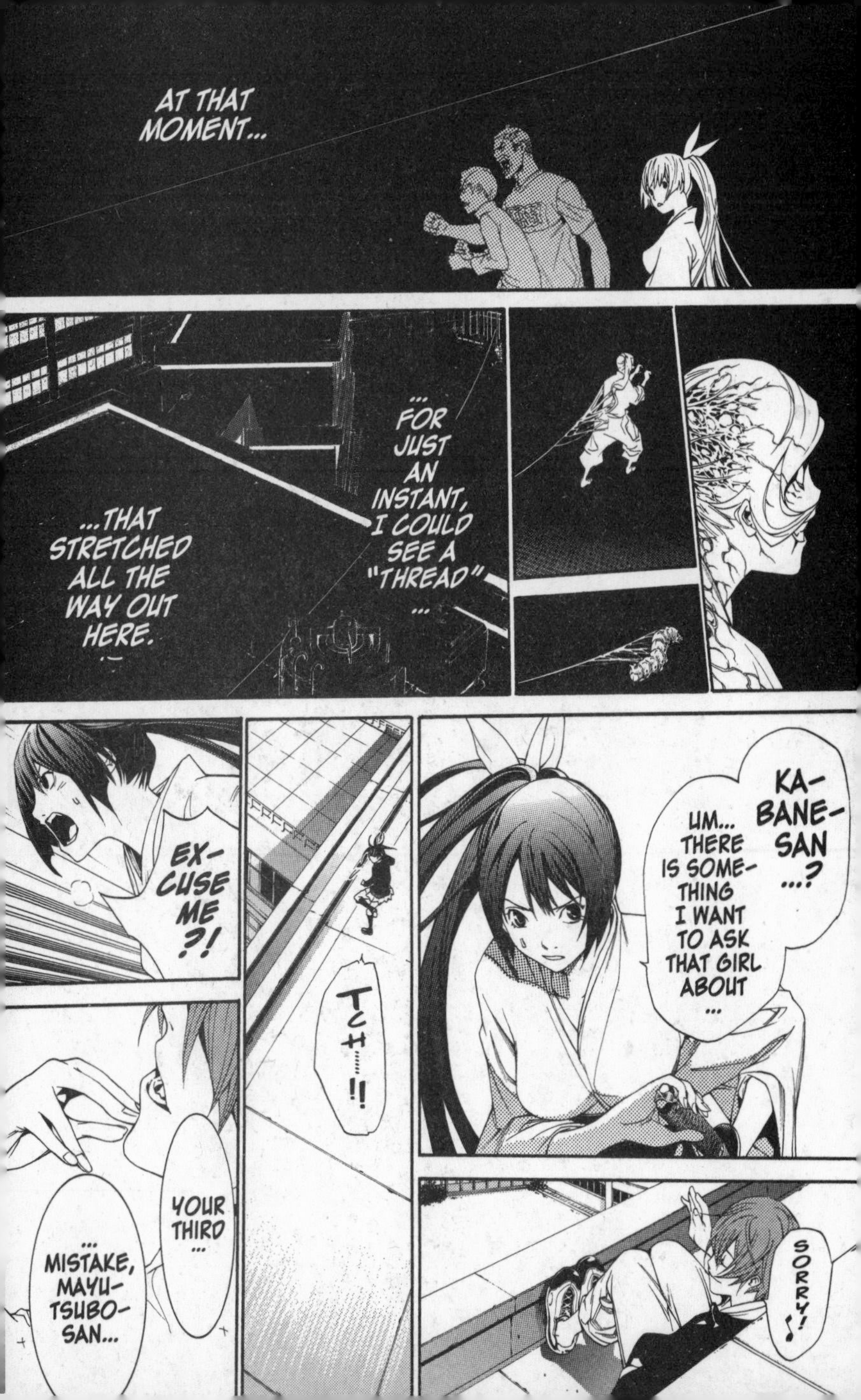
AT THAT MOMENT...
...FOR JUST AN INSTANT, I COULD SEE A "THREAD"...
...THAT STRETCHED ALL THE WAY OUT HERE.
KA-BANE-SAN ...?
UM... THERE IS SOME-THING I WANT TO ASK THAT GIRL ABOUT ...
SORRY!
TCH.....!!
EX-CUSE ME ?!
YOUR THIRD ...
... MISTAKE, MAYU-TSUBO-SAN...

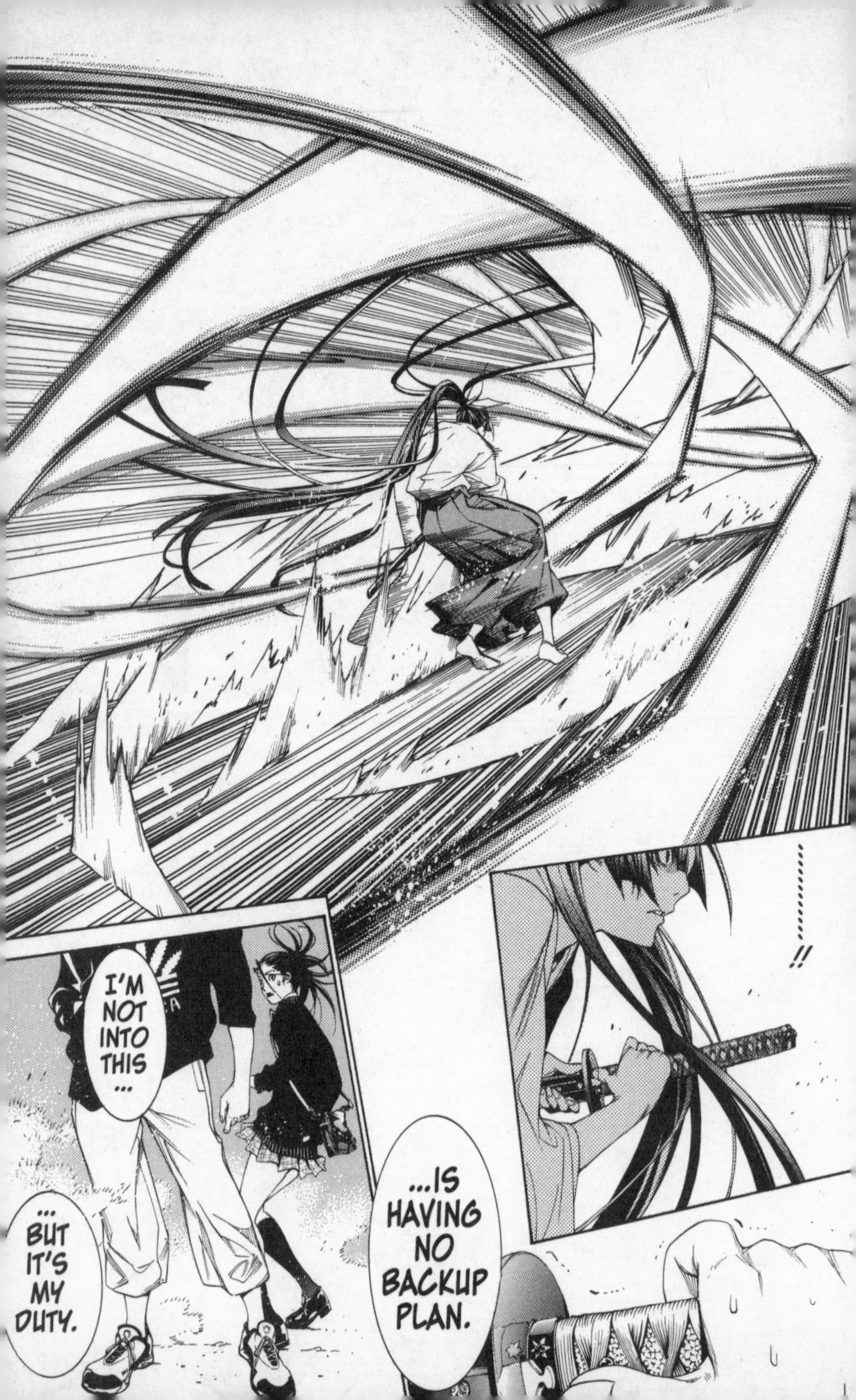
......
!!
...IS HAVING NO BACKUP PLAN.
I'M NOT INTO THIS...
...BUT IT'S MY DUTY.

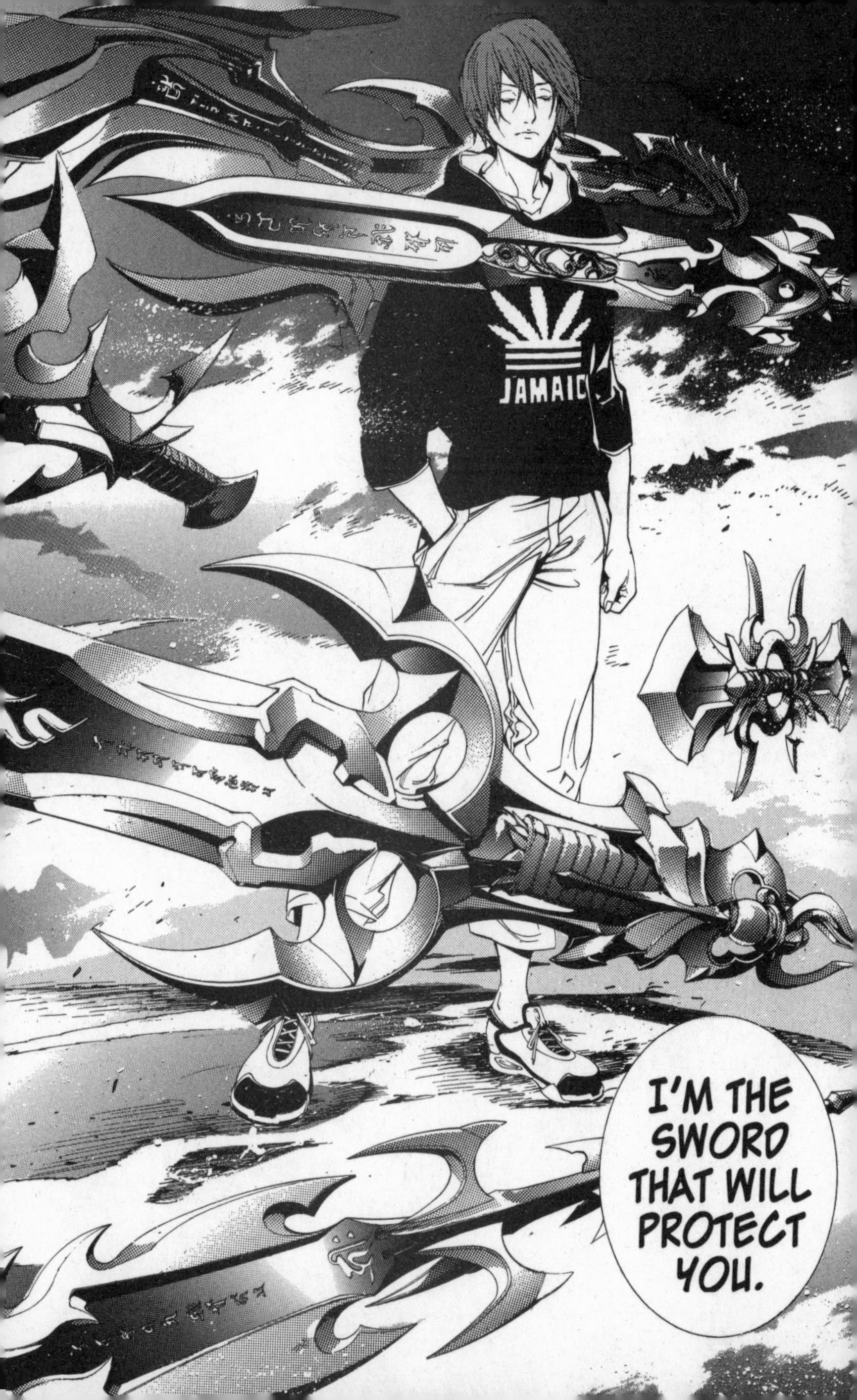
I'M THE SWORD THAT WILL PROTECT YOU.

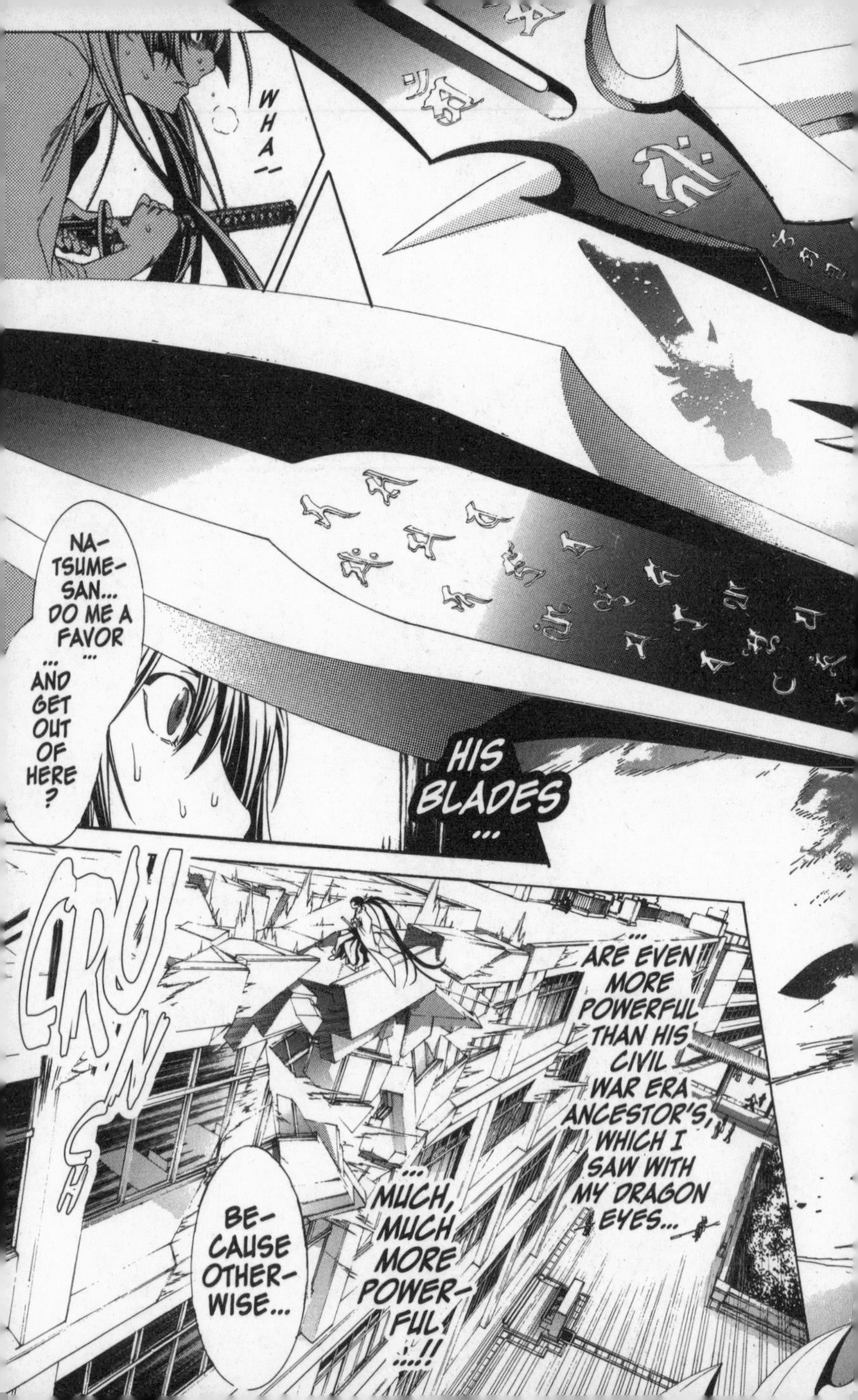
WHA--
NA-TSUME-SAN... DO ME A FAVOR... AND GET OUT OF HERE?
HIS BLADES...
CRUNCH
...ARE EVEN MORE POWERFUL THAN HIS CIVIL WAR ERA ANCESTOR'S, WHICH I SAW WITH MY DRAGON EYES...
...MUCH, MUCH MORE POWERFUL...!!
BE-CAUSE OTHER-WISE...

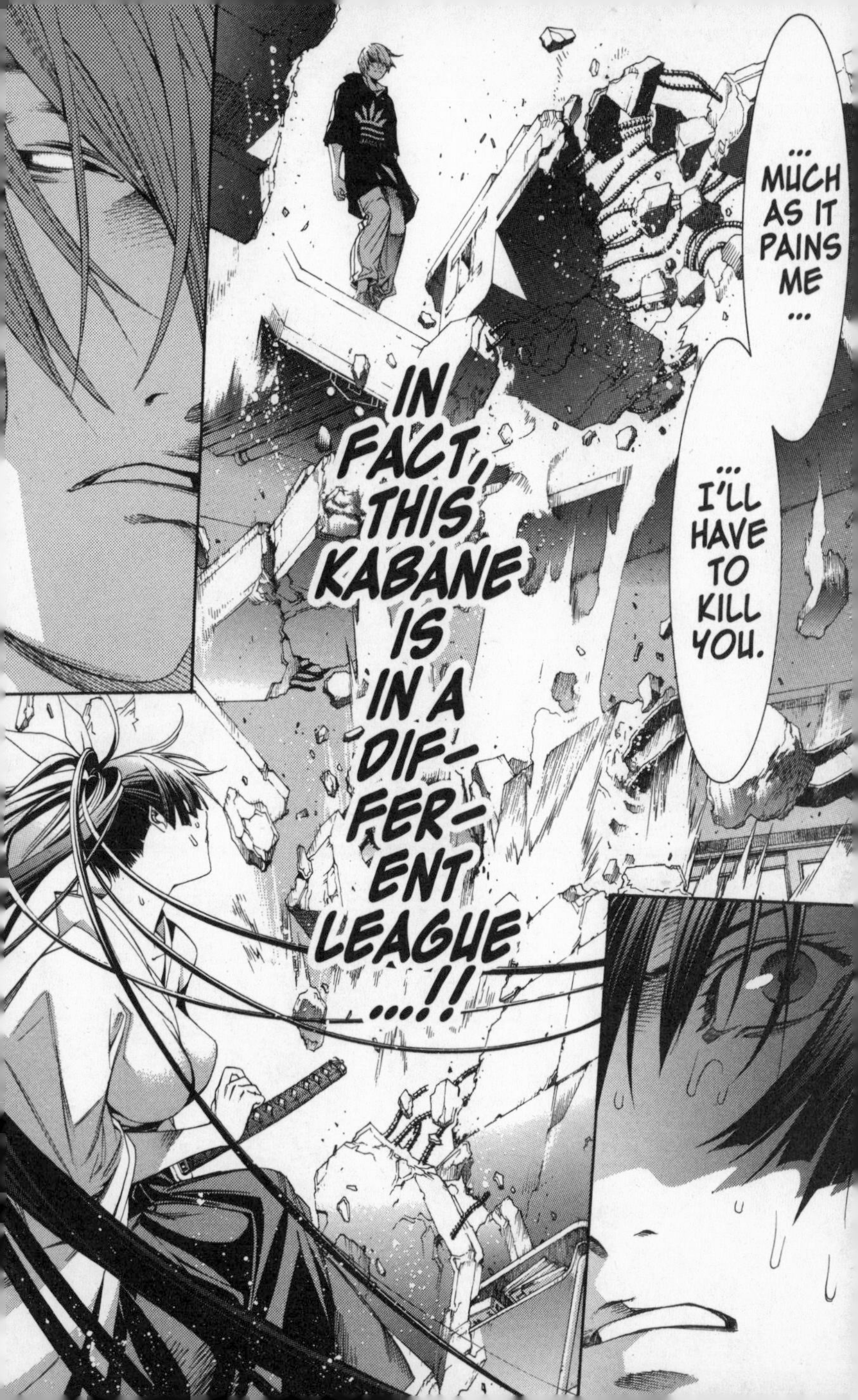
...MUCH AS IT PAINS ME...
...I'LL HAVE TO KILL YOU.
IN FACT, THIS KABANE IS IN A DIF-FER-ENT LEAGUE...!!

FIGHT:105

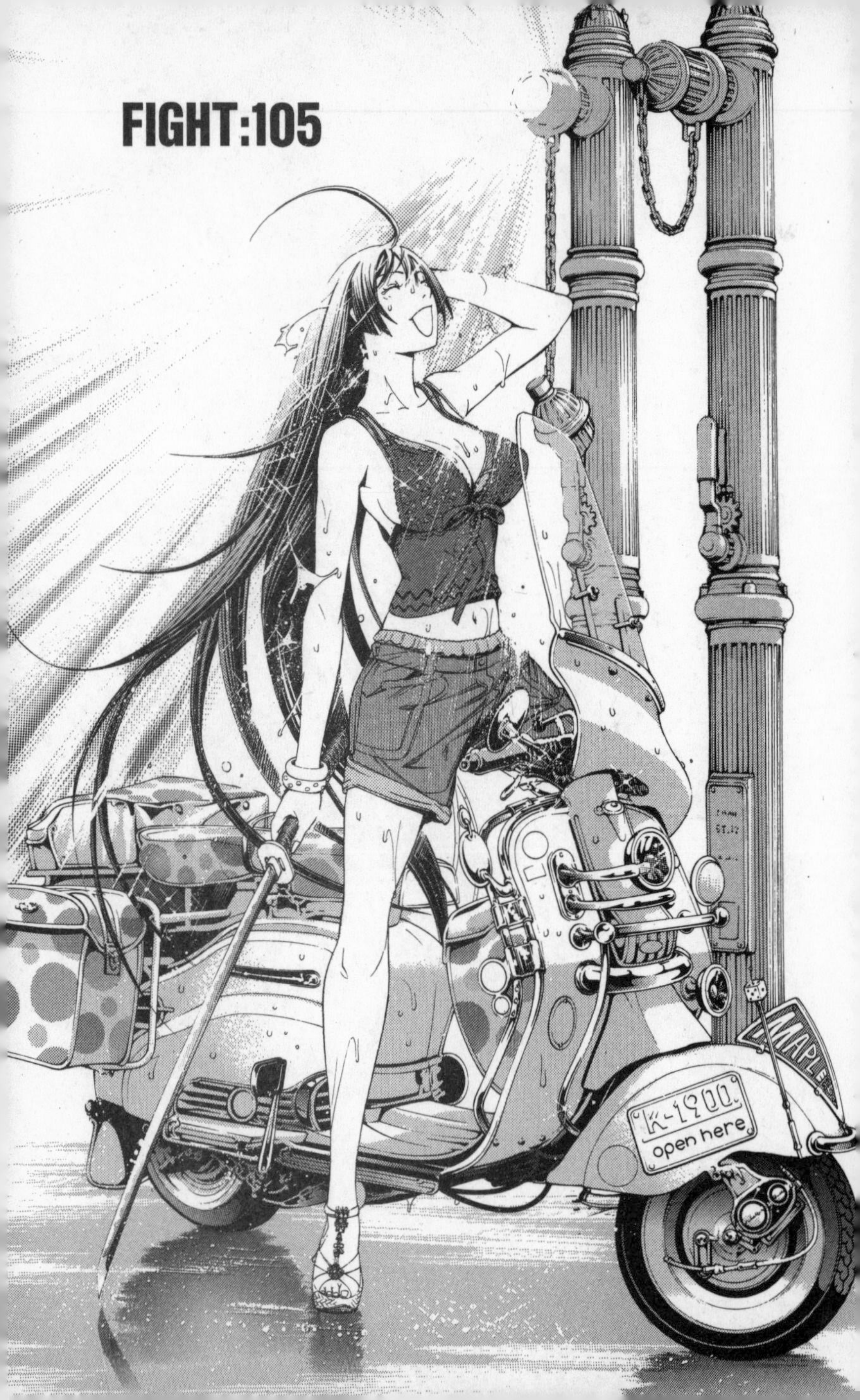
MAPLE
K-1900
open here

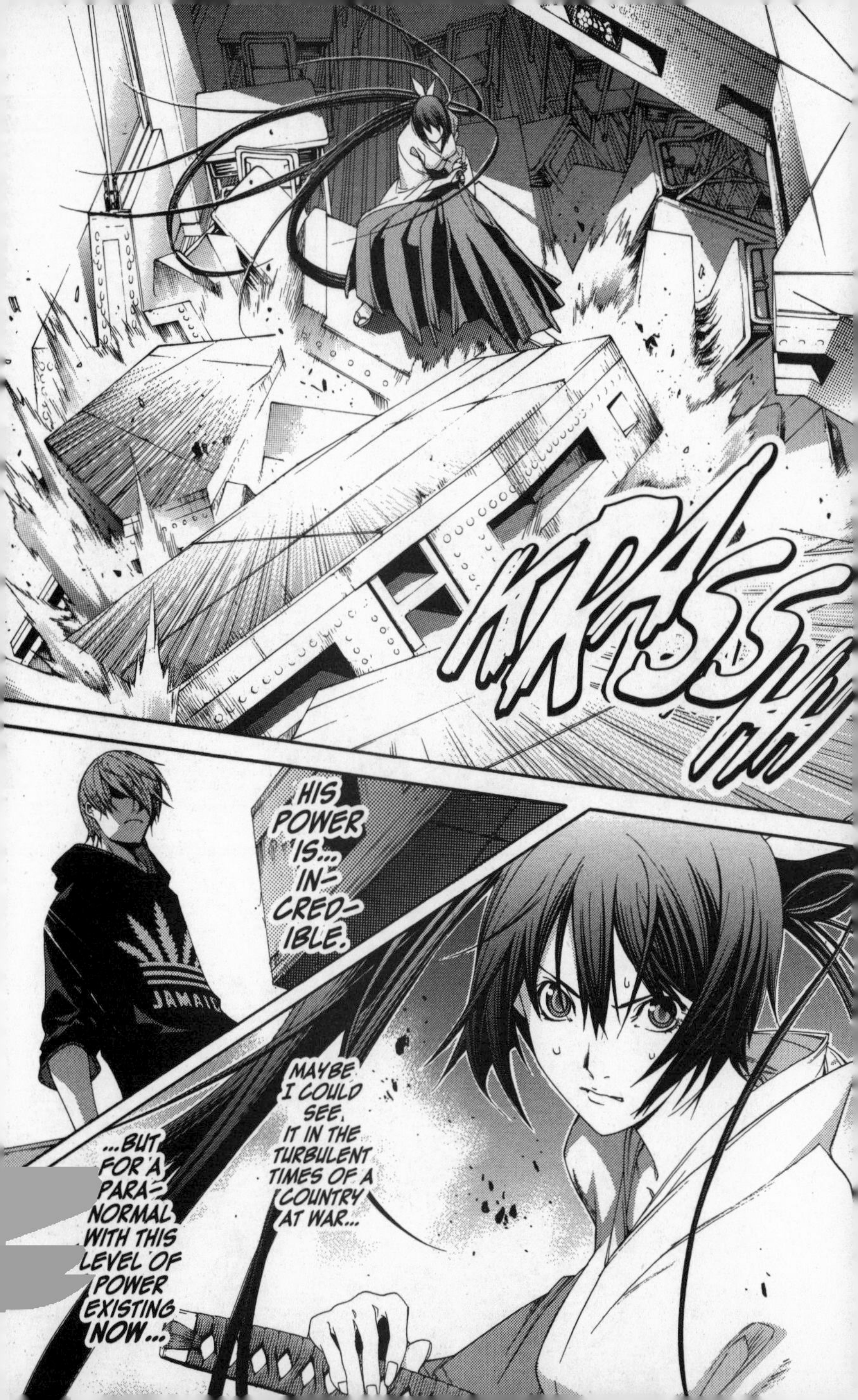
KRASSH
HIS POWER IS... IN-CREDIBLE.
MAYBE I COULD SEE IT IN THE TURBULENT TIMES OF A COUNTRY AT WAR...
...BUT FOR A PARA-NORMAL WITH THIS LEVEL OF POWER EXISTING NOW...

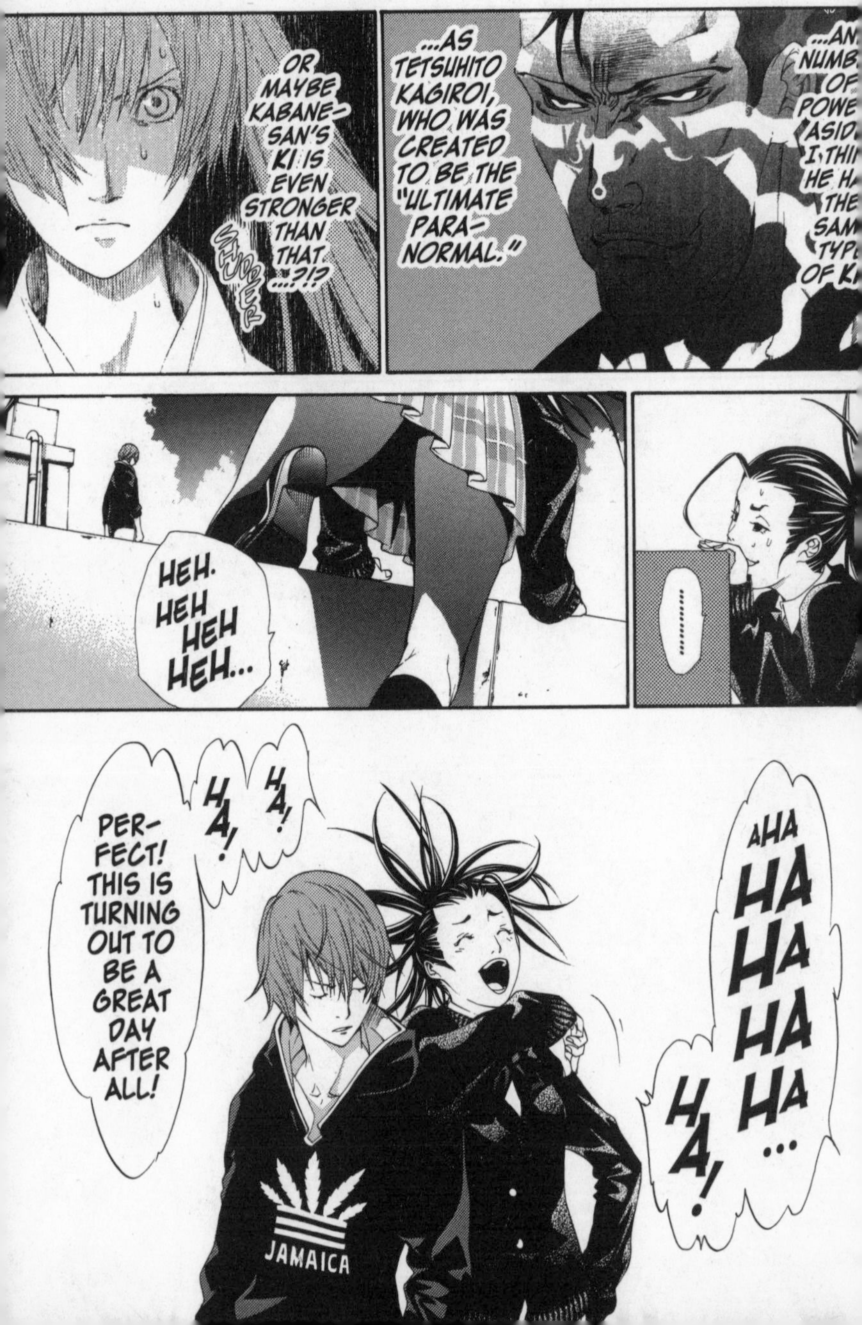
...AN NUMB OF POWE ASID I THI HE HA THE SAM TYP OF K
...AS TETSUHITO KAGIROI, WHO WAS CREATED TO BE THE "ULTIMATE PARA-NORMAL."
OR MAYBE KABANE-SAN'S KI IS EVEN STRONGER THAN THAT. ...?!?
SHUDDER
......
HEH. HEH HEH HEH...
AHA HA HA HA HA HA...
HA!
HA! HA!
PER-FECT! THIS IS TURNING OUT TO BE A GREAT DAY AFTER ALL!

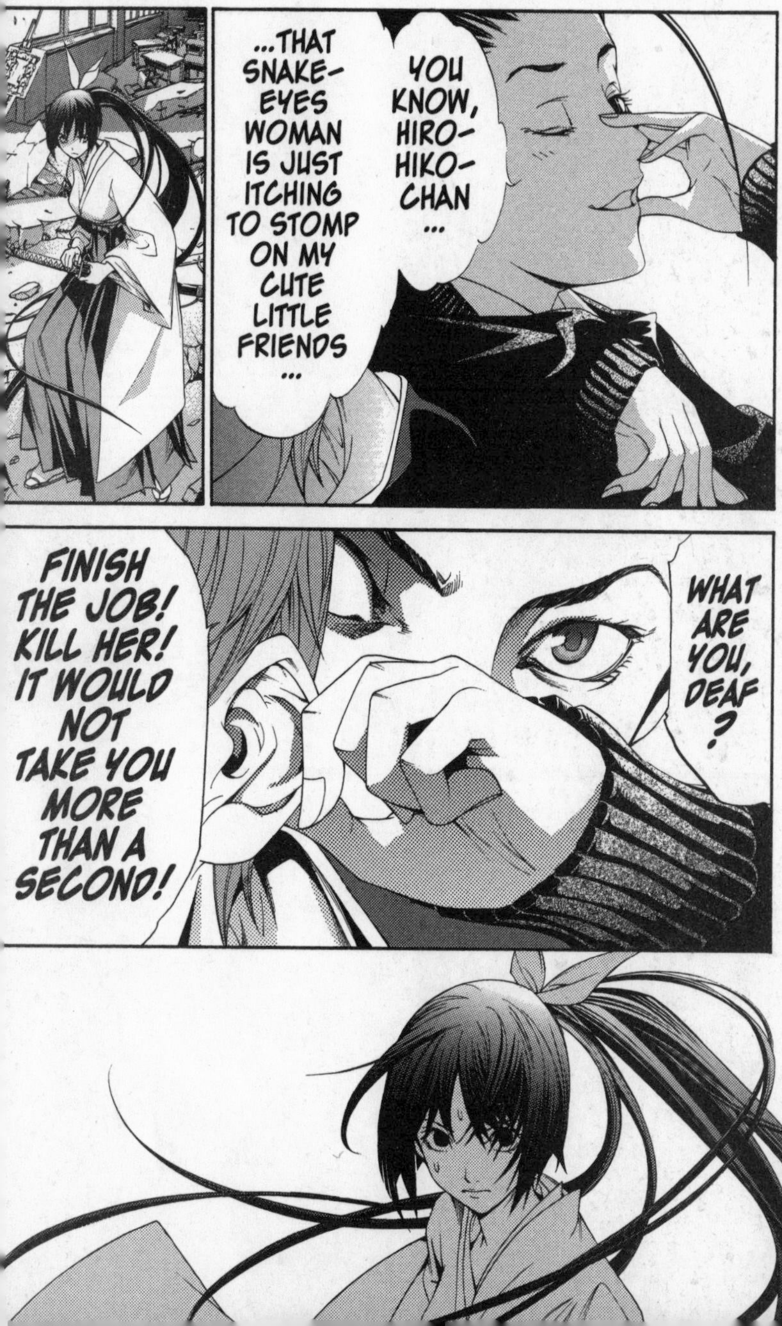
YOU KNOW, HIRO-HIKO-CHAN...
...THAT SNAKE-EYES WOMAN IS JUST ITCHING TO STOMP ON MY CUTE LITTLE FRIENDS...
WHAT ARE YOU, DEAF?
FINISH THE JOB! KILL HER! IT WOULD NOT TAKE YOU MORE THAN A SECOND!

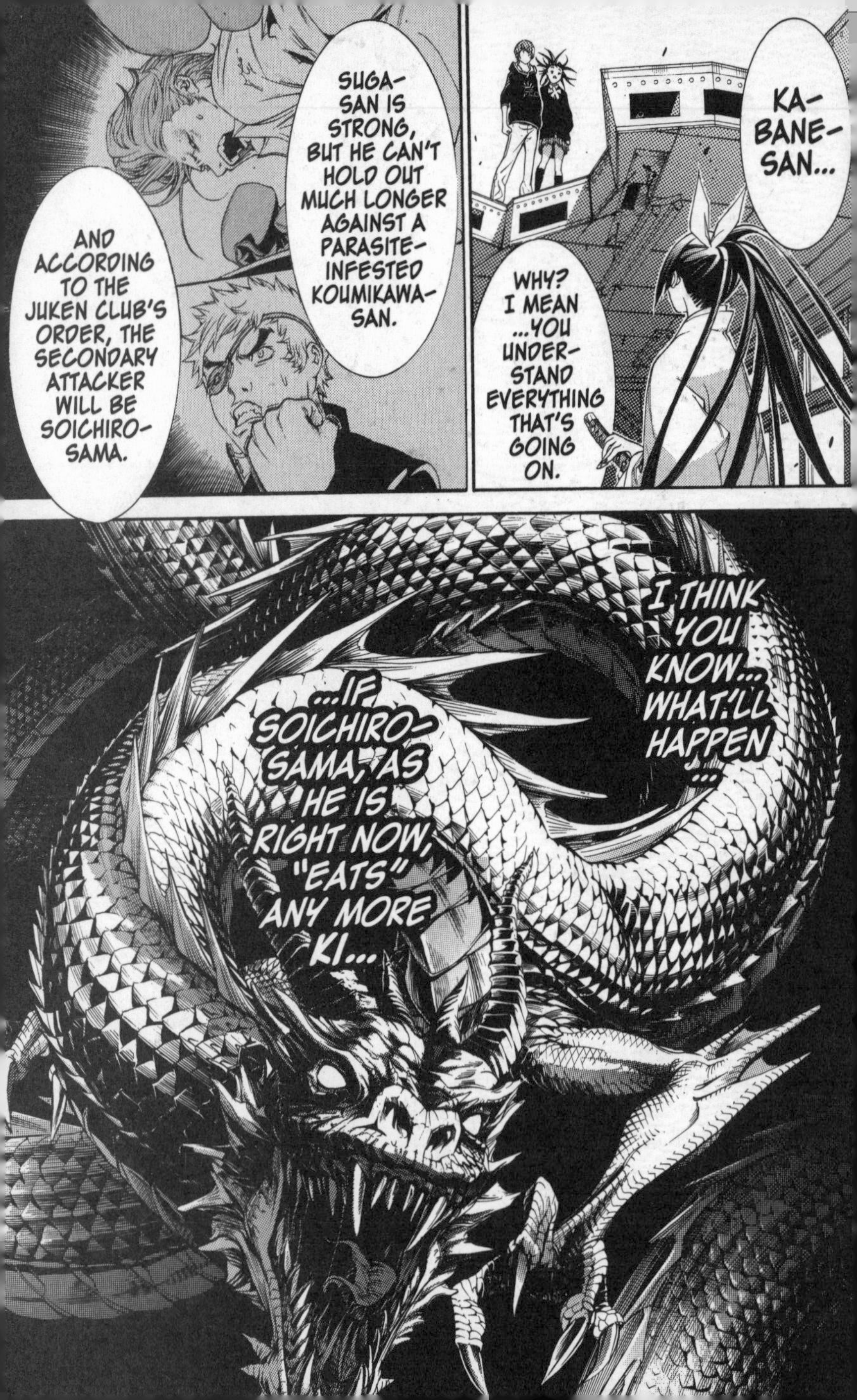
KA-BANE-SAN...
WHY? I MEAN ...YOU UNDER-STAND EVERYTHING THAT'S GOING ON.
SUGA-SAN IS STRONG, BUT HE CAN'T HOLD OUT MUCH LONGER AGAINST A PARASITE-INFESTED KOUMIKAWA-SAN.
AND ACCORDING TO THE JUKEN CLUB'S ORDER, THE SECONDARY ATTACKER WILL BE SOICHIRO-SAMA.
I THINK YOU KNOW... WHAT'LL HAPPEN...
...IF SOICHIRO-SAMA, AS HE IS RIGHT NOW, "EATS" ANY MORE KI...

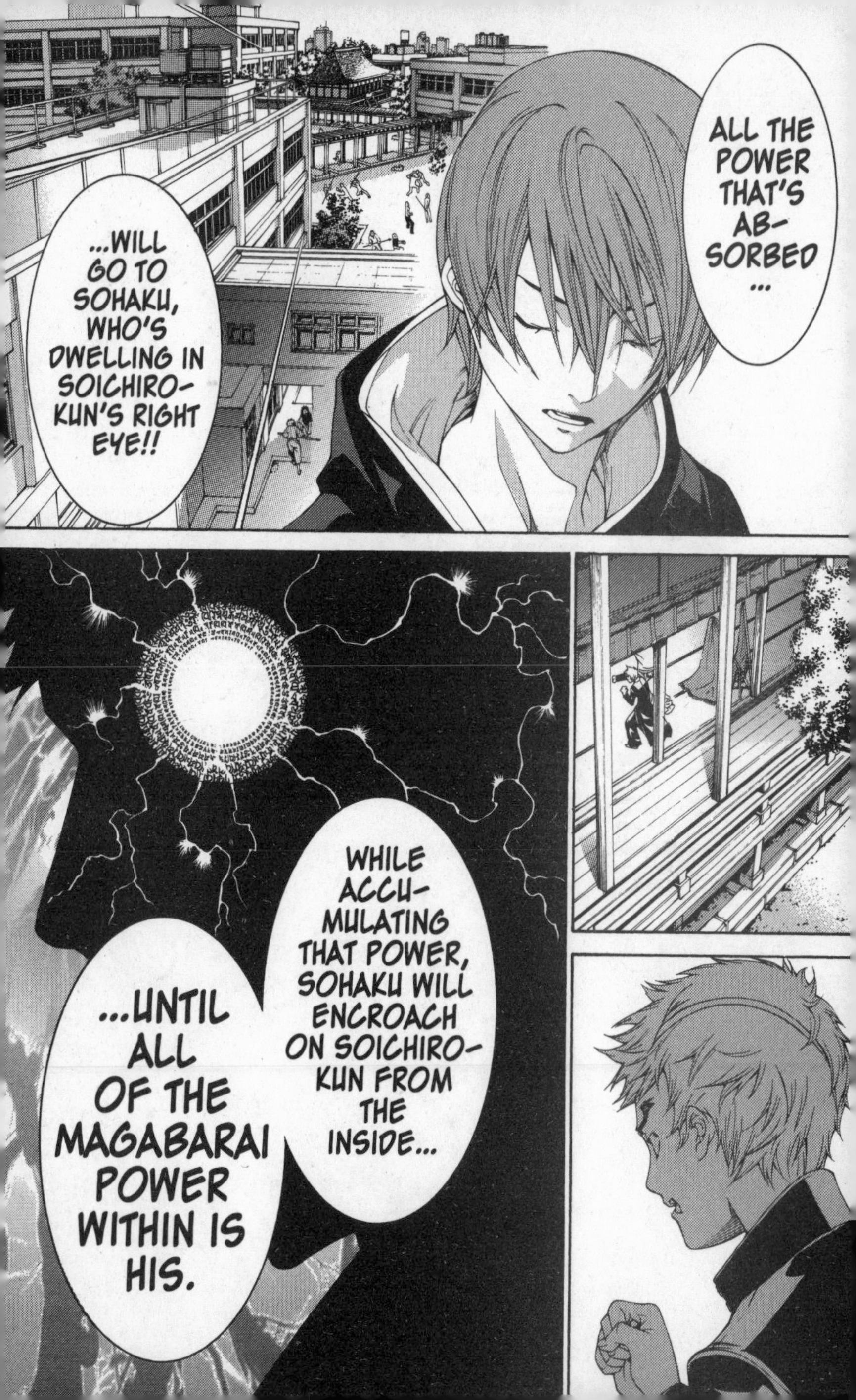
ALL THE POWER THAT'S ABSORBED...
...WILL GO TO SOHAKU, WHO'S DWELLING IN SOICHIRO-KUN'S RIGHT EYE!!
WHILE ACCUMULATING THAT POWER, SOHAKU WILL ENCROACH ON SOICHIRO-KUN FROM THE INSIDE...
...UNTIL ALL OF THE MAGABARAI POWER WITHIN IS HIS.

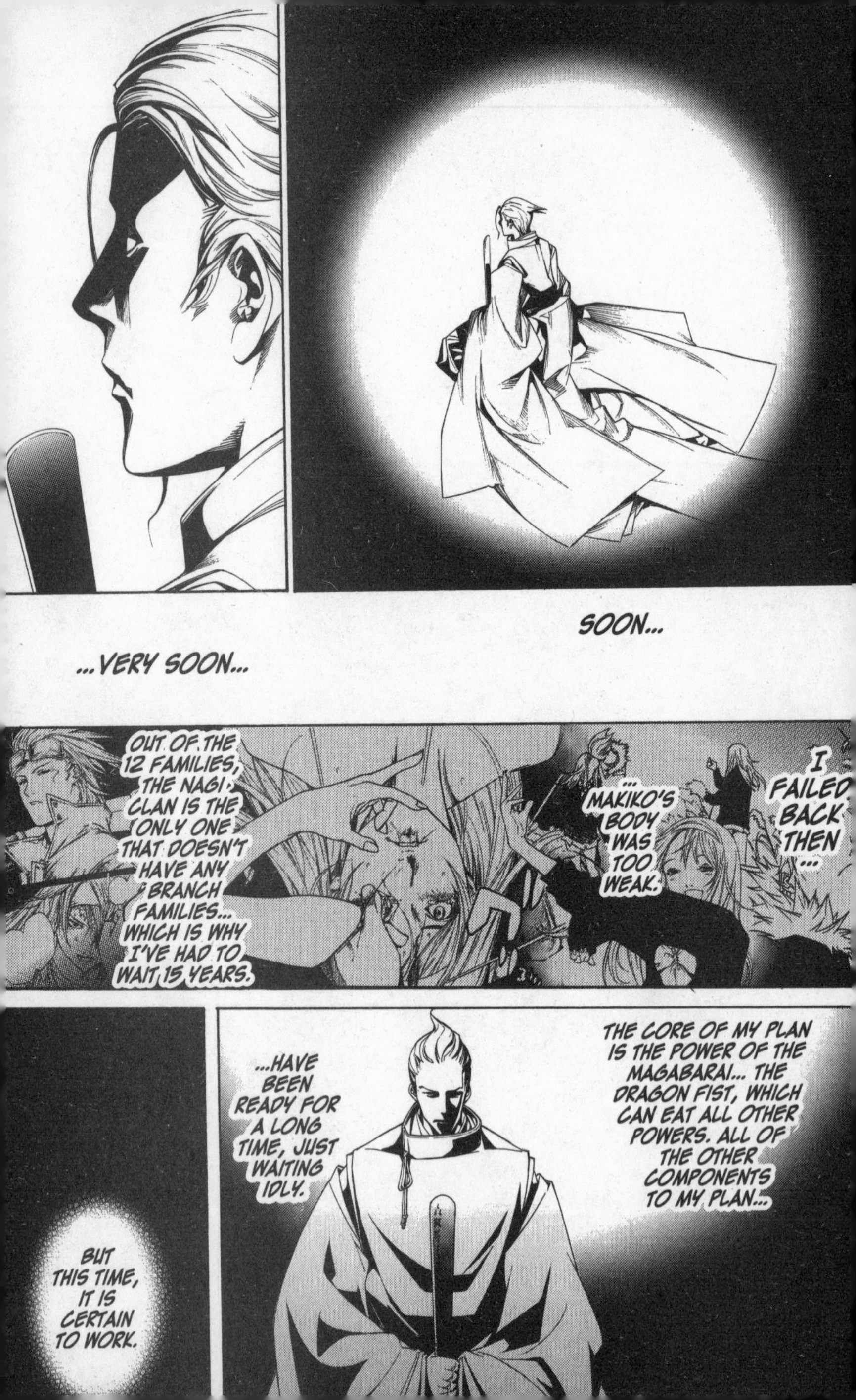
SOON...
...VERY SOON...
I FAILED BACK THEN...
...MAKIKO'S BODY WAS TOO WEAK.
OUT OF THE 12 FAMILIES, THE NAGI CLAN IS THE ONLY ONE THAT DOESN'T HAVE ANY BRANCH FAMILIES... WHICH IS WHY I'VE HAD TO WAIT 15 YEARS.
THE CORE OF MY PLAN IS THE POWER OF THE MAGABARAI... THE DRAGON FIST, WHICH CAN EAT ALL OTHER POWERS. ALL OF THE OTHER COMPONENTS TO MY PLAN...
...HAVE BEEN READY FOR A LONG TIME, JUST WAITING IDLY.
BUT THIS TIME, IT IS CERTAIN TO WORK.

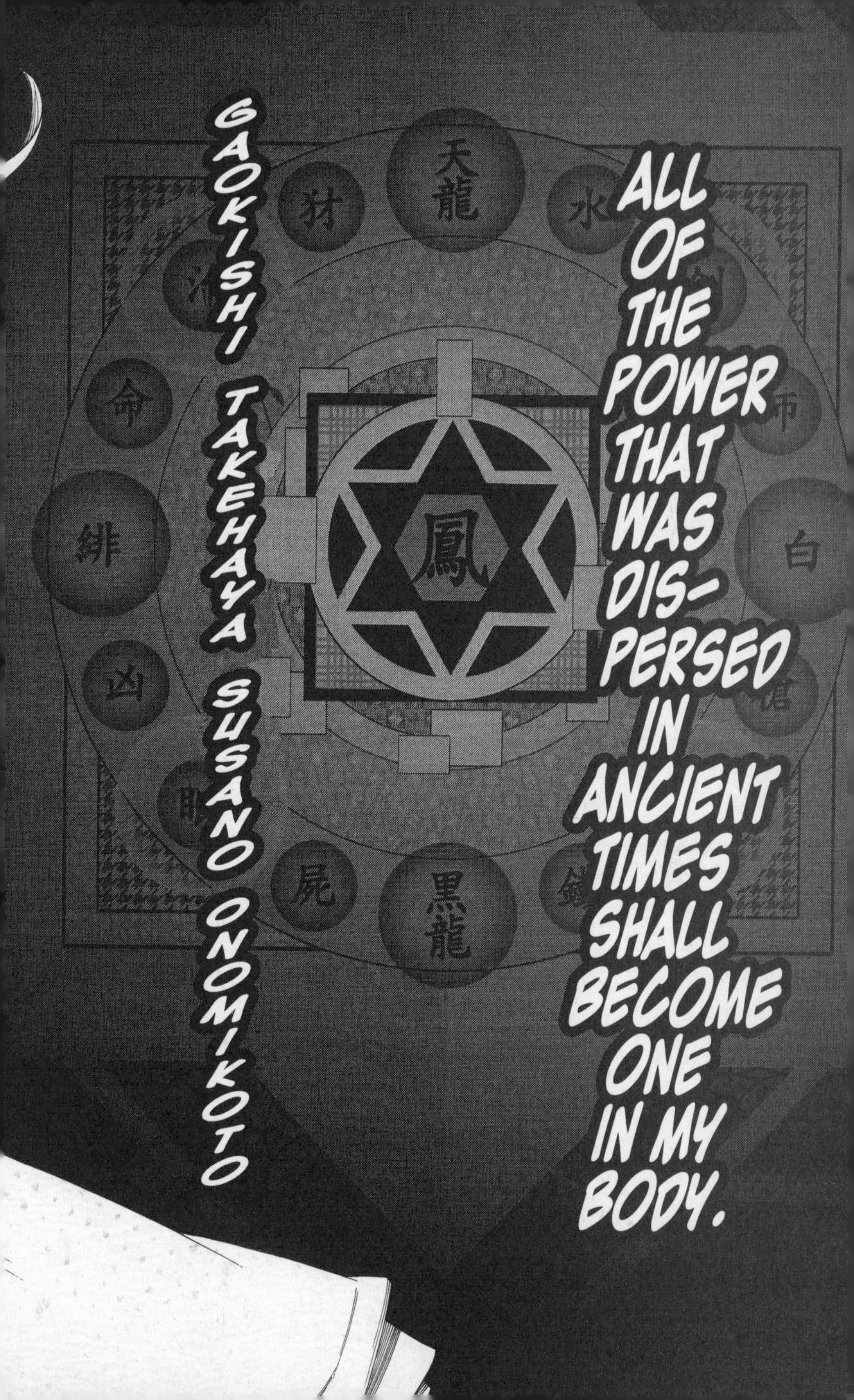
ALL OF THE POWER THAT WAS DISPERSED IN ANCIENT TIMES SHALL BECOME ONE IN MY BODY.
GAOKISHI TAKEHAYA SUSANO ONOMIKOTO

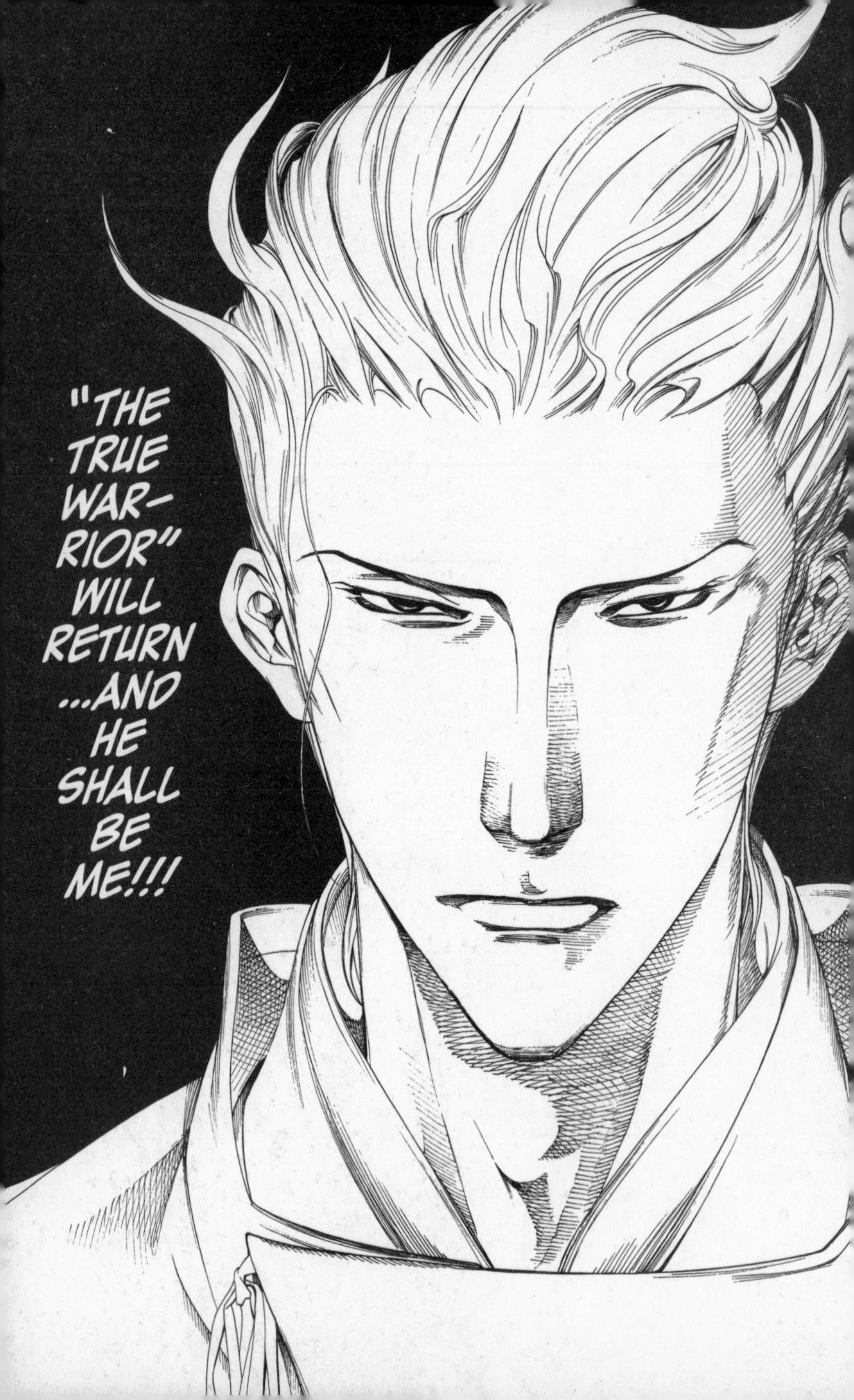
"THE TRUE WAR-RIOR" WILL RETURN ...AND HE SHALL BE ME!!!

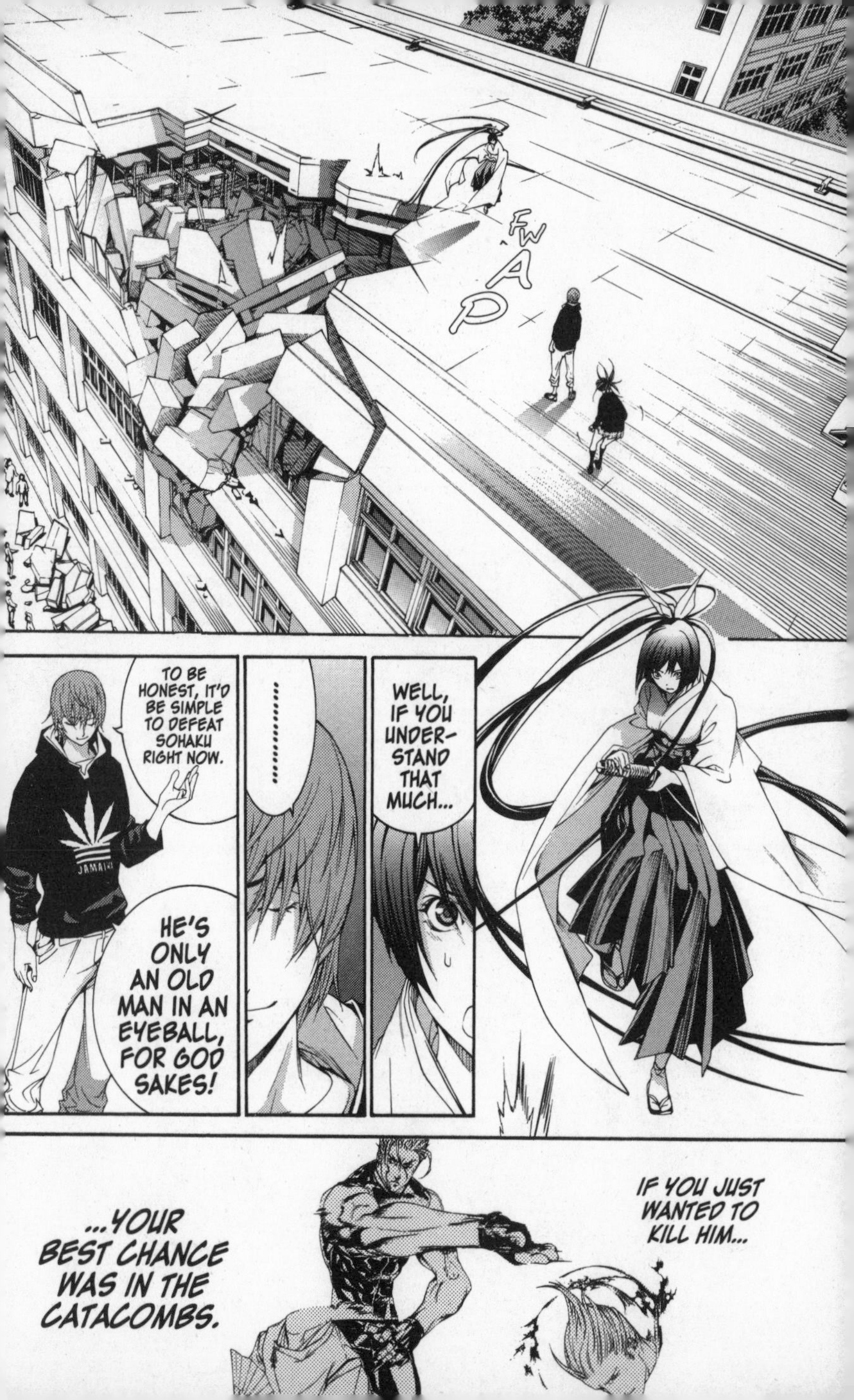
FWAP
WELL, IF YOU UNDER-STAND THAT MUCH...
....
TO BE HONEST, IT'D BE SIMPLE TO DEFEAT SOHAKU RIGHT NOW.
HE'S ONLY AN OLD MAN IN AN EYEBALL, FOR GOD SAKES!
IF YOU JUST WANTED TO KILL HIM...
...YOUR BEST CHANCE WAS IN THE CATACOMBS.

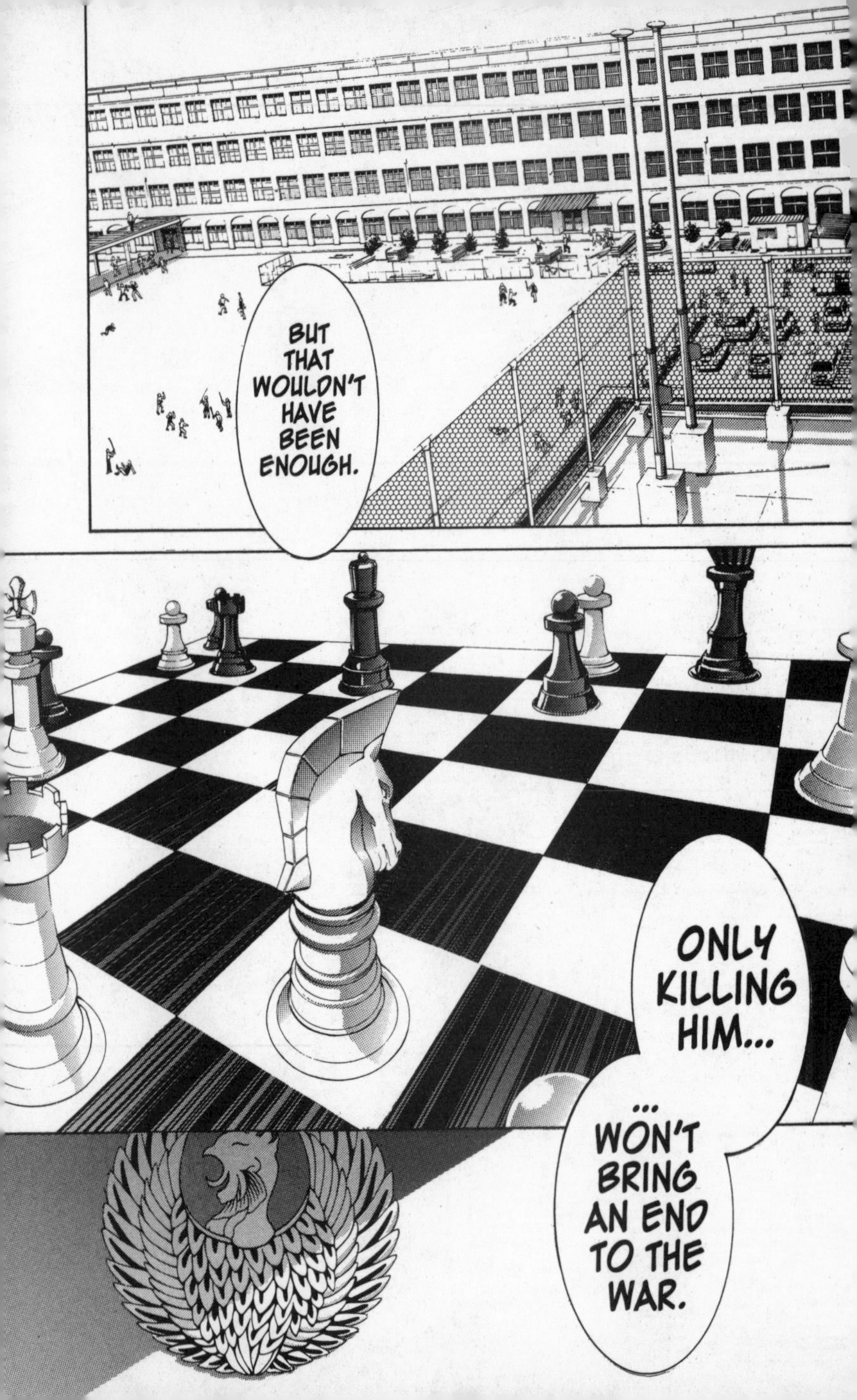
BUT THAT WOULDN'T HAVE BEEN ENOUGH.
ONLY KILLING HIM...
...WON'T BRING AN END TO THE WAR.

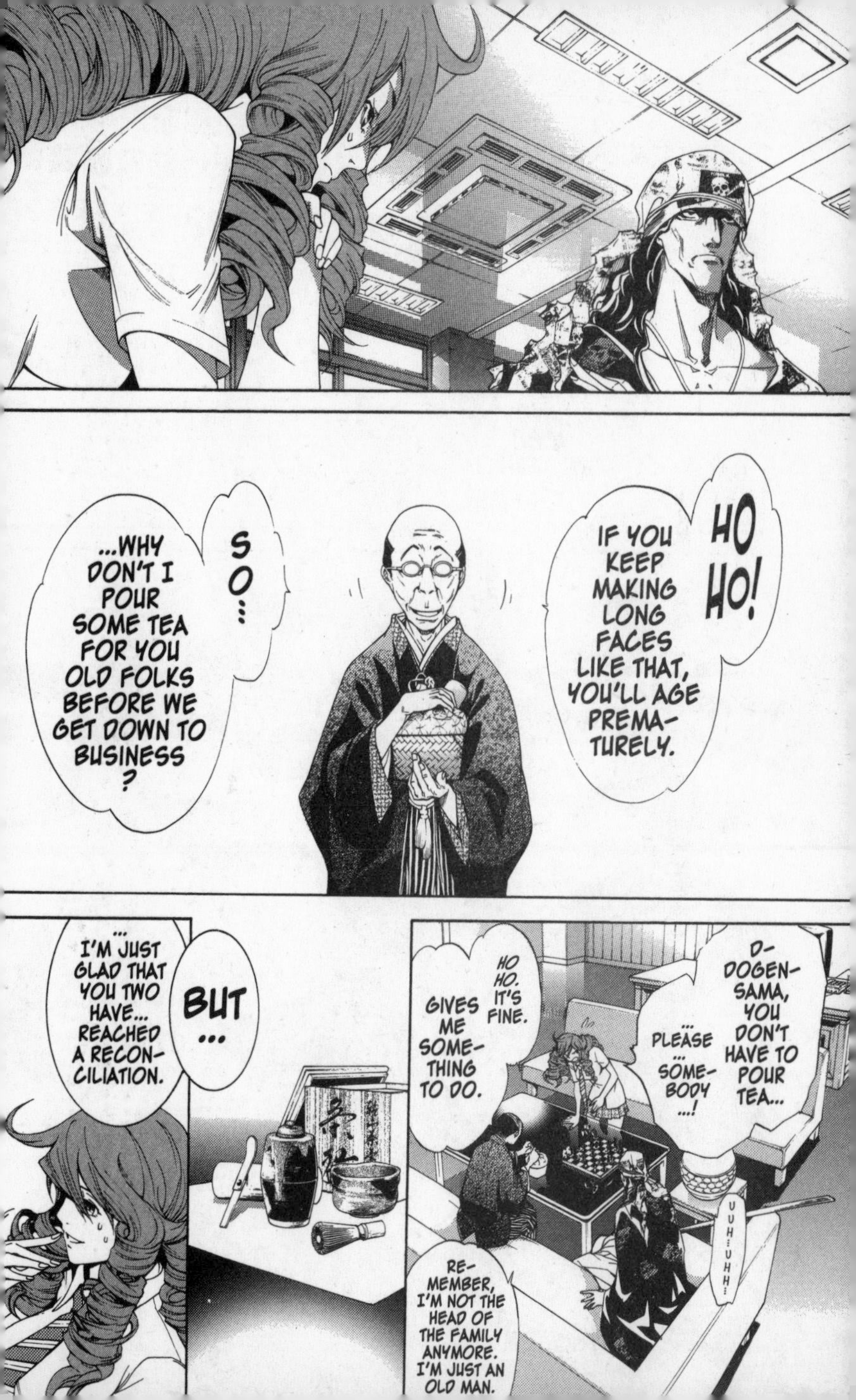

HO HO!
IF YOU KEEP MAKING LONG FACES LIKE THAT, YOU'LL AGE PREMATURELY.
SO...
...WHY DON'T I POUR SOME TEA FOR YOU OLD FOLKS BEFORE WE GET DOWN TO BUSINESS?
D-DOGEN-SAMA, YOU DON'T HAVE TO POUR TEA...
...PLEASE ...SOMEBODY ...!
HO HO. IT'S FINE.
GIVES ME SOMETHING TO DO.
UUH...UHH...
REMEMBER, I'M NOT THE HEAD OF THE FAMILY ANYMORE. I'M JUST AN OLD MAN.
BUT...
...I'M JUST GLAD THAT YOU TWO HAVE... REACHED A RECONCILIATION.

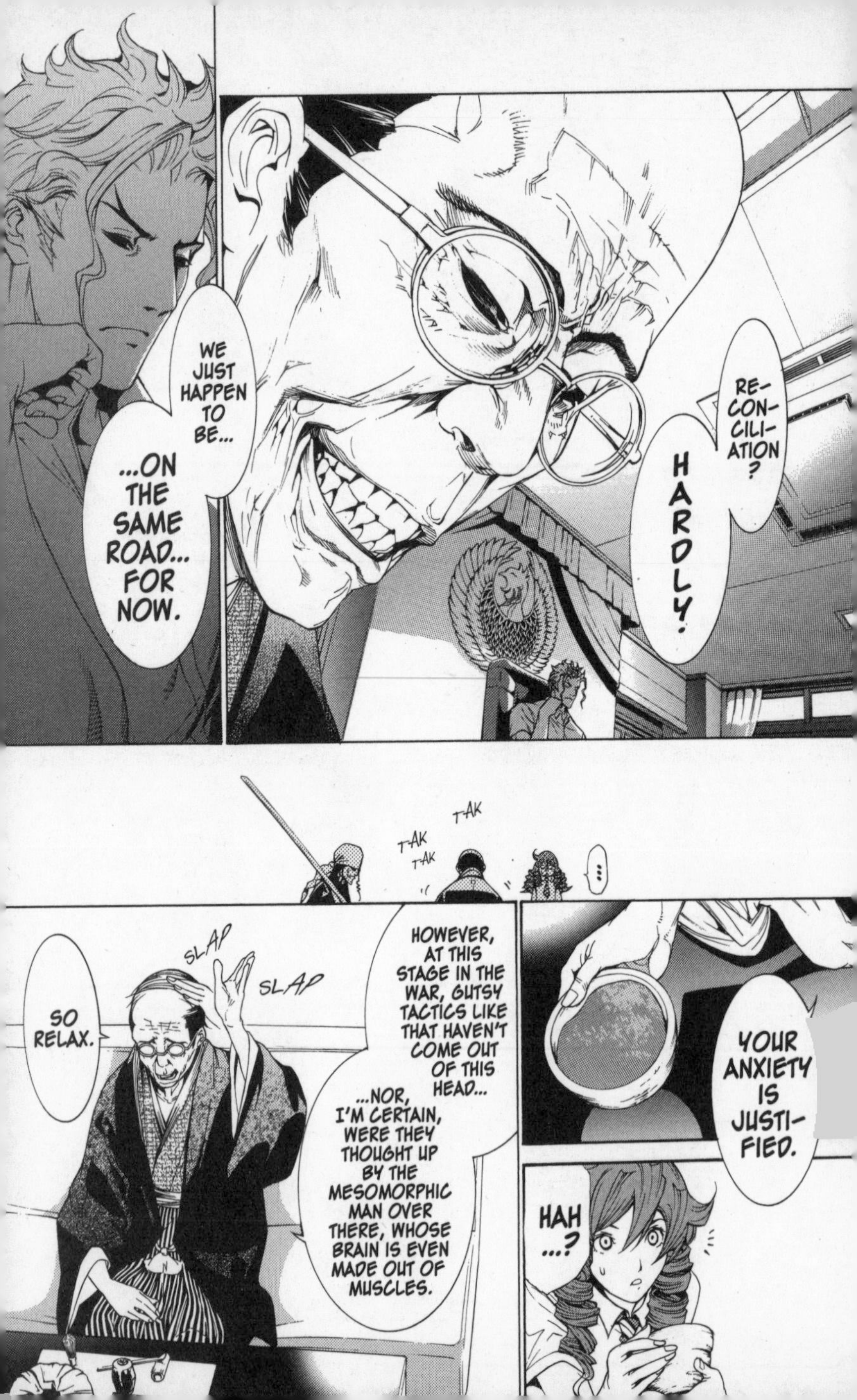
RE-CON-CILI-ATION?
HARDLY.
WE JUST HAPPEN TO BE...
...ON THE SAME ROAD... FOR NOW.
T-AK
T-AK
T-AK
...
YOUR ANXIETY IS JUSTI-FIED.
HAH ...?
HOWEVER, AT THIS STAGE IN THE WAR, GUTSY TACTICS LIKE THAT HAVEN'T COME OUT OF THIS HEAD...
...NOR, I'M CERTAIN, WERE THEY THOUGHT UP BY THE MESOMORPHIC MAN OVER THERE, WHOSE BRAIN IS EVEN MADE OUT OF MUSCLES.
SLAP
SLAP
SO RELAX.

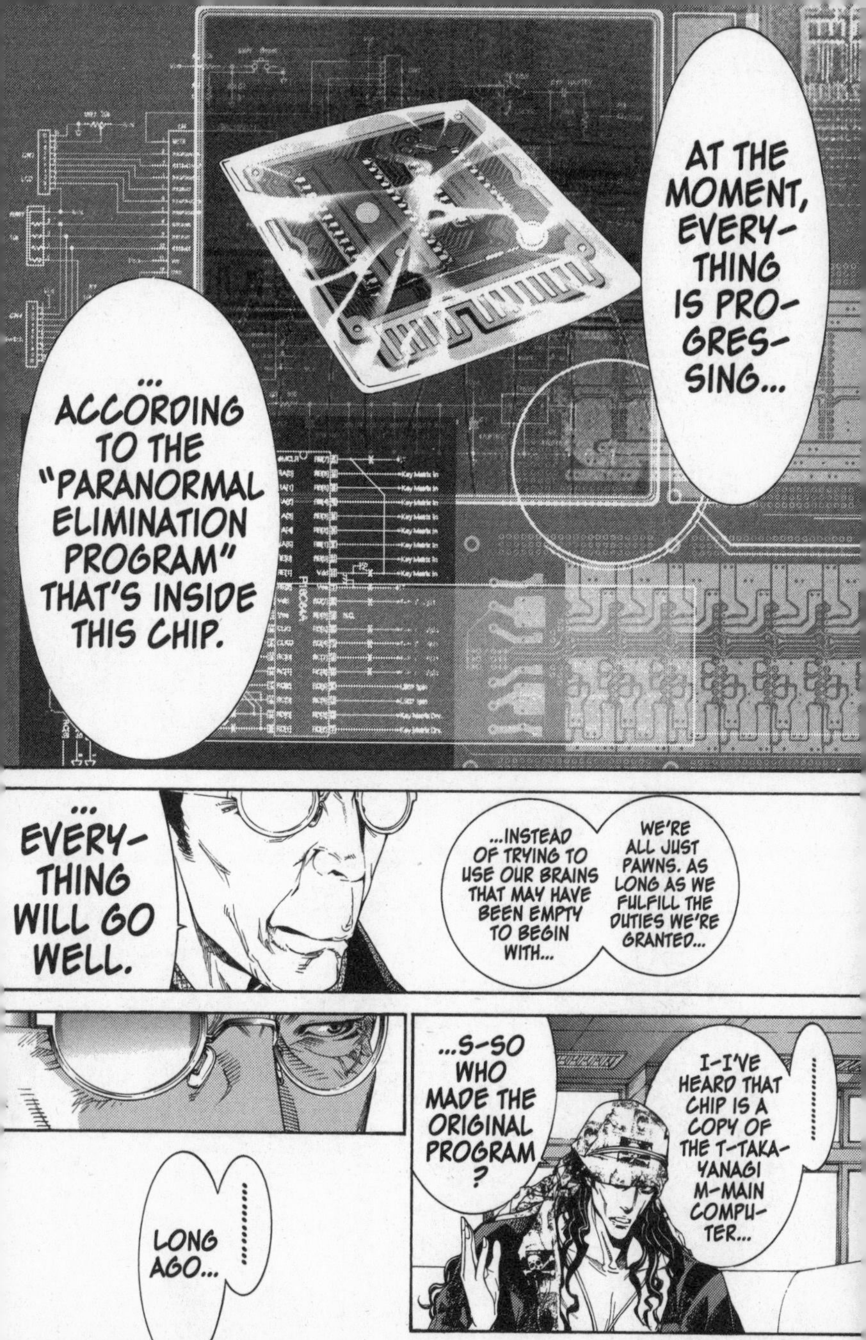
AT THE MOMENT, EVERY-THING IS PRO-GRES-SING...
...ACCORDING TO THE "PARANORMAL ELIMINATION PROGRAM" THAT'S INSIDE THIS CHIP.
WE'RE ALL JUST PAWNS. AS LONG AS WE FULFILL THE DUTIES WE'RE GRANTED...
...INSTEAD OF TRYING TO USE OUR BRAINS THAT MAY HAVE BEEN EMPTY TO BEGIN WITH...
...EVERY-THING WILL GO WELL.
....
I-I'VE HEARD THAT CHIP IS A COPY OF THE T-TAKA-YANAGI M-MAIN COMPU-TER...
...S-SO WHO MADE THE ORIGINAL PROGRAM?
....
LONG AGO...

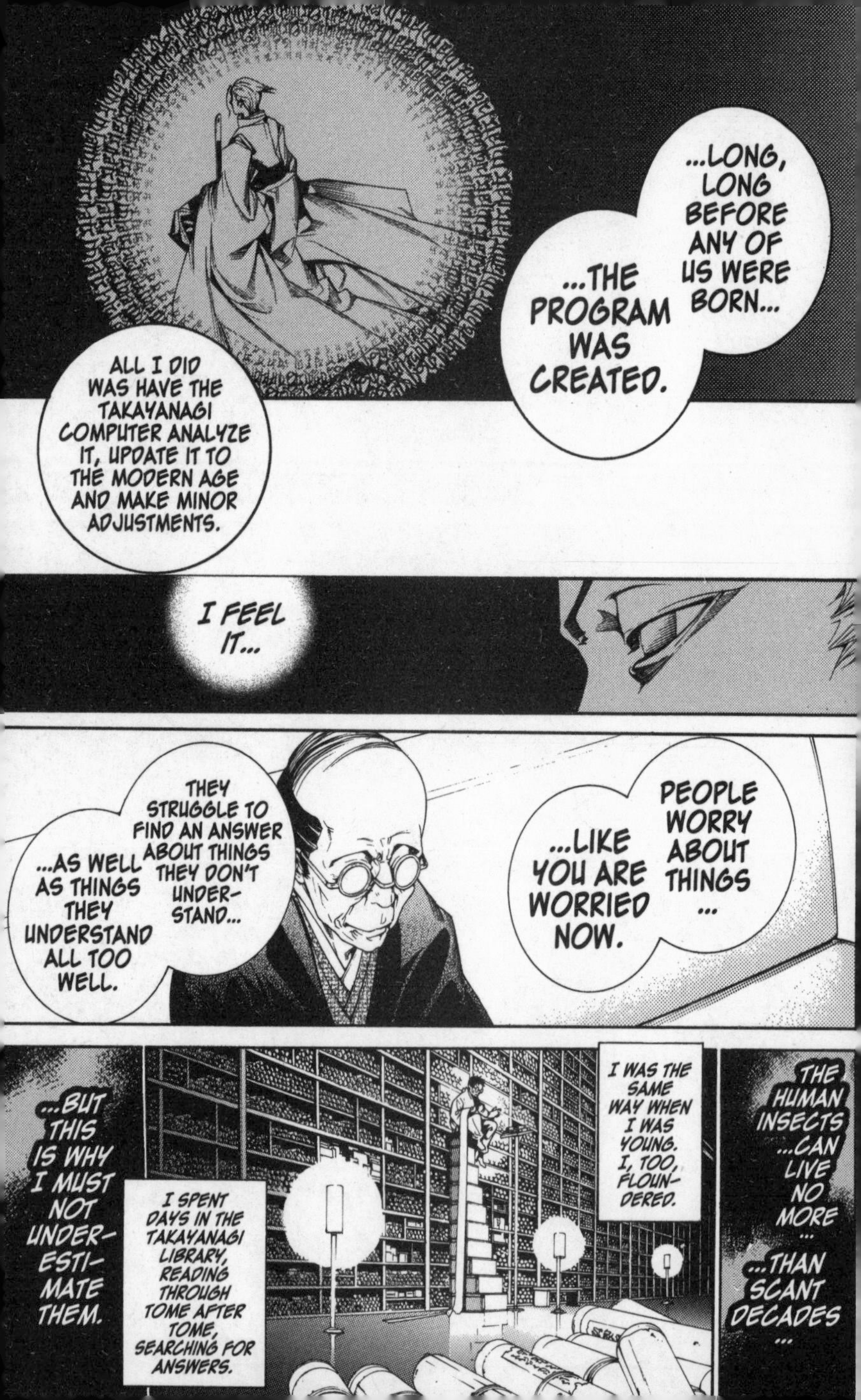
...LONG, LONG BEFORE ANY OF US WERE BORN...
...THE PROGRAM WAS CREATED.
ALL I DID WAS HAVE THE TAKAYANAGI COMPUTER ANALYZE IT, UPDATE IT TO THE MODERN AGE AND MAKE MINOR ADJUSTMENTS.
I FEEL IT...
PEOPLE WORRY ABOUT THINGS ...
...LIKE YOU ARE WORRIED NOW.
THEY STRUGGLE TO FIND AN ANSWER ABOUT THINGS THEY DON'T UNDER-STAND...
...AS WELL AS THINGS THEY UNDERSTAND ALL TOO WELL.
THE HUMAN INSECTS ...CAN LIVE NO MORE ...
...THAN SCANT DECADES ...
I WAS THE SAME WAY WHEN I WAS YOUNG. I, TOO, FLOUN-DERED.
I SPENT DAYS IN THE TAKAYANAGI LIBRARY, READING THROUGH TOME AFTER TOME, SEARCHING FOR ANSWERS.
...BUT THIS IS WHY I MUST NOT UNDER-ESTI-MATE THEM.

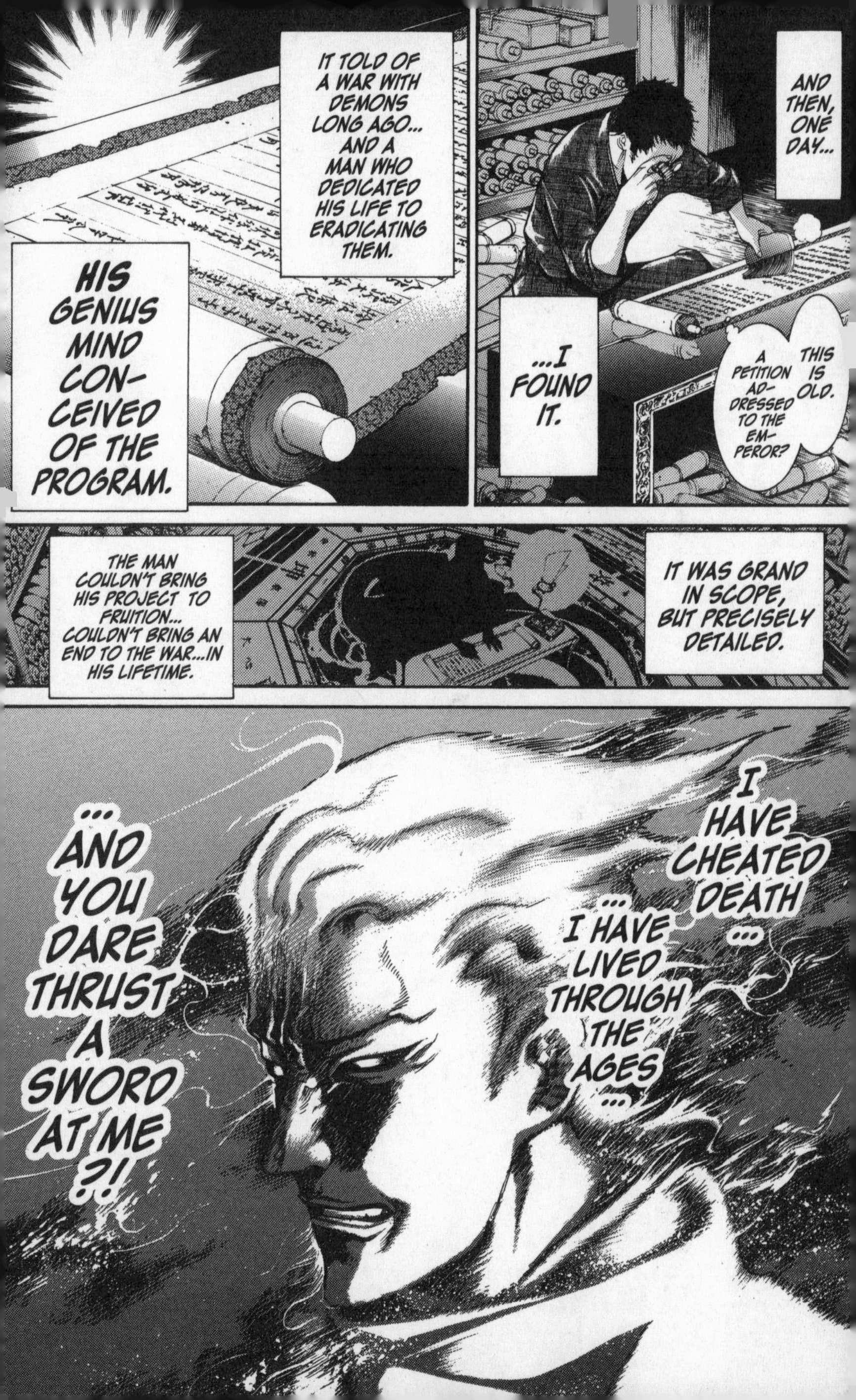
AND THEN, ONE DAY...
THIS IS OLD.
A PETITION ADDRESSED TO THE EMPEROR?
...I FOUND IT.
IT TOLD OF A WAR WITH DEMONS LONG AGO... AND A MAN WHO DEDICATED HIS LIFE TO ERADICATING THEM.
HIS GENIUS MIND CONCEIVED OF THE PROGRAM.
IT WAS GRAND IN SCOPE, BUT PRECISELY DETAILED.
THE MAN COULDN'T BRING HIS PROJECT TO FRUITION... COULDN'T BRING AN END TO THE WAR...IN HIS LIFETIME.
I HAVE CHEATED DEATH...
...I HAVE LIVED THROUGH THE AGES...
...AND YOU DARE THRUST A SWORD AT ME?!

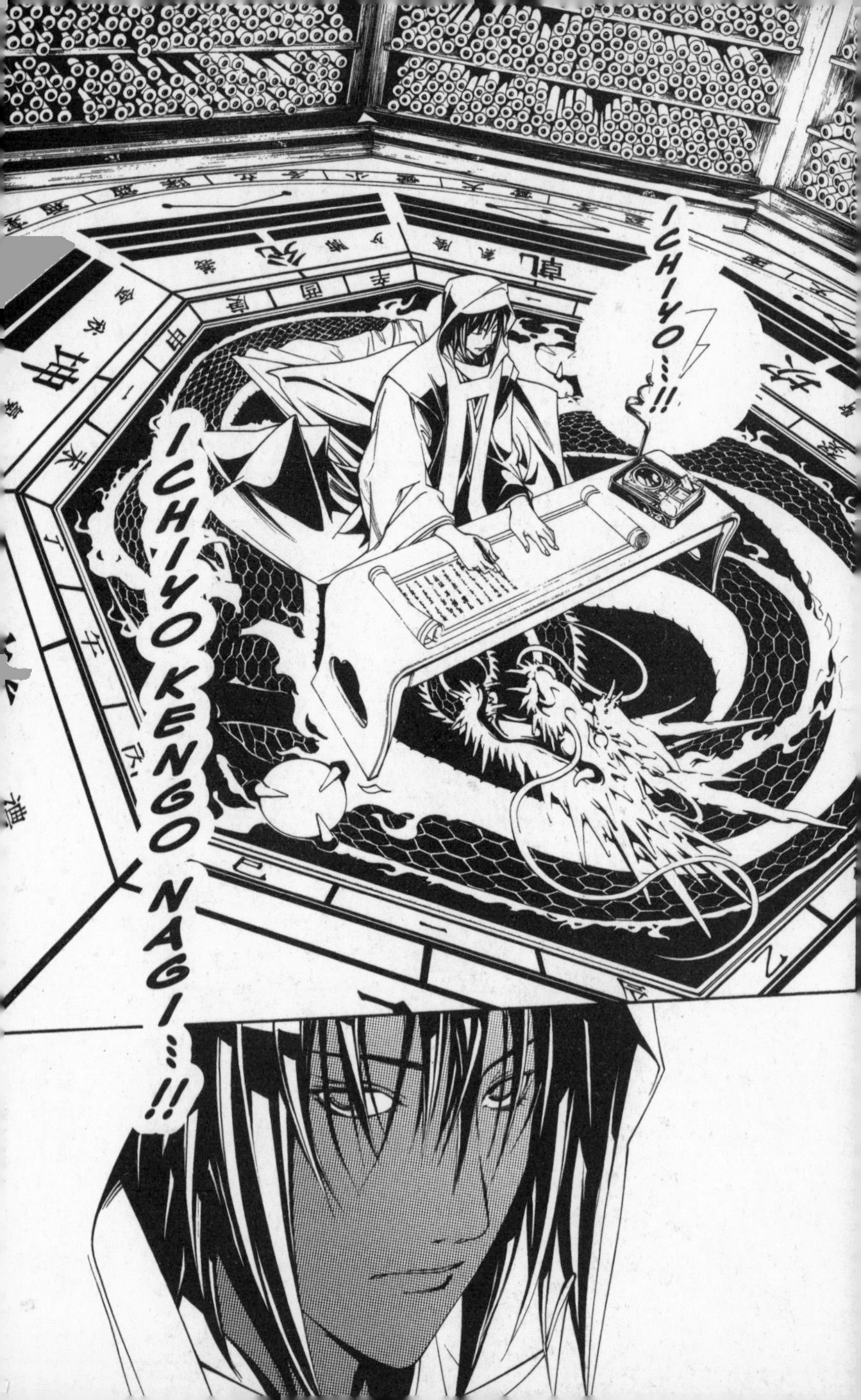
ICHIYO...!!
ICHIYO KENGO NAGI...!!

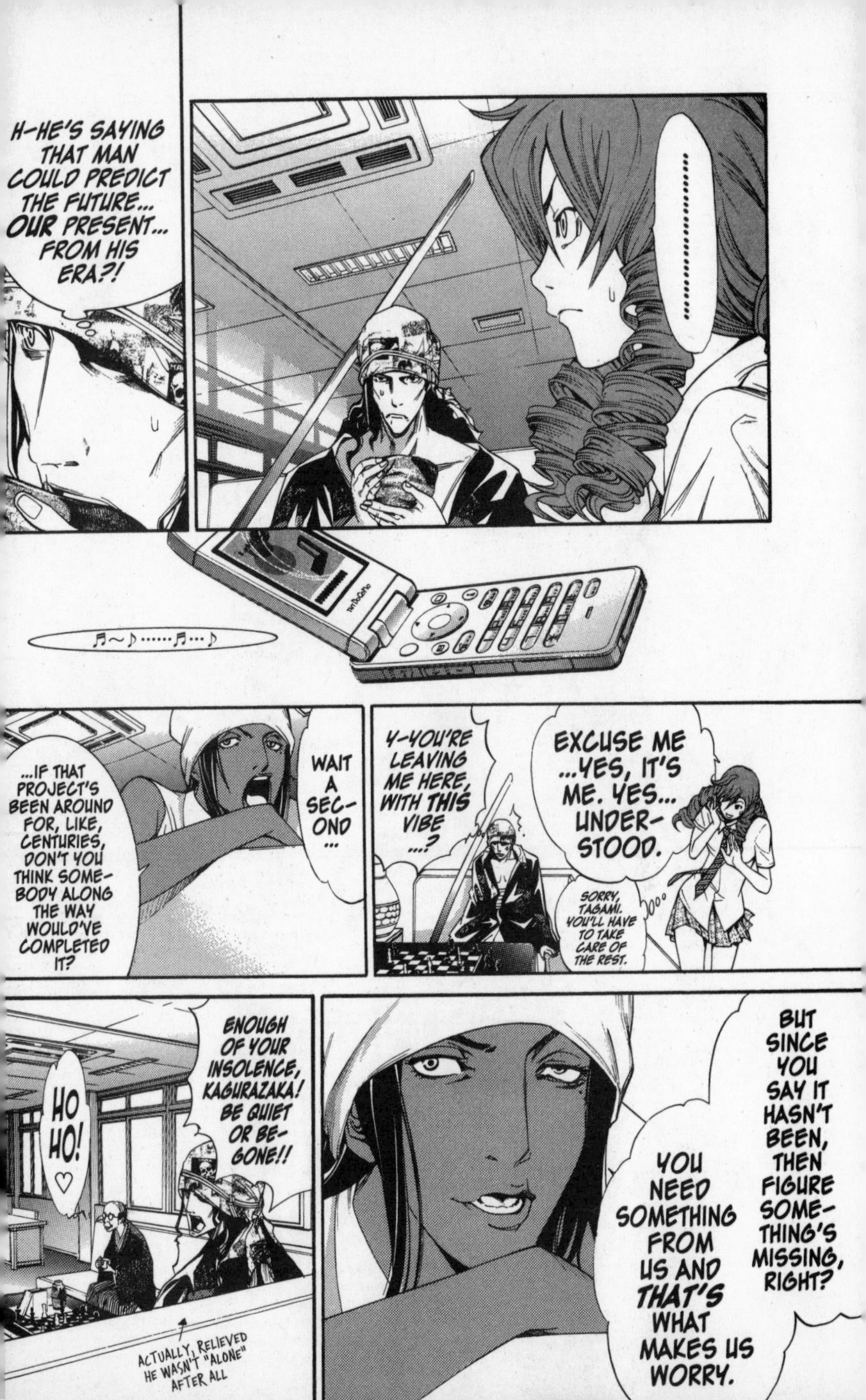
......
H-HE'S SAYING THAT MAN COULD PREDICT THE FUTURE... OUR PRESENT... FROM HIS ERA?!
♬～♪……♬…♪
EXCUSE ME ...YES, IT'S ME. YES... UNDER-STOOD.
Y-YOU'RE LEAVING ME HERE, WITH THIS VIBE ...?
SORRY, TAGAMI. YOU'LL HAVE TO TAKE CARE OF THE REST.
WAIT A SEC-OND ...
...IF THAT PROJECT'S BEEN AROUND FOR, LIKE, CENTURIES, DON'T YOU THINK SOME-BODY ALONG THE WAY WOULD'VE COMPLETED IT?
BUT SINCE YOU SAY IT HASN'T BEEN, THEN FIGURE SOME-THING'S MISSING, RIGHT?
YOU NEED SOMETHING FROM US AND THAT'S WHAT MAKES US WORRY.
ENOUGH OF YOUR INSOLENCE, KAGURAZAKA! BE QUIET OR BE-GONE!!
HO HO! ♡
ACTUALLY, RELIEVED HE WASN'T "ALONE" AFTER ALL

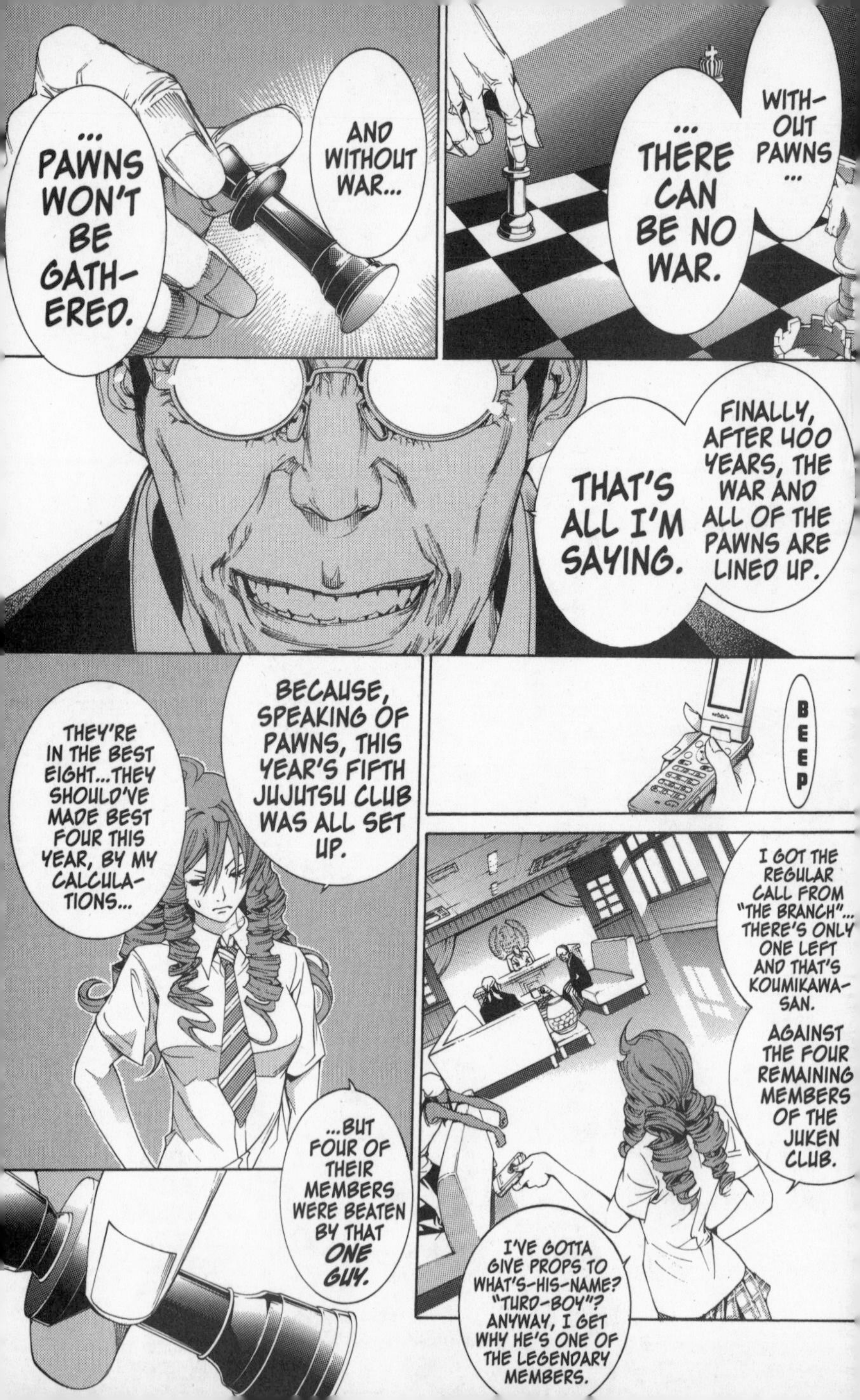
WITH-OUT PAWNS ...
... THERE CAN BE NO WAR.
AND WITHOUT WAR...
... PAWNS WON'T BE GATH-ERED.
FINALLY, AFTER 400 YEARS, THE WAR AND ALL OF THE PAWNS ARE LINED UP.
THAT'S ALL I'M SAYING.
BEEP
I GOT THE REGULAR CALL FROM "THE BRANCH"... THERE'S ONLY ONE LEFT AND THAT'S KOUMIKAWA-SAN.
AGAINST THE FOUR REMAINING MEMBERS OF THE JUKEN CLUB.
I'VE GOTTA GIVE PROPS TO WHAT'S-HIS-NAME? "TURD-BOY"? ANYWAY, I GET WHY HE'S ONE OF THE LEGENDARY MEMBERS.
BECAUSE, SPEAKING OF PAWNS, THIS YEAR'S FIFTH JUJUTSU CLUB WAS ALL SET UP.
THEY'RE IN THE BEST EIGHT...THEY SHOULD'VE MADE BEST FOUR THIS YEAR, BY MY CALCULA-TIONS...
...BUT FOUR OF THEIR MEMBERS WERE BEATEN BY THAT *ONE GUY.*

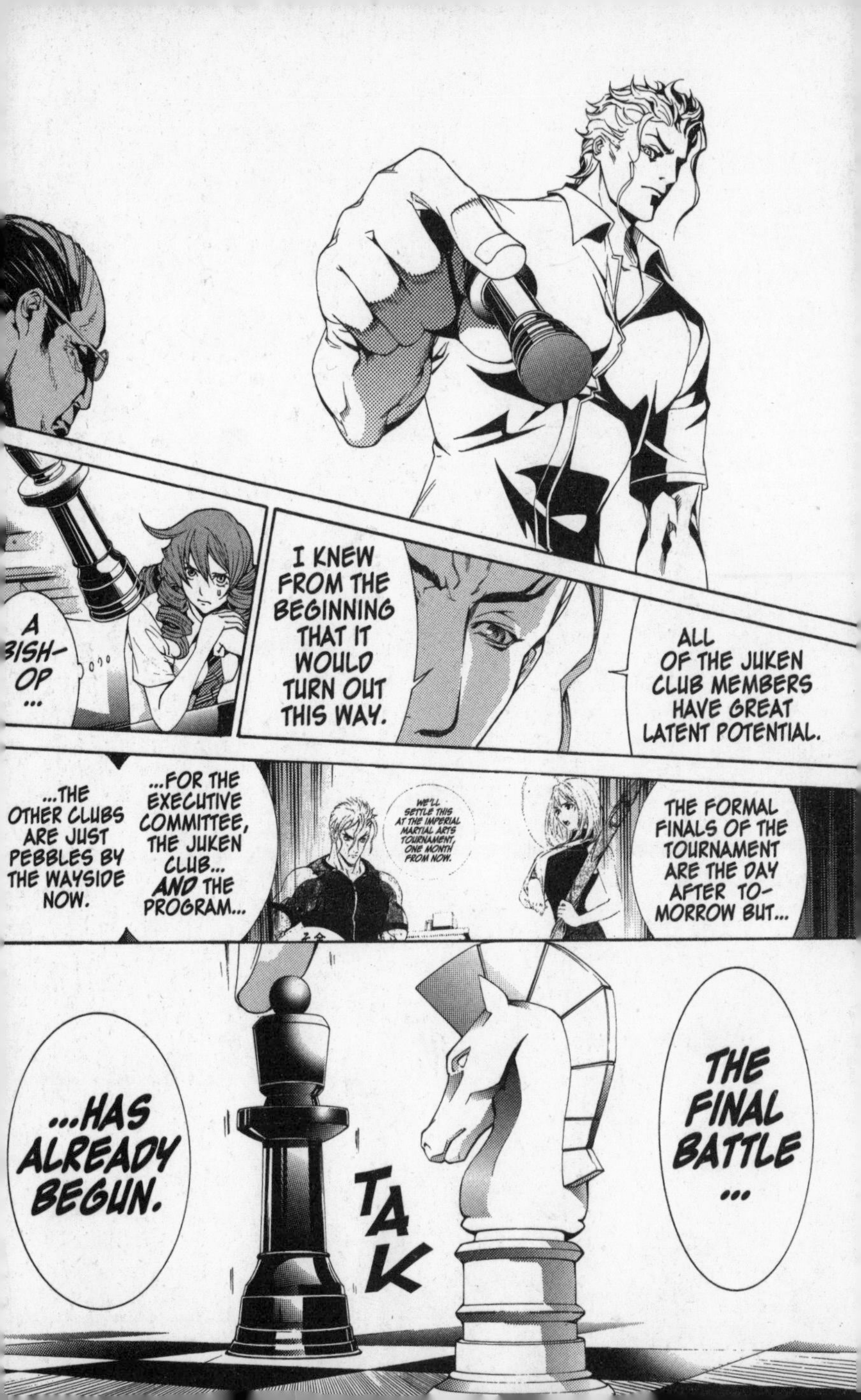
ALL OF THE JUKEN CLUB MEMBERS HAVE GREAT LATENT POTENTIAL.
I KNEW FROM THE BEGINNING THAT IT WOULD TURN OUT THIS WAY.
A BISH-OP...
THE FORMAL FINALS OF THE TOURNAMENT ARE THE DAY AFTER TO-MORROW BUT...
WE'LL SETTLE THIS AT THE IMPERIAL MARTIAL ARTS TOURNAMENT, ONE MONTH FROM NOW.
...FOR THE EXECUTIVE COMMITTEE, THE JUKEN CLUB... AND THE PROGRAM...
...THE OTHER CLUBS ARE JUST PEBBLES BY THE WAYSIDE NOW.
THE FINAL BATTLE...
TAK
...HAS ALREADY BEGUN.

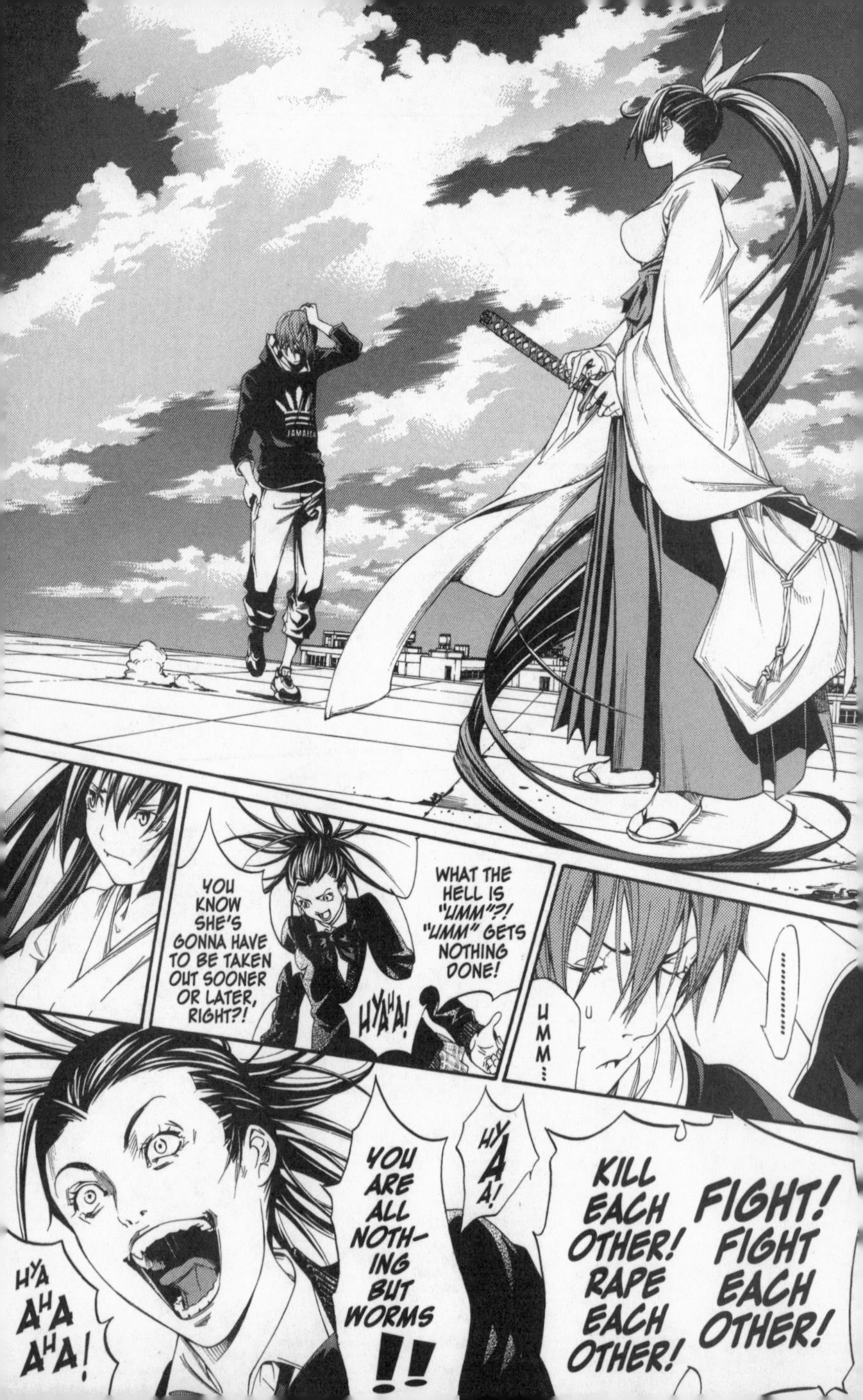
......
UMM...
WHAT THE HELL IS "UMM"?! "UMM" GETS NOTHING DONE!
YOU KNOW SHE'S GONNA HAVE TO BE TAKEN OUT SOONER OR LATER, RIGHT?!
HYAHA!
FIGHT! FIGHT EACH OTHER!
KILL EACH OTHER! RAPE EACH OTHER!
HYAA!
YOU ARE ALL NOTH-ING BUT WORMS!!
HYAAHAAHA!

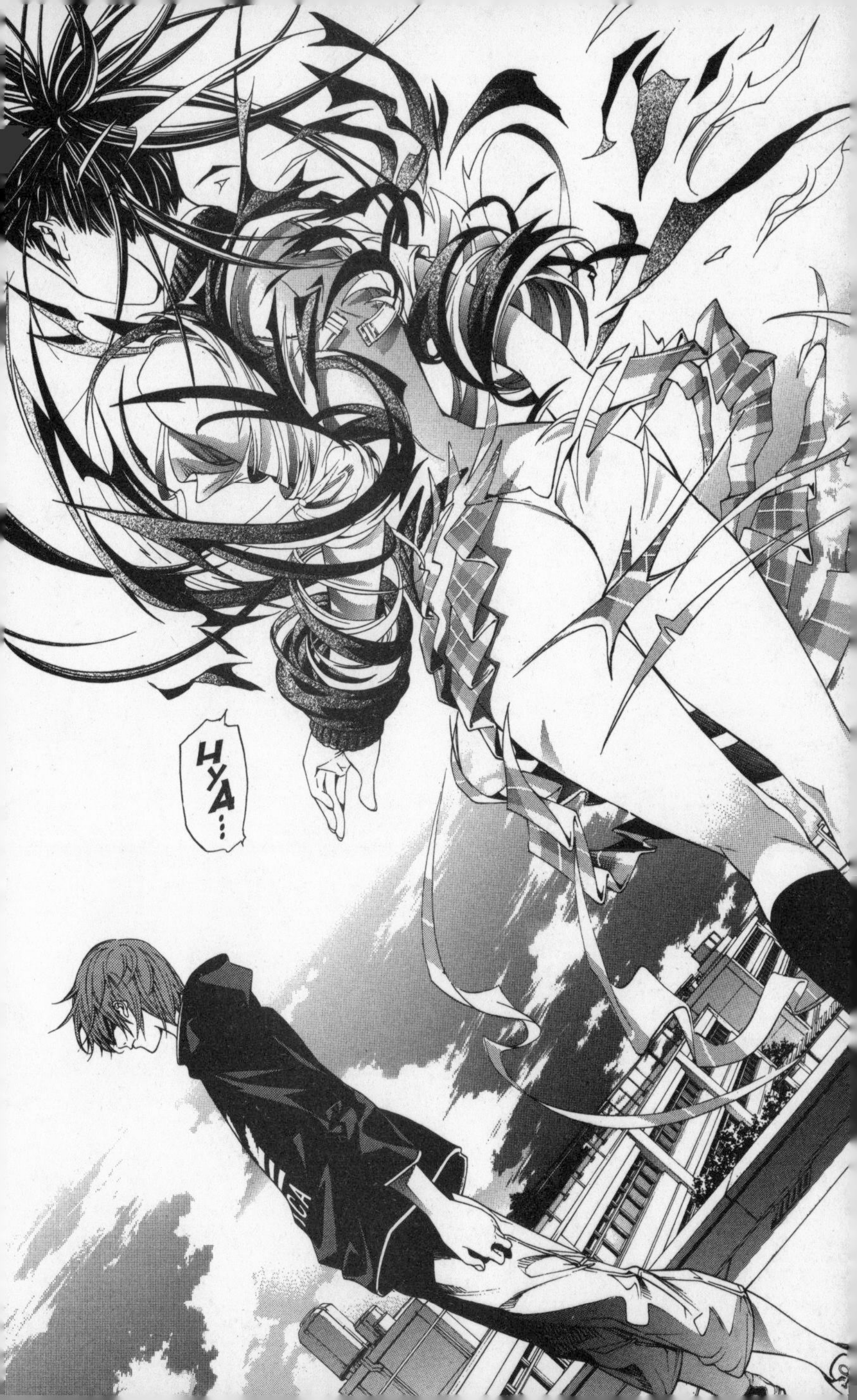
HYA...

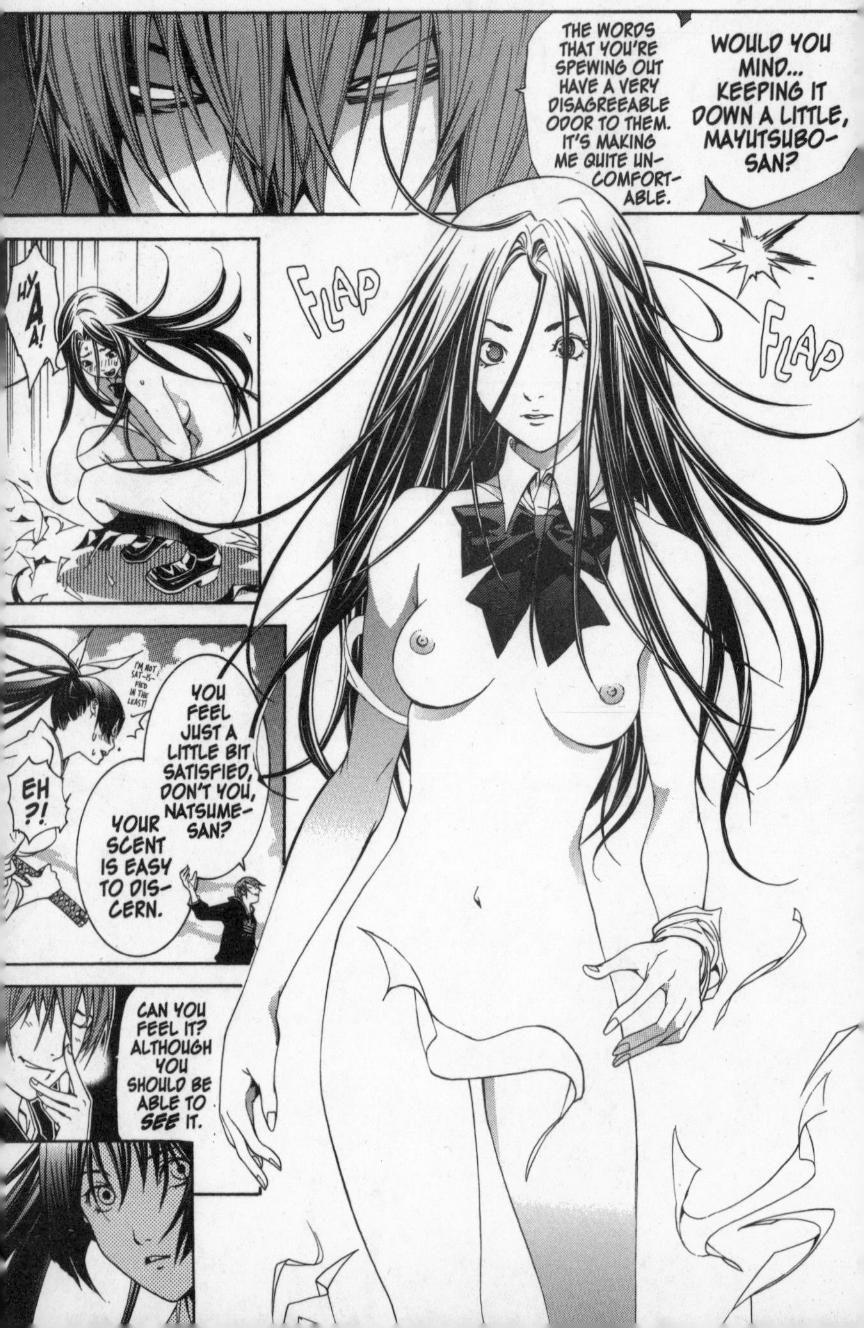
WOULD YOU MIND... KEEPING IT DOWN A LITTLE, MAYUTSUBO-SAN?
THE WORDS THAT YOU'RE SPEWING OUT HAVE A VERY DISAGREEABLE ODOR TO THEM. IT'S MAKING ME QUITE UN-COMFORT-ABLE.
FLAP
FLAP
HYAA!
YOU FEEL JUST A LITTLE BIT SATISFIED, DON'T YOU, NATSUME-SAN?
I'M NOT SAT-IS-FIED IN THE LEAST!
EH?!
YOUR SCENT IS EASY TO DIS-CERN.
CAN YOU FEEL IT? ALTHOUGH YOU SHOULD BE ABLE TO SEE IT.

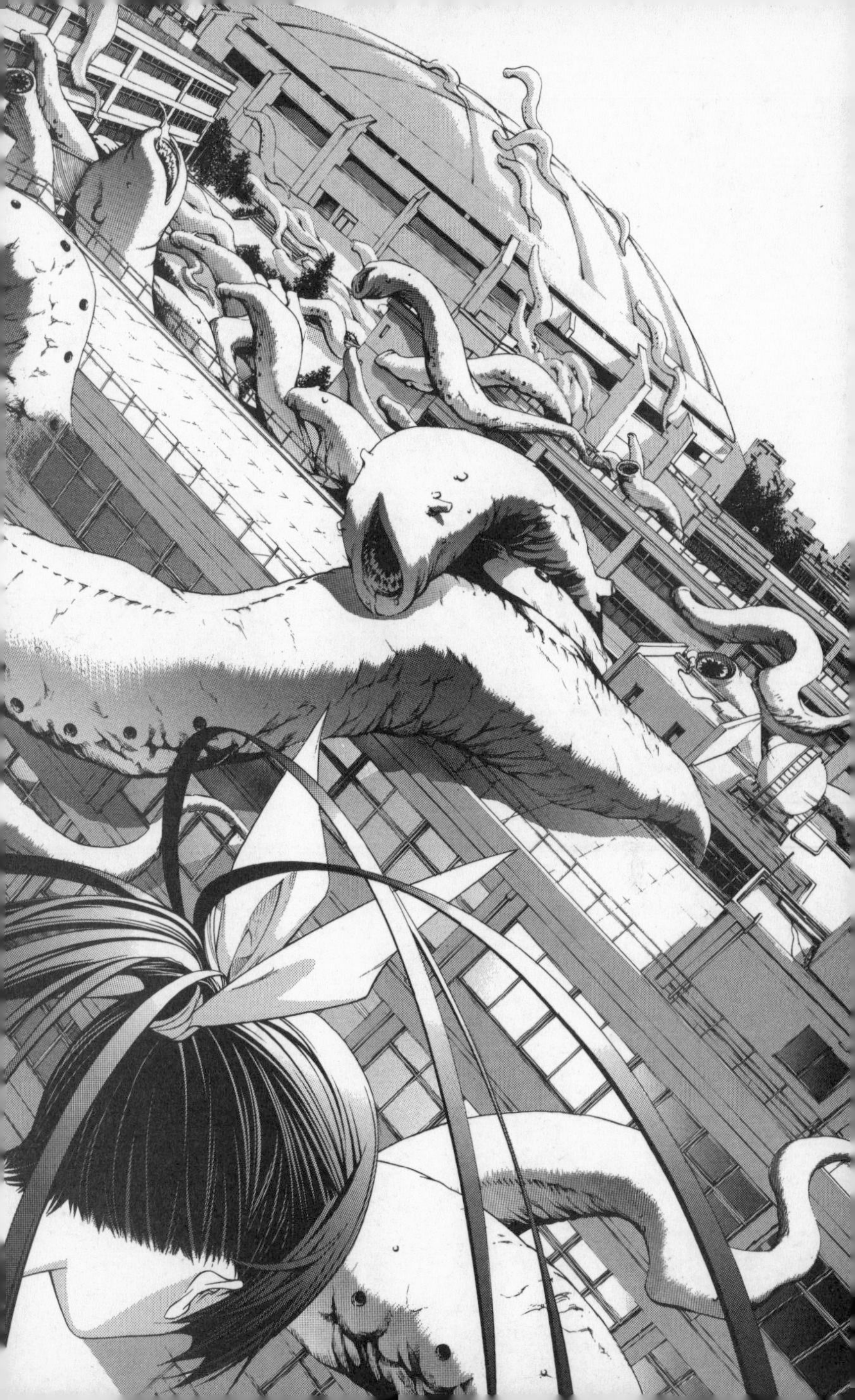

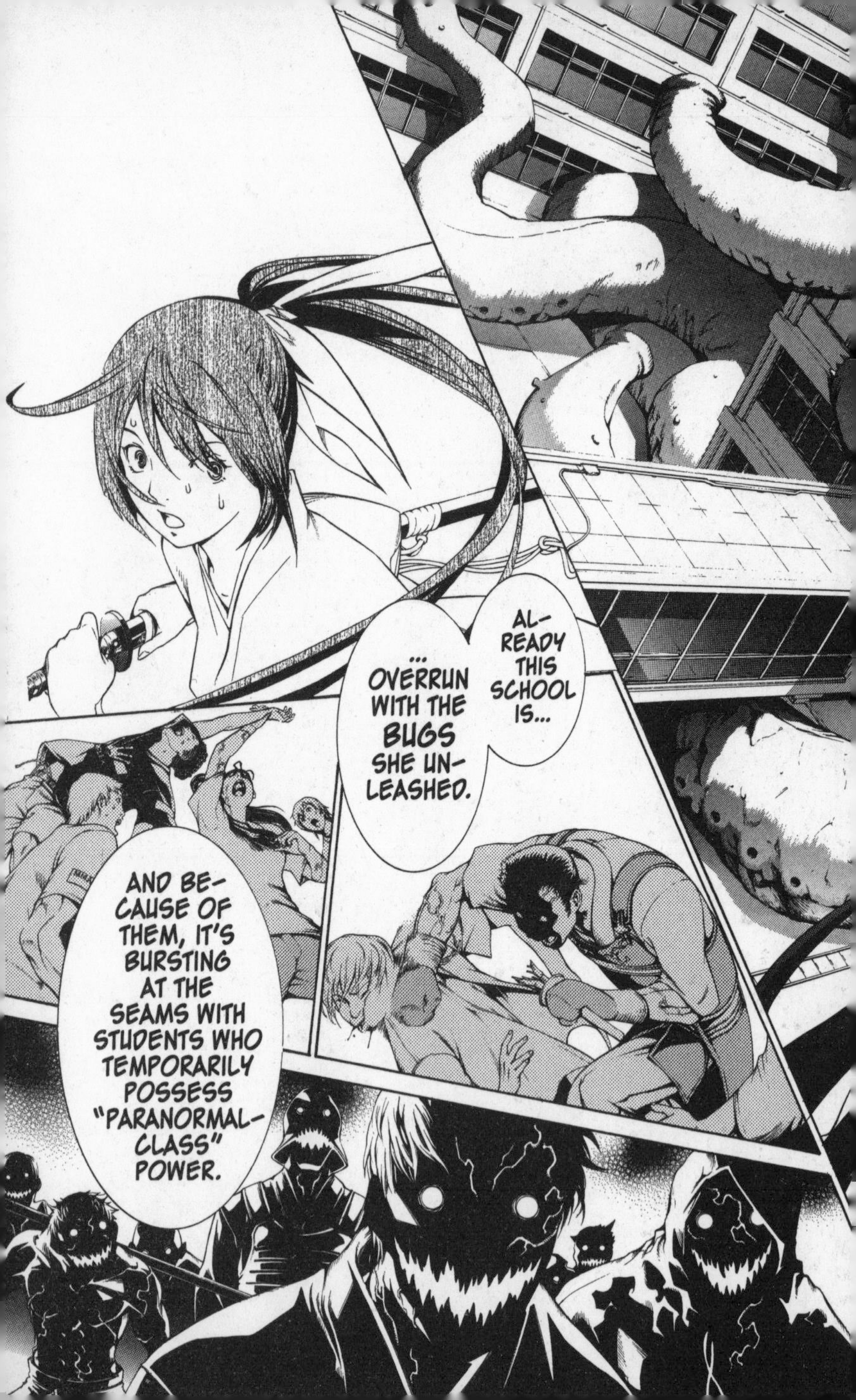
ALREADY THIS SCHOOL IS...
...OVERRUN WITH THE BUGS SHE UNLEASHED.
AND BECAUSE OF THEM, IT'S BURSTING AT THE SEAMS WITH STUDENTS WHO TEMPORARILY POSSESS "PARANORMAL-CLASS" POWER.

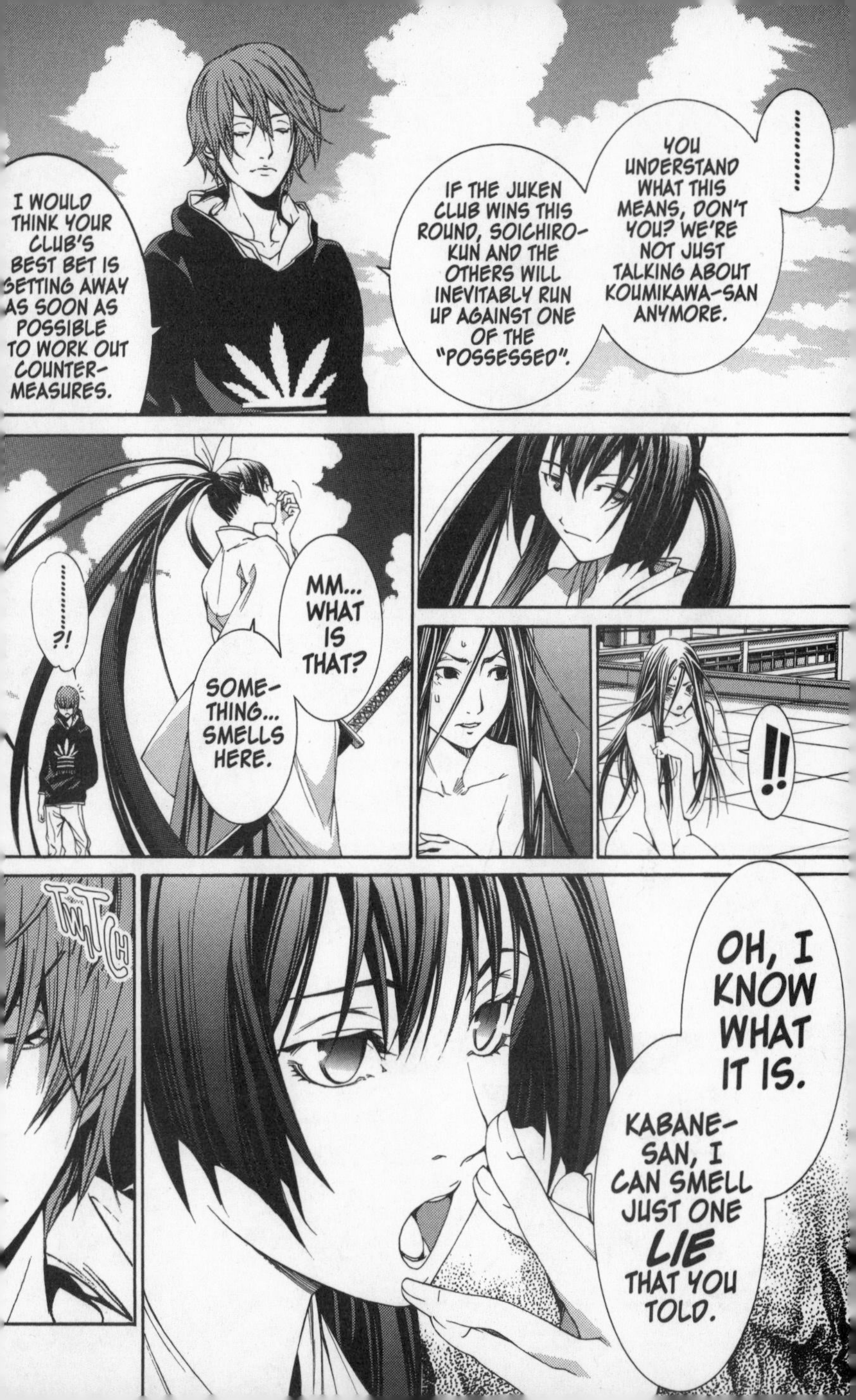
......
YOU UNDERSTAND WHAT THIS MEANS, DON'T YOU? WE'RE NOT JUST TALKING ABOUT KOUMIKAWA-SAN ANYMORE.
IF THE JUKEN CLUB WINS THIS ROUND, SOICHIRO-KUN AND THE OTHERS WILL INEVITABLY RUN UP AGAINST ONE OF THE "POSSESSED".
I WOULD THINK YOUR CLUB'S BEST BET IS GETTING AWAY AS SOON AS POSSIBLE TO WORK OUT COUNTER-MEASURES.
!!
MM... WHAT IS THAT?
SOME-THING... SMELLS HERE.
......?!
OH, I KNOW WHAT IT IS.
KABANE-SAN, I CAN SMELL JUST ONE LIE THAT YOU TOLD.
TWITCH

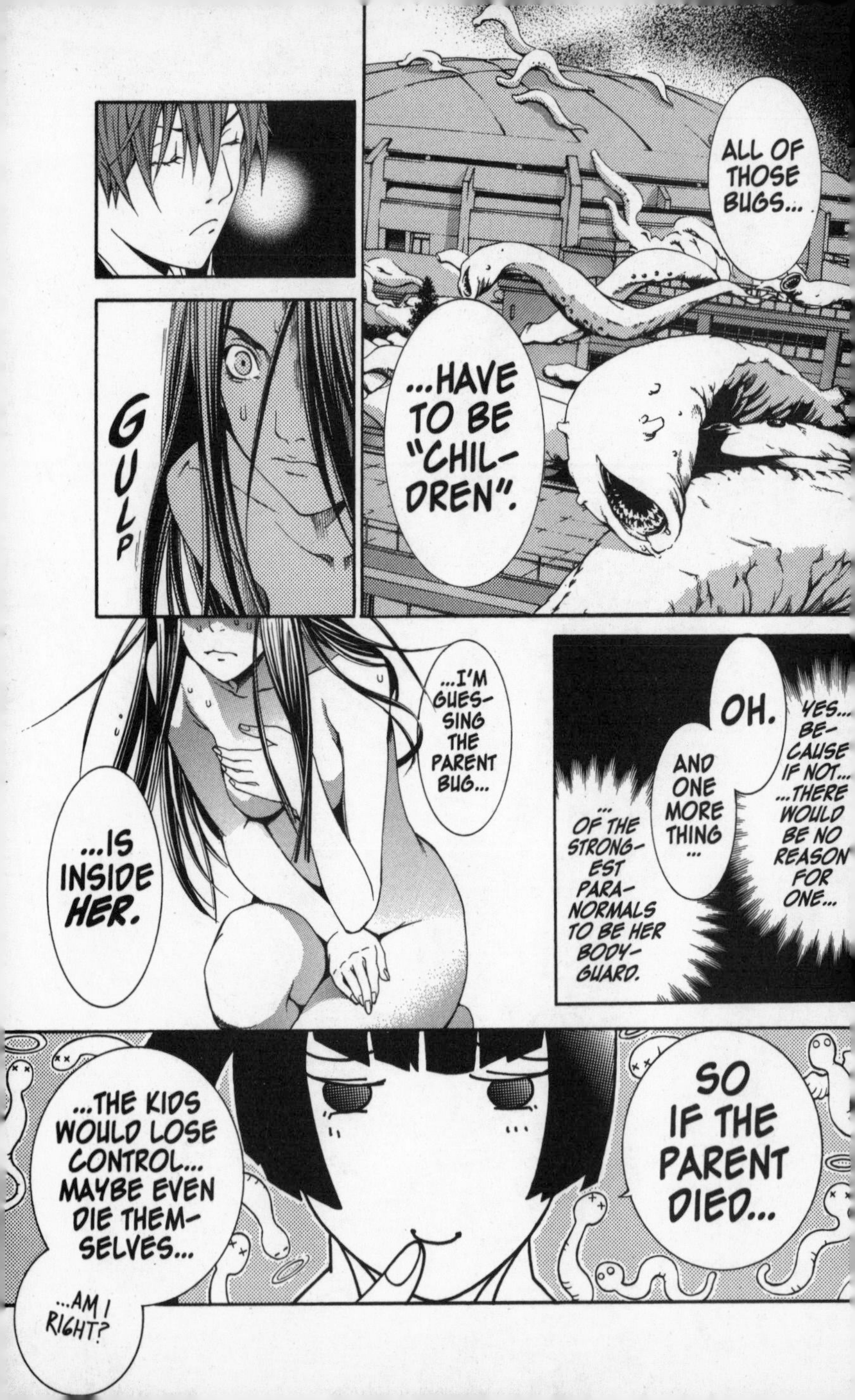
ALL OF THOSE BUGS...
...HAVE TO BE "CHILDREN".
GULP
YES... BECAUSE IF NOT... ...THERE WOULD BE NO REASON FOR ONE...
...OF THE STRONGEST PARANORMALS TO BE HER BODYGUARD.
OH.
AND ONE MORE THING...
...I'M GUESSING THE PARENT BUG...
...IS INSIDE HER.
SO IF THE PARENT DIED...
...
...THE KIDS WOULD LOSE CONTROL... MAYBE EVEN DIE THEMSELVES...
...AM I RIGHT?

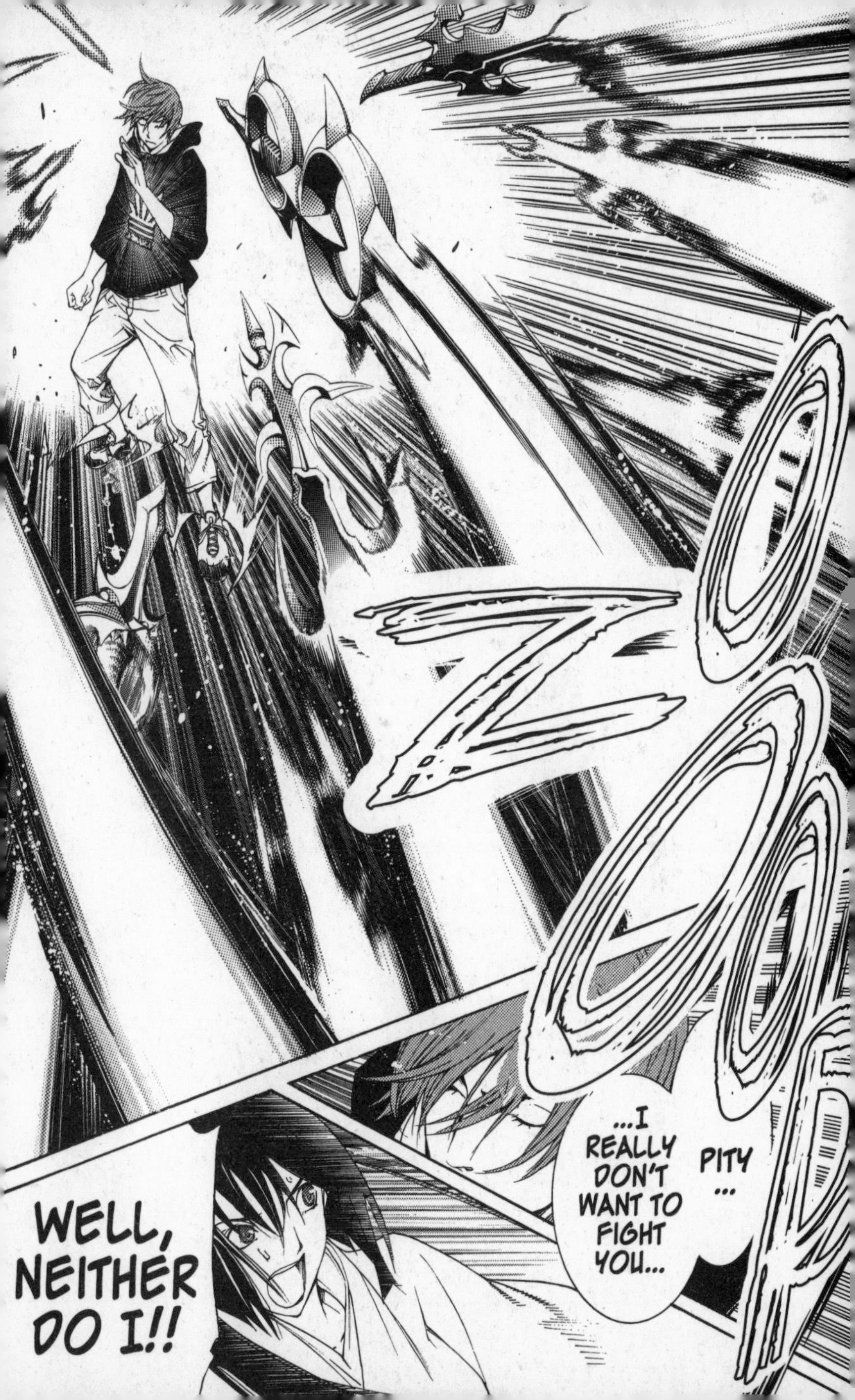
PITY ...
...I REALLY DON'T WANT TO FIGHT YOU...
WELL, NEITHER DO I!!

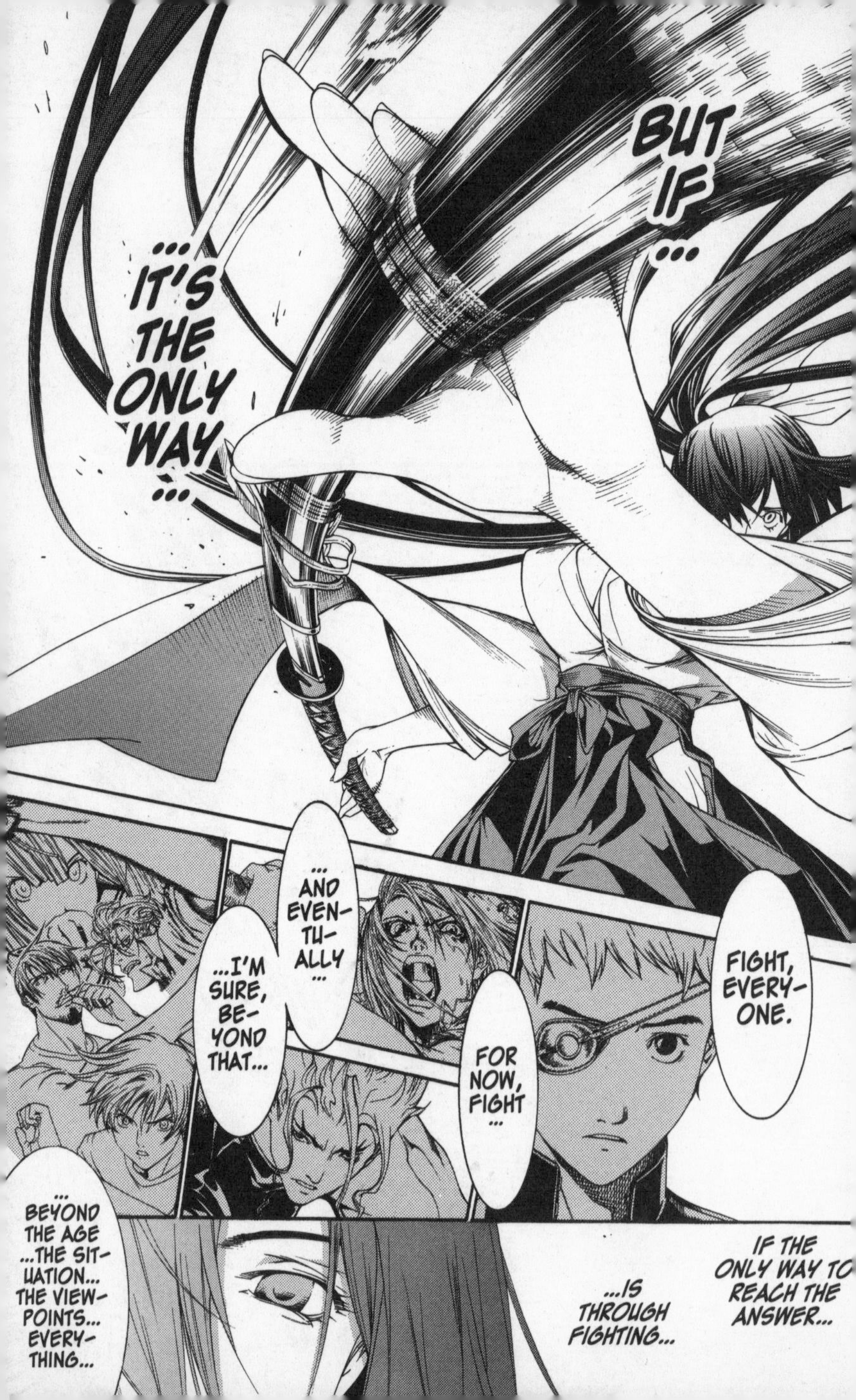
BUT IF...
...IT'S THE ONLY WAY...
FIGHT, EVERY-ONE.
FOR NOW, FIGHT...
...AND EVEN-TU-ALLY...
...I'M SURE, BE-YOND THAT...
...BEYOND THE AGE ...THE SIT-UATION... THE VIEW-POINTS... EVERY-THING...
IF THE ONLY WAY TO REACH THE ANSWER...
...IS THROUGH FIGHTING...

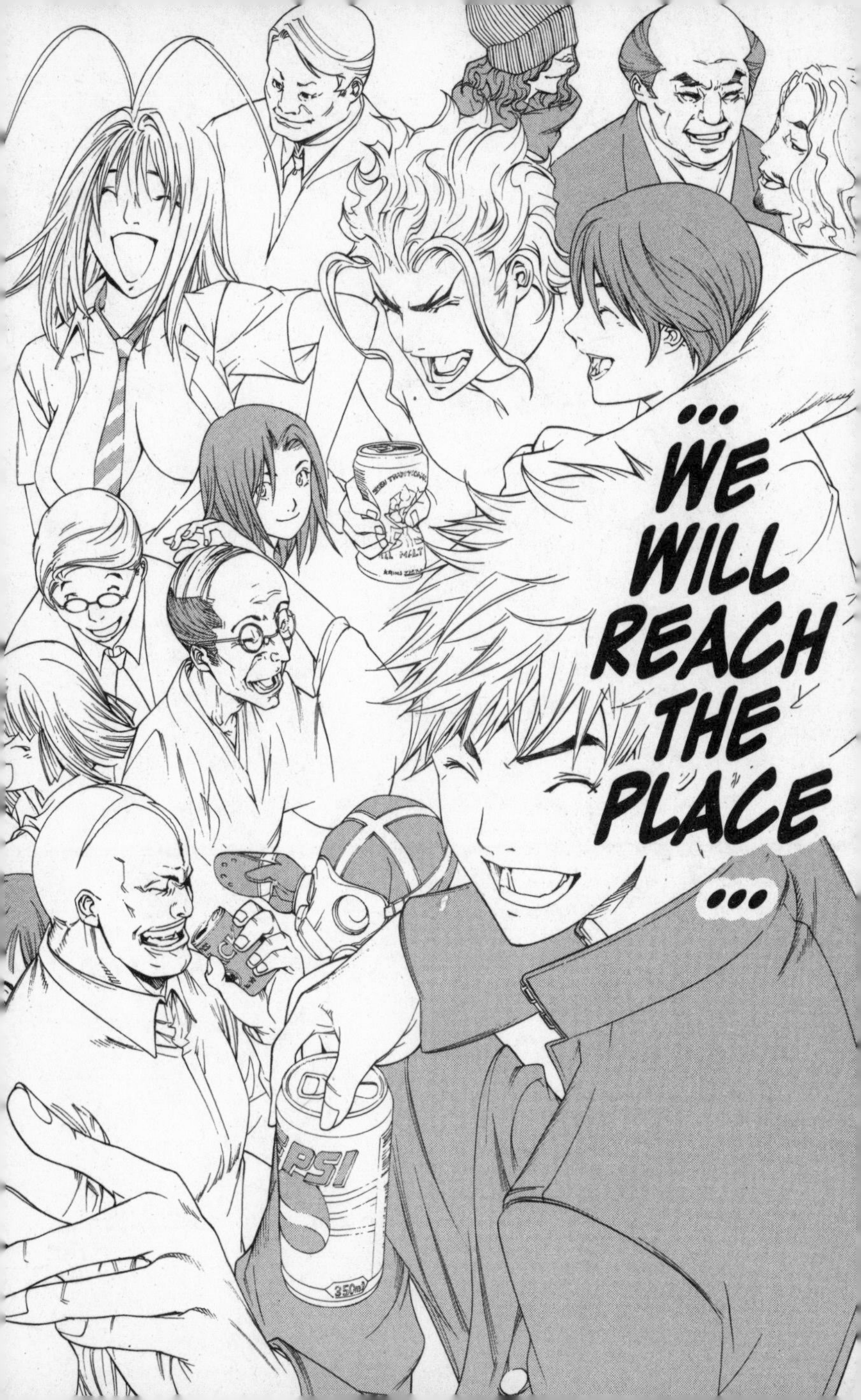
...WE WILL REACH THE PLACE...

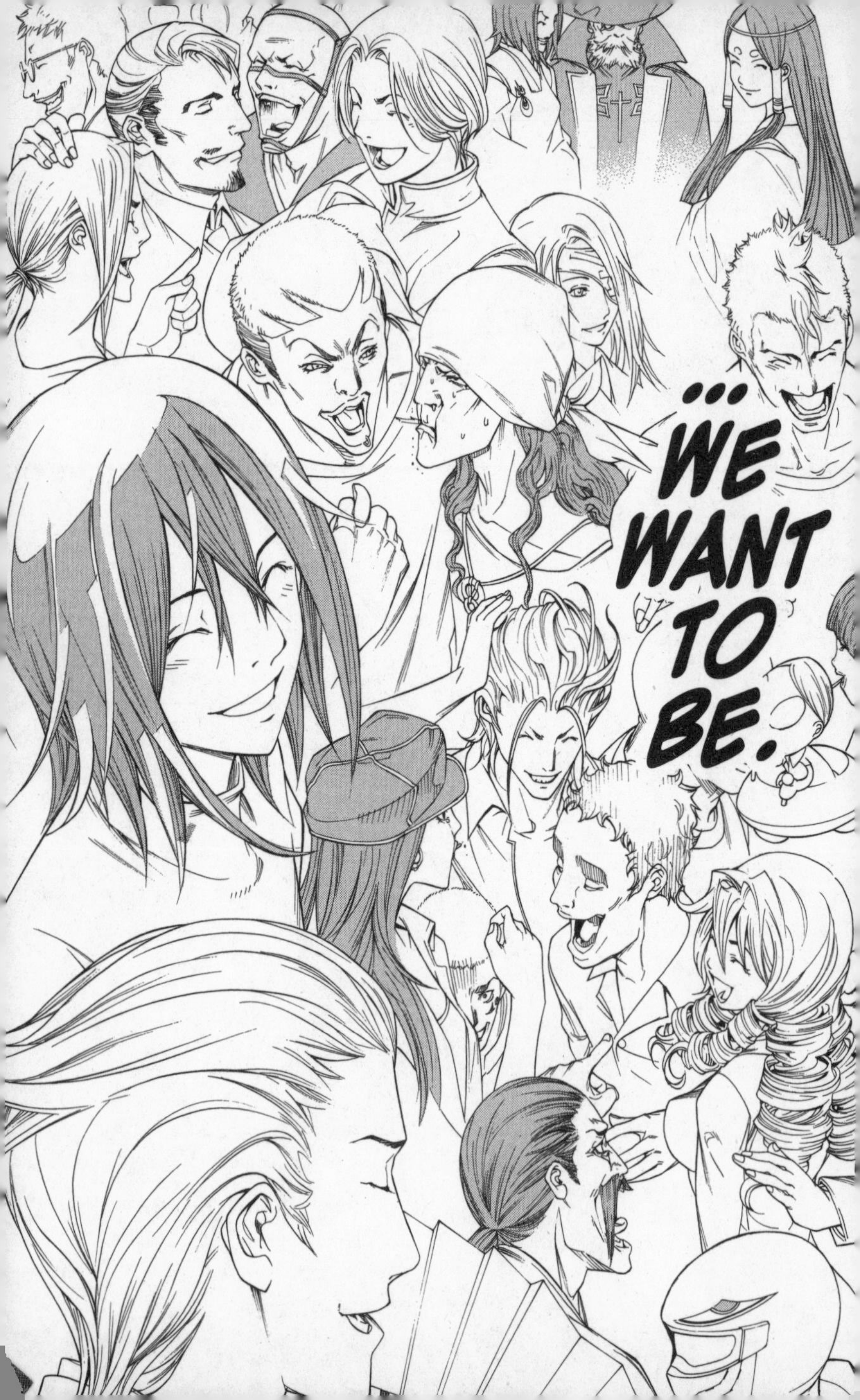
...WE WANT TO BE.

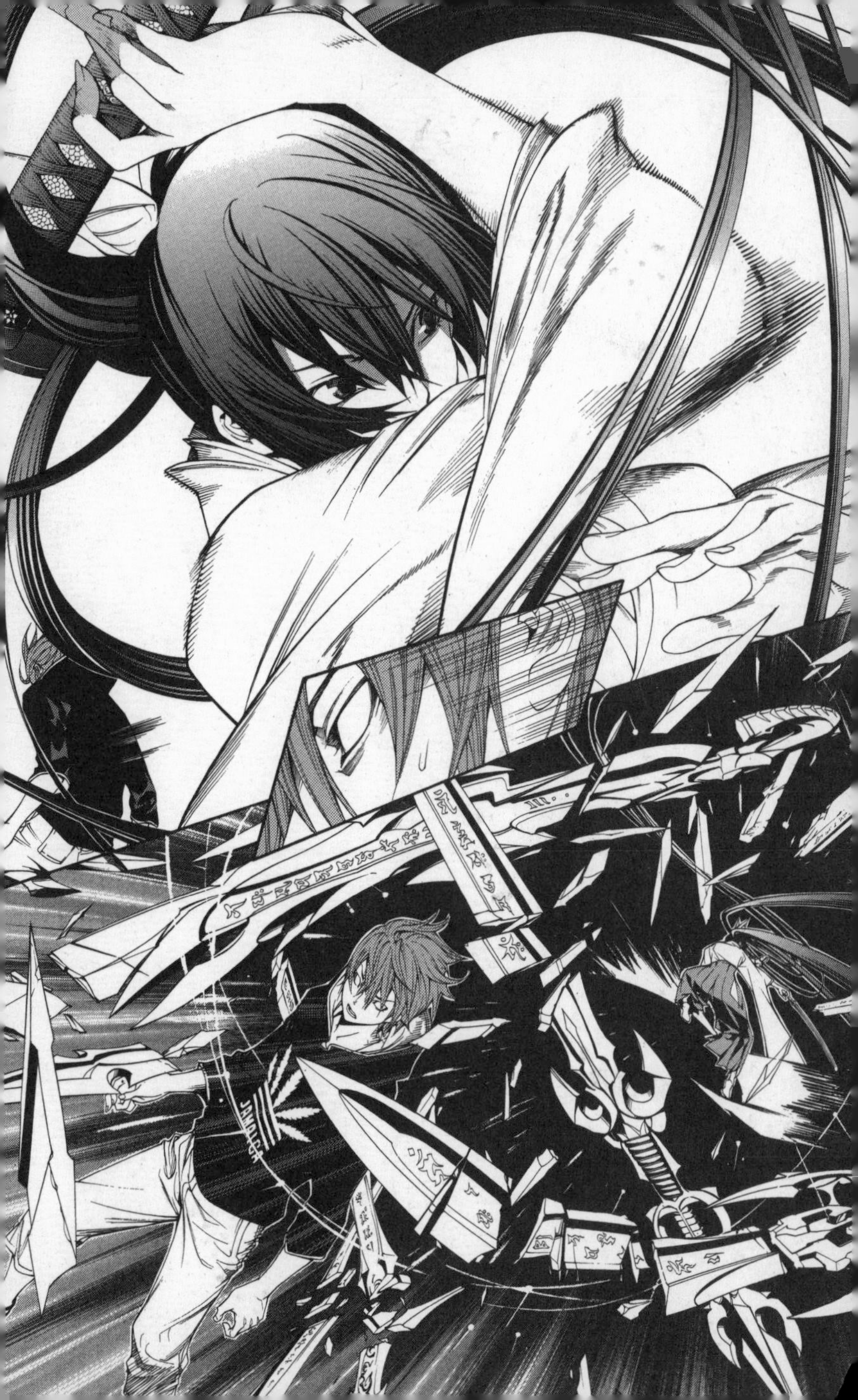
JAMAICA

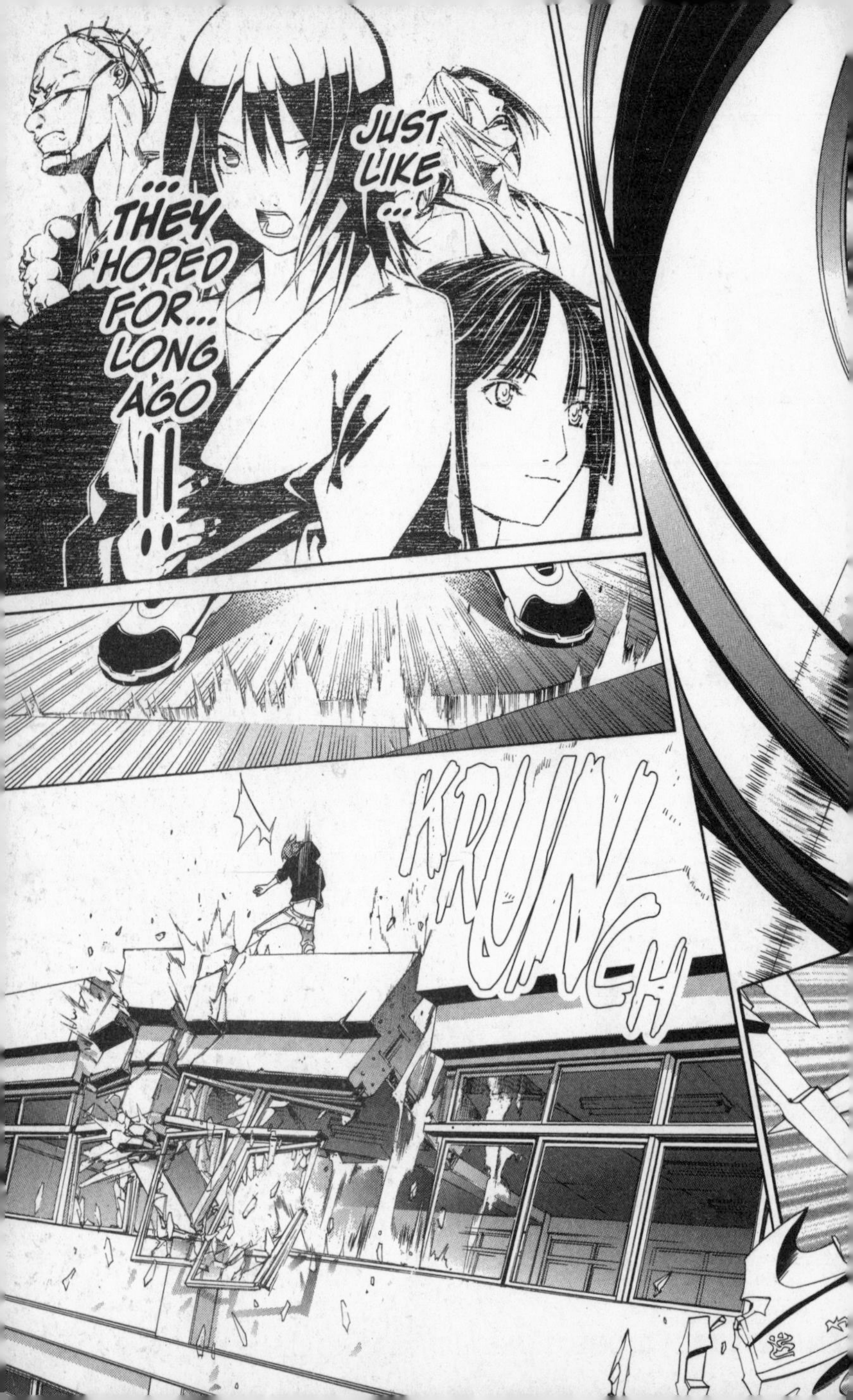
JUST LIKE ...
... THEY HOPED FOR... LONG AGO !!
KRUNCH

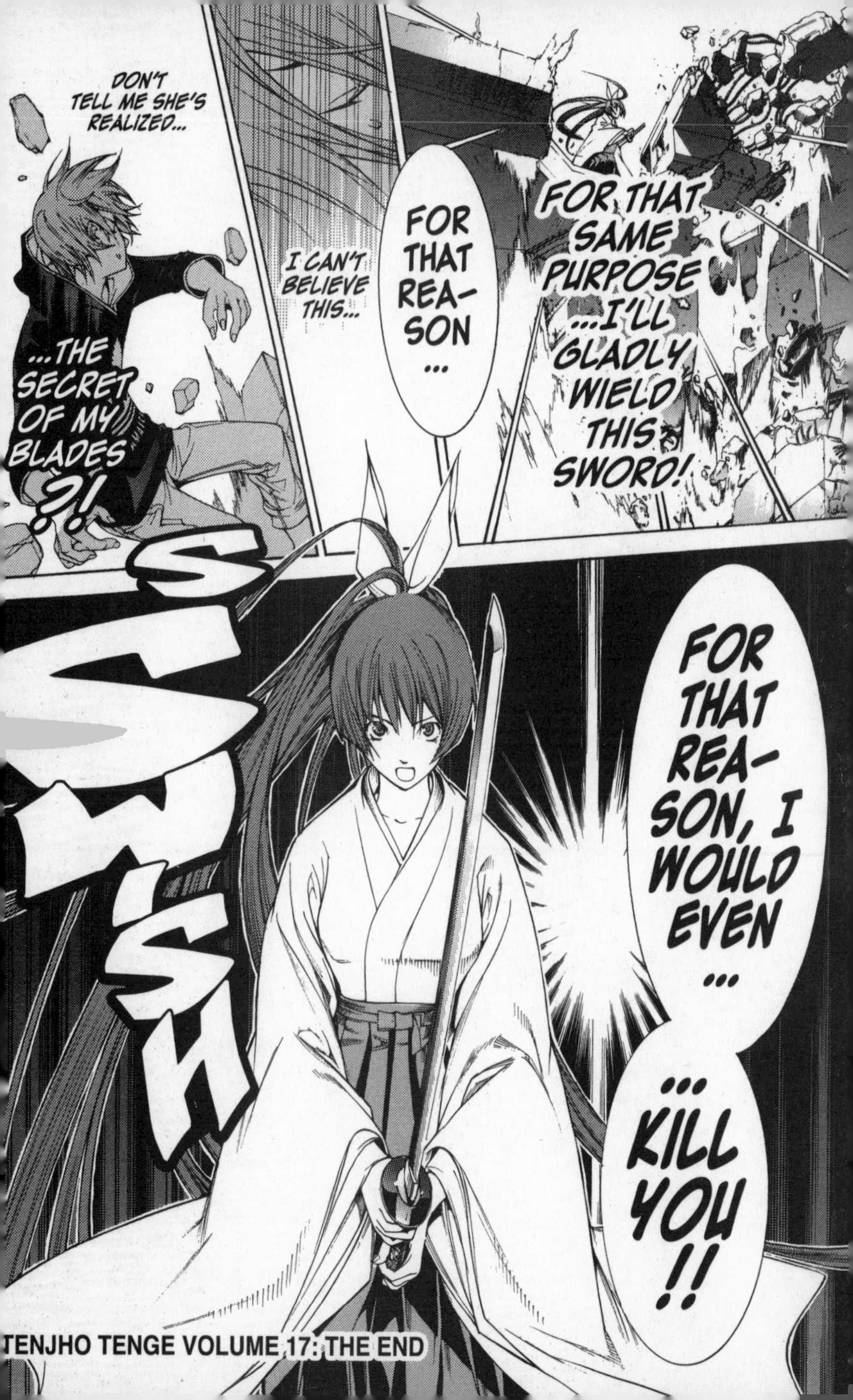
FOR THAT SAME PURPOSE ...I'LL GLADLY WIELD THIS SWORD!
FOR THAT REA-SON ...
I CAN'T BELIEVE THIS...
DON'T TELL ME SHE'S REALIZED...
...THE SECRET OF MY BLADES ?!
FOR THAT REA-SON, I WOULD EVEN ...
... KILL YOU !!
SWISH
TENJHO TENGE VOLUME 17: THE END

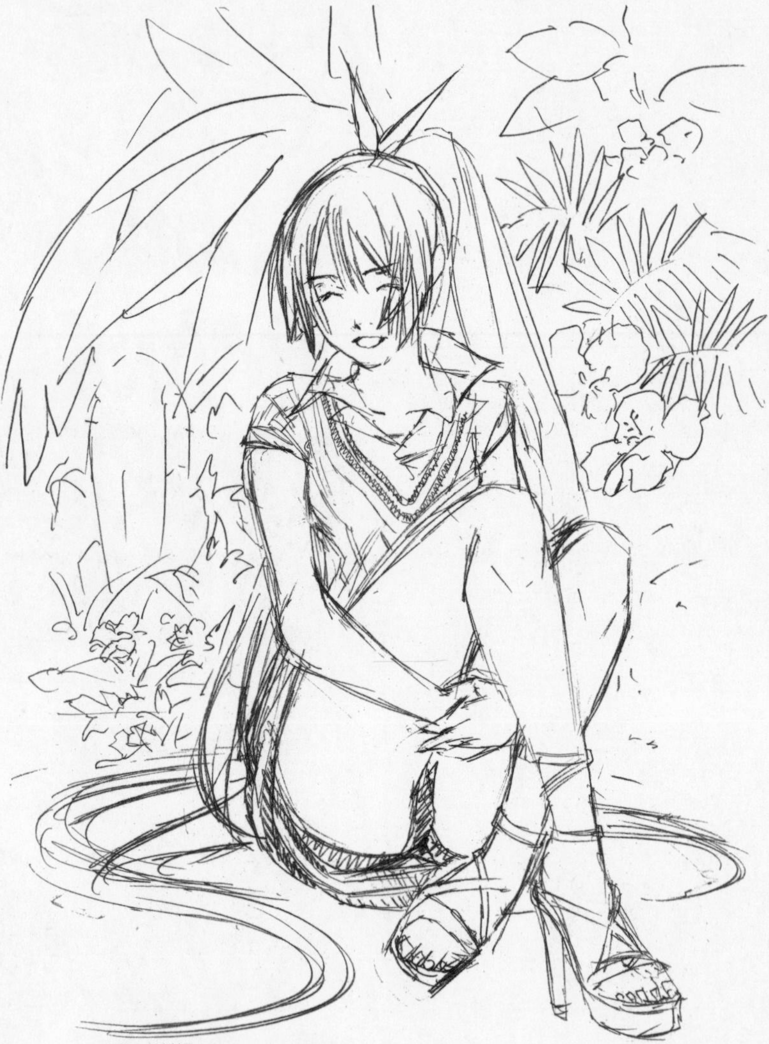

Editor Yoichi Hasegawa
Chief Editor Ayami Sakurada
Binding Michiru Kobayashi

With thanks to: Kokoro Takei
Masayoshi Tazuchi Takeshi Fujita Yo Mamura Akira Takagishi Takashi Onishi Masaru Aoki Yoshisuke Matsuo Motoko Shinohara

The stories in this volume were originally published in "UltraJump" January-June 2007.

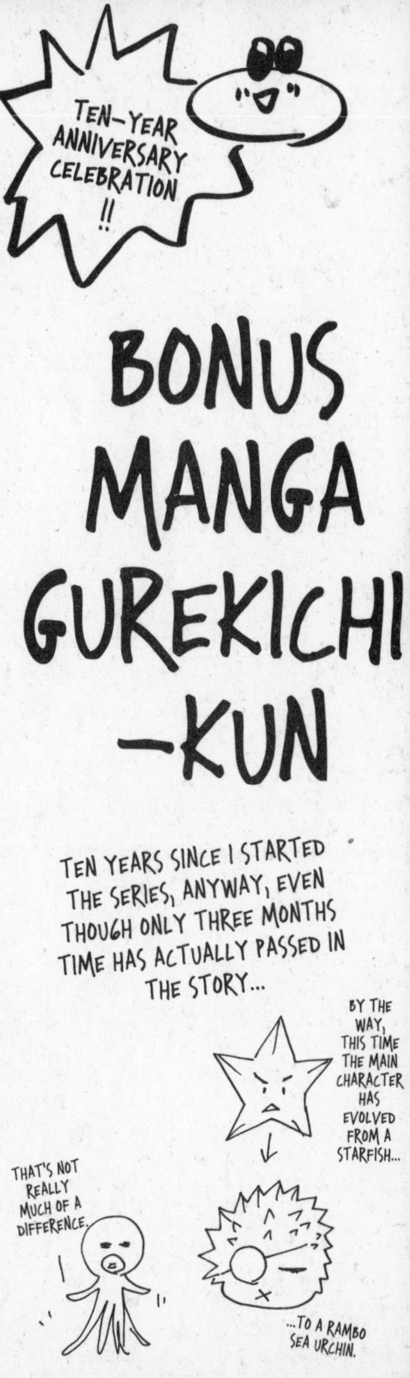
TEN-YEAR ANNIVERSARY CELEBRATION!!
BONUS MANGA GUREKICHI-KUN
TEN YEARS SINCE I STARTED THE SERIES, ANYWAY, EVEN THOUGH ONLY THREE MONTHS TIME HAS ACTUALLY PASSED IN THE STORY...
BY THE WAY, THIS TIME THE MAIN CHARACTER HAS EVOLVED FROM A STARFISH...
...TO A RAMBO SEA URCHIN.
THAT'S NOT REALLY MUCH OF A DIFFERENCE.

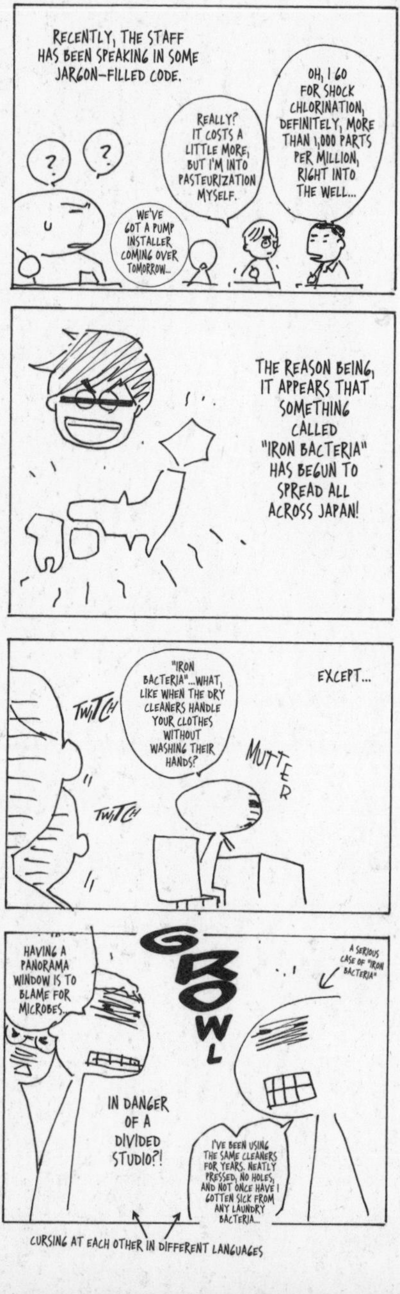
RECENTLY, THE STAFF HAS BEEN SPEAKING IN SOME JARGON-FILLED CODE.
OH, I GO FOR SHOCK CHLORINATION, DEFINITELY, MORE THAN 1,000 PARTS PER MILLION, RIGHT INTO THE WELL...
REALLY? IT COSTS A LITTLE MORE, BUT I'M INTO PASTEURIZATION MYSELF.
WE'VE GOT A PUMP INSTALLER COMING OVER TOMORROW...
?
?
THE REASON BEING, IT APPEARS THAT SOMETHING CALLED "IRON BACTERIA" HAS BEGUN TO SPREAD ALL ACROSS JAPAN!
EXCEPT...
"IRON BACTERIA"...WHAT, LIKE WHEN THE DRY CLEANERS HANDLE YOUR CLOTHES WITHOUT WASHING THEIR HANDS?
MUTTER
TWITCH
TWITCH
A SERIOUS CASE OF "IRON BACTERIA"
GROWL
HAVING A PANORAMA WINDOW IS TO BLAME FOR MICROBES.
I'VE BEEN USING THE SAME CLEANERS FOR YEARS. NEATLY PRESSED, NO HOLES, AND NOT ONCE HAVE I GOTTEN SICK FROM ANY LAUNDRY BACTERIA...
IN DANGER OF A DIVIDED STUDIO?!
CURSING AT EACH OTHER IN DIFFERENT LANGUAGES

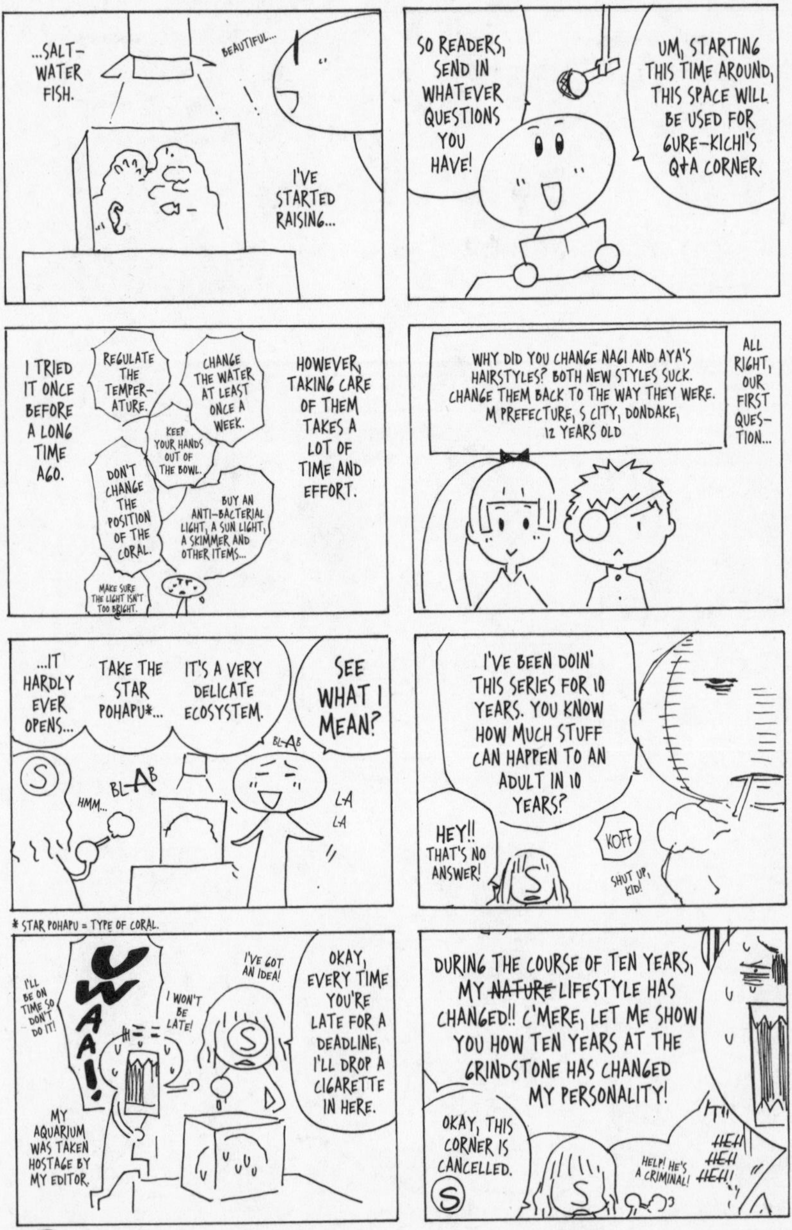
UM, STARTING THIS TIME AROUND, THIS SPACE WILL BE USED FOR GURE-KICHI'S Q+A CORNER.
SO READERS, SEND IN WHATEVER QUESTIONS YOU HAVE!
I'VE STARTED RAISING...
...SALT-WATER FISH.
BEAUTIFUL...
ALL RIGHT, OUR FIRST QUESTION...
WHY DID YOU CHANGE NAGI AND AYA'S HAIRSTYLES? BOTH NEW STYLES SUCK. CHANGE THEM BACK TO THE WAY THEY WERE. M PREFECTURE, S CITY, DONDAKE, 12 YEARS OLD
HOWEVER, TAKING CARE OF THEM TAKES A LOT OF TIME AND EFFORT.
CHANGE THE WATER AT LEAST ONCE A WEEK.
REGULATE THE TEMPERATURE.
I TRIED IT ONCE BEFORE A LONG TIME AGO.
KEEP YOUR HANDS OUT OF THE BOWL.
BUY AN ANTI-BACTERIAL LIGHT, A SUN LIGHT, A SKIMMER AND OTHER ITEMS...
DON'T CHANGE THE POSITION OF THE CORAL.
MAKE SURE THE LIGHT ISN'T TOO BRIGHT.
I'VE BEEN DOIN' THIS SERIES FOR 10 YEARS. YOU KNOW HOW MUCH STUFF CAN HAPPEN TO AN ADULT IN 10 YEARS?
KOFF
SHUT UP, KID!
HEY!! THAT'S NO ANSWER!
SEE WHAT I MEAN?
IT'S A VERY DELICATE ECOSYSTEM.
TAKE THE STAR POHAPU*...
...IT HARDLY EVER OPENS...
BL-AB
LA LA
BL-AB
HMM...
* STAR POHAPU = TYPE OF CORAL.
DURING THE COURSE OF TEN YEARS, MY ~~NATURE~~ LIFESTYLE HAS CHANGED!! C'MERE, LET ME SHOW YOU HOW TEN YEARS AT THE GRINDSTONE HAS CHANGED MY PERSONALITY!
HEH HEH HEH!!
HELP! HE'S A CRIMINAL!
OKAY, THIS CORNER IS CANCELLED.
OKAY, EVERY TIME YOU'RE LATE FOR A DEADLINE, I'LL DROP A CIGARETTE IN HERE.
I'VE GOT AN IDEA!
I WON'T BE LATE!
UWAAAI!
I'LL BE ON TIME SO DON'T DO IT!
MY AQUARIUM WAS TAKEN HOSTAGE BY MY EDITOR.

NOTE: MY EDITOR ACTUALLY LOVES ANIMALS AND IS A GOOD PERSON...MAYBE. THE END!!